## Preliminary Edition Notice

You have been selected to receive a copy of this book in the form of a preliminary edition. A preliminary edition is used in a classroom setting to test the overall value of a book's content and its effectiveness in a practical course prior to its formal publication on the national market.

As you use this text in your course, please share any and all feedback regarding the volume with your professor. Your comments on this text will allow the author to further develop the content of the book, so we can ensure it will be a useful and informative classroom tool for students in universities across the nation and around the globe. If you find the material is challenging to understand, or could be expanded to improve the usefulness of the text, it is important for us to know. If you have any suggestions for improving the material contained in the book or the way it is presented, we encourage you to share your thoughts.

This text is not available in wide release on the market, as it is actively being prepared for formal publication.

If you would like to provide notes directly to the publisher, you may contact us by e-mailing studentreviews@cognella.com. Please include the book's title, author, and 7-digit SKU reference number (found below the barcode on the back cover of the book) in the body of your message.

# HOW TO THINK CRITICALLY

*Preliminary Revised First Edition*

## Kenneth Hochstetter

College of Southern Nevada

**cognella®**

SAN DIEGO

Bassim Hamadeh, CEO and Publisher
Kristina Stolte, Senior Field Acquisitions Editor
Amy Smith, Senior Project Editor
Casey Hands, Production Editor
Jess Estrella, Senior Graphic Designer
Alexa Lucido, Licensing Coordinator
Kim Scott/Bumpy Design, Interior Designer
Natalie Piccotti, Director of Marketing
Kassie Graves, Vice President of Editorial
Jamie Giganti, Director of Academic Publishing

Cover image copyright © 2014 Depositphotos/tanor.
Design Image: Copyright © 2010 Depositphotos/ildogesto.

Printed in the United States of America.

cognella® | ACADEMIC PUBLISHING
3970 Sorrento Valley Blvd., Ste. 500, San Diego, CA 92121

# CONTENTS

## ACTIVE LEARNING

This book has interactive activities available to complement your reading.

Your instructor may have customized the selection of activities available for your unique course. Please check with your professor to verify whether your class will access this content through the Cognella Active Learning portal (http://active.cognella.com) or through your home learning management system.

# CRITICAL THINKING
## *A First Look*

Each of us have various beliefs and opinions about the world, some mundane and some about very deep and important issues. However, far too frequently many of us fail to slow down to reflect and think about our beliefs, let alone think about them critically. The goal of this chapter is to give a better idea of just what thinking critically about our beliefs would amount to, and to offer some motivation for doing so. We will get an overview of what critical thinking is, the appropriate attitude for thinking critically, and the stages of critical thinking. Further, we will consider why it matters, and some obstacles to engaging in it. Here are a few key words to master as we work through this chapter:

## KEY WORDS

| | |
|---|---|
| Critical Thinking | Open-Minded |
| Global Skepticism | Self-Refuting |
| Humble | Skepticism |
| Judgment | Subjectivism |
| Local Skepticism | |

## A First Look at Critical Thinking

### 🔍 KEY CONCEPT: CRITICAL THINKING

**Critical thinking** involves being disposed to examine any statement, belief, or argument one encounters with an open mind, appropriate humility, patience, and wonder in the pursuit of truth and knowledge, using knowledge of and skill at applying methods of problem solving, linguistic analysis, data interpretation, evidence assessment, argument evaluation, logical inquiry, and reasoning, with a willingness to render judgments about any statement, belief, or argument and adjust one's beliefs as a result.

Let's unpack this key concept. First, note that *critical thinking* does *not* mean *negative* thinking. Even though the word "critical" is often negative—critical condition, critical state, you're being critical, and the like, in this context, it does not mean negative thinking—though it can involve rejecting a statement or belief as false or irrational, or pointing out that an argument is fallacious. The "critical" in *critical thinking* means that one is forming a **judgment** based on **active**, **disciplined**, and **methodical** application of **objective criteria** in the evaluation of a **statement** or **belief**, or the **quality** of an **argument**. The judgment may be that a statement or belief is true or false, or that an argument is good or bad. The ultimate goal is to gain **knowledge**.

Each of the bold terms in the previous paragraph are key terms that will be discussed further at some point in the book, beginning with the following few. Engaging in critical thinking involves being *active* in one's thinking. It is not a passive mental process in which one simply receives information. It takes mental work. It also involves being *disciplined* in one's mental activity. To be disciplined amounts to engaging in training to be self-controlled in some activity (in this case, thinking) in order to develop a habit of behavior (or in this case, *thought*). Further in one's disciplined active thinking, one is being *methodical*, which amounts to following systematic and established ways of thinking, using *objective criteria*. We will discuss these objective criteria, as well as the other key terms, throughout the book.

Critical thinking has a scope, a method, and a goal. The *scope* is broad, ranging over *any* statement, belief, or argument. The *method* includes the use of background beliefs, reflection, and careful reasoning. And the *goal* is the formation or affirmation of rational and hopefully true beliefs, the repudiation or elimination of irrational beliefs and false beliefs, and ultimately to gain knowledge, which in turn affects every area of our lives, including our thoughts, desires, emotions, and actions.

"Critical thinking" has been defined or described in various (compatible) ways. One quite comprehensive description is by Edward Glaser, as follows:

> The ability to think critically ... involves three things: (1) an **attitude** of being disposed to consider in a thoughtful way the problems and subjects that come within the range of one's experiences, (2) **knowledge of the methods** of logical inquiry and reasoning, and (3) some **skill** in applying those methods. Critical thinking calls for a persistent effort to examine any belief or supposed form of knowledge in the light of the evidence that supports it and the further conclusions to which it tends. It also generally requires ability to recognize problems, to find workable means for meeting those problems, to gather and marshal pertinent information, to recognize unstated assumptions and values, to comprehend and use language with accuracy, clarity, and discrimination, to interpret data, to appraise evidence and evaluate arguments, to recognize the existence (or non-existence) of logical relationships between propositions, to draw warranted conclusions and generalizations, to put to test the conclusions and generalizations at which one arrives, to reconstruct one's patterns of beliefs on the basis of wider experience, and to render accurate judgments about specific things and qualities in everyday life.[1]

---

1.  Edward M. Glaser, *An Experiment in the Development of Critical Thinking*, Teacher's College, Columbia University, 1941, https://www.criticalthinking.org/pages/defining-critical-thinking/766.

## The Appropriate Attitude for Thinking Critically

There is a *lot* to unpack in Glaser's description. Let's begin where Glaser does—namely, having the right *attitude*. Glaser notes that to be a critical thinker, one must have "an attitude of being disposed to consider in a thoughtful way the problems and subjects that come within the range of one's experiences." This involves several things.

First, one must be *open-minded*. This does not mean that one treats all beliefs, statements, and arguments as equal. In fact, the very reason we engage in critical thinking is because we do *not* believe that all statements, beliefs, and arguments are equal. If they were all equal, there would be no need for critical thinking, but rather one would simply select whatever belief one wants from a list of equals. For example, the belief that the earth is flat would be equal (in every way) to the belief that the earth is spherical. If all beliefs were equal, then simply flip a coin, or choose the one that makes you feel good. However, we *know* that these are *not* equal, but we can still be open-minded in our consideration of each. What this (being open-minded) amounts to is having a *willingness* to consider any statement, idea, belief, or argument and reflect upon it, and especially a willingness to consider the possibility that one's own beliefs are false, that one's own reasoning is bad, and that perhaps one is engaging in some illicit rhetoric. It does not imply that one accepts all such ideas, but only that one is willing to consider them.

Hand in hand with open-mindedness is being appropriately *humble*. This involves having an appropriate view of oneself in the world of other thinkers. It is simultaneously recognizing what one, in fact, knows (as opposed to *thinks* one knows), while knowing that one does not know everything, and having a willingness to learn from others and from new experiences.

This disposition that Glaser mentions also involves having a *wonder* about the world, and an eagerness to gain understanding, find truth, and ultimately to obtain knowledge. If all one cares about is adopting a belief that is convenient for one's lifestyle and interests, one may not be a very good critical thinker. Instead, one must be disposed to seek the truth wherever it may lead.

Further, it involves *patience* and *persistence*. Often one must be patient in seeking the truth and applying the methods we will be discussing. If one is rushed, one will often make more mistakes in reasoning, and perhaps adopt false beliefs, thereby putting up roadblocks to gaining knowledge. Along with patience, critical thinking requires that one be *persistent* in one's willingness to examine various statements, beliefs, or arguments (one's own included) in light of evidence and good reasoning, not giving up if the task becomes difficult.

In sum, the appropriate empirical local skepticism for critical thinking includes having a disposition to persistently examine any statement, belief, or argument one encounters with an open mind, appropriate humility, patience, and wonder in the pursuit of truth and knowledge.

Glaser next mentions that critical thinking involves having knowledge of the methods of critical thinking, as well as possessing knowledge of and skill at applying methods of problem solving, linguistic analysis, data interpretation, evidence assessment, argument evaluation, logical inquiry, and reasoning, with a willingness to render judgments about any statement, belief, or argument and adjust one's beliefs as a result. Throughout this book we will be discussing the methods of critical thinking and improving our skills at applying them.

**EXERCISE 1.1**

**Review Questions**

1. True or false: Critical thinking amounts to nothing more than attacking other people's beliefs.

2. True or false: One applies critical thinking only to the evaluation of others' beliefs and reasoning, but not to one's own beliefs and reasoning.

3. In a sentence or two, briefly summarize what critical thinking is.

4. What does it mean to say that critical thinking involves being *active* and *disciplined*?

5. What does it mean to say that critical thinking involves being *methodical*?

6. What is the *scope*, the *method*, and the *goal* of critical thinking?

7. True or false: Being *open-minded* amounts to treating all beliefs and ideas as equal.

8. What does it mean to be *humble* in the context of being a critical thinker?

9. Can one fully engage in critical thinking if one is not filled with *wonder* about the world? Why or why not?

10. Why does critical thinking involve *patience* and *persistence*?

## The Stages of Critical Thinking

There are several stages in the process of engaging in critical thinking, including, but not necessarily limited to, the following. In the *first stage*, which we'll call the *awareness stage*, one focuses one's awareness on a statement, for example (though it could also be a belief or argument). One then questions the statement and wonders whether it is true, rational, or even coherent. Suppose that the statement is:

> The cosmos is all there is, or ever was, or ever will be.[2]

The statement is coherent and may even initially strike one as true and obvious. But, as critical thinkers, we want to slow down a bit, inquire about this statement, and ask a few questions about it. For example, what is meant by *cosmos*? Does it include only the matter and forces making up *our* universe? Does it include the *multiverse*? Does it mean that everything is physical and composed of matter? Does it imply that there is no God? Or, does it imply that there are no immaterial souls? So, one should wonder about this statement, and perhaps feel uneasy about it.

The second stage is the *reflection stage*. In this stage one begins to reflect upon ways of solving the issue of whether the statement is true, should be believed, is rational, and the like. One may consider one's background knowledge and consider how the statement fits in with what else one believes or knows about the world. And, one begins making inferences. With the statement we are discussing, one may infer that if by *cosmos* one means to refer to and only to the sum total of

---

2. You may recognize this as astronomer Carl Sagan's opening statement his 1980 series *Cosmos*.

the *material* stuff in our universe,[3] then the statement entails that there is no immaterial God, or souls, or abstract objects. So, if one has good reason to think God exists as part of one's background beliefs, one is likely to reject the statement as false, or at least not immediately accept it. But as critical thinkers, we want to be sure. So, these are some questions we will want to ask in our inquiry: What reasons are there for accepting the statement? Did Sagan have some good reasons for thinking the statement is true? Do the reasons for the statement, if there are any, defeat the reasons for believing that God exists, for example? Is there evidence for other immaterial objects besides God, such as abstract objects, that may also defeat the statement?

The third stage is the *discovery stage*. In this stage, one begins to answer the questions one asked in the reflection stage. One consults experts or others who have done work on the subject. One considers the relevant writings of philosophers on the existence of God, souls, and abstract objects. For example, one may discover Thomas Aquinas's arguments for God's existence, and find the arguments compelling. Or, one may reflect on various religious experiences one has had. One may investigate the recent findings in cosmology. One may discover that Sagan had no evidence for the statement, and certainly no scientific evidence for it, as one cannot have scientific evidence for it. If relevant (which is not in the case for the statement above), one does some experimentation. One then engages in careful reasoning based on one's findings.

The final stage is the *judgment stage*. In this stage, one makes judgments about which statements one should accept in light of one's evidence that one has or discovered in the discovery stage. So, for example, one may decide that in light of one's available evidence, experiences, and background knowledge, there really is an immaterial God. And thus, one will make the judgment that the statement above is false, since it implies that there is no God. One then decides that one will make adjustments to one's overall belief system and conduct one's life accordingly.

Once one goes through the stages of critical thinking, one's task as a critical thinker is not over, since even after one reaches the last stage, further questions worth exploring arise, and the process begins again. For example, if one concludes that God exists in the thought process above, several more questions arise, each of which brings more questions. Here are just a few: *What kind of being is God? What is his character? Why does God allow evil and suffering? What is God's relationship to the cosmos? What is God's relationship to me?* And, of course, there are countless others. In short, the critical thinking process should be an ongoing, daily activity.

**FIGURE 1.1**

---

3.  By "sum total material stuff in the universe" I mean the material, ranging from the very large such as planets, stars, and galaxies, to the very small such as atoms, quarks, leptons, bosons, and perhaps strings, to the physical forces, including gravity, electromagnetism, and the strong and weak nuclear forces. It includes that and only that which is composed of matter, forces that act upon the matter, and fields.

**EXERCISE 1.2**

Review Questions

1. What is involved in the *awareness stage* of critical thinking?
2. What is involved in the *reflection stage* of critical thinking?
3. What is involved in the *discovery stage* of critical thinking?
4. What is involved in the *judgment stage* of critical thinking?
5. True or false: Once one has gone through all the stages of critical thinking for some statement, belief, or argument, one's task as a critical thinker is finished.

## Why Critical Thinking Matters

With the rough idea of what critical thinking is in hand, let's have a look at why it matters. In short, it matters because *thinking* is involved in *every* thing we do, *every* decision we make, *every* act of reasoning we engage in, which in turn often affects our emotions. Thus, whether one's thinking is good or bad, it affects every area of one's life. Thus, it matters! Here are a few areas of life that are impacted by critical thinking: learning and exploring, self-evaluation, and self-defense. Each of these is closely related to the other.

### Learning and Exploring

Learning involves gaining knowledge, understanding, or a new skill, each of which involves being open-minded and humble enough to receive the new (to oneself) facts or skills. As we saw above, these are traits of a critical thinker. To gain knowledge and understanding involves more than simply being aware of a statement and believing it; it involves accepting the statement in a way that grounds it as *knowledge*, as opposed to, say, making a lucky guess. This "grounding it as knowledge" often involves going through the stages of critical thinking—being reflective of a particular statement; asking good questions about the statement or noticing puzzles about the statement; drawing from appropriate sources to help one answer one's questions or solve the puzzles; and using good, careful reasoning to draw a conclusion and form a judgment. Additionally, because critical thinking involves these stages, it helps one with reading comprehension, as well as with one's listening and observation skills, which in turn is important for learning.

### Self-Evaluation

A central, and incredibly important, aspect of self-evaluation is asking, and correctly answering, the question:

*What should I believe?*

Asking and then answering this question is important given that what one believes affects *every* aspect of one's life. It is important to ask not just about the big questions (*Does God exist? Do we have free will? Is the cosmos all there is?*) but also about smaller and more mundane questions.

In order to even ask the question in a serious manner, one must (at least somewhat) have the appropriate attitude to which Glaser referred—open-minded, humble, patient, and like attitudes. And, of course, to answer it correctly in such a way that one is not just making a lucky guess, one must go through (at least some of) the stages of critical thinking. By carefully going through the stages of critical thinking with the appropriate attitude, one is more likely to end up with true and rational beliefs, and avoid false and irrational beliefs, and is ultimately more likely to gain knowledge.

### Self-Defense

We are constantly bombarded or in some way confronted with statements of all sorts—about what we should believe, how we should behave, which product to buy, what foods to eat, and many more. Many such statements are *false*, and some are ridiculous and even irrational. And frequently lying behind many of the statements—whether true or false, rational or irrational—is bad reasoning or illicit rhetorical devices. By understanding and being skilled at the methods of critical thinking, which involves being aware of various logical fallacies and rhetorical devices and how to spot them, one is much better equipped to avoid being duped by them. One is more likely to avoid being manipulated by so-called experts and authorities speaking in areas in which they are not experts or authorities. Further, by being a good critical thinker, one is more likely to defend one's own beliefs by rational means rather than by using logical fallacies, appeals to emotion, or other illicit rhetorical devices.

---

**EXERCISE 1.3**

Review Questions

1. Why is critical thinking important for learning?
2. How does critical thinking help with self-evaluation?
3. How does critical thinking help with self-defense?

---

## Obstacles to Critical Thinking

There are many obstacles to critical thinking, but the focus will be on a few important obstacles and how to overcome them. These can be divided into six categories: *wrong attitude, emotional obstacles, social pressures, skepticism, relativism,* and *lacking the knowledge and skills of critical thinking methods.* As we discuss these, you'll notice that many are closely related. So, the categorization is a bit arbitrary but still may be helpful in thinking about these obstacles.

### Wrong Attitude

The first obstacle to critical thinking is having the *wrong attitude*. Recall that the *right* attitude of a critical thinker is being disposed to be an active, disciplined, open-minded, humble, patient, and persistent thinker. Thus, if one lacks this attitude, or some aspect of it, then one is already shutting oneself off from, and putting up an obstacle to, critical thinking. This wrong attitude can be had in many ways. Here are a few.

### Lack of Care

First, it should be obvious that to even begin critical thinking, one must *care* about truth and knowledge, about examining beliefs and arguments, as opposed to only caring about what serves one's own desires and interests. If one simply does not care about truth, knowledge, and good reasoning, then probably one would not take time to overcome this wrong attitude; indeed, it is doubtful such a person would even be reading this book. So, the first step is caring about how you think and what you believe.

One way to help motivate this care is to appeal to your love for yourself, family, and friends. While it may *appear* that this conflicts with what was just said—namely, caring only about one's own desires and interests—it is actually not in conflict, *because* of what is meant by "love of self." What is intended is this: each person cares for themselves in *appropriate* ways, such as ensuring that one is fed, clothed, and sheltered, and has other needs taken care of. Beliefs and reasoning play an important role in this. Take diet, for instance. If one has a *false* belief about what foods are good or bad, such a false belief affects what the person eats, and thus one's health. Thus, having true beliefs about what foods are healthy or unhealthy is very important. To arrive at such true beliefs *requires* at least some critical thinking. One must think about which "authorities" to trust and how to interpret experiences related to diet. Thus, critical thinking matters here. The same is true *in every important matter* regarding tending to one's needs. But critical thinking also matters for other issues we care about—such as morality, religion, and politics. Critical thinking plays, or can fail to play, a central role in one's beliefs about these very important areas of thought and belief, which one already cares about.

The same is true of caring for one's family and friends. *How should I raise my children? Do I practice corporal punishment? Do I spoil them?* To answer these and many other important questions *in a way that leads to truth requires* critical thinking. Again, one must think about which "authorities" to trust, and how to interpret experiences related to child-rearing. The same applies to interacting with friends and caring for them. In short, *everyone* loves one's self in the ways mentioned—for example, food, shelter, clothing—and cares to some degree about morality, religion, and politics. And presumably *everyone* loves someone as a family member or as a friend. Given this love, one should also therefore care about critical thinking.

### Close-Minded

Related to *caring* about critical thinking is *being open-minded*. Being a critical thinker involves being open-minded in the ways discussed above. In contrast, one may be *close-minded*, unwilling to seriously consider statements about certain issues, or to consider that one's own beliefs may be false or one's reasoning bad. Clearly, such a person has an attitude that is an obstacle to thinking critically and has cut themselves off from new and perhaps freeing ideas.

While close-mindedness can result from various things, two driving forces are having self-esteem that is too high and having self-esteem that is too low. The first of these is having a "superior than thou attitude." This involves taking one's self and one's beliefs as being superior to other people's beliefs. It is exaggerating one's own worth and beliefs to the degree that they are superior to others'. As a result, one will tend to (a) insist that one is always right and (b) fail to take the claims and beliefs of others seriously, or at least not as seriously as one should.

Now it may be true that your belief *is* superior to another's in some way—perhaps yours is based in good reasoning and evidence, whereas another's is not grounded at all but simply a "gut feeling." However, when one has the *attitude* that one's beliefs *in general* are better than others' beliefs, then *that attitude* results in close-mindedness and reflects a lack of critical thinking about one's own beliefs.

The other extreme that leads to being close-minded is having self-esteem that is too low. This attitude can be more difficult to detect, as it is often an unconscious, under-the-surface driving force. However, it has a similar result. Because one has low self-esteem, one will try to protect oneself by stubbornly insisting that one's own beliefs *must be* true, or that one *must be right* about every issue or "win" every argument. It is a subconscious way that a person protects themselves. If one becomes vulnerable to being wrong or being corrected, one may think others will think less of them or that their self-worth decreases.

To fix both closed-mindedness in general, and the *superior* or *inferior* attitude specifically, is difficult, and requires the person to become vulnerable in a way that may be uncomfortable at first. One must become vulnerable to being corrected by others or to being wrong and acknowledge that one's reasoning is bad. The low self-esteem thinker must not only learn to become vulnerable in these ways, but must also come to learn that one's self-worth is *not* in what they believe but is in their very being—that one is a rational thinker, equally valuable to every other thinker. Becoming vulnerable is difficult and gaining a correct understanding of one's self worth is even more difficult. Both may require counseling, which is beyond the scope of this book. The goal here is simply to note an important obstacle to critical thinking and to provide some guidance on how to fix it. In short, being an open-minded thinker (and thus *not* a "superior than thou" or "I must always be right" thinker) is a necessity to becoming a critical thinker.

### Lack of Patience and Discipline

The last *wrong attitude* obstacle that we will discuss is that a thinker may lack discipline or patience in one's thinking. This can come about in at least two ways. First, one may be a *passive thinker*. To be a critical thinker, one must have an attitude of being willing to be an active and disciplined thinker—exploring, reasoning, reflecting, and more. If one is too lazy to engage in this and simply believes whatever one is told (in the extreme) or believes whatever "feels right" at the time because it takes too much mental energy to engage in careful thought, then clearly one will *not* be a critical thinker.

On the other hand, it may not be laziness, but *impatience* that prevents one from pursuing an issue to the extent that is required for critical thinking. Critical thinking often requires that a person focus and concentrate on an issue, or follow an argument, for an extended period of time—perhaps hours, or days, and in some cases weeks or months or years![4]

---

4. For example, Einstein spent the last 30 years of his life (including moments before his death) critically thinking about trying to find a unified field theory.

To overcome this obstacle of being a lazy or impatient thinker, one must simply be willing to engage in the mental work that is required, and for the length of time that it is required, to solve the problem or issue. To the extent that one is not willing to engage in this disciplined activity, one has thereby become a *slave* to others. One will not be thinking for oneself but will be subject to believing *what others say* or be subject to *whatever one feels*, thereby in an important sense becoming a slave to others and one's emotions.

## Emotional Obstacles

Emotions are a very important aspect to our lives and interpersonal interactions. However, if not careful, one may allow one's emotions to rule over one's thinking, thereby becoming an obstacle to critical thinking. There are many ways this can occur.

### Pride and Fear

Above we discussed having self-esteem that is too high as a *wrong attitude* obstacle. This can very easily lead to *pride*, not in the sense of taking pleasure in or feeling satisfied with one's accomplishments (which can be a good thing, if at the appropriate degree), but rather *pride* in the sense of being unwilling to be wrong or admit wrong since one believes that "I already know *I'm* right."

Additionally, above we discussed having self-esteem that is too low as a *wrong attitude* obstacle. This can lead to *fear* of being wrong or looking bad because one admits that one is wrong. This fear can hinder one from being open to critical thinking. Since these were addressed above, we won't elaborate here, but simply note that one must keep one's pride and fear in check, and instead be appropriately humble and courageous if one wants to be a critical thinker.

### Emotional Attachment to Idea

We naturally feel quite emotional about issues important to us. And, there are certain moral issues that stir up considerable emotions for various reasons. And, of course, people are quite emotionally attached to various political and religious ideas. While it is certainly okay to be emotionally attached to one's cherished beliefs, the emotional attachment *can* get so strong that it interferes with thinking critically about the issues.

Here are a few things that one can do to help overcome this. First, one can and should take time to reflect on the fact that all these ideas about which one has deep emotional attachment have opposing ideas, many of which also *have strong supporting evidence*. The suggestion here is *not* that all beliefs are equal or that all have equal evidence. Indeed, they do not, which is why we engage in critical thinking. However, the fact that there are opposing views supported with good reasons should help one understand that *perhaps* one has missed something, which in turn may help one not be so emotionally attached to a particular view.

Second, and related, one can and should take time to reflect that one is not the *only* thinker in the world, and that others have had experiences and learned things one has not, and that perhaps one can learn from others.

Third, and in light of the first two points above, one can and should practice being quick to listen and slow to speak. One should train to first *truly* listen to (read) what others have to say, and then speak one's own views and replies. This takes time, effort, and retraining. This may help one to see that perhaps one has misunderstood some aspect of the opposing view, which in turn may help one to emotionally relax one's emotional attachment to one's own view.

Finally, to help overcome one's emotional attachment to a particular idea, one should attempt to emotionally detach from the idea and instead look at the matter as an *exercise* in seeing the logical connections between various statements. In doing this, one may see that there are certain statements that one thinks are true that entail some other statement that one believes to be false—that is, one may become surprised about the implications of one's views. Doing this as a purely mental exercise may help one overcome the emotional attachment.

Each of these practices may also help one to be more open-minded as well.

### Gut Feeling

The final emotional obstacle is the "gut feeling" one may have that some statement is true. If one does have this *gut feeling*, this *could* interfere with one thinking critically about the statement.

To be clear, there is a difference between having a "gut feeling" that some statement is true versus having what is called *rational intuition* about a particular statement. Rational intuition will be discussed in chapter 3, but the rough idea is that there are some very basic logical statements which are such that just by understanding them, we can "intellectually see" that they are true. For example, once one understands the following statement, one can just "intellectually see," by *rational intuition*, that it is true:

*If Adam is taller than Bob, then Bob is not taller than Adam.*

In contrast is having a "gut feeling." Having a gut feeling is *not* "intellectually *seeing*" that a statement is true but is instead *having a feeling* that it is true. Typically, it does not concern basic statements that one can perhaps know by rational intuition, but instead concerns statements that require some sort of evidence in order to know that they are true. So, for example, perhaps someone has a "gut feeling" that some conspiracy theory is true, such as *humans never landed on the moon and the government is deceiving us about this*. The fact is that no amount of *gut feeling* alone can inform anyone that humans never landed on the moon and that the government is deceiving us about this.

To overcome this difficulty, one must come to accept that except for certain basic statements, we need some sort of evidence to determine whether some statement is true or false. One should also adopt an attitude of humility and acknowledge that there is a lot one simply does not know.

### Social Pressures

Whether we like to admit it or not, to some degree we are all influenced by those around us. Such influences can, of course, be very good and beneficial. Other times they can be bad. One example of social pressure being bad is when it creates an obstacle to thinking critically. This can occur in various ways.

One way arises simply from our tendency to adopt the beliefs of those around us, especially if we are passive thinkers. For example, John may for a time frequently watch one news station and find himself leaning left politically, but then later choose to watch another news station over a period of time and find himself leaning right politically. It can happen without even realizing it. So, we need to be mindful of this and make a conscious effort to actively think critically under such circumstances.

Another way we can be affected by social pressures arises from our desire to be part of the group. We want to fit in and be like others. As a result, we can find ourselves adopting the beliefs of others without thinking critically about them. Again, the solution is to be mindful of this and make a conscious effort to actively think critically even with our desire to fit in with the group and be sure that our desire does not overpower our critical thinking.

## Skepticism

Skepticism comes in various forms. In its strongest form, it is the belief that knowledge is impossible in *every* area of inquiry; and in weaker forms, it is the belief that knowledge of certain things is impossible. It shouldn't be difficult to see how skepticism is an obstacle to critical thinking. But, let's examine it a bit.

### Global Skepticism

We can call the strongest form of skepticism, according to which knowledge in general is impossible, *global skepticism*. Probably there are not many global skeptics, if there are any, as *this* sort of skepticism is impossible to defend! For if knowledge is impossible, period, then knowledge that global skepticism is true is impossible. And if one *did* claim to know it, their statement is *self-refuting*. A self-refuting statement is one that lays down standards that undermine the very statement. A fairly clear example is the statement:

> *There are no true statements.*

If this statement is *true*, then by its own standards, it cannot be true, since it says that there are no truths. Thus, it is *self*-refuting.

The same is true of the *knowledge claim* to *know* that global skepticism is true. To see why, consider the *knowledge claim* about global skepticism:

> *I know that knowledge of anything is impossible.*

Clearly, the second part of the statement (knowledge is impossible) undermines the first part of the statement (I know that …), and thus the statement is self-refuting.

So, while global skepticism certainly puts an obstacle in front of critical thinking (given that knowledge is impossible, there is little motive to think critically), since (a) we cannot know that it is true, if it is true, and (b) the knowledge claim about it is self-refuting, one ought not be a global skeptic, and thus remove this obstacle to critical thinking.

### Local Skepticism

*Local skepticism*, in contrast, is skepticism only about a particular area of thought. It comes in many forms. For example, one form (which is a bit on the strong side) limits knowledge to what can be known directly by observation or by the scientific method. Let's call it "empirical local skepticism." We can put it this way:

<u>Empirical Local Skepticism</u>: We can only know what is verifiable by direct observation or by the scientific method.

This sort of skepticism entails that while we can know, for example, whether there is a water bottle on the counter, we cannot know, for example, whether there is a God. Or, perhaps we can know, for example, whether water is composed of $H_2O$, we cannot know, for example, whether humans have a soul. In the first instances in these examples, one may think that we *can* have knowledge because it is simply a matter of observing the world or engaging in science. But in the second instances in these examples, we *cannot* know just by observation or by science, and thus we simply cannot know the answers, or so says this form of skepticism.

This skepticism does not put up as large a barrier to critical thinking as does global skepticism, but it certainly places up a large barrier. While such a thinker might accept that critical thinking is useful in the sciences, it is useless in many other areas. For example, since direct observation does not require critical thinking (or so someone might say—though one could challenge this[5]), and since direct observation yields knowledge, then we simply don't need critical thinking here. And, in any area not knowable by direct observation or by science, we simply cannot have knowledge, in which case, again, critical thinking is useless. Thus, this way of thinking puts the brakes on thinking critically in many areas of thought.

The first thing that can be said to this skeptic is that much of our knowledge of the world comes from science, and science definitely requires critical thinking, as this local skeptic admits. Thus, at the very least critical thinking should be valued and learned by this skeptic *for the sake of doing science.*

However, we should go further and counsel this local skeptic to reject their skepticism altogether and remove the skeptical obstacle to thinking critically in the other areas as well. The reason is similar to the reason given to the global skeptic—namely, that knowledge of empirical local skepticism is impossible.

Consider it once again:

<u>Empirical Local Skepticism</u>: We can only know what is verifiable by direct observation or by the scientific method.

Notice that empirical local skepticism lays out criteria for knowing something—namely, that it is verifiable by direct observation or by the methods of science. So, *if* empirical local skepticism is true, then we can *know* that it is true *only if* we can verify it (empirical local skepticism) by direct observation or by the methods of science. However, what direct observation or scientific experiment could verify empirical local skepticism? Perhaps one might suggest that we

---

5. Delving into this would require us to go far beyond the scope of this book. However, to get one started thinking about this, consider the difference between *simple seeing, seeing as,* and *seeing that.* Simple seeing is having a sensory experience (in this case, *seeing*) of some aspect of the world, but *not* forming any concept about what one is seeing. One the other hand, *seeing as* and *seeing that* require one to form a concept along with their sensory experience. *Seeing as* is having a sensory experience (in this case, *seeing*) and conceptualizing what is seen in some way—for example, seeing the sign *as red. Seeing that* is one step further. It is not only applying a concept to the sensory experience, but it is applying *the correct* concept—the one that corresponds to reality. Arguably, knowledge based on sensory experience (e.g., direct observation) requires *seeing that,* which in turn may require critical thinking.

can justify by direct observation or science that until now all that we have known is by direct observation or by science. But even this seems impossible. How can we directly observe or apply our scientific methods to all the past scenarios? It is even more difficult to show that *we can verify* by direct observation or science that the *only* way of knowing is by direct observation or science. Again, what direct observation or scientific experiment shows that?!? Thus, if empirical local skepticism is true, we *cannot* know that it is true by the very standards laid out by the principle. Thus, since the standards of knowledge laid out by the principle prevent us from knowing the principle, there is no reason to embrace it, and thus we should not embrace it, especially since it undermines critical thinking in so many areas of human thought.

Perhaps the local skeptic here would offer a revision in order to justify knowledge of the principle, such as follows:

> Empirical Local Skepticism Revised: We can only know what is verifiable by direct observation or by the scientific method, and we can know this very principle.

The problem with this revision is that the added clause at the end is something not knowable by observation or science, as noted, and thus to choose only *that* non-observable, non-scientific statement (i.e., *empirical local skepticism is true*) as knowable is arbitrary and unjustified. Why limit the knowable non-observable, non-scientific statements to just that? Why not include *God exists* on the list?

But perhaps the skeptic here would not claim something so strong as empirical local skepticism, but rather something weaker. For example, perhaps the local skeptic would simply give a list of things we cannot know, even with critical thinking (e.g., philosophical matters). Thus, they may adopt the following:

> *We cannot know any statements of philosophy, such as that God exists, or that some act is morally wrong, or that we have a soul, or any other philosophical statement.*

While this sort of skepticism does not put an obstacle in front of critical thinking in general, it certainly places an obstacle in front of some of the most important issues that we think about, and thus is a problem.

But again we must ask, *why* think we cannot know such things as whether God exists or whether we have a soul? Interestingly, to answer this, one will probably engage in critical thinking! And, often one will do a very poor job of it. Or, if one has not arrived at this form of skepticism by thinking critically, then one wonders whether the skeptic here has any rational grounds for their skepticism, or rather simply arrived at it with a "gut feeling" or lazy thinking (not wanting to think deeply about important matters), or perhaps driven by other emotional attachments, or perhaps by social pressures. In any case, if the skepticism did not arise from thinking critically, then it is probably irrational and groundless. Thus, the rational choice is to reject this local skepticism.

Even if we ultimately cannot *know* whether such statements as those about God, free will, and the like are true, still we can have rational or irrational thoughts about the matter, and critical thinking is the difference maker here. Thus, once again, the rational choice is to reject local skepticism and remove this obstacle to thinking critically.

## Subjectivism

Another extreme in one's thinking is subjectivist thinking, or subjectivism. More and more these days one hears or even says things like, "That is my truth," or, "That may be true for you, but not for me," or, "It depends on whose truth you are talking about." The idea of *subjective* truth, as expressed in the above statements, is often expressed in relation to morality, religion, or politics. However, it can be found in other areas of thought as well. This idea that there is subjective truth is dangerous, and it is an obstacle to thinking critically! In chapter 2 *truth* will be discussed and reasons will be given for why subjectivism is mistaken. But here we'll just consider why it is dangerous and an obstacle to critical thinking. To overcome it is much like overcoming skepticism—namely, being aware of its negative implications.

Before evaluating the idea of "my truth," or "true for me," let's briefly get the idea of *subjectivism* before us. In its strongest form, subjectivism is the belief that believing a statement makes it true, for *every* statement; and in weaker forms it is the idea that believing a statement makes it true for *some* but not all statements. The idea of "true for me" can be understood to be one form of subjectivism. Let's examine it.

What exactly is meant by this idea of "*p* is true for me," where *p* stands for some statement? For example, one may say, "It's true for me that the earth is flat." How should we understand this?

Option #1: "*p* is true for me" means "I believe *p*"

If this is what the saying means, then there are two problems. One, if *p* is false, then the statement is not *true* for me, it is *false* for me. Thus, it is misleading to say it is "*true* for me," which statement contains the word "true," when in fact it is *false*. Two, and importantly, it shuts down critical thinking. If one believes that some statement is "true for me," one is unlikely to think critically about it, but rather one has already made the judgment that it is "*true* for me."

Option #2: "*p* is true for me" means "whether true or false, I'll act as if *p* is true"

If this is what is meant, then fine—behave as you will. But it may be that your behavior is contrary to the *truth* and may (probably will) lead to problems for you. For example, suppose you say, "It is true for me that next year I'll have an extra $250,000." You then proceed to purchase a 2020 Audi R8 (with a loan you could not afford with your current salary minus the supposed, but not yet received, extra $250,000). However, suppose that it is false that you *will have* the extra $250,000. You will then have borrowed for a vehicle you cannot afford, and it will likely be repossessed.

Or worse, suppose you say, "It is true for me that handling an inland taipan snake without protective armor is totally fine." You then proceed to play with the deadly snake. You will likely be dead shortly! Not only is the thinking expressed in Option #2 potentially deadly, it again shuts down critical thinking. If one decides that one is going to behave as if some particular statement is true, whether it is or not, then one is unlikely to think critically about it.

Option #3: "*p* is true for me" means "*p* is about the way things really are, independent of appearances, but only relative to me"

For example, suppose *p* stands for "The earth is flat," and thus "It's true for me that the earth is flat." And what one means by this is that the earth really is (in itself, apart from appearances) flat, but only relative to me. If this is what is meant, then the idea is clearly mistaken. Reality simply does not mold itself to a single individual. If reality is *p*-wise (e.g., flat earth-wise), then it is *p*-wise (e.g., flat earth-wise), period, not relative to one individual. We will elaborate in the next chapter, but for now let's consider why it shuts down critical thinking.

Suppose for a moment that one believes that reality really does mold itself to whatever one believes, and thus one means it to be taken *literally* when one says that "*p* is true for me." This person should be aware of two consequences of their thinking. First, this way of thinking implies that reality, in itself, is filled with contradictions—the earth is both flat and not flat, there is a God and there is not a God, since there are those with beliefs on both sides of each issue. Given this, we have the second implication—namely, that this way of thinking implies that not only is critical thinking useless, but science, math, and nearly all other disciplines are useless. We can just believe what we want and we have the truth, as reality is constantly molding itself to our beliefs. There is no need for thinking critically.

In summary, if one is to be a critical thinker, one must remove such obstacles as thinking that believing something is sufficient to make it true. Instead, one must understand that belief is one thing and truth another. One must further accept that we are able to *discover truth* by rational reflection together with experience, or at least arrive at rational belief in this way.

**EXERCISE 1.4**

**Review Questions**

1. How does lack of care affect critical thinking?

2. In what way does self-esteem that is too high or too low affect open-mindedness?

3. How does being lazy-minded or impatient affect critical thinking?

4. In what way does being a passive thinker make one a slave?

5. How do pride and fear affect critical thinking?

6. How can one overcome emotional attachment to an idea?

7. What is having a "gut feeling" that a statement is true? How is this an obstacle to critical thinking?

8. How might one's natural desire to be part of a group affect one's thinking critically?

9. What does it mean to say that a statement is self-refuting?

10. What is the difference between global skepticism and local skepticism?

11. How is skepticism an obstacle to critical thinking?

12. Why should we reject skepticism in general?

13. What does it mean for a statement to be subjective?

14. What are three things that might be meant by the phrase "*p* is true for me?"

15. How is subjective thinking an obstacle to critical thinking?

## Lack of Knowledge of or Skills in the Methods

The last obstacle to critical thinking is simply lacking knowledge of the methods of critical thinking, or lacking the skills needed to engage in critical thinking. To overcome this difficulty is obvious: study critical thinking and practice its methods. The rest of this book is devoted to helping provide knowledge of the methods and to provide exercises to help the student develop the skills of engaging in critical thinking.

## Recap

In this chapter, we considered a somewhat lengthy description of *critical thinking*, the appropriate *attitude* to have as a critical thinker, and the various *stages* of critical thinking. We next reflected upon *why critical thinking matters*, as well as discussed obstacles to critical thinking and how to overcome them. Below are some important concepts and definitions:

- **Critical Thinking**: Being disposed to examine any statement, belief, or argument one encounters with an open-mind, appropriate humility, patience, and wonder in the pursuit of truth and knowledge, using knowledge of and skill at applying methods of problem solving, linguistic analysis, data interpretation, evidence assessment, argument evaluation, logical inquiry, and reasoning, with a willingness to render judgments about any statement, belief, or argument and adjust one's beliefs as a result.
- **Open-Minded**: Being willing to consider any statement, idea, belief, or argument and reflect upon it, and especially a willingness to consider the possibility that one's own beliefs are false, that one's own reason is bad, and that perhaps one is engaging in some illicit rhetoric.
- **Skepticism**: Holding that knowledge in some form is impossible.
  - **Global Skepticism**: Belief that knowledge of *anything* is impossible.
  - **Local Skepticism**: Belief that knowledge of *particular areas of thought* is impossible.
- **Subjectivism**: In its strongest form, it is the belief that believing a statement makes it true, for *every* statement; in weaker forms it is the belief that believing a statement makes it true for *some* but not all statements.

# 2

# BELIEF, TRUTH, AND KNOWLEDGE

As we saw in chapter 1, the goal of critical thinking is to increase one's *true beliefs* and decrease one's false beliefs and ultimately to achieve *knowledge*. But *what exactly is a belief*, and importantly, *what is a true belief*? And *what is it to know something*? There appears to be some confusion about each of these concepts: *belief*, *truth*, and *knowledge*. So, in this chapter, we will discuss these very important concepts, which we must understand as critical thinkers. Along the way we will also distinguish between *absolute* vs. *relative statements* on the one hand, and *objective* vs. *subjective statements* on the other. Below are some important key words and phrases to master as we work through this chapter:

## KEY WORDS

| | |
|---|---|
| Absolute Statement | Law of Excluded Middle |
| Belief | Law of Non-Contradiction |
| Circular Definition | Objective Statement |
| Contradiction | Opinion |
| Counterexample | Relative Statement |
| Judgment | Subjective Statement |
| Knowledge | Truth |

## Belief

Let's begin with the concept of a *belief*. As the terms are typically used in philosophy, "belief," "opinion," and "judgment" are synonymous. We will follow this convention, and so whether we call it a "belief," "opinion," or "judgment," we are talking about the same thing. We will primarily call it "belief." A *belief* is a *mental state of a person*. It is a mental state of the person *accepting a statement as true*. For example, consider the following statement:

*The earth has exactly one moon.*

To believe this statement is to just accept it as being *true*. Alternatively, we could put this as *accepting that reality is a certain way* (and thus, for the belief here, it is accepting that *in reality* the earth has only one moon).

Note that *the belief* is different from *the statement*. For one thing, for one to *believe* the statement, first one must be aware of and understand the statement. However, the statement could exist if neither of these were the case. There are statements that we don't understand, and many that we are unaware of, and thus we don't believe such statements. It is *not* that we think such statements are false. Rather, we simply lack the belief that they are true. Nevertheless, the statements still exist. Thus, a statement is one thing, and believing it another.

Note further that not just any mental state is a belief. One could have a *thought*, for example, without believing the thought. For example, consider the following statement:

> *The earth has exactly three moons.*

We are right now *thinking* the above statement, since we just read it. Thus, we now have the thought that the earth has three moons. However, we don't *believe* this (it is hoped), since we don't accept it as true. Indeed, we believe that it is *false*. So, a thought is one kind of mental state, and a belief another.

Further, and very importantly, just because one accepts a statement as true when one believes it, it does *not* follow that the statement accepted really is true. If the statement believed is true, then the belief is true, and if the statement accepted is false, then the belief is false. So, it is one thing to believe a statement and another for the belief to be *true*. For example, if one believes that the earth has three moons, then one accepts this as being true. But, since this statement is *false*, the belief is *false*. What makes a belief true or false, then, is not the mere fact that someone believes it. What makes it true or false is the same thing that makes a statement true or false, which we will discuss in the next section.

This point about a belief being true applies to every type of belief, ranging from historical beliefs, to scientific beliefs, to religious beliefs, to moral beliefs, and any belief in any area of thought. So, that means that not all religious and moral beliefs are true. Some are false, just as some historical and scientific beliefs are false. For example, if someone believes that there are 16 gods, but there are not 16 gods, then the person's belief is false. The same is the case with "opinion" and "judgment," since these are synonymous with "belief."

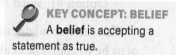

**KEY CONCEPT: BELIEF**
A **belief** is accepting a statement as true.

(*Belief, opinion,* and *judgment* are synonyms.)

---

**EXERCISE 2.1**

Review Questions

1. What is a belief?
2. True or false: A *statement* and a *belief* are the same thing.
3. True or false: *Belief, opinion,* and *judgment* are three names for the same mental state.

4. True or false: The mere act of having a belief makes the belief true.

5. True or false: Opinions are neither true nor false; they are just opinions.

6. True or false: A *thought* and a *belief* are the same thing.

## Truth

In the New Testament of the Bible, we have the record of Jesus at his trial before Pontius Pilate.[1] During his interaction with Pilate, Jesus said that he (Jesus) was sent into the world to testify to the truth and that those on the side of the truth listen to him. Pilate then asked Jesus, "What is truth?" However, Pilate immediately departed and did not wait for Jesus's answer.[2] Jesus did not provide an answer at that time. But, let's explore this question and see whether we can find an answer. So, our question is: *What is truth?*

In answer to this general question, one often hears a variety of general, vague, and even obscure answers, including, "Truth is Love," "Truth is relative," "Truth is in the eyes of the beholder," "God is truth," "Science is truth," and, "There is no truth." What should we make of these answers, or even the original question itself? Perhaps the reason why we get such a diverse and obscure set of answers is that the original question is itself too general. Perhaps it will help if we make it more specific. One way to make it more specific is this:

*What is it for a statement to be true?*

This is more precise, since we are now focusing on a *statement* as opposed to the general question above. So, what is it for a *statement* to be true? In what does its truth consist? What is *required* for a statement to be true? What would *guarantee* it?

### Misguided Attempts at Defining Truth

As a first attempt to answer this question, someone may offer this:

Option #1: What makes a statement true is that most believe it.

This answer might initially seem to have something going for it. After all, how could most of us be wrong? The evidence, however, tells us that this is not right. There are countless cases in which most people believed something but were mistaken. Here is just one example: prior to Copernicus (AD 1473–1543) nearly everyone believed that the earth was the center of the solar system, and that the sun, moon, planets, and stars revolved around the earth. So, 700 years ago, for example, nearly everyone (if not everyone) believed:

*The earth is the center of the solar system.*

---

1. Pontius Pilate was the Roman governor of Judaea from AD 26–36 under the emperor Tiberius. Pilate presided over the trial of Jesus and ordered his crucifixion.

2. See the Gospel of John 18:28–40, especially verses 37 and 38.

However, we now know that they were wrong—that this is *false*. Thus, anyone who believed (believes?) that had (has) a *false* belief. So, the mere fact that most people believe something cannot be what makes it true.

Further, there are many *true* statements that no one believes, in large part because we are unaware of such statements. Nevertheless, they are still true. Thus, since we can have *false* beliefs, and since there are truths that we do not believe, belief is one thing and truth another, and thus a *true statement* does **not** consist in belief.

Perhaps what makes a statement true is that there is evidence for it. So, perhaps the following is the right answer:

Option #2: What makes a statement true is that there is evidence for it.

This is certainly better than Option #1. After all, having evidence seems to play an important role in how we *know*, at least in part for some things, that some statement is true. While this is a good attempt, unfortunately it won't do either. The reason is that we often have evidence for a *false* statement. Here is an example:

Suppose that Sam murders his neighbor Fred. However, suppose that Sam is very crafty. He has carefully studied crime scene investigation and has learned how to cover his tracks and make it look like someone else committed the crime. As a result, he leaves evidence that his other neighbor Jim murdered Fred. So, when the detectives and crime scene investigators gather all the evidence, they conclude that it was Jim who murdered Fred.

In the story, the detectives have evidence, and perhaps even very good evidence (if Sam was good at his deception), that the following statement is true:

*Jim murdered Fred.*

Despite the evidence, however, this is *false*. While the above story is fictional, we know that there are actual cases where this occurs—namely, that the evidence points to the guilt of an innocent person. We also know that it happens in the sciences. Consider again the statement about the earth being the center of the solar system:

*The earth is the center of the solar system.*

Not only did most (all) believe this at one time, but astronomers had *good evidence* for it. This is one reason why it was hard for Copernicus and Galileo to get scientists to accept that it is false.

Further, there are statements that are *true* for which there is *no evidence*. For example, consider the following statement:

*Exactly 68 million years ago, dinosaur Carl ate dinosaur Marty for lunch.*

Of course, they were not at the time named "Carl" and "Marty," but are so named now to refer to the *specific* dinosaurs. The point is that a *specific* dinosaur (whom we're calling "Carl") ate another *specific* dinosaur (whom we're calling "Marty"). Further, and to the point, while there is evidence that some dinosaurs ate others, there is no evidence for the statement above—that the *specific* dinosaur (Carl) ate the other *specific* dinosaur (Marty). Nevertheless, it may well be true.

So, since there can be evidence for *false* statements, and since some *true* statements can lack evidence, truth is one thing and evidence another, and having evidence is **not** what makes a statement *true*.

Alternatively, one might suggest that what makes a statement true is that it is impossible to prove it false. So, we have

Option #3: What makes a statement true is that *it is impossible to prove it false.*

While it is true that if it is *impossible* to prove a statement false then it is probably true, this is too strong. After all, there are some statements which, while they are in fact true, could have been false, and had they been false then we would be able to prove them false, at least in principle. For example, it is *actually true* that Barack Obama was elected to be the 44th president of the United States. However, it is *possible* that he wasn't, and that John McCain won instead. That is, things *could* have gone differently, such that McCain won. Had McCain won, then Obama would not have been elected to be the 44th president of the United States. So, consider the following statement:

*Barack Obama was elected to be the 44th president of the United States.*

While it is actually true, it *could have been* false. And, had it been false, then we would have been able to *prove it to be false*. So, since it is possibly false and is such that had it been false, we would be able to prove it to be false, it follows that it is *possible* to prove it false, even though it is actually true. Therefore, Option #3 is too strong.

But there is another problem with Option #3—namely, it is *circular*. A definition of a term is circular if one uses the term (or one of its synonyms) in the definition. For example, if one says that *what makes a statement true is that it is true*, one has not told us what makes it true, but rather has given a circular definition. If we don't know what it is for a statement to be true, we won't know what one means when one says *it is true if and only if it is true*. Now consider Option #3, which says that a statement is true if it cannot be proven *false*. To say that a statement is *false* means that *it is not true*. Thus, Option #3 amounts to this: A *statement is true if it is impossible to prove that it is not true*. But this uses "true" in the definition, in which case it is circular. So, since Option #3 is too strong and circular, it won't do.

Someone may be led to conclude from this that there isn't anything that makes a statement true. They may think that either there is no such thing as a true statement, or that while there are true statements, there is nothing that makes them true. Let's consider these in order. The first of these is expressed in Option #4:

Option #4: There are no true statements.

This won't work. After all, Option #4 itself expresses a statement. Thus, if what it says is true, then it cannot be true. That is, what it says is true only if it is false. Thus, option #4 is self-refuting.[3] So, we don't want to go to the extreme of saying that there are no true statements.

The next option is that there are true statements, but nothing that makes them true:

---

3. See chapter 1 for more on self-refutation.

Option #5: There are true statements, but *nothing makes a statement true*.

This doesn't seem to be correct either. Consider the following statement:

*Utah is in the United States.*

Surely this is *made true* by that fact that Utah *really is* in the United States. So, it cannot be correct to say that *nothing makes a statement true*.

## Correct Account of Truth

The last point gets us much closer to the answer to our question, however. Consider again our statement: *Utah is in the United States.* Isn't what makes it true the *existence of certain conditions* in *reality* (or alternatively, the *structure of reality*)—namely, that in reality Utah is in the United States? It seems that the answer is "Yes!" But the same can be said of other statements. Consider again the following statement:

*The earth has exactly one moon.*

Surely what *makes* this *true* is the structure of reality—namely, that *in reality* the earth has exactly one moon.

We can generalize and get to what is the *correct answer* to our question—namely, Option #6:

Option #6: What makes a statement true is the *structure of reality*.

This account of truth goes back at least to the ancient Greek philosophers and is a common-sense view. It is the view that we will adopt, and indeed we accept as *correct*.

Let's investigate it further.

> **KEY CONCEPT: TRUTH**
> A statement is **true** if and only if *the structure of reality* matches the statement.

### Laws of Non-Contradiction and Excluded Middle

Given that truth consists in the structure of reality being a certain way, and given two fundamental features of reality, we can state two important axioms about truth—namely, the *law of non-contradiction* and the *law of excluded middle*. Let's discuss these.

Both laws are rooted in fundamental features of the structure of reality. The *law of non-contradiction* is rooted in the fundamental feature of reality that in reality there cannot be any contradictions. A *contradiction* is something both *being* and *not being* part of the structure of reality simultaneously. Here are some examples of contradictions:

- *Esther exists and does not exist simultaneously.*
- *The car is simultaneously entirely red and not entirely red.*
- *The Burj Khalifa is taller than Shanghai Tower and also not taller than Shanghai Tower, at the same time.*

However, a fundamental feature of reality is that reality not only *does not* but *cannot* contain contradictions. As a result, the *law of non-contradiction* governing all statements follows:

Law of Non-Contradiction: No statement can be both true and false simultaneously.

The other fundamental feature of reality is that for any pair of contradictions, one or the other is an aspect of the structure of reality—that is, it cannot be that *neither* is an aspect of the structure of reality. So, consider the first of the three contradictory pairs above. Either Esther exists in reality, or she does not, but it cannot be that neither of these is the case. If reality contains Esther in its structure, then *Esther exists* is true. If reality lacks Esther in its structure, then *Esther does not exist* is true. There are no other options! The same is the case for *every* contradictory pair. This yields the *law of excluded middle* governing all statements:

> Law of Excluded Middle: For any statement S and its contradiction not-S, either S is true or not-S is true, and there are no other logically possible options.

As a side note, there may be *manmade* systems of logic in which either or both laws are not included, and thus *in the logical system*, there may be contradictions or statements that are neither true nor false, but such systems do *not* correspond to reality. In *reality*, two fundamental features are and must be that there are no contradictions, and that for any contradictory pair, one or the other is true, and it cannot be that neither is true.

### Generality

Second, the account that truth consists in reality having a certain structure is *general*. It covers statements about *anything*. For example, we make statements about the concrete *physical* world, such as:

> *Water is composed of $H_2O$.*

This is true, according to the account if and only if in *reality, independent of appearance and what we believe*, water *really* is composed of $H_2O$. Otherwise, it is false.

People also make statements about the concrete *non-physical* world. For example:

> *God (of Christianity) is omnipotent.*

This is true according to our account if and only if *in reality, independent of appearances and our beliefs*, God exists and is omnipotent. And we make statements and have beliefs about countless other matters. Here are just a few more:

> $2 + 2 = 4.$

> *Murder is wrong.*

> *Santa Claus is jolly.*

The account covers all of these. In each case, what makes the statement true, if indeed it is true, is *the structure of reality* independent of our appearance. If reality contains the appropriate states of affairs, then the statement is true. It is false otherwise.

It should be noted that a statement may be true or false, *even if* we do not *know* that it is true or false. For example, suppose no one knows whether Bigfoot exists. Still, if in reality Bigfoot exists, then the statement *Bigfoot exists* is *true*, even if we don't know it—indeed, even if there is no evidence for it, and no one believes it.

**Reality Independent of Appearances**

Third, let's consider further this idea of *reality* and, more exactly, *reality independent of appearances*. Things *appear* to us in all sorts of ways. Some of these appearances do *not* reflect how things *really* are. For example, a straight stick *appears* bent in water, the sun *appears* to go around the earth, and some actions *appear* to be right, when in fact they're wrong. Other appearances *do* reflect reality. But truth consists not in how things *appear* to us, but in how things *really* are. For example, in *reality* the earth revolves around the sun, and it merely *appears* that the sun revolves around the earth. Thus, consider the two statements below (the first true and the second false):

> The earth revolves around the sun.

> The sun revolves around the earth.

It is *not* the case that the first of these is true *because* we believe it, but rather *it is true because of the structure of reality, independent of appearances*. Thus, even prior to Copernicus, the first statement was true and the second false, even though humans believed otherwise.

Further, reality may well consist in a variety of different types of states of affairs. There could very well be *physical* concrete states of affairs (e.g., *water being composed of $H_2O$*) as well as *nonphysical* concrete states of affairs (e.g., *God being omnipotent*) as well as *in abstract* states of affairs (e.g., *the number 2 being even*).

**Knowledge of Reality**

One may ask:

> *Who's to decide which states of affairs exist?*

If this question is intended to be taken *literally* (to be asking who *creates* the structure of reality), then the answer varies. For some aspects of reality, no one "decides" (creates) *that* aspect—the states of affairs just exist (e.g., *the existence of God*). For other aspects of reality, perhaps God created them. Still for others, humans created them.

However, perhaps the question really means:

> *How do we <u>know</u> which states of affairs exist in reality?*

The answer to this is difficult to say, but probably we know what exists in a variety of ways, including observation, scientific method, philosophy, and other ways of knowing. We'll consider this a bit more in chapter 3. However, fortunately we do not have to answer this in order to say in general what it is for a statement to be true, as opposed to how we *know* that it is true. A statement is *true* if and only if *the structure of reality* is a certain way, and the statement is otherwise false, even if we do not *know* what reality is like.

## EXERCISE 2.2

### Review Questions

1. In general, what makes a statement true?
2. True or false: Whether a statement is true or false is based on whether we have evidence for the statement.
3. True or false: If *everyone* believed that ghosts exist, then this would make it true that ghosts exist.
4. What is the *law of non-contradiction*?
5. True or false: There are some statements that are both true and false at the same time.
6. True or false: If one person sincerely believes that God (of Christianity) exists and another person sincerely believes God (of Christianity) does not exist, both of them are right (i.e., both have true beliefs).
7. What is the *law of excluded middle*?
8. True or false: There are some statements that are neither true nor false.
9. What does it mean to say that the theory of truth is *general*?
10. True or false: The statement that *abortion is wrong* is neither true nor false.

## Absolute vs. Relative and Objective vs. Subjective

We can make two distinctions about our account. The first distinction is between *absolute* vs. *relative* statements, which has to do with whether a statement changes in truth-value; and the second distinction is between *objective* vs. *subjective* statements, which concerns whether a statement depends on our beliefs to make it true.

### Absolute Statements

A statement is *absolute* (true or false) if and only if it *never changes* in truth-value, no matter what time, place, or circumstance. It is either true everywhere, always, and in all circumstances, or false everywhere, always, and in all circumstances. The paradigm examples of absolute statements are mathematical statements, though of course one can cite many other examples as well, including logical, philosophical, religious, and other statements. Below are two examples of absolute mathematical statements.

2 + 2 = 4

2 + 2 = 17

While the first is true and the second false, both are *absolute*, because in each case the statement *never* changes in truth-value. The first is *always* true, in every circumstance, and the second is *always* false, in every circumstance.

## Relative Statements

In contrast to absolute statements are relative statements. A statement is *relative* (true or false) if and only if it *changes* in truth-value, relative to time, to place, or to circumstance. Some statements are *relative to time*—for example, the age of an object. Suppose that Mary was born exactly 10 years ago. Then the statement below is true *now*:

> Mary is 10 years old.

However, one year ago it was false, and it will be false next year as well.

Other statements have their truth-value *relative to place*. For example, the climate in Colombia is tropical, but not so in Nevada. So, if one utters the statement below while standing in downtown Bogota, one will have said something true, but if one were to utter it while standing in downtown Las Vegas, one will have said something false:

> The climate here is tropical.

And still other statements are *relative to circumstance*. For example, it is illegal to drive 45 mph on a road with the posted speed limit of 35 mph, *unless* one is driving an emergency vehicle (police, ambulance, fire truck) in an emergency. Thus, for an ordinary citizen (Kyle), in an ordinary circumstance, the statement below is false:

> Kyle's speed of 45 mph on this road with a speed limit of 35 mph is legal.

It is false, unless Kyle is an ambulance driver (for example) racing a patient to the hospital.

## Objective Statements

The second distinction is objective vs. subjective statements. A statement is *objective* (true or false) if and only if it has its truth-value (true or false) *independent* of what anyone believes. So, even if everyone thought or believed otherwise, an objectively true statement is still *true*, and an objectively *false* statement is still *false*. Our mental life is simply *irrelevant* to the truth-value of an *objective* statement. Many examples of objective statements are obvious:

> Water is composed of $H_2O$.

> Las Vegas is in Nevada.

> The earth revolves around the sun.

Note that while the above examples are examples of *true* objective statements, there are also *false* objective statements:

> Water is composed of $NH_4$.

> Las Vegas is located on the moon.

> The sun revolves around the earth.

Other objective statements may be less obvious to some, but they are still objective. Consider two such examples:

> God (of Christianity) exists.
>
> Humans are composed of a material body and an immaterial soul.

Some may find it surprising that these two statements are *objective*. But it can easily be shown that they are. Consider the first. Can anyone cause God to exist *in reality* simply by *believing* that God exists in reality, or cause *reality* to lack God simply by *believing* that there is no God in reality? The answers are clearly *No!* One cannot cause the creator of the universe to exist *in reality* simply by believing that he exists *in reality*. Whether God exists or not is simply not up to us. He either exists or he doesn't, independent of what we think. Thus, the statement is objective (true or false). All the same points can be made about the second statement. Whether humans have a soul is simply not brought about because someone believes it. Our beliefs simply do not have such power.

## Subjective Statements

A statement is *subjective* if and only if the mere act of believing it makes it *true*. Thus, the truth-value (true or false) of a subjective statement is *dependent* on what someone believes. Notice that subjective statements (if there are any) are extremely relative—they are relative to each individual person!

### There Are No Subjective Statements

There are good reasons to *deny* that there are any subjective statements—that is, the subjective category is *empty*. First, every type of statement appears to be *objectively* true or false, and second, which is the more powerful reason, beliefs simply do not have the power to cause reality to be structured in particular ways. Of course, a belief may (and often does) lead a person to *act* upon that belief, which *action* may in turn cause reality to be structured in a particular way. But that is the *person* causing a state of affairs *in virtue of a belief*, not the belief itself causing the state of affairs. Thus, since beliefs cannot cause reality to be a certain way, and since all cases appear objective, we can conclude that all statements are objective.

However, let's consider a couple of potential *counterexamples*. A *counterexample* is an exception to a general principle, rule, definition, or statement, which may show the principle, rule, definition, or statement to be false. In the case at hand, if the following examples *really* are examples of subjective statements, then they are *counterexamples* to the statement that *there are no subjective statements* and prove the claim to be false.

Let's reconsider the following statement, which someone may suggest is *subjective* and thus to be a counterexample to the claim that there are no subjective statements:

> God (of Christianity) exists.

Some have considered religious beliefs subjective and thus would treat the statement above as a counterexample to the claim that all statements are objective. However, it was already shown why this statement is *objective* in truth-value (either objectively true or objectively false). It is so because no one causes, or can cause, God to exist simply by believing that God exists (or causes God's non-existence by being an atheist). Now suppose that someone *believes* that the statement is true. While the *existence* of their belief depends on them, the *truth-value* of their belief (being true or false) does *not* depend on them, and thus the *truth-value* is objective. Thus, the statement is not a counterexample to the claim that all statements are objective.

Alternatively, someone may offer something like the following statement as a counterexample to the claim that there are no subjective statements:

> *Spinach tastes good to me.*

It may be suggested, contrary to the claim, that the statement above is subjectively true for the person uttering it—after all, it is about the person's own taste!

Reply: While the *existence* of the person's *taste* is dependent upon that person, it does not thereby follow that the *truth-value* of a *statement* about that taste is subjective. A good case can be made that it is objective. To see why, consider the following question, which will be put in first person to help make the point:

> *What causes me to like spinach?*

Did I believe that I like spinach (e.g., prior to ever tasting it), which in turn *caused* me to like spinach (without having tasted it)? *No!* I cannot cause myself to like something *merely* by believing that I do. Rather, *first I taste the spinach*. Having tasted it, I find myself liking it. *Then* this state of affairs in reality (*that I like the spinach*, having already tasted it) causes me to believe that I like spinach, *and* this state of affairs in reality (*that I like the spinach*, having already tasted it) grounds the *truth* of the statement (and belief) that "*I like spinach.*" Thus, it is not the *belief* that *I like spinach* that grounds the *truth* of the belief—that is, the belief does *not* make itself true. Rather, the *existence of the taste* (state of affairs in reality) grounds *the truth of* the belief. Figure 2.1 illustrates this point:

**FIGURE 2.1**

Let's continue in first person for a moment. Since the fact that I believe that I like spinach did *not* cause me to like it, but rather *my taste caused my belief,* and since the *truth* of my belief is grounded not in itself (the belief), but in the existence of my taste, my belief that I like spinach does *not* ground the truth of the statement *"I like spinach."* Therefore, the above example about taste is *not* a counterexample to the claim that all statements are objective in truth-value.

The final potential counterexample to the claim is to cite moral statements—claiming that they are subjective. However, rather than discuss the moral cases at length, consider that beliefs lack the power to cause the structure of reality to be a certain way, *including moral states of affairs.* While this point about morality requires a lot more discussion, consider that if merely believing that an act is right is what makes it right, then one can justify murder, rape, genocide, torturing babies for fun, and all sorts of other things. If believing that an act is right makes the act right, then all those acts mentioned are right for someone *simply because the person believes them.* And if the acts are right, then blame and punishment of these acts makes no sense. Surely that thinking is wrong!

In wrapping up this section, let's note the relationships between *absolute, relative, objective,* and *subjective* statements. First, the categories of *absolute* and *relative,* on the one hand, and *objective* and *subjective,* on the other hand, are *mutually exclusive.* This means that no statement can be both *absolute* and *relative,* as this would be contradictory. The same for *objective* and *subjective*—no statement can be in both categories. And this fact is not relative to what we think but is an objective fact.

However, while no statement can be both *absolute* and *relative* or both *objective* and *subjective,* there are *objective* statements that are absolute and others that are relative. And, any subjective statement (if there were any) is relative. All absolute statements are objective. Figure 2.2 diagrams the relationships:

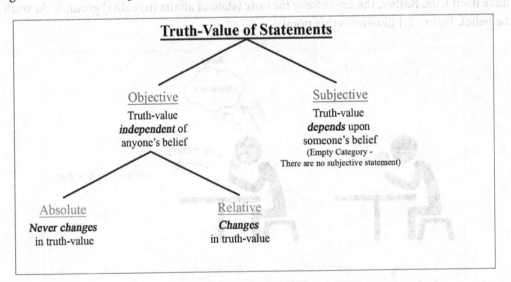

**Truth-Value of Statements**

Objective
Truth-value
*independent* of
anyone's belief

Subjective
Truth-value
*depends* upon
someone's belief
(Empty Category -
There are no subjective statement)

Absolute
**Never changes**
in truth-value

Relative
**Changes**
in truth-value

**FIGURE 2.2**

## EXERCISE 2.3

Review Questions

1. What does it mean to say that a statement is *absolute*?
2. True or false: All absolute statements are true.
3. What does it mean to say that a statement is *relative*?
4. True or false: The statement *2 + 2 = 4* is relative.
5. What does it mean to say that a statement is *objective*?
6. True or false: All objective statements are true.
7. What does it mean to say that a statement is *subjective*?
8. True or false: There are *no* subjective statements.
9. True or false: All relative statements are also subjective.
10. True or false: If a statement is absolute, then it is also objective.
11. Consider the proposition expressed by the sentence, "The Bible is the inspired word of God." Into which of the following categories does it fall?
    a. Relative
    b. Subjective
    c. Objective
    d. None of the above
12. True or false: The statement *"Every human has a soul"* is a subjective statement.
13. True or false: The statement *"That rose appears beautiful to me"* is an objective statement.

## Knowledge

The final concept we will discuss in this chapter is that of *knowledge*. Our discussion will be brief just to get the rough idea of the concept before us. To begin, we should distinguish between three senses of "knows." So, consider the following:

John knows ...

(a) ... his mother.

(b) ... how to ride a bike.

(c) ... that 2 + 2 = 4.

In (a), we have an example of what may be called "*knowledge by acquaintance.*" It involves being aware of something as an object of experience or thought, and not derived from any process of reasoning or reliance on knowledge of some other truth. So, in (a) we have a case of John being aware of his mother. This form of knowledge does not involve any conceptual judgment about some statement but is simply acquaintance. Of course, one may *also* make a judgment along with one's awareness, but the awareness itself does not involve any judgment.

In contrast, we have (b). This is what has been called "*know how*." It is possessing some skill or ability. In the example given in (b), John possess the skills to ride a bike.

Lastly, there is (c). It is this one that we are most interested in for critical thinking, as it involves knowing that a *statement* is *true*. It has been called "*propositional knowledge*." Since propositional knowledge is of particular interest to us as critical thinkers, let's give at least a partial analysis of it.

First, note that it involves knowing that a *statement* is *true*. One cannot know that a statement is *true* if it is *false*! Thus, as a start, we have:

> *A person knows that a statement is true only if the statement is true.*

One lesson from this is that we should be careful about our knowledge claims. We often mistakenly say things like, "We used to *know* that the earth was the center of the universe, but now we know otherwise." Well, as a matter of fact, we never *knew* that the earth was the center of the universe, because it was (is) *false*. Rather we *believed* it. But we had a *false* belief, and thus lacked knowledge.

So, the first part of our analysis of knowledge is that the known statement must be *true*. However, the mere fact that some statement is true does *not* entail that someone knows that it is true. More is needed for knowledge than that the statement in question is true. What is needed, of course, is that the *person* in question at the very least is acquainted with the statement *and* accepts it as true—that is, *believes it*. For surely if the person does not believe that the statement is true, the person cannot very well *know* that it is true. Thus, we have:

> *A person knows that a statement is true only if the person believes the statement.*

So, for a person to have propositional knowledge of a statement, the statement must be true and the person must believe it.

However, a *mere* true belief (i.e., true belief and *nothing* more) is insufficient for knowledge, as one may simply be believing the truth *by luck*, for example. Here is an example to show it:

> Suppose that Mary drives to the mall and parks her car in parking garage A, which looks amazingly like garage B. After several hours of shopping, Mary cannot recall if she parked in garage A or B, since she often parks in B, and it looks very similar to A. As she is sitting trying to recall where she parked, her friend Betty comes along. Mary confesses that she is embarrassed that she cannot remember where she parked. Betty tells her that she is in luck, as she saw Mary's car when she was walking into the mall, and it is parked in garage A. Mary believes Betty's report and proceeds to walk toward garage A.

However, suppose that Betty did *not* really see Mary's car, but only one that looked very similar to Mary's car. Thus, while it is true that Mary's car is parked in garage A, Betty would have given the same report even if it were not true. Thus, Mary got *lucky* that Betty happened to see a car that looked just like Mary's in garage A, and that she (Mary) is also parked in A. Surely we would say that Mary does not *know* that her car is in garage A, even though she has a true belief that it is. She does not know in this case (even with her true belief) because she got *lucky* that her belief is true. Something more is needed for knowledge.

Philosophers agree that *true belief* is required for knowledge, and nearly all also agree that more is needed. However, there is a great deal of disagreement about what more is needed. One thought is that what more is needed is what is called "justification." In order to know the statement, the person must have a true belief and *be justified* in having this belief. To be justified means roughly that the believer is some way in right standing in holding the belief—for example, the belief is more likely to be true, or that those beliefs were formed in a responsible manner, or that one is within one's rational rights to believe the statement. Thus, some have accepted that the right analysis of knowledge is this:

A person knows that a statement is true if and only if ...

(a) ... the statement is true,

(b) ... the person believes that the statement is true, and

(c) ... the person is justified in believing that the statement is true.

However, some have questioned whether this is the right analysis, as there seem to be counterexamples. For example, consider the Mary case above. We already established that Mary has a true belief that her car is in garage A. But isn't Mary also *justified* in believing this, since her friend Betty is usually reliable? Surely, believing Betty's report is the right thing to do in the scenario. Thus, surely, she is *justified*. But we also saw that Mary lacks knowledge in this case, since she was lucky that her belief is true, even if justified.

Because of scenarios like the Mary case, other philosophers have offered different accounts of knowledge, such as that what is needed along with true belief is that there is a causal relationship between what makes the belief true and the person's belief that it is true. Still others have suggested that what is needed along with true belief is that the person's cognitive faculties are functioning properly, aimed at truth, and operating in an appropriate environment. And still others offer other accounts.

We will not take the time to elaborate or evaluate each of these accounts, as that would go far beyond the scope of this book. Rather, the idea is simply to give the rough idea of knowledge. What we should take away from this is the concept that knowledge requires a true belief and something more. While we have not established here what the more is, surely critical thinking can increase one's likelihood of gaining knowledge in a scenario where without the critical thinking one may not have gained knowledge.

**KEY CONCEPT: KNOWLEDGE**
A person **knows** that a statement is true if and only if ...

(a) ... the statement is **true**,
(b) ... the person **believes** the statement, and
(c) ... **something more** (e.g., justification, causal link, warrant).

**EXERCISE 2.4**

Review Questions

1. True or false: A person can know a *false* statement.
2. True or false: It is possible to know a statement even if you do not believe the statement.
3. True or false: *Anytime* someone has a *true belief* about a statement, it is *guaranteed* that they know the statement.
4. True or false: If a person knows a statement, this *guarantees* that the statement known is *true*.
5. True or false: Knowing that a statement is true consists in the statement being true, the person (the knower) believing the statement, and something more that rules out luck, malfunction, and other conditions that undermine knowledge.

## Recap

In this chapter, we discussed three important concepts for critical thinking—*belief, truth,* and *knowledge*. We also looked at the distinction between *absolute* vs. *relative statements* on the one hand, and *objective* vs. *subjective statements* on the other. We saw an argument for the claim that there are no subjective statements—that it is an empty category. Finally, while we did not settle on the correct definition of "knowledge," we at least got the rough idea before our mind and noted that with critical thinking we increase our chances of gaining knowledge, even if we cannot say exactly what it is. Below are some important concepts and definitions:

- **Belief**: A person believes a statement if and only if the person accepts it is true.
  - Note that *belief, opinion,* and *judgment* are synonyms.
- **Contradiction**: A contradiction consists in something both being and not being part of the structure of reality simultaneously.
- **Counterexample**: A counterexample is an exception to a general principle, rule, definition, or statement, which may show the principle, rule, definition, or statement to be false.
- **Knowledge**: A person knows that a statement is true if and only if (a) the statement is true, (b) the person believes the statement, and (c) something more.
- **Law of Excluded Middle**: For any statement $S$ and its contradiction not-$S$, either $S$ is true or not-$S$ is true, and there are no other logically possible options.
- **Law of Non-Contradiction**: No statement can be both true and false simultaneously.
- **Truth**: A statement is true if and only if the structure of reality is a certain way.
  - **Absolute Statement**: A statement is absolute if and only if it never changes in truth-value.
  - **Relative Statement**: A statement is relative if and only if it changes in truth-value, relative to time, place, or circumstance.

- **Objective Statement**: A statement is objective if and only if its truth-value is independent of what anyone thinks or believes.
- **Subjective Statement**: A statement is subjective if and only if someone believing it makes it true.

## Figure Credits

Fig. 2.1a: Copyright © 2016 Depositphotos/deisey.
Fig. 2.1b: Copyright © 2011 Depositphotos/mocoo2003.

# 3

# EVALUATING STATEMENTS

*Defining Terms, Clarifying Terms, Judging Statements*

Critical thinking involves making and evaluating statements, among other things. An important aspect of both is clarifying the meaning of a sentence, defining terms in a sentence, and drawing upon truth-indicating sources to judge the statement to be true or false. In this chapter, we will study these important aspects of critical thinking, including considering *vagueness, ambiguity, generality, types of definitions, types of statements, sources of belief,* and *methods for attaining knowledge.* As we work through this chapter, be mindful of the following key terms:

---

**KEY WORDS**

| | |
|---|---|
| Ambiguity | Intuitive Truth |
| Definition | Necessary Condition |
| Empirical Statement | Principle of Charity |
| Generality | Sufficient Condition |

---

## Vagueness

Vagueness and ambiguity occasionally get confused or blurred. But these are two different things. To say that a word or phrase is *vague* means that it is *not precise*, and thus has borderline cases, such that there are contexts in which we know that the term applies, others in which we know that it does *not* apply, and contexts in which it is impossible to say objectively whether the term applies. As a result, if a sentence contains a vague term, then there will be occasions in which we cannot say whether the sentence is true or false. Thus, we want to make vague terms more precise to avoid this problem. Let's consider some examples.

## Examples of Vagueness

Here are some vague words:

- *bald*
- *hot*
- *many*
- *old*
- *rich*
- *small*

There are cases in which these terms clearly *do* apply, and thus sentences that contain these terms are clearly true. For example:

1. 50-year-old Michael Jordan is bald.
2. The sun is hot.
3. There are many trees in the Amazon.
4. The Parthenon is old.
5. Bill Gates is rich.
6. Quarks are small.

And, there are cases in which these terms clearly do *not* apply, and thus sentences that contain these terms are clearly *false*. For example:

7. Felicity Jones is bald.
8. Icebergs are hot.
9. There are many trees on the moon.
10. A newborn baby is old.
11. The homeless man is rich.
12. The universe is small.

However, there are borderline cases where we just cannot tell whether the term applies, and thus we are unable to tell whether a sentence containing one of the words is true or false. Rather than give examples, consider that there is simply no answer to the following questions:

- What is the maximum amount of hair of a bald person?
- What is the minimum temperature of a hot temperature?
- What is the minimum number of members of a group of many?
- What is the minimum age of an old person?
- What is the minimum dollar amount of a rich person?
- What is the maximum height of a short object?

Vagueness in a sentence can sometimes amount to nothing more than a slight annoyance, such as when your Uber driver informs you that he will be arriving a *little* late to take you home from work. But it can also be incredibly important, such as if the IRS informs us that "No rich person will be receiving a stimulus check." Will you be getting a check?

Vagueness comes in degrees, as you may have noticed. Sometimes there are situations in which a vague term is precise enough for the given context. For example, suppose that Fred shows up soaking wet and is asked how he got wet. He replies that "Mary dumped *a lot* of water over my head!" which is precise enough, even though it contains the vague expression "a lot."

But there are other situations in which a vague term is too vague for us to know whether the sentence containing it is true or false, or too vague for our concerns. It is with these that we are concerned and need to make more precise for the given context. For example, consider these sentences:

> *John makes <u>a lot</u> of money each year.*
>
> *The dog is doing <u>something</u> in the kitchen.*

The underlined word or phrase in each is too vague. Here is a way to make them more precise:

> *John makes more than $250,000 annually.*
>
> *The dog is eating from the trash can in the kitchen.*

However, if one encounters a sentence with a vague term and is not able to make it more precise, then one will have to withhold judgment about the sentence, neither accepting it as true nor rejecting it as false.

---

**🔍 KEY CONCEPT: VAGUENESS**

A **vague** word or phrase is one that is *not precise*, and thus has borderline cases, such that there are contexts in which we know that the term applies, others in which we know that it does *not* apply, and contexts in which it is impossible to say objectively whether the term applies.

---

**EXERCISE 3.1**

Each sentence below contains an *italicized* vague word or expression. Re-write each sentence to make the vague expression more precise. (Note that the goal is only to make the sentence more precise; it is not to make it true.)

**\*1.** The hurricane will hit the city *sometime* tomorrow.

**2.** If you eat *too much* fried food, you will get cancer.

**3.** Only *small* cars are permitted on this bridge.

**\*4.** If you drive *fast*, you will get a speeding ticket.

**5.** In order to win the lottery, you must show up to the booth *early*.

**6.** Do not go outside when there is *too much* smog in the air.

**\*7.** This movie is intended for *mature* audiences only.

**8.** No *old* people can ride on this roller coaster.

**9.** Wanted: *Tall* people to help hang Christmas lights.

**10.** Stay away from the *blue* snakes, as they are very poisonous.

## Ambiguity

In contrast with vagueness (which is imprecision), *ambiguity* occurs when a sentence has at least two meanings, and the context does not clarify which meaning is intended. Just as vagueness can pose a problem with evaluating statements, ambiguity does as well. If it is not clear what a sentence means, then it is not clear whether it is true or false. While the best we can and need to do with vagueness is make vague terms more precise, we can and must *eliminate* ambiguity if we are to evaluate a sentence. How to do this will be discussed below.

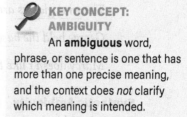

**KEY CONCEPT: AMBIGUITY**
An **ambiguous** word, phrase, or sentence is one that has more than one precise meaning, and the context does *not* clarify which meaning is intended.

### Three Types of Ambiguity

Ambiguity arises in all sorts of ways and contexts. We will focus on three types for the sake of illustration: lexical, syntactic, and collective-distributive. While there are other sorts of ambiguity, being aware of these three will be instructive for dealing with other cases. We'll conclude the section by considering how to eliminate ambiguity by practicing the principle of charity.

### Lexical Ambiguity

*Lexical ambiguity* (also called *"semantic ambiguity"*) involves homophones (words with the same pronunciation but different meanings), which are sometimes homonyms (homophones with the same spelling). In purely verbal contexts, which do not involve written words, ambiguity can arise when a homophone is used. For example, suppose that one says, or hears, the following:

> *Russell Crowe was sighted in his car.*

Since "sighted" and "cited" are homophones, the sentence is ambiguous in *purely verbal* contexts in which someone merely *says* (but does not write) this sentence, or merely *hears* it but does not read it. In such contexts, it is ambiguous between whether he was *seen* or *given a citation.*

Whether written or spoken, lexical ambiguity occurs when the word is a homonym, and context does not clarify the meaning. For example, consider the following out of context, or in a context that does not clarify the meaning:

> *The glasses are in the kitchen.*
>
> *George held the bat in his hand.*
>
> *Marcy doesn't like the chair.*

One way that lexical ambiguities can be made unambiguous is by substituting an unambiguous word or phrase for the ambiguous word. For example:

> *The spectacles are in the kitchen.*
>
> *George held the Chiroptera in his hand.*
>
> *Marcy doesn't like the presiding officer.*

Additionally, lexical ambiguities can be made unambiguous by inserting a word that modifies the ambiguous word, which eliminates the ambiguity. For example:

> *The wine glasses are in the kitchen.*

> *George held the baseball bat in his hand.*

> *Marcy doesn't like the wicker chair.*

## Syntactic Ambiguity

*Syntactic ambiguity* occurs as a result of the *syntax* of the sentence, resulting from word ordering or from the scope of the quantifier. Let's consider each.

### Word Order

Sometimes syntactic ambiguity results from the word ordering in the sentence. Consider the following examples:

> *Dillon chased the dog in pajamas.*

> *The missing puppy was found by Freddy.*

> *Headline: Firemen help burn victim.*

In the first, who was wearing the pajamas, Dillon or the dog? In the second, did Freddy find the puppy, or did someone else find it located next to Freddy? In the third, did the firemen burn the victim, or did they assist the victim who was already burned?

The way to eliminate ambiguity with examples like these is to re-order the words and perhaps add some words. So, for example:

> *While wearing his pajamas, Dillon chased the dog.*

> *Freddy found the missing puppy.*

> *Headline: Firemen burned a victim.*

### Scope

Other occasions in which syntactic ambiguity results is when there is ambiguity regarding the *scope* (what is referenced) of either a quantifier (e.g., "every," "none," "some," "a," "the"), a verb, an adverb, or an adjective. Here are some examples:

> *Every woman kissed a man.*

> *A dollar is found in every wallet.*

> *The kids left with the tall men and women.*

> *The students were captivated by the entertaining lecture and illustrations.*

The first two examples involve ambiguity resulting from ambiguity in the scope of the *quantifiers*. Which quantifier has scope over the other? Does "*every* woman" have scope over "*a* man" or vice versa? Read one way, it is saying:

1. *There is one man (man1), such that every woman kissed him (man1).*

Read another way, it is saying:

2. *For every woman, there is at least one man (man1, man2, or man3, etc.) that she kissed.*

There is a similar scope issue with the second example. It is ambiguous between whether there is exactly one dollar (dollar$_1$), such that *it* (dollar$_1$) is found in every wallet, or for every wallet, the wallet contains at least one dollar (dollar$_1$, dollar$_2$, or dollar$_3$, etc.).

In the third and fourth examples, the ambiguity arises because the scope of the adjectives is unclear. Consider the third example:

*The kids left with the tall men and women.*

Are both the men *and* the women tall? Or, are only the men tall, and the kids left with them, and some women (who may or may not have been tall). And consider the fourth example:

*The students were captivated by the entertaining lecture and illustrations.*

Are both the lecture and illustrations entertaining, or is the lecture alone entertaining, and the students were captivated by it and the illustrations (which may or may not have been entertaining)?

To eliminate the ambiguity with these, one simply re-writes the sentence so that the scope of the quantifier, verb, adverb, or adjective is clear. For example, we could re-write the four examples this way:

*There is a man, such that every woman kissed him.*

*For every wallet, that wallet contains at least one dollar.*

*The kids left with the women and tall men.*

*The students were captivated by the lecture and illustrations, both of which were entertaining.*

## Collective-Distributive Ambiguity

*Collective-distributive ambiguity* occurs when a sentence contains a word or phrase that refers to a group, and it is unclear whether reference is being made to the members of the group taken collectively or individually (distributive). Here are some examples:

*Three men pulled the plane.*

*Nurses make more money annually than doctors do.*

In the first case, does "three men" refer to them collectively, such that the three men *together* pulled the plane in one event, or does it refer to them individually, such that each man pulled the plane in three different events? In the second case, is it saying that *nurses'* collective annual income is greater than that of *doctors'* collective annual income (since there are many more nurses than there are doctors), or is it saying that each nurse makes more money than each doctor?

To eliminate this kind of ambiguity, one simply re-writes the sentence so that it is clear whether one is referring to the members collectively or individually. For example, we could re-write the examples this way:

> *Together, the three men pulled the plane.*
>
> *Each nurse makes more money annually than each doctor does.*

Wrapping up this section, it is important to take away that we need to recognize and eliminate ambiguity. It is less important that one classify the ambiguity as *lexical*, *syntactic*, *collective-distributive*, or *other*. Although in an exercise, we will classify them as part of our practice of dealing with ambiguity.

## Eliminating Ambiguity and the Principle of Charity

We need to eliminate ambiguity by choosing *exactly one* of the possible meanings of a sentence or term. But how do we decide which interpretation to give a word or sentence? One way to decide is to rely on clues from the context, even if the context does not ultimately settle which interpretation is intended. Here's an example:

> *In the Gospel of Luke, 10:18–19, a rich ruler asked Jesus, "Good Teacher, what shall I do to inherit eternal life?" Jesus replied with, "Why do you call Me good? No one is good except God alone."*

There is ambiguity in Jesus's question and sentence (let's not concern ourselves here with which type of ambiguity it is). Jesus could be saying one of at least the following two things:

- That he (Jesus) *is* good, and thus *is* God, and whether this rich ruler understands this fact in calling him "good."

Or,

- That he (Jesus) is a mere man, and not God, and thus that he (Jesus) is not good, and thus the rich man should not be calling him "good."

The immediate context does not definitely settle which is the intended meaning. For example, Jesus does not go on in the immediate context to say, "Yes, I am good, and thus I am God." However, there are *hints* in both the immediate and broader context that Jesus intended the first interpretation above—that he is good and God.

In the immediate context, one hint is that no one in the passage (not Jesus, nor the rich man, nor anyone else) *denies* Jesus is either good or God. This is a significant hint, as one would have thought that Jesus would explicitly say that he is not God if he wasn't. And the rich man does not change how he addresses Jesus. And, in the broader context of the New Testament, Jesus has called himself *good* (e.g., the Gospel of John 10:11). The point here is that whether one agrees with the interpretation, there are hints in the passage that help us to determine how to interpret that statement.

Another way to settle on which interpretation to give to an ambiguous phrase or sentence is to use what is called the *principle of charity*, defined as follows:

> Principle of Charity: When interpreting someone's sentence, assume the best possible interpretation that maximizes the truth or rationality of the sentence.

So, if there are two ways to interpret an ambiguous sentence, and both are compatible with the context, then the principle of charity urges us to interpret it in the way the most benefits the author or speaker—that is, the way that makes the sentence more rational and more likely true.

For example, consider again the ambiguous statement:

> *Nurses make more money annually than doctors do.*

In most contexts, it would be demonstrably false if interpreted to be saying that each nurse makes more money than each doctor, and indeed probably the author or speaker of the sentence would not intend that distributive interpretation. Thus, the principle of charity urges us to give its collective interpretation: *The collective annual salary of nurses is greater than the collective salary of doctors.*

---

**EXERCISE 3.2**

Each sentence below is ambiguous. For each, (a) specify whether the ambiguity is *lexical*, *syntactic*, or *collective-distributive*, and (b) then re-write each sentence to eliminate the ambiguity. (Note that the goal is only to make the statement unambiguous; it is not to make it true.)

**\*1.** Betsy told Sally that she has a bee on her shoulder.

**2.** Two boys lifted the box.

**3.** The medic helped the snake bite victim.

**\*4.** Acacia has a unique and healthy bark.

**5.** There is a nut behind the wheel.

**6.** The police officer threatened the man with a gun.

**\*7.** Paul and Kyle rowed a boat.

**8.** I saw the fisherman heading to the bank.

**9.** The cow is ready to kill.

**10.** The farmer is unhappy with his new pen.

## Generality

Generality, like vagueness and ambiguity, can cause problems for determining whether a sentence is true or false, and thus must be dealt with. Generality is lack of specificity, and thus sentences can contain a general word or phrase that results in lack of clarity. It can do this while simultaneously being unambiguous and precise, and thus generality is a different issue than vagueness and ambiguity. For example, consider the sentence:

>   *Jim was at his grandmother's house on Saturday.*

This statement is precise enough for the context, and thus vagueness is not a problem. Further, there is only one meaning, and thus it is unambiguous. However, it is too general, as it does not specify whether Jim was at his maternal or fraternal grandmother's house, and thus we don't know whether this is true, unless of course we independently knew that he has only one grandmother.

Or consider these sentences:

>   *Dogs are excellent for home security.*

>   *Betty was found guilty.*

Setting aside any issues of vagueness or ambiguity, each of these may be too general for a given context. The first is likely false, given that there are many dogs that are not great guard dogs. It would be more defensible to say something like:

>   *German shepherds are excellent for home security.*

The second may be too general for certain contexts, such as if one is determining whether Betty is a good person, or the right person for a job. We need to know of what she was found guilty. Was she found guilty of murder? Was she found guilty of violating a curfew law in order to help a friend in need?

It should be noted that generality can be useful, especially in the sciences. However, the point here is that it can also be problematic in some contexts. The fix is to make the term in question more specific, which is context relative. The idea is to make it specific enough for the context in question.

---

**KEY CONCEPT: GENERALITY**

 A sentence is too **general** when it lacks specificity by containing a word or phrase that is too general for the context, preventing clarity of the intended meaning.

---

**EXERCISE 3.3**

Follow the instructions for each below.

>   **\*1. Which of the following is the general word?**
>   taipan, snake, mulga, red-bellied black, eastern brown
>
>   **2. Which of the following is the general word?**
>   chair, bed, desk, stool, furniture

3. **Which of the following is the general word?**

   hexagon, pentagon, shape, circle

*4. **Re-write the sentence to make the italicized general expression more specific:**

   The bank is *on J Street*, but *approach carefully* because of the *creature* that is *outside*.

5. **Re-write the sentence to make the italicized general expression more specific:**

   Do not buy that *product* from Walmart, since it is *unsafe*.

6. **Re-write the sentence to make the italicized general expression more specific:**

   *School* in *this country* is *overpriced*.

*7. **Which of the following pairs of sentences is more specific?**

   a. Taking illegal drugs is dangerous.

   b. Smoking meth is very hazardous to our health.

8. **Which of the following pairs of sentences is more specific?**

   a. There is an exam in October.

   b. The Introduction to Philosophy class will have an exam Friday, October 16.

9. **Which of the following pairs of sentences is more specific?**

   a. Mark enjoys reading.

   b. Mark enjoys reading philosophy books.

10. **Which of the following pairs of sentences is more specific?**

    a. There is a God.

    b. The triune God of Christianity exists.

# Defining Terms

Central to understanding the meaning of a sentence is understanding the words within it. Typically, having the general idea of the meaning of the various words is good enough to understand the sentence. However, occasionally a word needs to be defined in to order for us to understand it. Thus, it's important to get a handle on definitions, both for the sake of evaluating definitions, as well as for defining ourselves. So, in this section we will look at different types of definitions, the purpose of definitions, and tools for evaluating definitions. We'll begin with the purpose of definitions.

## Purpose of Definitions

There are a variety of purposes for defining a word. We will consider four:

### To Inform About Common Usage

One purpose for defining a word is to inform about how the word is commonly used. This can be useful in many contexts. For example, one occasion in which this may arise is when one needs to be informed about how a term is used by a different generation. A teenager, for example, may need to inform her parent of the way in which a word is used among her friends. For example, a parent may overhear her teen say,

*I'm going out to get some cheddar from Ben.*

This may puzzle the parent, who is wondering why her daughter would be getting *cheese* from her friend Ben. The teen may then inform mom that by "cheddar" she means "money." Her purpose is to inform mom about the common usage of the word among teens.

Or, perhaps one is learning a new language. Often a very helpful definition, at least for conversation, is to be informed about how the word is *commonly* used in the society in which the language is spoken.

### To Make a Word More Precise

Alternatively, one may define a term in order to make it more precise for a given context. For example, while "computer" might be precise enough in some contexts, there are others in which using that term alone in a sentence without making it more precise simply won't do. There are desktop computers, microcomputers, notebook computers, smartphone computers, PDAs, super-computers, and more. So, we may ask someone if they have a computer and want to define what we mean precisely, in which case we might say, "Do you have a computer, as in a *desktop* or *laptop*?"

### To Define a New Word

Sometimes new words are introduced for various purposes. This often happens in philosophy and the sciences. In cases such as these, one defines in order to introduce the new word. For example, in the 1980s, philosophers introduced the term "perdurantism" to name a view about the persistence of objects in time, which they defined, roughly, as the view that objects persist by having different temporal parts at different times.

Or, for example, the physicist Murray Gell-Mann was awarded the Nobel Prize for his discoveries in quantum physics. He adopted the word "quark," defining it, roughly, as an elementary particle that makes up protons and neutrons.

But, of course, introducing and defining a new word need not be limited to philosophy and physics, but can occur in any area of thought.

### To Give the Essence of Something

Some concepts are incredibly important, such as *knowledge, truth, justice, morally right, person,* and many more. For these, it is not enough to inform about common usage or make them more precise. Instead, we want to get at the *nature* or *essence* of these concepts. So, for some terms, the purpose of defining is to specify the essence of the thing being defined. This is a very important purpose of defining in order to increase our understanding of reality. This is also the most difficult to carry out, as we will discuss below.

## Types of Definitions

With the various purposes of defining specified, let's next consider various types of definitions, three of which we will consider: *ostensive, synonym,* and defining in terms of necessary and sufficient conditions.

### Ostensive Definition

One way to define a term is by *pointing to, listing,* or *naming* examples of things to which the word in question applies. This is called defining by *ostension.* For example, one might say by "dog" I mean *that,* and then point to a dog. Or, one might offer a list: A "dog" is a beagle, German shepherd, golden retriever, poodle, pug, and the like.

Ostensive definitions are not very deep, in the sense that they do not specify the *essence* of the things to which the word applies. Nevertheless, they can be useful, particularly if one's purpose is to provide the common use of a term.

### Defining by Synonym

Another way to define a term is to offer synonyms of the term. For example, one may offer the following definition by synonym: "superficial" means the same as "cursory, frivolous, one-dimensional, perfunctory, or trivial" or, for another example, "apathetic" means the same as "callous, indifferent, laid-back, passive, stoic, or uninterested."

This sort of definition is also not very deep and may not be helpful if one does not choose synonyms that are familiar to one's intended audience. However, like ostensive definitions, definition by synonym can be a useful for the purpose of providing the common use of a term.

### Defining in Terms of Necessary and Sufficient Conditions

A very important and deep definition is one that provides the *necessary* and *sufficient conditions* to be the thing to which the term applies. To understand this important type of definition, let's consider the concepts of necessary condition and sufficient condition.

#### Necessary Condition

A *necessary condition* is a condition that *must* be met; it is *required.* For example, a *necessary condition* for something to be square is that *it have four sides.* A *necessary condition* for something to be a *dog* is that it be an *animal.* We often introduce a necessary condition with the phrase "only if." Consider:

Something is square *only if* it has four sides.

Something is a dog *only if* it is an animal.

By providing the necessary conditions for something, one is thereby specifying the minimum requirements to be met for that something. However, one is *not* thereby (necessarily) specifying conditions, such that once they are met, the thing in question *is* a thing of that type. For example, suppose something is an animal. It thereby meets a necessary condition for being a dog. However, the *mere fact* that this thing in question is an animal, while necessary for being a dog, is not enough for something to be a dog. This leads us to *sufficient conditions.*

#### Sufficient Condition

A *sufficient condition* is a condition that *guarantees.* For example, a *sufficient condition* for something to be an *automobile* is that is a *truck.* That is, an object being a *truck* guarantees that it is an *automobile.* Or, for example, something being a *snake* is a *sufficient condition* for it to be a *reptile* (the former guarantees the latter). We often introduce a sufficient condition with the word "if." Consider:

> *If* something is a truck, then it is an automobile.
>
> *If* something is a snake, then it is a reptile.

By providing the sufficient conditions for something, one is thereby specifying conditions that *guarantee* that something. However, one is *not* thereby (necessarily) specifying conditions that are *required* for that something. For example, while something being a truck does guarantee that it is an automobile, something can be an automobile and not be a truck.

### Defining in Terms of Necessary and Sufficient Conditions

This brings us to *defining in terms of necessary and sufficient conditions*. In these definitions, one specifies the *individually necessary* and *jointly sufficient conditions* for the application of a term, the use of a concept, the occurrence of some event, or an object to be a certain type of thing. Given that "if" introduces a *sufficient condition*, and "only if" introduces a *necessary condition*, the form of such a definition will be:

> [term to be defined] *if and only if* [the conditions]

We often use "iff" to stand for "if and only if."

If there are multiple conditions on the right side of "if and only if," each individual condition is necessary (hence the conditions are individually necessary), and taken together (jointly) they are sufficient. Thus, each condition is *required* and together they *guarantee*.

For example, one definition of *knowledge* that was considered in chapter 2 was put in terms of necessary and sufficient conditions, as follows:

A person *knows* that a statement is true *iff*

1. the statement is true,
2. the person believes the statement, and
3. the person is justified in believing the statement.

While this definition of knowledge was questioned in chapter 2, we can still consider it for the sake of illustrating how defining in terms of necessary and sufficient conditions works. In the above definition of knowledge, each condition listed is *necessary* for *knowledge*, and all three taken together are sufficient for *knowledge*. So, each condition *must* be satisfied if one is to know the statement, and once *all* the conditions are satisfied, then the person is guaranteed to have knowledge.

In some cases, there may be just *one* condition which is both necessary and sufficient. For example, in the definition given of *truth* in chapter 2, just one condition was offered as being both necessary and sufficient:

> A statement is *true iff* reality is as the statement says it is.

In this definition, the one condition (reality is a certain way) is both necessary and sufficient for *truth*.

Definitions in terms of necessary and sufficient conditions are very important since they get at the *essence* of the thing in question (if they are correct). Such definitions specify what the thing *really* is, and thus if correct, help to provide us with knowledge of the world.

## Evaluating Definitions

Definitions are very important for critical thinking and knowledge. However, they can go awry, and thus as critical thinkers, we should be familiar with some mistakes that can be made. While there are several ways definitions can be unacceptable, we'll consider five.

### Too Broad

First, a definition can be *too broad*. This occurs when the definition of some term entails that the term applies to things that are not in the reference of the term. For example, suppose "automobile" is defined as follows:

> Something is an automobile *iff it is a motorized craft that transports people.*

Even though it is true that automobiles are motorized crafts that transport people, the definition is too broad, since it also applies to things that are not automobiles. For example, it entails that boats and airplanes are automobiles, since boats and airplanes are motorized crafts that transport people. Therefore, it won't work *as a definition.*

### Too Narrow

Clearly the way to fix a definition that is too broad is to make it narrower in its reference. However, one must be careful not to make it *too narrow*. This occurs when the definition of some term entails that the term does *not* apply to things that *are* in the reference of the term. For example, suppose "automobile" is defined as follows:

> Something is an automobile *iff it is a craft that transports people on land, powered by an internal combustion engine.*

While this way of defining "automobile" does not entail that boats and airplanes are automobiles, and thus is not too broad in that sense, it fails in the other direction of being **too narrow**. It is too narrow in at least two ways. First, not all automobiles have internal combustion engines, as some have an electric motor. Second, not all automobiles are limited to transporting people *on land*, as there are amphibious automobiles that can travel both on land and on (and under) water. And there are some that can fly!

Clearly the way to fix a definition that is too narrow is to make it broader in its reference, though one must be careful to not make it too broad.

### Too Broad and Too Narrow

Furthermore, a definition can be both *too broad* and *too narrow*. For example:

> Something is an automobile *iff it is a craft that transports people on land, water, or air, and is powered by an internal combustion engine or an electric motor.*

This is *too broad* since it entails that something like a Razor electric scooter is an automobile, since a Razor is a craft that transports people on land and is powered by an electric motor. But a Razor is not an automobile. It is *too narrow* since it entails that a Stanley steam car, for example, is not an automobile, though it clearly is.

### Circular

Another way that a definition can be unacceptable is to be *circular*. A circular definition is one in which the term being defined is in the definition. Circular definitions can be explicitly circular, such as in the following:

>    An act is morally right iff it conforms to morally right principles.

This is obviously and explicitly circular.

However, a definition can be implicitly circular, such as in the following example:

>    A statement is true iff it is not false.

While the word "true" does not explicitly occur in the definition, it is implicitly there, since "not false" is just another way of saying *true*.

Or a definition can be circular by containing a cognate of the term being defined, as in this example:

>    A geologist is a person who studies geology.

This is circular since "geologist" and "geology" are cognates, both deriving from the root word "geo," meaning "earth." This is unacceptable because anyone who does not know what the term "geologist" means is unlikely to know what its cognate "geology" means, and it's extremely unlikely that one will know the root word "geo."

We can generalize that all circular definitions (whether explicit or implicit, or using a cognate) are unacceptable because anyone who does not know what the term means will not be enlightened by the circular definition.

### Vague, Ambiguous, or Obscure

Definitions can also be unacceptable by containing *vague*, *ambiguous*, or *metaphorical* terms. Here are some examples of each, respectively:

- A person is a *terrorist* iff the person uses *violence* and *threats* to *intimidate* or *coerce*, particularly for *political reasons*.
- An insult is *offensive* speech or action. (Rude or on the attack.)
- *Life* is the climbing of a mountain.

The first of these is unacceptable as the underlined words in the definition are each *vague*. Thus, we won't always know when someone counts as a terrorist. The second is unacceptable as the word "offensive" is ambiguous between *rude or disrespectful* and *attacking*, or *both*. The third won't do as the phrase "the climbing of a mountain" is a metaphor and thus not very informative.

In sum, creating and evaluating definitions are important aspects of critical thinking. With the knowledge of some of the varieties and purposes of definitions in hand, as well as knowing some ways that definitions can be unacceptable, we are now in a better position to approach definitions in our critical thinking.

---

**EXERCISE 3.4**

In each passage below, a term is being defined. Determine (a) which term is being defined and (b) what type of definition is being given.

   *1. "Racism" means bigotry.

   2. An amphibious vehicle is a flat-bottomed motor vehicle that can travel on land or water.

   3. The BMW i8 is my idea of a spectacular electric sports car.

   *4. Eastern Orthodox is an example of a Christian denomination.

   5. A mammal is a warm-blooded vertebrate animal that has hair or fur nourishes its young with milk secreted by mammary glands and (typically) gives birth to live offspring.

   6. "Epiphany" is another word for enlightenment.

   *7. A person is an immaterial conscious substance with self-consciousness and the ability to act, and if human, the person inhabits and interacts with a material body.

   8. "Esoteric" means abstruse.

   9. That big dog is a Great Dane.

   10. A religion is a conceptual system that provides an interpretation of the world and the place of human beings in it; bases an account of how life should be lived given that interpretation; and expresses this interpretation and lifestyle in a set of rituals, institutions and practices.[1]

---

1.  Keith Yandell, *Philosophy of Religion: A Contemporary Introduction* (London: Routledge, 1999), 16.

---

**EXERCISE 3.5**

Each of the definitions below is problematic in some way. Identify the problem with each definition as *too broad, too narrow, too broad and too narrow, circular,* or *vague, ambiguous, or obscure.*

   *1. An act is morally right to do iff it is the morally appropriate thing to do.

   2. A computer is a machine that sits at a single location on or near a desk or table due to its size and power requirements, and is designed to accept data, perform prescribed mathematical and logical operations at high speed, and display the results of these operations.

   3. Love is two people touching each other's soul.

   *4. A racist is anyone who says something offensive to or about someone of a different race than that of the speaker.

5. A philosopher is someone who studies, writes, and thinks about philosophy.

6. An animal is a dog iff it is a mammal that typically has fur, four legs, a long snout, an acute sense of smell, nonretractable claws, and barks.

*7. A planet is a celestial body that is in orbit around the sun, has sufficient mass for its self-gravity to overcome rigid body forces so that it assumes a hydrostatic equilibrium (nearly round) shape, and has cleared the neighborhood around its orbit.

8. The inner light is the light that illuminates the self and the world from within.

9. Something counts as art iff someone finds it to be beautiful.

10. A person is a Christian iff the person believes that God exists.

## Judging Statements

Having arrived at a sufficiently precise, unambiguous sentence with all terms well defined, and we understand the statement being expressed, we need to evaluate it—is it true or false? But *how* do we test a particular statement? After all, not all statements can be known to be true or false in the same way. Some statements can be tested by simple observation, whereas others require engaging in scientific method. Some we can derive by reason from other statements, and others we cannot but are the very axioms of reason. Some we can know by our awareness of our own minds, whereas others require testimony from others.

Given this, one cannot, for example, rationally judge a statement to be false or unknowable simply because it cannot be justified *by scientific method*—for instance, if it is a statement that is not justifiable by science, such as a philosophical statement. This would be like declaring that there is no wood in the field since a *metal detector* did not detect any.

So, it will be useful to sketch out various categories into which statements fall, and sketch out some methods for verifying or falsifying statements in the various categories. However, the discussion to follow will *not* be an *exhaustive* survey of the various categories and methods, but merely a sketch of some. The purpose is two-fold: first, to show that we can neither categorize all statements the same nor come to know each by the same methods; and second, to illustrate some of the categories into which various statements fall, as well as some methods of thinking critically about various statements in the categories. The idea is to help show how to categorize and then evaluate *some* statements, which can then be applied to other statements as we think about them critically.

Before turning to the categories and methods, note that the categories below are *objective* and *mutually exclusive*. To say they are *objective* means that whether a statement falls into a category is *independent* of what anyone thinks or believes about the statement. For example, the broadest two categories that will be discussed below are *empirical* and *non-empirical*. Whether a statement is *empirical* or *non-empirical* has nothing to do with how the statement is viewed or what is believed about the statement. If it is non-empirical, for example, it is *objectively* non-empirical.

To say the categories are *mutually exclusive* means that if a statement falls into one category, it cannot also fall into another category *at the same level*. For example, if a statement is *empirical*, it cannot also be *non-empirical*. These are mutually exclusive categories. Let's turn to our categories, and to the methods for verifying or falsifying statements in each.

## Empirical Statements

One general category into which statements fall is *empirical*. An *empirical statement* is a statement that one can verify or falsify by *experience* of some sort. But not all empirical statements can be verified or falsified in the same way. Below we'll discuss some more specific empirical categories and ways to verify or falsify statements in each category.

### Sensory Experience

Perhaps the most obvious kind of empirical statements are those verifiable or falsifiable by *sensory experience*. This covers any statement that can be verified or falsified by using our five senses. Many such statements can be verified or falsified by direct observation. For example,

> *The tree in my backyard has no leaves.*

> *Fred's new car has only three wheels.*

> *The river has overflowed its banks.*

While we *can* verify or falsify these statements in other ways (such as personal testimony—to be discussed below), we can also verify or falsify them by simply going out and observing the world using our five senses.

Other statements in this category are *indirectly* verifiable or falsifiable by combining observation with other methods of knowing. One such method is the *scientific method*, which roughly is verifying or falsifying certain statements with a combination of observation and reasoning. Of course, there is more *detail* to the scientific method, including systematic observation and experimentation, inductive and deductive reasoning, and the formation and testing of hypotheses and theories, but ultimately verifying and falsifying a statement with scientific method comes down to observation and reasoning.

However, not all empirical statements can be verified or falsified by science, nor even with sensory experience in general. Consider the following.

### Personal Testimony

Consider statements about the contents of the mind of *another*. While I can know the contents of *my* mind immediately and directly (more on which later), I cannot know the contents of *your* mind immediately and directly. Perhaps there are *some* statements about *your* mind that I can *reason* to by analogy—by comparing *your* behavior in some context to *my* behavior based on my mental life in a similar context. For example, I may observe you bang your knee against a coffee table and then fall to the floor, grab your knee, cry, and writhe. From this I may *infer* that you are in pain (the contents of your mind), by comparing your behavior to my past behavior in a similar situation after banging my knee, a situation in which I felt pain. Thus, by observation and reasoning by analogy, I can, *perhaps*, know:

> *You are in pain now.*

Of course, I could be mistaken. You might be acting, and not experiencing pain at all. But it is reasonable for me to conclude that you are in pain, and perhaps even know that you are, based on my observation and reasoning. Still, I am not *observing* your pain, nor *experiencing* it, but rather I am only observing your *behavior* in the context, and then *reasoning* to some statement about the contents of your mind based on my observation.

But there are other occasions or contexts in which no matter how much I observe your behavior or your body, I simply *cannot* know the contents of your mind in that moment, not even with careful reasoning about the matter. And no amount of scientific knowledge will help me either *in these contexts*. In such contexts, the only way for me to know the contents of your mind is if *you* report to me the contents of your mind. That is, some statements are verifiable or falsifiable only by another's *personal testimony*. For example:

> *Mary is thinking about what she needs to purchase at the grocery store.*

No matter how much we observe Mary or reason about Mary *in this context*, unless she tells us what she is thinking about right now, we cannot verify or falsify the statement by observing her. She must report to us her thoughts for us to know her thoughts.

Whether I am observing another's behavior and then reasoning to some statement about the contents of their mind or receiving their report about the contents of their mind, *my* knowledge of another's mind is still *empirical*, since it is grounded in, or based on, some experience I am having. I *observe* the person's behavior and then reason based on the *observation*, or I receive their testimony about the contents of their mind by way of some *sensory experience*.

### Introspection

Other statements that are *not* verifiable or falsifiable by observation or science are those about *one's own mind*. Each person is simply directly aware of their own current mental life, not by observation or reasoning, but simply by virtue of it being *one's own mental life*. For example, I know the following statement:

> *I am thinking about introspection right now.*

I know this, not by any observation of the world, nor by reasoning, but rather by *introspection*, by simply being aware of my own mental life immediately and directly.

### Other Experiences

There are perhaps other empirical statements in addition to those verified or falsified by *sensory experience*, *personal testimony*, or *introspection*. For example, *memory* is another sort of empirical method of verifying or falsifying certain empirical statements. Others would argue that a *religious experience* of various sorts is another way.

As critical thinkers, we must be mindful of whether we are evaluating an empirical or non-empirical statement, and if empirical, what sort of empirical statement it is. And we want to avoid the mistake of treating all empirical statements the same, and especially attempting to verify or falsify them with the same methods. The methods of science will work for verifying whether there are quarks, for example, but such methods will not work for telling me what you are thinking right now (in some contexts) or whether I am currently in pain.

## Nonempirical Statements

In contrast with empirical statements, there are *nonempirical* statements. These are statements that are verifiable or falsifiable *apart from* or *independent of* experience. Indeed, nonempirical statements simply cannot be verified or falsified by experience, except for *some occasions* in which we might be able to know some of them by the testimony of an authority on the particular case telling us that some particular nonempirical statement is true. There are at least three categories of statements that are nonempirical—*intuitive statements, innate statements,* and *statements known by reasoning from either intuitive statements or innate statements.* Let's consider each.

### Intuitive Statements

One kind of nonempirical statement that we may encounter is an *intuitive* statement. This is a statement that once we fully understand and reflect upon it, we can just "see" intellectually that it is *true.* For example:

> *Nothing can be both entirely red and entirely non-red simultaneously.*
>
> *Every object is self-identical.*
>
> *If Adam is taller than Bob, then Bob is not taller than Adam.*

These are statements that are not only *true* but are such that we can just "see" that they are true by understanding them, apart from any experience. Furthermore, we *cannot* know them by observation or other experience (with the exception that in certain contexts we might be able to know some of them by the testimony of an authority on the matter in question. Nor can we reason to them from statements that are more obvious than they are. Rather, we know them by *rational intuition,* which is simply our capacity as rational beings to "see" that they are true once we understand them. Since these are statements that cannot be known by experience (with the aforementioned exception) nor by reasoning to them from more obvious truths, we should not judge any statement to be an intuitive truth if such a statement *can* be known by experience or by reasoning from more obvious truths. But if we do encounter an intuitive truth, we can judge it to be a true statement and then use it in our thinking about the world.

However, we must be careful in judging a statement to be an intuitive truth, as not all *potential* candidates are *real cases.* Consider the following statement, for example:

> *Every event has sufficient cause.*

Some have taken it to be an intuitive truth, whereas others question whether it is even true, let alone an intuitive truth. So, while there are some clear cases of intuitive truths, we should be careful in judging a statement to belong in this category.

### Statements Known Innately

Some (for example, the philosophers Plato and Descartes), but by no means all, thinkers have suggested that there are some statements that we simply know as part of our being. That is, we do <u>not</u> *acquire* the knowledge—we do *not* <u>learn</u> such statements; we do not *come to know them having previously not known them*—rather we come into being with the knowledge. That is, we know them *innately*. Perhaps God instilled such knowledge in us when creating us, or perhaps knowing these is just part of what it is to be a rational being. But whatever the details, some maintain that we have some innate knowledge. If we do, then since we come into being knowing these *innate* statements, then we know them *apart from* or *independent of* any experience.

So, what statements would count as *innate*? The answer to this is not agreed upon by those who believe in innate knowledge. But some candidate answers include some of the very basic statements that others would perhaps count as intuitive truths, others add basic moral truths, and others that God exists. Thus, some candidates for innate knowledge are:

> *Everything is self-identical.*
>
> *Murder is wrong.*
>
> *God exists.*

And there are others, but these are some representative answers.

The difference between an *intuitive statement* and an *innate statement* is that we *learn* or *acquire* intuitive statements, but we do not *learn* or *acquire* innate statements (since we simply come into being knowing them). So, while both are *nonempirical*, one kind (innate statements) "comes with the package" and the other kind (intuitive statements) is *added* as we think and learn about the world.

### Statements Known by Reasoning from Either Intuitive Truths or Truths Known Innately

There are many statements that we cannot verify or falsify by any experience, nor are they intuitive truth, nor are they innate. Rather they can be verified or falsified only by reasoning to them from statements that are known intuitively or innately. We'll very briefly sketch two cases where this occurs: a philosophical case and a case from mathematics.

#### A Philosophical Case

A great many philosophical statements are verifiable or falsifiable *only by arguments* or reasoning. Consider the following statement, for example:

> *Endurantism is the best view of persistence.*

In a word, *persistence* concerns things existing over a period of time, and *endurantism* is one of the competing theories about *how* things persist, specifically that things persist by being wholly present at each moment of their existence.

We simply cannot *observe* whether an object persists by enduring versus persisting by perduring (which is another view of persistence). So how would we know that the statement above is true, assuming that we can know it? In short, by reasoning to it from other things we accept, including intuitive or innate truths. For example, someone may argue for the statement above in roughly the following way:

> *It is an obvious intuitive truth that people perform various actions—throw a ball, whistle a tune, run a mile. It is also an intuitive truth that to perform an action, the person must perform each component of the act—for example, for a person to run a mile, the person*

*must run each quarter of the mile. The only view that entails that a person can perform each component of an action, and thus perform the action, is endurantism. Thus, endurantism is the best view of persistence.*

The point, once again, is that we *can* know whether philosophical statements are true or false, but for many such statements, we *must* arrive at that knowledge by way of reasoning to them from other statements that we know intuitively or innately.

### A Mathematical Case

There are all sorts of statements in mathematics, including axioms (self-evidence basic statements, known by rational intuition), theorems (which are statements arrived at with arguments, axioms, and rules of inference), hypotheses (a statement offered for proof or falsification), and more. The axioms are among the *intuitive* truths discussed above. But other statements can be verified or falsified *only by* reasoning to them from axioms (which are intuitive truths or innate). For example, consider:

*Triangle ABC is congruent to triangle DEF.*

We cannot verify or falsify this statement by observation in many instances at least. Rather, we can verify or falsify it only by reasoning to it from other things we know about the triangles, plus the axioms in the background, plus rules of inference.

## Summary and Cautions

We'll conclude this section with a summary of the points about judging statements true or false, and a brief statement about the nature of *proof* for a statement.

### Summary

Two important points were made in the previous section:

First, not all statements are of the same sort. Some are about a person's *own* mental life, and others are about the mental life of *another*. Some are about the observable physical universes, and others are about philosophical matters, and others are about mathematical matters.

Second, there are *different* criteria for verifying or falsifying statements in the different categories. With some, direct observation will do, whereas with others, we need to combine observation and reasoning. With others, observation plays no role at all, because they are knowable by rational intuition, and still others may be innate. Finally, others are knowable only by reasoning to them from intuitive truth or innate statements.

Therefore, as critical thinkers we must be mindful of whether we are evaluating an empirical statement or a nonempirical statement, and then further categorize it in order to use the appropriate methods for verifying or falsifying a statement of that type. And we want to avoid the mistake of treating all statements the same, and especially attempting to verify or falsify them with the same methods—such as by science. The methods of science will work for verifying whether there are quarks, but such methods will not work for telling me what you are thinking right now, or whether I am currently in pain, or whether endurantism is the best view of persistence. Nevertheless, each statement *can* be verified or falsified by the appropriate methods.

## On Proof of a Statement

In order to make a rational and confident judgment that some statement is true, does one need **proof** of the statement? Some believe that we do. For example, one occasionally hears the following sorts of claims or questions about *proof*:

> *What's your proof that endurantism is true?*

> *That's a nice argument for God's existence, but it's no proof that God exists.*

> *Only science can prove whether we have free will.*

What should we make of these questions and statements? How should we understand "proof?" How does it relate to our judgment about whether some statement is true or false? For example, must we reduce our confidence in accepting that some statement is true if it hasn't been "proven"?

To answer these questions, let's discuss what it means for a statement to be "proven." We'll consider two ways to understand "proof"—deductive inference and scientifically "proven," and then conclude with a general remark about this.

### Deductive Inference

One use of the word "proof" is that it refers to a type of inference in which one derives one statement from others, using valid inference rules. Deductive and valid inference will be discussed in detail in later chapters, but here we can consider a sketch of the idea. This sort of argument or inference occurs both in mathematics and in formal logic. For example, in our geometry class, we did *proofs*, which consisted of considering certain statements as "givens," and then applying inference rules to derive a conclusion. Such is a proof. The same occurs in logic.

Suppose that one has "proof" of a statement in this *deductive inference* sense. Does it justify one in concluding that the statement is *true*, and that one *knows* it? Not necessarily! Suppose that one starts with *false* givens or assumptions. Then even if the application of the rules to derive a statement is perfect, it does not follow that the derived statement is true. For example:

> Given: Rhode Island is a larger state than Texas.

> Given: Texas is a larger state than Alaska.

From these two givens, we can derive the following from the transitivity of "larger than":

> *Rhode Island is a larger state than Alaska.*

We have thereby "proven," in one sense of the word, the statement.

However, since we began with false assumptions / givens, this sense of "proof" does not justify us in judging the derived statement to be true, *if* we don't independently know that the givens / assumptions are true. Thus, if by "proof" one means that it is a mathematical inference, having proof is not necessarily what we need to be confident in judging a statement to be true.

### Scientifically "Proven"

You may have heard the following sorts of statements:

*Special theory of relativity has been proven.*

*The existence of Bigfoot has not been proven.*

What is (typically) meant by "proven" in statements like these is that the statement in question is part of or derived from *science*. So, for example, there is an abundance of scientific evidence for the special theory of relativity (the theory introduced by Einstein regarding the relationship between space and time), which is nearly universally accepted among scientists. Thus, it is said to be "proven." In contrast, the existence of Bigfoot does not enjoy support among scientists, and there is certainly no scientific evidence for it. Thus, it is *not* "proven."

So, must we have proof in this sense in order to be justified in judging a statement true? *No!* We do *not* need such scientific evidence in order to be confident in judging a statement to be true, for two reasons. First, some statements simply *cannot* be verified or falsified by science, as they are not about the material universe. For example, the following statement is simply beyond to purview of science:

*Endurantism is the best view of persistence.*

As discussed, this is not an empirical statement. Nevertheless, we can have great confidence in judging it to be true, for example, if the philosophical arguments for it are good. Indeed, we can have as much confidence in our judgment of it as we can in judging a statement of science.

Second, we do *not* need such scientific evidence in order to be confident in judging a statement as there are some statements that even science itself relies upon, and thus we cannot justify them by science. For example, consider the statement:

*Our sensory experiences are reliable sources of information about reality.*

This statement cannot be justified by science, as science itself presupposes it. Nevertheless, we can be, and should be, confident in judging it to be true. So, for the two reasons given (that there are nonempirical statements, and statements that science presupposes), having "scientific proof" is *not* required in order for us to have confidence in judging a statement to be true.

Further, having such "scientific proof" does *not* guarantee that the statement in question is true. Scientific evidence is certainly impressive, and unless we have very good evidence to the contrary, we should trust the findings of science. However, scientific conclusions are *not* guaranteed to be true. Evidence of this is that all past and now rejected scientific theories are now considered false. But they *were* scientific theories. So, if being a scientific theory guarantees truth, then we should have maintained believing the previous theories.

So, while having scientific evidence is impressive, since it neither guarantees truth nor is it required for us to be confident in judging a statement to be true, having "scientific proof" is not necessarily what we need to be confident in judging a statement to be true.

### General Lesson

The general lesson to draw is this. While both mathematical and scientific proof have their place, and each is impressive in serving its purpose, it is a mistake to conclude that one cannot be confident in judging a statement true or false if is not proven in one of these senses of "proof" or even in a other ways the term is used. Instead, we should recognize what kind of statement is under consideration and then seek out the *appropriate* evidence for *that kind* of statement, if evidence is required (with some statements, evidence is not required, such as with introspective statements and intuitive statements). We then appropriately judge the statement in question true or false relative to the degree of evidence. The more evidence, the greater the confidence.

### EXERCISE 3.6

Review Questions

1. What is an empirical statement? What is a nonempirical statement?
2. Write three empirical statements.
3. Write three nonempirical statements.
4. What are three general empirical categories?
5. What are two general nonempirical categories?
6. What is rational intuition?
7. True or false: For *any* statement, we can know the statement only by the methods of science.
8. True or false: We can be confident in a statement only if it has been proven.
9. True or false: We cannot know any philosophical statements, since they are not knowable by experience.
10. True or false: There are some statements that we can know independent of any experience.

## Recap

In this chapter, we considered the importance of clarifying statements, including making *vague* terms more precise and eliminating *ambiguity*. We then discussed various types of *definitions*, purposes of definitions, and how to evaluate a definition. Finally, we turned to the evaluation of statements. We noted the importance of identifying what kind of statement is being evaluated, and then the importance of using appropriate criteria to judge a statement of that kind. And, we noted that we should not judge a statement false or unknowable merely because we cannot test it with a particular set of criteria (such as scientific criteria) when that criteria is *not* relevant for a statement of that kind. Below are some important concepts and definitions:

- **Ambiguity**: To say that a statement or term is *ambiguous* means that it has more than one precise meaning, and the context does *not* clarify which meaning is intended.
  - **Lexical Ambiguity**: *Lexical ambiguity* occurs when a statement contains a word or phrase that is ambiguous.
  - **Syntactic Ambiguity**: *Syntactic ambiguity* occurs when a statement is ambiguous because of its word ordering or the scope of its quantifiers.

- **Collective-Distributive Ambiguity**: *Collective-distributive ambiguity* occurs when a sentence contains a word or phrase that refers to a group, and it is unclear whether reference is being made to the members of the group taken collectively or individually (distributive).
- **Definition**: A *definition* provides the meaning of a term.
  - **Ostensive Definition**: An *ostensive definition* is one in which a term is defined by *pointing to, listing,* or *naming* examples of things to which the word in question applies.
  - **Definition by Synonym**: A *definition by synonym* is one in which a term is defined by listing *synonyms* of the term.
  - **Definition in Terms of Necessary and Sufficient Conditions**: A *definition in terms of necessary and sufficient conditions* is one in which one specifies the *individually necessary* and *jointly sufficient conditions* for the application of a term, the use of a concept, the occurrence of some event, or an object to be a certain type of thing.
- **Empirical Statement**: An *empirical* statement is a statement that one can verify or falsify by *experience* of some sort.
- **Nonempirical Statement**: A *nonempirical* statement is a statement that one knows or can know *apart from* or *independent of* experience.
- **Generality**: A *statement is too general* when it lacks specificity by containing a word or phrase that is too general for the context, preventing clarity of the intended meaning.
- **Intuitive Truth**: To say that a statement is an *intuitive truth* means that once we fully understand and reflect upon it, we can just "see" intellectually that it is *true*.
- **Necessary Condition**: A *necessary condition* is a condition that *must* be met; it is *required*.
- **Principle of Charity**: When interpreting someone's statement, the *principle of charity* urges one to assume that the best possible interpretation that maximizes the truth or rationality of the statement.
- **Sufficient Condition**: A *sufficient condition* is a condition that *guarantees*.
- **Vagueness**: To say that a word or phrase is *vague* means that it *not precise*, and thus has borderline cases, such that there are contexts in which we know that the term applies, others in which we know that it does *not* apply, and still others in which it is impossible to say objectively whether the term applies.

# 4 AN INTRODUCTION TO REASONING AND ARGUMENTS

In our daily lives we are flooded with things to think about, including experiences, memories, ideas, questions, commands, claims, theories (including conspiracy theories), and more! Such things can be expressed as *sentences*. However, while many sentences, such as questions, commands, and exclamations, may be worthy of critical thought, they do not actually assert that anything is the case—that is, none asserts something that is either true or false, such as the following:

- *What are the details of President Trump's temporary halt on green cards?*
- *When will we be having lunch?*
- *Slow down!*
- *Bye for now.*
- *Go-Pack-Go!*

The first two are questions, the third a command, the fourth a salutation, and the last a cheer, and thus none say anything true or false.

We certainly think about sentences of those sorts. However, we are also confronted with *statements*—sentences which are true or false (i.e., *they assert that something is or is not the case*). It is primarily *these* sorts of sentences (i.e., *statements*) that we think about and *should* think about *critically* to determine whether we should accept them or reject them—to judge whether the sentence is true or false and to what degree we should accept it.

Of course, not all statements *require* critical thinking, such as:

- *I'll have a tuna fish sandwich for lunch today.*
- *Mary had trouble sleeping last night.*
- *The Packers won the game on Sunday.*

Typically, those sorts of statements are either uninteresting or well established and simply don't require critical thinking to determine whether they should be accepted.

However, other statements (many others) require our careful attention and critical thought to determine whether we should accept them as true or reject them as false, as well as to what degree we should accept or reject (given that our acceptance of a statement comes in degrees of strength). So, for example, consider the following statements:

- *There really is an all-powerful God.*
- *We ought to punish the government of China for concealing the deadliness of Covid-19.*
- *The only way to really know something is by the methods of science.*
- *As long as an act does not harm anyone, it is perfectly fine to do.*

Those statements are *interesting, not obvious, not a given*, and thus *require* our critical thought to determine in a rational way whether they should be accepted as true or rejected as false.

- *How would you determine whether you should accept or reject the statements just above?*
- How do *you* determine whether your acceptance or rejection of these is *rational*?

What is *often required* for answering these questions, and for thinking about various statements in a *rational* way, is *reasoning* and *arguments*, in which we appeal to other statements that we already know to be true. Whether a statement requires critical thought or not can be clear, but also not so clear. The recommendation is to give *critical* thought to any statement that is interesting and not obviously true. In such a case, we apply reasoning and arguments.

- But what is involved in *reasoning* and *arguments*; what are these?

In the remainder of this chapter, we will answer this question.

Before delving into reasoning and arguments, you may be wondering *why it matters* and *how it applies to you*. There are two reasons. First, as a matter of fact we humans are rational beings that <u>already</u> *naturally* engage in reasoning and in the creation / evaluation of arguments. So, thinking about reasoning and arguments matters for the sake of improving our natural rational skills.

Second, what we believe affects every area of our lives. If one believes that the mere act of going into a social situation **will** cause one to get some disease (e.g., Covid-19), then one will probably remain in social isolation indefinitely. This can lead to serious psychological problems. But suppose there is **not** a rational, good reason to support this idea. Then one's choice to be socially isolated is either groundless or based on bad reasoning, and thus one is bringing unnecessary hardship into one's life based on lack of or poor reasoning. So, reasoning and arguments have practical consequences, and thus thinking about how to improve our reasoning and creation / evaluation of arguments is important for our everyday lives.

In this chapter we take an introductory look at reasoning and arguments, as well as learn exercises for improving our skills at identifying the presence of an argument, distinguishing the parts of arguments, recognizing various indicator words and phrases, and recognizing implicit assumptions and implications. Some key words and phrases to master as we work through this chapter are the following:

## KEY WORDS

Argument

Argument Content

Argument Standard Form

Argument Structure

Circular Reasoning

Conclusion

Implicit Conclusion

Implicit Premise

Indicator Words

Inference

Reasoning

Syllogism

### EXERCISE 4.1

For each sentence below, specify whether it expresses or does not express a *statement*.

**\*1.** The first Vince Flynn book is better than the second.

**2.** Keep going!

**3.** The Green Bay Packers selected a quarterback for their first pick in the 2020 NFL draft.

**4.** How many dogs do you own?

**\*5.** I hope the flood waters do not rise too high.

**6.** Good morning.

**7.** Christians believe that God is a tri-personal being.

**8.** Do you believe that Brett Kavanaugh is guilty?

**9.** My head really hurts today.

**\*10.** Stay away from that snake!

**11.** What an exciting game!

**12.** That is a beagle.

**13.** There is no other intelligent life in the universe beside humans on earth.

**14.** Why is there so much evil in the world?

**\*15.** That woman is very beautiful.

## Reasoning vs. Argument

The terms *reasoning* and *argument* are central to critical thinking. Not everyone makes a clear distinction between these, and indeed they are often blurred or used interchangeably. In our treatment of them, we will attempt to not only distinguish them, but to make a clear distinction between them. While we may be using the terms differently than others, our use of them is close to standard usage and will do for our purposes. Having made the distinction, we will go on to focus on arguments.

## Reasoning

As the term will be used in this text, *reasoning* is a process of proceeding from one statement to another. More exactly, it *typically* involves beginning with certain assumptions (accepting a statement as true) and proceeding to a conclusion (another statement) based on these assumptions, though it does not have to involve drawing a conclusion. If one *is* drawing a conclusion based on the assumptions, let's say that the person is drawing an *inference* from the assumptions to a conclusion. So, some reasoning involves inference from assumptions to a conclusion, whereas other cases of reasoning do not involve drawing an inference but are cases of simply thinking through various statements but falling short of drawing an inference to a conclusion.

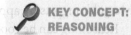

**KEY CONCEPT: REASONING**

**Reasoning** is an activity or process of proceeding from one statement to another statement, typically beginning with assumptions and proceeding to a conclusion based on those assumptions.

Much can be said about reasoning. But our focus will be on arguments, and so our look at reasoning will be brief. As mentioned, reasoning is *typically* from assumptions to a conclusion. This process can be a simple linear process. For example, suppose that John reasons:

> *We know that Fred or Bob are the only two possible people who could have broken the bottle, and we know it was not Fred, and so it must have been Bob.*

Notice that John's reasoning is rather simple and linear, beginning with the assumptions (known or not) that Fred or Bob are the only possible options, and it wasn't Fred, to the conclusion that it was Bob.

Or, reasoning can be more complex, with a tree-like structure. Adam reasons:

> *Since my car engine has been having many problems, I need to get it fixed if I want to continue driving my car, but I do not want to pour so much money into this old engine; and since the transmission in my car has been having so many problems, I need to get it fixed if I want to continue driving my car, but I do not want to pour so much money into this old transmission; therefore, I will buy a new car.*

Here there are two lines of reasoning, one from the fact that the car *engine* is having troubles and that Adam does not want to pour money into the old engine to justify buying a new car, and the other from the fact that the car *transmission* is having troubles and that Adam does not want to pour money into the old transmission to justify buying a new car.

Or, reasoning can be circular. Consider the following exchange between Mark and John, illustrating a famous example:

> *Mark and John stumble across three equal-sized gold nuggets. John takes two and hands one to Mark.*
>
> Mark: *Why do you get two and I get only one?*
>
> John: *I am the leader of this operation.*
>
> Mark: *What makes you the leader?*

John: *I have two gold nuggets.*

You can probably see John's circular reasoning, in which he is trying to justify that he is the leader by appealing to the fact that he has two gold nuggets, and trying to justify that he gets two gold nuggets by appealing to the fact that he is the leader.

Reasoning can be good or bad, occur in the privacy of one's mind, or in an exchange between two or more people. It can be aimed at finding truth or knowledge, or to persuade someone of something, whether true or not. It can be static, relying on fixed assumptions, or dynamic, adjusting one's assumptions and conclusions throughout the process. It can be purely theoretical, where one is reasoning about some abstract idea with no practical application, or practical, where one is reasoning about what to do, how to behave, or how to live.

## Arguments

> 🔍 **KEY CONCEPT: ARGUMENT**
>
> An **argument** is a collection of at least two statements, in which at least one of the statements is a reason for thinking that another of the statements is true.

It is not uncommon to use the word "argument" to mean an exchange (often heated) of diverging or opposing views, such as "I just had an argument with my father!" However, as we will use the term "argument," such an exchange is *not* necessarily an argument. As we will use the term, an *argument* is a *collection of statements* (a minimum of two) in which at least one of the statements *supports* (or is a reason for) another statement. The *supporting* statements (the reasons) are called *premises*, and the *supported* statement is the *conclusion*. Here are two examples:

- *All men are mortal, and Socrates is a man. Thus, Socrates is mortal.*
- *There are 32 teams in the NFL, and so there are at least 10 teams in the NFL.*

Notice that in each case, we have a collection of statements in which at least one of the statements is being offered as a reason for thinking another is *true*.

The examples above are written in normal paragraph form. Often, however, arguments are presented in what is called "*standard form.*" *Standard form* presentation of an argument occurs when one separates (and perhaps numbers) the statements, and in some way separates the premises from the conclusion. Below are three examples of how an argument can be written in standard form, where each is a different way of writing the argument in standard form (though these are not the only ways of doing so):

| Example #1 of Standard Form | Example #2 of Standard Form | Example #3 of Standard Form |
| --- | --- | --- |
| Premise: All men are mortal. | 1. All men are mortal. | All men are mortal. |
| Premise: Socrates is a man. | 2. Socrates is a man. | Socrates is a man. |
| Conclusion: Socrates is mortal. | 3. So, Socrates is mortal. | ∴ Socrates is mortal. |

In the rest of this chapter, as well as in the rest of the book, arguments will be presented in standard form so that the structures can more easily be seen. However, occasionally, especially for homework exercises, arguments will be presented in non-standard form to provide practice in identifying arguments and their parts.

## Differences Between Argument and Reasoning

As the terms "argument" and "reasoning" are being used in this book, there are several differences between arguments and reasoning, even though one can reason through an argument.

- First, reasoning is a *process*, but an argument is a static collection of statements (*not* a process).
- Second, reasoning takes place over time as one moves from one statement to another, making assumptions and drawing conclusions. In contrast, an argument is an unchanging, fixed collection.
- Third, in reasoning, one can make adjustments through the process, perhaps changing one's assumptions or even changing one's conclusion, as one works through the process. By comparison, there is never a change in the premises or conclusion in an argument. If any premise or the conclusion is removed, added, or changed, a *different* argument is *thereby* created.
- Fourth, reasoning is often goal-directed, such as trying to arrive at knowledge or persuade someone of something. But an argument is not goal-directed but is simply a collection as described.

Hereafter the focus will be exclusively on arguments, though what will be said about what makes an argument good or bad, as well as how one evaluates arguments, can be carried over to reasoning.

## Focus on Arguments

Let's turn our attention to arguments, which will remain our focus hereafter. Above, two examples of arguments were given, written in non-standard form. Consider them in standard form:

### Argument #1

Premise: All men are mortal.

Premise: Socrates is a man.

Conclusion: Socrates is mortal.

### Argument #2

Premise: There are 32 teams in the NFL.

Conclusion: There are at least 10 teams in the NFL.

As a first point, note that the argument, in each case, is *the entire collection* of statements. So, for example, in Argument #1 the argument is the *entire collection* of the *three* statements. It is *not* the last statement. So, if asked, "What is the argument in Example #1?" it would be a mistake to say that the argument is that *Socrates is mortal*. That is the *conclusion* of the argument. The argument is the entire collection of the three statements. And, of course, similar points can be made about Argument #2.

Moreover, while arguments must have a minimum of two *statements*—at least one premise and one conclusion (as illustrated in Argument #2), they can and often do have more premises. Many common argument forms have exactly two premises and one conclusion. Such an argument is called a "syllogism"—that is, a syllogism is an *argument* in which there are exactly two premises and one conclusion (such as Argument #1).

However, there is no limit to how many premises an argument can have. Consider:

Premise: The universe exists.

Premise: However, the universe might not have existed.

Premise: Something must explain why it exists rather than not.

Premise: The best explanation is that there is a God who created it.

Conclusion: [Therefore,] God exists.

Here we have an argument with four premises and one conclusion. And we could have an argument with many more premises, or as few as just one premise and one conclusion, as seen above with the example about the number of NFL teams. Moreover, there can be other complexities in the structure of arguments, four of which will be discussed below in the section entitled "Four Caveats about Arguments." Figure 4.1 shows the various structures that we have discussed thus far:

| Minimum Argument Structure | | More Complex Argument Structures | |
|---|---|---|---|
| Premise | (*Syllogism*) | Premise$_1$ | Premise$_1$ |
| Conclusion | Premise$_1$ | Premise$_2$ | $\vdots$ |
| | Premise$_2$ | Premise$_3$ | Premise$_n$ |
| | Conclusion | Premise$_4$ | Conclusion |
| | | Conclusion | |

**FIGURE 4.1**

## Content vs. Structure

Arguments have *content* and *structure*. The *content* consists of the statements making up the argument. For example, Argument Example #1 contains three statements in its *content*:

**Argument #1**

Premise: All men are mortal.

Premise: Socrates is a man.

Conclusion: Socrates is mortal.

In contrast, argument Example #2 contains two statements in its content:

### Argument #2

Premise: There are 32 teams in the NFL.

Conclusion: There are at least 10 teams in the NFL.

We judge the content (i.e., the individual statements) to be *true* or *false*. For example, since there really are 32 teams in the NFL, the premise in Argument #2 is *true*. If there were more or fewer teams, the premise would be false. Our study of evaluating statements in chapter 3 should be used to evaluate the content of an argument.

The structure of an argument is the relationship between the premises and conclusion. We judge the structure in terms of how well the premises support the conclusion. Thus, we judge the structure as either *good* or *bad*. It would be a mistake to say that the *argument* (the *collection*) is true or false, since only the individual statements in it are true or false. Structured collections, which is what an argument is, cannot be true or false. Rather, we judge the argument structure to be good or bad.

As an analogy, we can think of an argument as being like a building, where the supporting beam(s) (as few as one [1]) are like the premises of the argument, and the roof is like the conclusion. The supporting beams can give good or not so good support to the roof, in which case we would judge the structure to be good or bad. Likewise, the premises give good or not so good support to the conclusion, in which case we judge the argument to be good or bad. Our focus in the rest of this chapter and in the next few chapters will be on *structure* of arguments.

### EXERCISE 4.2

For each of the following arguments, specify how many statements make up the content, and identify each statement.

*1. Only fish can sing, and since Marlin is a fish, it follows that Marlin can sing.

2. My frequent drinking does not mean that I am an alcoholic since it doesn't affect my work.

3. The Green Bay Packers will win all of their games next season, because they will fix all their weaknesses during the off-season, and any team that will fix all their weaknesses over the off-season will win all their games the next season.

*4. If the universe exhibits design, then God exists, and since the universe exhibits design, it follows that God most certainly does exist.

5. China is the origin of the various coronaviruses, since SARS emerged from China in 2003, SADS emerged from China in 2012, and the devastating Covid-19 emerged from China in 2019.

6. No three-year-old in the past has ever been able to understand quantum physics, and since Betty's baby is three years old, you can be sure that Betty's baby does not understand quantum physics.

*7. The US leaders had no clear plan for maintaining order once Saddam Hussein's government had been toppled. So, the United States should not have invaded Iraq.

8. The last five German shepherds that I have owned have been excellent watch dogs, and thousands of German shepherd owners have had the same experience with their German shepherds. Further, I have read dozens of reliable authorities about German shepherds, who say that they have this quality. So, probably, my next German shepherd will also be a good watch dog.

9. John driving the family to the airport guarantees that he drove the SUV, and since we know he drove the SUV, you can be sure that he drove the family to the airport.

*10. If a fetus is a human person, then it is morally wrong to kill it without good reason. And, if it is wrong to kill it without good reason, then most abortions are morally wrong. Therefore, most abortions are morally wrong, since fetuses are human persons.

### EXERCISE 4.3

For each of the following arguments, specify whether it is a *syllogism*.

*1. You can login to the site, since you have a current password, and if you have a current password, then you can login to the site.

2. Sam bombed his last two logic tests. So, probably he'll not do well on his next logic test.

3. Some of those oranges are bad, and every bad fruit should be thrown away. Therefore, some of those oranges need to be thrown away.

4. Saul just had two cups of coffee, and whenever he has two cups of coffee, he is very hyperactive, and whenever he is very hyperactive, he tends to get into trouble, and so he is likely to get into trouble.

*5. The car is red, since it is red and square-shaped.

6. If taxes are lowered, I will have more money to spend. Thus, I'll have more money to spend, since taxes have been lowered.

7. All frogs are amphibians, since all toads are frogs and all toads are amphibians.

*8. Coach Johnson once fell asleep during a game, and so probably he's not a very good coach, since any coach who falls asleep during a game is not a very good coach.

## Arguments vs. Non-Arguments

Having stated what an argument is, let's compare it to some examples of non-arguments to help highlight what an argument is.

### Non-Argument Case 1—Single Statements

First, a *single statement by itself* is never an argument. It does not matter if it is believed, stated with great emotion, or conflicts with other statements; by itself, it is *not* an argument. The reason is that an argument is a structured *collection* of *at least two* statements. There are a couple of cases where there *appears* to be multiple statements, when in fact there is only one. Let's consider these.

#### Single Compound Statements

One example of a single statement that may *appear* to be multiple statements is a *compound* statement. A compound statement is a *single* statement but composed of simpler statements. Consider a *conditional* statement (which is an "*If ... then ...*" statement):

> If Carl has $1 million in his savings account, then Carl has more than $10,000 in his savings account.

This is a *single* statement—a conditional, though it is composed of two simpler statements. However, in the context of a conditional, the simpler statements are *not* being *asserted* as true, but rather one is specifying a connection between the two simpler statements, namely that the first simpler statement entails the second—for example, *Carl having $1 million in his savings account* entails that *Carl has more than $10,000 in his savings account*. Notice that the above conditional is *true* even if the simpler component statements are false. This is so because in a conditional, we have a single expression of a relationship between statements, but we are not expressing those simpler statements as true. The point here is that while a conditional may *appear* to be multiple statements, and thus may *appear* to be an argument, by itself it is a *single* compound statement and thus *not* an argument.

Another example is a *disjunction*. For example:

> Either water is composed of $H_2O$, or there are 10 billion people on earth.

Here again, while it may *appear* that there are multiple statements, there is only a *single* compound statement. Notice that in the disjunction, one is *not* asserting that water is composed of $H_2O$, nor that there are 10 billion people on earth. Rather, a *single* thing is being asserted—namely, that at least one of these simpler statements is true. So, once again, while a disjunction may *appear* to be multiple statements, and thus may *appear* to be an argument, by itself it is a *single* compound statement and thus *not* an argument. *The point is to be careful not to judge a single compound statement by itself to be an argument.*

#### Multiple Sentences

A second case in which there *appears* to be multiple statements but in fact there is only one is when someone is writing or uttering multiple *sentences* but is only expressing a single *statement*. This can happen in a couple of ways. First, only a *declarative* sentence is an expression of a statement. Exclamatory (exclamation), imperative (command), and interrogative (question) sentences do not express statements. So, someone may be uttering or writing multiple sentences composed of exclamations, imperatives, or questions, but perhaps only one *declarative* sentence, in which case while they are expressing multiple *sentences*, they are making only a single *statement*, in which case they are *not* making an argument. Here is an example:

Paul: *Where are you going?*

Missy: *Why do you care?*

Paul: *Stop being so intense!*

Missy: *Fine! I'm going to the store.*

In this exchange between Paul and Missy, there are multiple *sentences*. However, only *Missy* is making a statement in her last sentence. Thus, there is no argument here, since there is only a single statement. And, of course, a case of multiple sentences but only a single statement need not be in an exchange between two people, but can be presented by one person.

Another way one can have multiple sentences but only a single statement is if one is expressing the same statement with multiple declarative sentences. For example:

*The Green Bay Packers are the best NFL team.*

*No team in the NFL is as good as the Green Bay Packers.*

*The Green Bay Packers are alone at the top of the NFL ranking scale.*

There are three declarative sentences just above, but they are *saying the same thing*, and thus we have just a single *statement*—namely, that *the Green Bay Packers are the best NFL team.* There are two points to note:

1.  A single statement by itself is never an argument.
2.  There are contexts in which it appears as though there are multiple statements but in which there is only a single statement and thus no argument.

### Non-Argument Case 2—Multiple Statements

A second point of comparison: *Not just any collection of two or more statements, even if structured, constitutes an argument.* Consider the following as an example:

*Fred had oatmeal and eggs for breakfast. Then after finishing his coffee, he went to the gym. When he returned home from the gym, he drank his protein shake. He then resumed writing his book.*

This short passage contains multiple statements, and they are structured—expressing an order of events. However, there is no argument. The reason is that they don't have the structure *appropriate* for an argument—namely, where at least one statement is offered as a reason for thinking another is true.

Another example of where there are multiple statements, and structured ones, which can be mistaken for an argument, is an explanation. In an *explanation*, one is stating *why* or *how* something is the case, but one is *not* giving a reason for thinking a statement is true. Of course, an explanation can be *part of* an argument, but by itself it is *not* an argument. However, an explanation can *appear* to be an argument, since (i) it is composed of multiple statements, and (ii) the statements are structured. Here's a simple example:

*The water is all over the floor as a result of a pipe in the ceiling leaking.*

Notice that the statement that *"There is water all over the floor"* is not in question in this context but is a given. And the statement that *"A pipe in the ceiling is leaking"* is being offered as the *cause of* (explanation of) the water on the floor—*how* there came to be water on the floor or *why* there is water on the floor. But, in this short passage, no reasons for thinking this statement to be true are offered. Thus, there is no argument.

There are two points to note here:

1.  Not just any collection of statements, even if structured, constitutes an argument.
2.  Explanations *appear* to be arguments, but they are not. Arguments give reasons for thinking a statement is true, whereas explanations state how or why a statement is true.

## Identifying Arguments and Their Parts

Above, several examples of arguments were presented in *standard form*. But recall that often arguments are *not* put in standard form. For example, here are three different non-standard form presentations of the same argument:

- *It is undeniable that all men are mortal, and since Socrates is a man, it follows that Socrates is mortal.*
- *Socrates is mortal, since he is a man, and all men are mortal.*
- *All men are mortal, and so Socrates is mortal, since he is a man.*

The argument above (however it is stated) is a simple argument, and perhaps it is easy to identify that it is an argument, as well as easy to identify its parts. However, it is not always easy to identify whether a passage contains an argument or to identify its parts if there is one. One difficulty in identifying the components is that when the argument is in non-standard form, the conclusion can be positioned anywhere in the argument. In the first example, the conclusion is positioned at the end, but in the second and third is it in the beginning and middle, respectively.

- *How do we identify whether there is an argument?*
- *How do we identify the parts of the argument, if there is one, if the statements are not presented in standard form?*

When beginning to learn to identify the presence of an argument and its parts, it is helpful to ask and answer the following questions:

Question #1: Is there more than one statement?

If the answer is *No*, then there is no argument present. Keep in mind that a compound statement is a single statement, despite initial appearance. Also keep in mind that the mere presence of multiple *sentences* does not necessarily mean that there are multiple *statements*.

On the other hand, if the answer to Question #1 is *Yes*, then there might be an argument, and we keep going. So, the next question to ask might be:

Question #2: Are there any indicating words or phrases?

Sometimes arguers insert *indicating words or phrases* into the argument. These are words or phrases that could indicate a premise, with certain indicators, or a conclusion, with others. Some common *conclusion indicators* are:

| CONCLUSION INDICATOR WORDS OR PHRASES | | |
|---|---|---|
| accordingly | hence | thus |
| as a consequence | in consequence | we may conclude that |
| as a result | it follows that | we may infer that |
| consequently | so | which entails that |
| for these reasons | therefore | which implies that |

This is not an exhaustive list of conclusion indicators, but only some common ones. You will find these, when they are used, positioned *before* the conclusion. Note that these indicators are *not* part of the conclusion, but only indicate it. So, for example, consider the argument:

> *Since all men are mortal, and Socrates is a man, it follows that Socrates is mortal.*

In this argument, the phrase *"it follows that"* is a conclusion indicator. However, it is not part of the conclusion. The conclusion is the statement: *Socrates is mortal.*

Likewise, there are *premise indicators*. Here are some common ones:

| PREMISE INDICATOR WORDS OR PHRASES | | |
|---|---|---|
| after all | because | inasmuch as |
| as | follows from | may be deduced |
| as shown by | for | otherwise |
| assuming that | given that | since |

Again, this is not an exhaustive list of premise indicators, but just some common ones. You will find these, when they are used, positioned *before* the premise(s). And, as with conclusion indicators, these indicators are *not* part of the premise(s), but only indicate the premise(s). So, for example:

> *Since all men are mortal, and Socrates is a man, it follows that Socrates is mortal.*

In this argument, the word *"since"* is a premise indicator, but it is not part of the premises. The premises are the statements: *All men are mortal*, and *Socrates is a man*.

Let's turn back to our question: *Are there any indicating words or phrases?* If the answer is *Yes*, then there *could* very well be an argument, especially with the conclusion indicators. These almost always indicate the presence of an argument. However, one must be careful, as sometimes these words or phrases could be used, but *not* as premise or conclusion indicators. For example, the word "so" can be used without indicating a conclusion:

> *He studied hard so he could pass the test.*

Here the word "so" does *not* indicate a conclusion. Rather, in this context, it indicates *purpose* or *goal*. The same statement would have been expressed as:

> He studied hard *for the sake of* passing the test.

Another example is with the word "*because.*" While it can indicate a premise, it can also indicate an explanation. Consider:

> The car stopped running <u>because</u> it is out of gas.

Here we do *not* have an argument but rather an *explanation*, where the statement "it is out of gas" plays the role of explaining why *the car stopped running*. So, in this passage, "*because*" functions as an explanation indicator and not as a premise indicator.

So, back to our question (*Are there any indicating words or phrases?*) and answer. If the answer is *Yes*, let this merely be an *indication* that there is an argument (as some evidence) but not a guarantee. We would consider this evidence and do a further test, which we will get to momentarily.

On the other hand, if the answer to our question (*Are there any indicating words or phrases?*) is *No*, that does *not* mean that there is no argument. There still could be an argument; it is just that the presenter of the argument failed to give any indicator words. For example:

> Socrates is mortal. He is a man, and all men are mortal.

Even though there are no indicating words, there is still an argument here.

So, while indicating words and phrases can be evidence of an argument, they don't always indicate an argument, and there may be an argument without them. However, they are often *good evidence* of the presence of an argument and thus can be used to identify one.

Further, *if* there are indicating words or phrases, and *if* they indicate premise or conclusion, not only do they help us identify that there is an argument, but they also help us identify its parts, which we need to do for evaluation. It should be clear how they do so. *Premise* indicators indicate *premises*, and *conclusion* indicators indicate *conclusions*. So, consider our argument with another indicating word added:

> *Because* all men are mortal, and *since* Socrates is a man, *it follows that* Socrates is mortal.

Not only do our indicating words strongly indicate an argument here, but "*because*" and "*since*" help us identify the two premises, and "*it follows that*" helps us identify the conclusion.

So far, we have two question / answer steps in our process of identifying arguments:

Question #1: Is there more than one statement?

- If *No*, there is no argument.
- If *Yes*, there might be an argument, and so keep going.

Question #2: Are there any indicating words or phrases?

- If *Yes*, this is evidence of an argument and evidence of its parts. Keep going.
- If *No*, there still might be an argument, and so keep going.

This brings us to our final question:

Question #3: Is it reasonable to interpret the passage in such a way that one or more of the statements in it are *reason(s) for thinking* another statement in the passage is *true*?

If the answer to Question #3 is *Yes*, then we can have confidence in concluding that there is an argument present, especially if there are indicating words or phrases. If the answer is *No*, then we can conclude that there is no argument. Each of these options will be illustrated below.

Consider the following argument:

*Ken loves the Green Bay Packers, since most people from Wisconsin love the Green Bay Packers, and Ken is from Wisconsin.*

Suppose that we didn't know it was an argument. We can run our question / answer process.

Question #1: Is there more than one statement?

*Answer:* Yes! So, we keep going.

Question #2: Are there any indicating words or phrases?

*Answer:* Yes! The word "since" is a premise indicator. So, this is some evidence that we have an argument and that the two statements following the "since," connected with "and," are the premises.

Question #3: Is it reasonable to interpret the passage in such a way that one or more of the statements in it are *reason(s) for thinking* another statement in the passage is *true*?

*Answer:* Yes! It makes sense to interpret the statements following the "since" as *reasons for thinking it is true* that Ken loves the Packers. Thus, we have an argument, and we have identified its parts.

We can present it in standard form as follows:

Premise: Most people from Wisconsin love the Green Bay Packers.
Premise: Ken is from Wisconsin.
Conclusion: [So,] Ken loves the Green Bay Packers.

But even if there were no indicating words or phrases in the argument, we could still arrive at the same results with our question / answer process. Consider:

*Ken loves the Green Bay Packers. Most people from Wisconsin love the Green Bay Packers, and Ken is from Wisconsin.*

Again, suppose that we did not know it was an argument. We would run our question / answer process:

Question #1: Is there more than one statement?

*Answer:* Yes! So, we keep going.

Question #2: Are there any indicating words or phrases?

*Answer:* No! But there may still be an argument, and thus we keep going.

Question #3: Is it reasonable to interpret the passage in such a way that one or more of the statements in it are *reason(s) for thinking* another statement in the passage is *true*?

*Answer:* Yes! It makes sense to interpret the second and third statements as *reasons for thinking it is true* that Ken loves the Packers. Thus, there's an argument. And we can present it in the same standard form.

Or we may go through the steps and discover that there is *no* argument. Consider:

*Fred had oatmeal and eggs for breakfast. Then after finishing his coffee, he went to the gym. When he returned home from the gym, he drank his protein shake. He then resumed writing his book.*

Suppose that we didn't know that this is a non-argument. We would go through our steps.

Question #1: Is there more than one statement?

*Answer:* Yes! So, we keep going.

Question #2: Are there any indicating words or phrases?

*Answer:* No! But there may still be an argument, and thus we keep going.

Question #3: Is it reasonable to interpret the passage in such a way that one or more of the statements in it are *reason(s) for thinking* another statement in the passage is *true*?

*Answer:* No! None of the statements, individually or together, is a reason(s) for another statement.

Thus, there is *no* argument here. Figure 4.2 shows an overview of the steps:

| Question | Answer | Action / Judgement |
|---|---|---|
| Question #1:<br>Is there more than one statement? | Yes | Maybe an argument;<br>continue investigating |
| | No | No argument |
| Question #2:<br>Are there any indicating words or phrases? | Yes | Evidence of an argument;<br>continue investigating |
| | No | May still be an argument;<br>continue investigating |
| Question #3:<br>Is it reasonable to interpret the passage in such a way that one or more of the statements in it are reasons for thinking another statement in the passage is true? | Yes | There *is* an argument!<br>Identify the premises and conclusion |
| | No | No argument |

**FIGURE 4.2**

**EXERCISE 4.4**

Determine which of the following passages contains an argument, and for any that contain an argument, identify the premise(s) and conclusion.

*1. Look, any animal that barks is a dog, and that animal is barking. Therefore, it is a dog.

2. If I was reading the newspaper in the kitchen, then my glasses are on the kitchen table.

3. Pornography is bad; after all, it misleads people about sexuality, and it portrays women as mere sexual objects and not as valuable humans.

4. Bob is likely to gain muscle mass because he works out regularly, and most people who work out regularly gain muscle mass.

*5. Do you really believe that North Korea's leader Kim Jung-un is perfectly healthy?

6. It is very hot outside, and most of the water has evaporated.

7. Jenna is a highly motivated runner, and thus she will finish the race, since all motivated runners finish the race.

8. Martha will take Introduction to Philosophy this fall, unless the class is full. In view of the fact that the class is already almost full, probably she will not be taking the class.

9. That truck's transmission will probably go bad soon, given that it's a Ford, and no Ford has a long-lasting transmission.

10. Stop driving so fast! Are you trying to kill me?

11. You know that this beverage will begin to cool more quickly in the freezer than in the refrigerator! Many people who don't understand physics think things will cool faster in the refrigerator. But they're sadly mistaken.

12. An observation is evidence for one theory over another theory if the observation is more probable given the first theory than it is given the second theory. Further, our observation that the universe is fine-tuned for life is far more probable given the theory that God exists than it is given the theory that there is no God. Consequently, we have good reason to think that God exists, relative to the fine-tuning of the universe.

13. There is no pile of rocks in the corner to be moved as my dad suggests, as can be seen from the fact that the ground is clearly visible.

14. It is clear that we know some things without proof. This follows from the fact that we do know some things, and if we do, then either some of the things that we know are known without proof or everything we know is by way of some proof from other premises that we know. However, we cannot prove every premise by other premises infinitely. [Paraphrase of the Aristotle]

*15. "Above all, avoid lies, all lies, especially the lie to yourself. Keep watch on your own lie and examine it every hour, every minute. And avoid contempt, both of others and of yourself: what seems bad to you in yourself is purified by the very fact that you have noticed it in yourself. And avoid fear, though fear is simply the consequence of every lie. Never be frightened at your own faintheartedness in attaining love, and meanwhile do not even be very frightened by your own bad acts." [Fyodor Dostoyevsky, *The Brothers Karamazov*]

16. There is a great deal of pollen floating outside right now. As a result, Davy cannot go outside, because he has bad hay fever, and if he is exposed to the pollen, his hay fever will cause him to have an asthma attack, and if he has an asthma attack, he'll have to go to the hospital, and if he goes to the hospital, he'll be exposed to all sorts of other viruses there, which could be devastating to his health.

17. We hold these Truths to be self-evident, that all Men are created equal, that they are endowed by their Creator with certain unalienable Rights, that among these are Life, Liberty, and the pursuit of Happiness—That to secure these Rights, Governments are instituted among Men, deriving their just Powers from the Consent of the Governed, that whenever any Form of Government becomes destructive of these Ends, it is the Right of the People to alter or to abolish it, and to institute new Government, laying its Foundation on such Principles, and organizing its Powers in such Form, as to them shall seem most likely to affect their Safety and Happiness. [From the United States' Declaration of Independence]

18. "In the beginning was the Word, and the Word was with God, and the Word was God. He was in the beginning with God. All things came into being through Him, and apart from Him nothing came into being that has come into being. In Him was life, and the life was the Light of men. The Light shines in the darkness, and the darkness did not comprehend it." [*Gospel of John 1:1–5*]

19. All human life has immeasurable value and is worth preserving, unless there is good reason to end it. Furthermore, a suffering (and perhaps dying) person's request to be helped to die (which may not be a competent, enduring, and genuinely voluntary request) is not good reason to justify helping to end their life. As a result, voluntary euthanasia is morally wrong.

*20. It is clear that time travel is impossible given the following: Suppose that a time traveler Mark steps into a time machine at a certain time and arrives at the time of the dinosaurs five minutes later, which means that the time between Mark's departure and arrival into the past is five minutes. But the time of the dinosaurs is millions of years ago, which means that the time between Mark's departure and arrival into the past is millions of years. But the time between his departure and arrival cannot be both five minutes and millions of years. [Paraphrase of David Lewis' discussion on p. 145 of his 1976 article, "The Paradoxes of Time Travel," *American Philosophical Quarterly*, 13, no. 2 (1976): 145–152.]

## EXERCISE 4.5

For each provided statement below, create an argument by contributing *at least* two additional statements to support (as premises) the provided statement (as conclusion).

*Example:*

Provided Statement: Space aliens often visit our planet earth. (To be the conclusion)

Added Statement 1: Often there are moving lights seen in the night sky. (Premise)

Added Statement 2: Moving lights in the night sky are caused by alien spacecrafts visiting our planet earth. (Premise)

Note that you do not have to believe the provided statement or the added statements, and the added statements can be entirely imaginary. This is merely an exercise in creating arguments.

Provided Statements:

1. Dogs make much better pets than do cats.
2. Most people love the taste of sardines.
3. Plants communicate with each other through the air and the soil.
4. *Seinfeld* was the greatest show of all time.
5. The United States should have completely open borders.
6. The United States should have completely closed borders.
7. God exists.
8. There is no God.
9. Abortion is morally permissible in any circumstance.
10. Abortion is never morally permissible.

## Four Caveats About Arguments

Above we saw that arguments can exhibit the following sorts of structures:

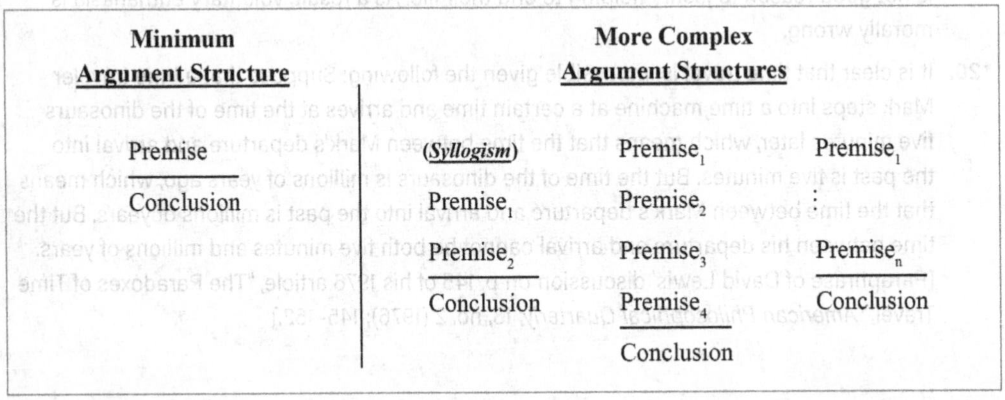

| Minimum Argument Structure | More Complex Argument Structures | | |
|---|---|---|---|
| Premise _____ Conclusion | (*Syllogism*) Premise$_1$ Premise$_2$ _____ Conclusion | Premise$_1$ Premise$_2$ Premise$_3$ Premise$_4$ _____ Conclusion | Premise$_1$ $\vdots$ Premise$_n$ _____ Conclusion |

**FIGURE 4.1** (repeated)

However, there are four caveats, complicating things a bit—namely, (a) the premises of an argument can be *dependent* upon each other to support the conclusion, or give *independent* support to the conclusion, (b) arguments can have *sub-conclusions*, (c) arguments can have more than one final conclusion, and (d) arguments can have *implicit* premises and an *implicit* conclusion.

## Dependent vs. Independent Premises

The first caveat about arguments concerns the relationship between the premises relative to the support they provide to the conclusion. On the one hand, the premises can *depend* on each other to support the conclusion. Consider the following *syllogism* for example:

Premise: If Barry will go to the movie, then Charles will go to the movie.

Premise: Barry *will go* to the movie.

Conclusion: [Therefore,] Charles will go to the movie.

In this argument, neither premise by itself supports the conclusion. Notice that the statement *"Charles will go to the movie"* is *not* supported by the statement *"If Barry will go to the movie, then Charles will go to the movie."* That statement (i.e., premise 1) is true, we may suppose, even if neither Barry nor Charles will go to the movie. Thus, premise 1 by itself provides no reason to think that the conclusion is true. The same is true of premise 2. The statement *"Barry will go to the movie"* by itself provides no support for *"Charles will go to the movie."* But *together* they *do* support the conclusion. Thus, the premises in this argument *depend* on each other to support the conclusion.

On the other hand, the premises can provide *independent* support to the conclusion. Consider the following example:

Premise: Violating the speed limit increases your chances of getting a speeding ticket.

Premise: Violating the speed limit increases your chances of getting into an accident.

Conclusion: [Therefore,] you should not speed.

In this argument, each premise by itself provides support for the conclusion. While they together make a stronger case for the conclusion, each would support the conclusion if the other premise were eliminated. Thus, the premises in this argument are *independent* of each other in support of the conclusion.

Further, while an argument with independent premises could be treated as two separate arguments for the conclusion, it can also be treated as a single argument with *independent* premises. Figure 4.3 illustrates dependent versus independent premise structures.

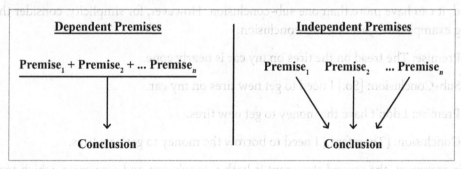

**FIGURE 4.3**

**EXERCISE 4.6**

For each argument below, state whether the premises provide dependent or independent support to the conclusion. (Note, identify the premises as "dependent" only if none of the premises alone supports the conclusion.)

*1. The package of strawberries that I bought at Smith's last week contained some moldy strawberries, and the package of strawberries that I bought at Smith's today contained some moldy strawberries. Thus, the strawberry packages at Smith's occasionally contain moldy strawberries.

2. A platypus can fly, since all birds can fly and a platypus is a bird.

3. Dr. Smith treated Kyle today, and he treated Miles today, and so Dr. Smith treated at least one person today.

*4. Either the water in this lake came from the north river or it came from the south river, but clearly it did not come from the south river, and therefore it came from the north river.

5. If the murder was committed in the library, then it was committed by Mrs. Peacock, and if it was committed by Mrs. Peacock, then it was not committed by Professor Plum. So, if the murder was committed in the library, it was not committed by Professor Plum.

6. You really stink, and you have mud all over yourself. You really need a shower.

*7. Some people in this room are artists. Some people in this room are realists. So, this room contains artists or realists.

8. If humans persist over time, then humans are immaterial souls inhabiting a body. Clearly, humans do persist over time, and thus humans are immaterial souls inhabiting a body.

9. Coffee is not bad for you, since if it were bad for you, the FDA would not approve it, but the FDA has approved it.

*10. Honey badgers are fearless and ferocious, and thus honey badgers are fearless.

## Arguments with Sub-Conclusion

The second caveat about argument structures is that an argument can have both a *main* conclusion and a *sub-conclusion* (which is both a conclusion and a premise for a further conclusion). Indeed, it can have more than one sub-conclusion. However, for simplicity, consider the following example with just one sub-conclusion:

Premise: The tread on the tires on my car is nearly gone.

Sub-Conclusion: [So,] I need to get new tires on my car.

Premise: I don't have the money to get new tires.

Conclusion: [Therefore,] I need to borrow the money to get new tires.

In this argument, the second statement is both a conclusion and a premise, which together with premise three, supports the last statement. Thus, the second statement is a *sub-conclusion*.

There are a couple of question-and-answer sets that can be used to help distinguish a sub-conclusion from the main conclusion. Question #1 helps to determine whether it is a conclusion at all:

Question #1: Is the statement *being supported* by other statements?

If the answer is *Yes*, then it is a conclusion (sub- or main). If the answer is *No*, then it is not a conclusion. For example, in the argument just above, the second and fourth statements are being supported, but the first and third are not. Thus, the second and fourth are conclusions.

If the answer to Question #1 is *Yes*, then move on to Question #2, which can help determine whether the conclusion is a sub-conclusion or a main conclusion:

Question #2: Is the statement *supporting* other statements?

If the answer is *Yes*, then it is a *sub*-conclusion. If the answer is *No*, then it is a *main* conclusion. So, for example, we can see that statement two in the argument above is being supported by the first statement, but it is also supporting (with the third statement) the fourth statement. Thus, the second statement is a sub-conclusion. In contrast, the fourth statement is being supported, but it is not doing any supporting. Thus, it is the main conclusion.

There is a third and separate question that can also be asked that may be helpful:

Question #3: Which statement seems to express the primary purpose of the argument?

For example, in the argument above, the primary purpose seems to be that I need to borrow money to get new tires. This is another sign that it is the main conclusion. Figure 4.4 illustrates *some* structures with sub-conclusions.

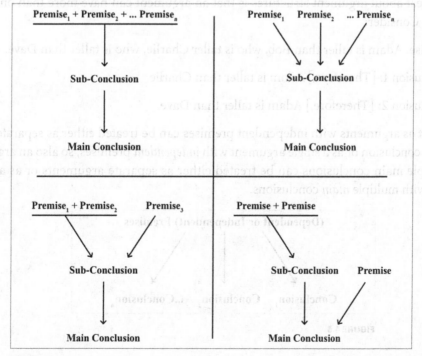

**FIGURE 4.4**

**EXERCISE 4.7**

For each passage below, identify the sub-conclusion(s) and the main conclusion.

**\*1.** The bees are angry because whenever you disturb their beehive, you are likely to make them angry, and you disturbed their beehive. Further, if you make the bees angry, you are likely to get stung. So, probably you will get stung.

**2.** Look, the bar is either open or it's closed. It is not closed because there are people inside. And, if it's open, Paul is inside. Therefore, Paul is inside the bar.

**3.** There is no doubt that Arnold is stronger than Sylvester, since Arnold has larger muscles than does Sylvester. Thus, if they compete in a lifting contest, Arnold will win!

**\*4.** Charles is nice, since he is from Wisconsin, and all people from Wisconsin are nice. There-fore, he'd make a good friend, since all nice people make good friends.

**5.** Physicalism is the view that everything is physical, including mental states. However, mental states are not physical states, which is evidenced by the fact that you can be as clever and creative as you like in telling me all the physical facts about the brain, including every kind of state, and their functional roles, and you will not have told me about anything mental. It follows that physicalism is false.

**6.** Timmy, I know that you broke the glass because it was either you, the cat, or the dog. It wasn't the dog because he was out at the groomer, and it wasn't the cat because she was in my room when the glass was broken in the kitchen, where you were.

## Arguments with More Than One Conclusion

A third caveat about argument structures is that an argument can have more than one *main* conclusion. Consider:

Premise: Adam is taller than Bob, who is taller Charlie, who is taller than Dave.

Conclusion 1: [Therefore,] Adam is taller than Charlie.

Conclusion 2: [Therefore,] Adam is taller than Dave.

And, just as arguments with independent premises can be treated either as separate argu-ments for a conclusion or as a single argument with *independent* premises, so also an argument with multiple main conclusions can be treated either as separate arguments or as a single argument with multiple *main* conclusions.

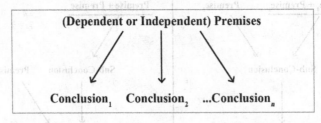

**FIGURE 4.5**

## Implicit Premises and Conclusion

A fourth caveat about argument structures is that some arguments may contain *implicit* premises or conclusions. A premise is *implicit* if it is *obviously* assumed, but not *explicitly* stated. Here's an example:

Premise: Anyone who handles a rock from Chernobyl will get cancer.

Conclusion: [Therefore,] you can expect Yuri to get cancer.

The *obvious* implicit *premise* here is:

Premise: Yuri handled a rock from Chernobyl. (*Implicit*)

Making implicit premises explicit can be very important when evaluating an argument, especially if the implicit premise is controversial, or even clearly false. But how do we decide whether a premise is *clearly* being assumed, and that we need to make it explicit for evaluation? This is an important question, since it may be that the arguer is *not* assuming anything implicit but is simply presenting a bad argument, in which the conclusion simply does not follow from the premises. In this case, we would **not** want to add any implicit premises, as there are none, but simply point out that the argument is flawed. However, other times the arguer *really is* assuming something and simply leaving it as an implicit premise. So, *how do we know when the arguer has an implicit premise*, and *how do we know what it is*?

Unfortunately, it is not always clear when an arguer is leaving a premise implicit, and what that implicit premise is. However, here are some things that can help. First, an implicit premise is **not** a statement that the evaluator of the argument arbitrarily invents, pulling it out of thin air. Rather, it will be a statement that is clearly connected to what is *explicitly* stated. Thus, when determining whether there is an implicit premise, pay attention to the **explicit** premises and to the conclusion that the arguer presents. Then ask:

*What seems obviously missing that would connect those premises to that conclusion?*

The answer is likely the implicit premise. Consider our example from above:

Premise: Anyone who handles a rock from Chernobyl will get cancer.

Conclusion: [Therefore,] you can expect Yuri to get cancer.

There clearly seems to be an implicit premise here. But we wouldn't just draw any statement out of thin air, such as that *Chernobyl is located in Ukraine*. That is just irrelevant to *this* argument. But if we pay attention to the *explicit* premise, and the conclusion, we see this structure: *All F are G* (premise form), and [therefore,] *x is G* (conclusion). Clearly what would connect these is our missing premise that: *x is F*. That is, what is *clearly* implicit is that *Yuri handled a rock from Chernobyl*.

But, again, note that there are not always implicit premises, but sometimes there are just bad arguments. Consider:

Premise: The hotdog that I had at Windy City had stale bread.

Conclusion: [Thus,] the food at Windy City is horrible.

There is no implicit premise in this case. It is just a *bad* argument. Thus, we would not want to attempt to draw out any implicit premises in this case.

While it will not always be clear whether one is dealing with an instance of an arguer having an implicit premise (as opposed to simply presenting a bad argument in which the conclusion simply does not follow from the premises), with practice the process of identifying any implicit premises, if there are any, will become more natural.

Similar points can be made about an implicit *conclusion*. A conclusion is *implicit* if it is *obviously* implied, but not *explicitly* stated. Consider:

> Premise: Snakes with triangular-shaped heads are poisonous.

> Premise: That snake has a triangular-shaped head.

The *obvious* implicit *conclusion* is:

> Conclusion: [Therefore,] that snake is poisonous. (*Implicit*)

### EXERCISE 4.8

Each argument below contains an explicit premise, an *implicit* premise, and an explicit conclusion. Identify the *implicit* premise and make it explicit.

> *Example:*
> Provided Argument: I bought this coffee at Trader Joe's, and so it is probably very good.
> Implicit Premise Made Explicit: Trader Joe's coffee tends to be very good.

Provided Arguments:

**\*1.** The Green Bay Packers are likely to win because they have Aaron Rodgers as quarterback.

**2.** Marcy deserves a promotion as a result of hard work over the past few months.

**3.** Felix is a long-haired cat. Therefore, he will shed a lot.

**\*4.** Most likely, Sally can now walk since she is two years old.

**5.** Jesus should be trusted—after all, he rose from the dead!

**6.** The United States has a very powerful and competent military, as shown by how quickly it defeated the Iraqi military.

**\*7.** My dad overate at dinner, and so he'll likely suffer from indigestion tonight.

**8.** Given that the North Korean government is a threat to the world, we may conclude that the North Korean government should be very carefully monitored.

**9.** It has been raining very heavily for two days, which implies that there will be flooding in the valley.

**10.** We'll go to the movie tonight, assuming that the theater is open.

### EXERCISE 4.9

Each argument below contains explicit premises but the conclusion is *implicit*. Identify the *implicit* conclusion and make it explicit.

> *Example*:
>
> Provided Argument: iPhones are excellent phones, and I just bought an iPhone.
>
> Implicit Conclusion Made Explicit: The phone I just bought is excellent.

Provided Arguments:

*1. My professor told me that practicing the homework exercises is good preparation for the test, and he knows what he is talking about.

2. If you smoke at least two packs of cigarettes a day, you are likely to get some form of cancer, and Victor smokes three packs of cigarettes a day.

3. Humans have been given dominion over animals, and it's morally permissible for humans to eat anything over which they have dominion.

*4. Most successful American entrepreneurs are very wealthy, and Bill is an American entrepreneur.

5. The grade on the exam is fair only if the grader was not sleepy while grading, but she was very sleepy while grading the exam.

6. If the universe is fine-tuned for life, then God exists, and physicists have told us that the universe is fine-tuned for life.

*7. We will either buy a Husky or a Bernese mountain dog for our next dog, but a Bernese mountain dog is very difficult to find.

8. If Sheldon wins the debate, his ego will be bloated, and if he has a bloated ego, he will likely gloat ad nauseam.

9. If Barry is good at mathematics, he is good at logic, but he is not good at logic.

10. Iguanas are reptiles, and reptiles are cold-blooded creatures.

## Recap

In this chapter, we discussed *reasoning* and *arguments*, and then focused on arguments. We differentiated *content* and *structure* of an argument, and distinguished arguments from non-arguments. We discussed steps to undertake to help identify whether an argument is present in a passage and how to identify its parts, if there is an argument. Finally, we discussed some caveats about argument structures. Below are some important concepts that should have been learned:

- **Argument**: A collection of at least two statements, in which at least one of the statements is a reason for thinking another of the statements is true.
  - **Argument Content**: The statements making up an argument.
  - **Argument Structure**: The relationship between the premises and conclusion.

- **Conclusion**: A statement in an argument that is being supported by other statements in the argument.
  - **Implicit Conclusion**: A conclusion that is assumed but not explicitly stated.
- **Premise**: A statement in an argument intended to support another statement in the argument.
  - **Implicit Premise**: A premise that is assumed but not explicitly stated.
- **Reasoning**: An activity of proceeding from one statement to another statement, typically beginning with assumptions and proceeding to a conclusion based on those assumptions.
  - **Inference**: Reasoning in which one draws a conclusion based on one's assumptions.
- **Standard Form**: Presenting an argument in such a way that each statement is clearly separated from the other statements, and such that the premises are distinguished from the conclusion.
- **Syllogism**: An argument with exactly two premises and one conclusion.

# A CLOSER LOOK AT ARGUMENTS

# 5

In chapter 4, we took an introductory look at arguments, and how to identify them and their parts. However, in order to expand our critical thinking skills, it is not enough merely to be able identify that an argument is present and what its parts are; we also need to know how to evaluate it, as well as how to create a good argument for ourselves. So, in this chapter, we take a bit more extensive look at arguments by considering the two types of arguments—*deductive* and *inductive*. We will learn what each is, as well as the following important related concepts: *valid* argument, *sound* argument, *strong* argument, and *cogent* argument. We will further discuss a couple of "everyday" methods for judging the validity of arguments—what we'll call the *thought experiment method* and the *abstraction and diagramming method*. Here are some key terms to master as we work through this chapter:

---

## KEY WORDS

| | |
|---|---|
| Cogent Argument | Strong Argument |
| Deductive Argument | Thought Experiment |
| Inductive Argument | Truth-Preserving |
| Sound Argument | Valid Argument |

## Introduction to Types of Arguments

### Review of Arguments

In chapter 4, we defined an argument as follows:

> An *argument* is a collection of at least two statements, in which at least one of the statements is a *reason for thinking* that another of the statements is *true*.

Again, the *supporting* statements (the reasons) are the premises, and the *supported* statement is the conclusion. We saw the following two examples:

### Example #1

Premise: All men are mortal.

Premise: Socrates is a man.

Conclusion: Socrates is mortal.

### Example #2

Premise: There are 32 teams in the NFL.

Conclusion: There are at least 10 teams in the NFL.

Further, we noted that when evaluating an argument, one must consider both the *content* and the *structure*. The *content* consists of the claims making up the argument, and we judge these in terms of their truth-value (we judge them to be true or false). The *structure* consists of the relationship between the premises and conclusion, and we judge it in terms of its *quality* (good or bad structure).

## Two Types of Arguments

Moving forward, we distinguish between two general types of arguments—*deductive* and *inductive*. If one looks up "deductive argument versus inductive argument" on Google, one finds a variety of definitions. A common, *and a misguided*, way to define these is that a deductive argument starts from a general principle in the premises and concludes with a specific statement, and an inductive argument starts from a specific statement (statement of observation) as premise and concludes with a generalized statement.

While anyone can use terms in any way they like, defining deductive as "general to specific," and inductive as "specific to general" fails to capture the essence of deductive and inductive arguments, respectively, and thus is misguided. As will be shown, inductive arguments can be "general to specific" and "specific to general," as well as "specific to specific" and "general to general." And deductive arguments can be "general to specific," as well as "specific to specific" and "general to general." Thus, the essence of deductive and inductive arguments is <u>not</u> captured with this idea of "general to specific" or "specific to general."

Instead, to capture, broadly, the *essence* of these arguments, we define them in terms of the *structure* that one is trying to create within one's argument. For a first pass, we can say that a *deductive* argument is one in which one is attempting to *prove* the conclusion with the premises; one is trying to create a *truth-preserving* structure—more on this momentarily. In contrast, an *inductive* argument is one in which one is attempting to *give evidence for*, but *not* prove, the conclusion with the premises. (Note that the difference between these is *not* a matter of content, as one can have very similar content within each type of structure.)

Before taking a closer look at each type, let's note and set aside a controversial issue. There is a type of argument called *"abductive argument"* or *"inference to the best explanation."* Some have considered this to be a *third* general type of argument, in addition to deductive and inductive arguments. However, others treat it as a type of *inductive* argument. The position adopted in this book is that as long as abductive argument is studied, it does not matter how it is classified. However, here are two reasons why one might want to treat it as an *inductive* argument. First, like all the *inductive* arguments that we will discuss, *abductive* arguments are non-deductive, in the sense that one is *not* attempting to *prove* the conclusion with the premises, but only to give evidence for the conclusion with the premises. Second, given the diversity of inductive arguments, there is not a clear way to distinguish abductive arguments from the variety of inductive arguments. Thus, for the purposes of this book, abductive arguments will be treated as a type of inductive argument and will be studied in chapter 9.

## Deductive Arguments

For our first pass, it was said that a *deductive* argument is one in which one is *attempting* to *prove* the conclusion with the premises. More exactly, it is an argument in which one is attempting to create a *valid* structure.

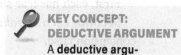

**KEY CONCEPT: DEDUCTIVE ARGUMENT**
A **deductive argument** is an argument in which one is attempting to create a valid structure.

A *valid* argument is one in which *it is impossible for the conclusion to be false, if the premises are true.* So, *if* the argument is *valid, then if* the premises are true, the conclusion *must* be true as well. This brings us back to the idea of *truth-preserving.* To say that an argument is *truth-preserving* is just another way of saying that the argument is *valid*—it is saying that *true* premises guarantee a true conclusion.

Note that we defined a deductive argument as an argument in which one is *attempting* to create a valid structure. We do not want to define it *being* valid, since then there would be no bad structured deductive arguments—ones that are *not* valid. But there are deductive arguments that have bad structures, that are not valid. If an argument is not valid, it is *invalid.* Many examples will follow.

**KEY CONCEPT: VALID ARGUMENT**
An argument is **valid** if and only if it is *impossible* for the conclusion to be false, if the premises are true.

### Validity: Structure vs. Truth

Often when students are first introduced to validity, they confuse *structure* and *content. Validity is a matter of structure, not content.* Put differently, it is the *structure* and not whether the premises are true or false, which grounds the validity of an argument. What matters is that *if* the premises are true, *then* the conclusion must be true as well. Or, as we defined it, what matters is that *it is impossible for the premises to be true and the conclusion to be false, simultaneously.* So, it is possible to have the following scenarios containing a *valid argument:*

**Scenario #1: Valid Arguments with True Premises and True Conclusion**

In the first scenario, we find *valid* arguments that have all true statements, both premises and conclusion. Here are three examples:

### Example #1 of a valid argument with all true statements

Premise: All birds are animals.

Premise: Cardinals are birds.

Conclusion: [Therefore,] cardinals are animals.

### Example #2 of a valid argument with all true statements

Premise: Las Vegas is in Nevada.

Premise: Nevada is in the United States.

Conclusion: [Therefore,] Las Vegas is in the United States.

### Example #3 of a valid argument with all true statements

Premise: The White House is white.

Premise: The White House is a house.

Conclusion: [Therefore,] the White House is white and a house.

There are a few points to be noted about these examples.

First, each has *true* statements throughout the argument.

Second, each is *valid*, since in each it is impossible for premises to be true and the conclusion false.

Third, two of the examples are *counterexamples* to the idea that deductive arguments have general principles as premises and a specific statement as a conclusion. While Example #1 has this format, Examples #2 and #3 do **not**. Both have more of a "specific to specific" format. This helps to make the point that one should <u>not</u> define a deductive argument as one that is "general to specific," but instead one should define it as was done above, to capture the essence of deductive arguments.

Fourth, while each example is an example of a *syllogism* (an argument with two premises and one conclusion), deductive arguments in general, and valid arguments in particular, don't have to be syllogisms. However, many of the examples that will be given are syllogisms, since it's easy to produce syllogisms that are clear examples of validity. Here are two examples of valid arguments that are not syllogisms:

### Example #1 of a valid argument that is not a syllogism

Premise: The earth is a planet.

Conclusion: [Therefore,] either the earth is a planet, or Barack Obama is Spider-man.

### Example #2 of a valid argument that is not a syllogism

Premise: A whale is a mammal.

Premise: If a whale is a mammal, then a whale has a heart.

Premise: If a whale has a heart, then a whale has a kidney.

Conclusion: [Therefore,] a whale has a kidney.

Scenario #1 cases are *valid* arguments with *true* premises. An argument of this sort—valid with true premises—is a *sound* argument.

> **KEY CONCEPT: SOUND ARGUMENT**
>
> An argument is *sound* if and only if it is *valid* and has *true* premises.

**Scenario #2: Valid Arguments with False Premises and False Conclusion**

In the second scenario, we find *valid* arguments that have all *false* statements, both premises and conclusion. While this is puzzling to some, it becomes problem free once one fully understands *validity*—namely, that it is a matter of *structure*, not content. Let's have a look at some examples:

### Example #1 of a valid argument with all false statements

Premise: If the earth has exactly three moons, then it has more than four moons.

Premise:  The earth does have exactly three moons.

Conclusion: [Therefore,] the earth has more than four moons.

### Example #2 of a valid argument with all false statements

Premise: Trump Tower is taller than One World Trade Center.

Premise: One World Trade Center is taller than Burj Khalifa.

Conclusion: [Therefore,] Trump Tower is taller than Burj Khalifa.

### Example #3 of a valid argument with all false statements

Premise: All dogs are cats.

Premise: All cats are birds.

Conclusion: [Therefore,] all dogs are birds.

We can make several points about each of these examples as well.

First, each has *false* statements throughout the argument.[1]

Second, and importantly, each is *valid*, since in each it is impossible for the premises to be true and the conclusion false. This may be difficult to grasp initially since the premises are false.

In order to help see that these are valid, for the moment ignore the fact that the premises are false and assume that they are true—that is, imagine that we live in a world in which the premises in each of the examples are true. Given this, we can see that the conclusion in each case would *have to be* true as well.

For example, consider the second example. Imagine we live in a world in which the premises are true. Wouldn't it follow by the transitivity of *taller than* that the conclusion is true as well? *Yes!* The same is true in each of the examples. If we *assume* that the premises are true, then the conclusion is guaranteed to be true as well. Or, as we put it in our definition, *it is impossible for the premises to be true and the conclusion to be false, simultaneously.*

Third, given our definition of *soundness*, while the arguments in the examples in Scenario 2 are examples of *valid* arguments, each is unsound.

---

1. The statements in the first and third examples are clearly false. In the second example, the statements are false since the height order of the buildings is the opposite of what is expressed in the argument—Burj Khalifa is the tallest of these (indeed, it is the tallest in the world), and Trump Tower is the shortest of these.

### Scenario #3: Valid Arguments with False Premises and True Conclusion

In the third scenario, we find *valid* arguments that have *false* premises with a *true* conclusion. This also may be puzzling to some, but again with understanding that it is *structure* that matters, this also becomes problem free. While valid arguments cannot have *true* premises with a *false* conclusion (since in a valid argument, true premises *guarantee* a true conclusion), valid arguments *can* have *false* premises with a *true* conclusion. Here are two examples:

#### Example #1 of a valid argument with false premises and true conclusion

Premise: World War I occurred before the American Civil War.

Premise: The American Civil War occurred simultaneous with World War II.

Conclusion: [Therefore,] World War I occurred before World War II.

#### Example #2 of a valid argument with false premises and true conclusion

Premise: Every dolphin is a man.

Premise: Benjamin Netanyahu is a dolphin.

Conclusion: [Therefore,] Benjamin Netanyahu is a man.

To repeat, for emphasis, what *cannot* occur is a *valid* argument that has *true* premises with a *false* conclusion, since a valid argument is one in which true premises guarantee a true conclusion.

### Invalid Arguments with All True Statements

Continuing to think about structure versus content, one must be careful not to judge an argument to be valid simply because all the statements in it are *true*, since *invalid* arguments can contain all true statements. In a valid argument, if the premises are true, then the conclusion is also true *because* the premises are true. That is the truth-preservation occurring in a valid argument. However, in the case of an *invalid* argument with all true statements, the statements are all true *independent* of each other—that is, the conclusion is not true *because* the premises are true, but independent of them.

Here are two *invalid* arguments with all true statements:

#### Example #1 of an invalid argument with all true statements

Premise: Some US citizens are women.

Premise: Some women are older than 30 years.

Conclusion: [Therefore,] some US citizens are older than 30 years.

#### Example #2 of an invalid argument with all true statements

Premise: If Aaron Rodgers plays in the NFL, then Aaron Rodgers lives in the United States.

Premise: Aaron Rodgers does live in the United States.

Conclusion: [Therefore,] Aaron Rodgers plays in the NFL.

In these examples, all the statements are true. However, the arguments are *invalid*, since it is *possible* for the premises to be true and the conclusion false simultaneously. Put differently, the conclusion is not *guaranteed* to be true *because* the premises are true. Rather, the claims are all true independent of each other. Thus, the arguments are *invalid*.

---

**EXERCISE 5.1**

Answer the review questions below about deductive arguments and the related concepts.

1. What is a deductive argument?
2. What does it mean for an argument to be *valid*?
3. What does it mean for an argument to be *truth-preserving*?
4. Is the validity of an argument a matter of content, structure, or both?
5. True or false: All deductive arguments are valid arguments.
6. What is the term for an argument that is valid and has true premises?
7. Can a *valid* argument have false premises and a false conclusion?
8. Can a *valid* argument have false premises and a true conclusion?
9. Can a *valid* argument have true premises and a false conclusion?
10. True or false: If all the statements in a deductive argument are *true*, then the argument is definitely *valid*.
11. True or false: If all the statements in a deductive argument are *false*, then the argument is definitely *invalid*.
12. True or false: All sound arguments are valid arguments.
13. What conclusion can be drawn about a *valid* argument that has a *false* conclusion?
14. True or false: A sound argument can have a false conclusion.
15. If the premises of a valid argument are true, what is the truth-value of its conclusion?

---

## Some Methods for Identifying Validity

How does one determine whether an argument is valid or invalid? There are a variety of methods for doing this. Some are found in formal logic systems, such as using Venn diagrams in *Categorical Logic* (chapter 6) or truth tables in *Propositional Logic* (chapter 7). But there are other methods one can use in everyday reasoning, two of which are examined below.

### Method #1: Testing Arguments for Validity with Thought Experiments

One method to determine whether an argument is valid or invalid is to use both the content and structure of a given argument and perform a thought experiment to judge the argument.

A *thought experiment* is a fictional scenario created using one's imagination to illustrate a point, explore a concept, hypothesize, entertain, test a theory, conceptual analysis, and more. In this first method, we will use thought experiments to test an argument for validity.

Let's apply it both to a valid and to an invalid argument from our examples above, beginning with an invalid example. So, consider once again the following:

Premise: Some US citizens are women.

Premise: Some women are older than 30 years.

Conclusion: [Therefore,] some US citizens are older than 30 years.

Suppose one did not know that this is an invalid argument. One can then use the thought experiment method to test it. To do this, one keeps the content, and *the structure of course*, since it is the latter that we are judging, and then creates a thought experiment, like the following:

Imagine that all US citizens aged 30 and older suddenly renounced their US citizenship—this, of course, includes both men and women. However, imagine that there remained both men and women US citizens aged 29 or younger.

If the details of this thought experiment were true, then the premises in the example would be true. There would be US citizens who are women, and there would be women in the world who are over 30 years old. However, the conclusion would be false, since there would not be any US citizens over 30 years old. Further, the details of the thought experiment are *possible*. This shows that it is *possible* for the premises of the example to be true, while its conclusion is false, simultaneously. Thus, our thought experiment shows that the argument is invalid.

We can also use a thought experiment to help us see that an argument is *valid*. Consider once again the following example from above:

Premise: Trump Tower is taller than One World Trade Center.

Premise: One World Trade Center is taller than Burj Khalifa.

Conclusion: [Therefore,] Trump Tower is taller than Burj Khalifa.

Again, for our thought experiment, keep the content and the structure. This one is rather easy; just imagine the following:

Imagine that Burj Khalifa is built first, at its current height of 2,717 feet. Then imagine that One World Trade Center is built later, and that designers want it to be taller than Burj Khalifa, and thus build it to be 2,720 feet. And then later Trump decides to build his tower and wants it to be still taller, and thus has it built to be 2,725 feet.

If the details of this thought experiment were true, then the premises and conclusion would be true. Furthermore, there is *no possible* scenario in which *the premises are true in that scenario, but the conclusion false in that scenario*, simultaneously. Thus, our thought experiment helps us to see that the argument is valid, in case it was not clear that it is.

So, this method of determining the validity of arguments is to use the content and structure of the argument and create a thought-experiment to judge the argument. While this can be an effective method, it is limited in two respects. First, it is limited to how creative one can be with thought-experiments. If one is simply not that creative, then this method can be more challenging. Second, it is limited to how familiar one is with the contents in the argument. If one is simply not familiar with the subject matter in the argument, then creating a thought experiment in which the premises (which one does not really understand) are true can be very difficult. Still, even with its limits, the thought experiment method can be a very useful tool.

### EXERCISE 5.2

Using the *thought experiment method*, create a thought experiment to determine whether the following deductive arguments are valid or invalid.

**\*1.** All mammals have hearts, and therefore plants are mammals, since plants have hearts.

**2.** No philosophy books are easy to read, and the text for this class is *not* easy to read. Therefore, the text for this class is a philosophy book.

**3.** It is clear that Ben is rich, because he owns an Audi, and rich people own Audis.

**\*4.** Scorpions are entirely transparent, since they have 16 legs, and anything with 16 legs is entirely transparent.

**5.** All good coaches begin practice on time. Coach McTaggart always begins practice on time. Therefore, Coach McTaggart is a good coach.

**6.** Obviously, the tallest mountain on earth is in Nebraska, since Mount Villaquest is the tallest mountain on earth, and it is located in Nebraska.

**7.** If Sam's vehicle is a Chevy, then it is amphibious, and if it is amphibious, then it can fly. So, if Sam's vehicle is a Chevy, then it can fly.

**\*8.** Susana is a philosopher, since only critical thinkers are philosophers, and Susana is a critical thinker.

**9.** A requirement to be the president of the United States is that one must be at least 85 years of age. Donald Trump is older than 85 years of age. Therefore, Donald Trump is president of the United States.

**10.** Princeton University is superior to Harvard University. This follows from the fact that Princeton University, but not Harvard University, is in Iowa, and if a university is in Iowa, then it is superior to Harvard University.

## Method #2: Testing Arguments for Validity by Abstraction and Diagramming

In the second method of determining the validity of an argument, one abstracts away from content, and then creates a diagram to help reveal whether the argument is valid or invalid. This method is a bit more complex than the counterexample method, as it involves more steps.

Before walking through the steps, consider why this is a valuable exercise in our everyday lives, as it may appear that it is impractical and time-consuming. We want to learn and become efficient at *abstracting* away from content in order to train ourselves to focus on structure and not be tripped up by content, and learning to become efficient at creating figures and diagrams (even mentally) can help us to quickly see whether the structure upon which we are focusing is valid or invalid. Regarding the time-consuming worry, while it is true that this method *initially* takes a bit more time than the thought experiment method, the more one practices this method, the quicker and more efficient one becomes at performing it, such that it can be just as quick and occasionally even quicker than the thought experiment method.

In our daily lives, we are often rushed, making us vulnerable to making mistakes in reasoning, being tripped up by content. But if one becomes more efficient at this method, it merely takes slowing down just a bit in our rushed lives (which is always a good thing) to perform this method to judge whether one's own or another's argument is good or bad (structurally).

Let's walk through the method with a couple of arguments. Consider the following argument:

Premise: Anyone who is not a Green Bay Packers fan is often disappointed.

Premise: Some NFL fans are not Green Bay Packers fans.

Conclusion: [Thus,] some NFL fans are often disappointed.

### Step 1—Abstract Away from Content
The first step in this *abstract and diagram method* is to ignore the content by abstracting away from it. This is done by replacing the concrete details in the content with place holders, such as letters. For example, with the example, we could do the following replacements:

| Content | Placeholder in Abstraction |
|---|---|
| Green Bay Packers fan | G |
| Disappointed person | D |
| NFL fans | xs |

To abstract away from the content, we replace the content with its placeholder. When we do with this with the argument we get:

Premise: Any non-G is a D.

Premise: Some xs are non-G.

Conclusion: [Thus,] some xs are D.

Note, since G is the place holder for *Green Bay Packers fan*, and since the premise is referencing anyone who is **not** a Green Bay Packers fan, we put non-G.

### Step 2—Create a Diagram of the Premises
The next step is to create a *diagram* representing the *premises in abstraction* and then observe the diagram to see whether the conclusion is also portrayed. If the conclusion **is** portrayed in the diagram (in which we diagrammed *only* the premises), then the argument is *valid*. If the conclusion is *not* portrayed, then the argument is invalid. The following illustrates how this can be done.

To begin our diagram, divide the world into Gs and non-Gs, as in figure 5.1:

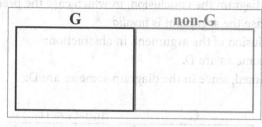

**FIGURE 5.1**

Next notice that the first premise in abstraction is:

Premise: Any non-G is a D.

Since it says that the non-Gs are Ds, we need to add some Ds to our diagram. *One way* to bring in the Ds is stipulate that they are *the same group as* the non-Gs. Thus, we get the following, in figure 5.2:

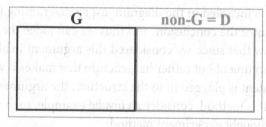

**FIGURE 5.2**

The first premise in abstraction is now portrayed in the diagram, since in the diagram *any non-G is also a D.*

Next consider the second premise in abstraction:

Premise: Some xs are non-G.

To diagram this premise, add some xs, making some of them *non-G.* One way to do it is as follows, in figure 5.3:

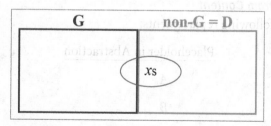

**FIGURE 5.3**

The second premise is now portrayed in the diagram, since some of the xs are non-Gs. At this point, the diagraming *stops. DO NOT* diagram the conclusion.

### Step 3—Observe and Judge

Finally, *observe* the diagram and determine whether the conclusion has already been portrayed in the diagram. If it *is* portrayed, then by simply diagraming the premises, the conclusion was *thereby* also diagrammed. Thus, the premises guarantee the conclusion, and the argument is *valid.*

On the other hand, if the conclusion is *not* already portrayed, then by diagraming the premises one did *not thereby* diagram the conclusion, in which case the premises do *not* guarantee the conclusion. In this case the argument is *invalid*.

So, consider the conclusion of the argument, in abstraction:

Conclusion: [Thus,] some *x*s are *D*.

Notice that it **is** diagrammed, since in the diagram some *x*s are D:

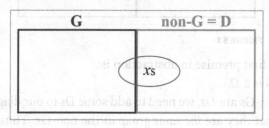

**FIGURE 5.3** (repeated)

Since the conclusion is included in the diagram *just by* diagraming the premises, we know that the premises guarantee the conclusion, and thus we can judge the argument to be valid.

Further, we also know that since we considered this argument in abstraction, it is not the content of the original argument but rather its structure that makes it valid. We further know that no matter what content is plugged in to the structure, the argument will still be valid.

To further illustrate this method, consider an *invalid* example, such as the following, which we examined with the thought experiment method:

Premise: Some US citizens are women.

Premise: Some women are older than 30 years.

Conclusion: [Therefore,] some U.S. citizens are older than 30 years.

We once again go through the steps:

**Step 1—Abstract Away from Content**

First, we could do the following replacements:

| Content | Placeholder in Abstraction |
|---|---|
| US citizens | A |
| Women | B |
| People older than 30 years | C |

Thus, the example in abstraction would be:

Premise: Some A are B.

Premise: Some B are C.

Conclusion: [Therefore,] some A are C.

*Step 2—Create a Diagram of the Premises*

Next, diagram *only* the *premises*. Figure 5.4 illustrates one way to diagram the first premise:

Premise: Some *A* are *B*.

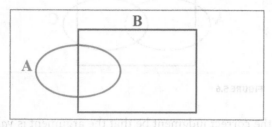

**FIGURE 5.4**

And, we could diagram the second premise, as illustrated in figure 5.5:

Premise: Some *B* are *C*.

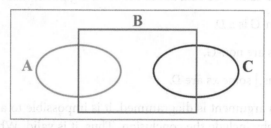

**FIGURE 5.5**

*Step 3—Observe and Judge*

Last, *observe* the diagram and determine whether the conclusion has already been portrayed in the diagram. The conclusion is:

Conclusion: [Therefore,] some *A* are *C*.

Notice that it is *not* included in the diagram of the premises, since no *A*s are *C*s in the diagram. Thus, we know that the argument is *invalid*.

At this point, one may wonder about how alternative diagrams affect the judgment that this argument is invalid. Consider again the argument and an alternative way of diagramming it.

Premise: Some *A* are *B*.

Premise: Some *B* are *C*.

Conclusion: [Therefore,] some *A* are *C*.

Suppose it had been diagrammed as follows in figure 5.6 instead of how it was diagrammed above:

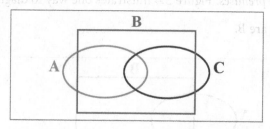

**FIGURE 5.6**

In this case, would the correct judgment be that the argument is *valid*? The answer is *No!* The reason is that while the second way of diagramming the argument is possible, *so is the first way of diagramming it.* Since the first way is *possible,* it shows that the premises in fact do *not guarantee* the conclusion, even though they *can be represented* in such a way that all the statements turn out to be true.

Notice that the same cannot be said about the valid argument that we considered:

Premise: Any non-G is a *D.*

Premise: Some *xs* are non-G.

Conclusion: [Thus,] some *xs* are *D.*

No matter how this argument is diagrammed, it is impossible to accurately diagram the premises and not thereby include the conclusion. Thus, it is valid. Whereas with the invalid example, while there are possible diagrams which represent all the statements being true, there are also possible diagrams like the one above in which the premises are true, but the conclusion false. Thus, it is *invalid.*

While the *abstract and diagram method* is a very useful in helping one to identify the validity of many arguments, its weakness is that there are certain arguments that simply cannot be diagrammed. Nevertheless, it is useful for many cases. In chapters 6 and 7, we will consider other ways for determining validity—the use of Venn diagrams in *Categorical Logic* (chapter 6) and the use of truth tables in *Propositional Logic* (chapter 7). Let's now turn to consider *inductive arguments.*

**EXERCISE 5.3**

Use the *abstract and diagram method* to determine whether the following deductive arguments are valid or invalid.

**\*1.** There were only three cats in the house last week, and no cats have left the house. Thus, there are only three cats in the house now.

**2.** All dogs are animals, and all dogs are mammals. Therefore, all animals are mammals.

**3.** Either you drive a four-door Jeep Wrangler, or your vehicle is garbage, and you are not driving a four-door Jeep Wrangler. Therefore, your vehicle is garbage.

*4. Of course, humans have immaterial souls—after all, they persist over time from birth to death, and this can be done only if they have an immaterial soul.

5. Professor Johnson, please believe me that I read the textbook, because I understand how to do the homework, and anyone who reads the textbook understands how to do the homework.

6. Marcy ate the last cookie, since she was the last person in the kitchen, and if she was the last person in the kitchen, then she ate the last cookie.

*7. Ladies and gentlemen of the jury, the defense has clearly established that it is true that whoever robbed the store had on a red shirt, wore glasses, and had a goatee. My client was not wearing a red shirt, was not wearing glasses, and did not have a goatee. Therefore, it follows that my client is not the robber.

8. Oh my gosh! My house is on fire! I know this because there is a ton of smoke coming from it, and anytime a house is on fire, a ton of smoke comes from it.

9. No Muslims are Christians, for the reason that while some Christians are Baptists, no Baptists are Muslims.

10. That animal that you found in the ocean is actually a mammal. The reason is that the animal that you found has tentacles, and all animals that have tentacles are squids, and all squids are mammals.

## Inductive Arguments

In contrast to a deductive argument, an *inductive* argument is one in which one is attempting to *give evidence for, but not prove,* the conclusion with the premises. More technically, an inductive argument is one in which one is attempting to produce a *strong* structure. Studying inductive arguments is just as important as studying deductive arguments, as we reason inductively just as much, in all areas of our lives—in our daily reasoning, in the sciences, in history, in philosophy.

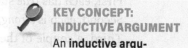

**KEY CONCEPT: INDUCTIVE ARGUMENT**
An **inductive argument** is an argument in which one is *attempting* to create a *strong* structure.

A *strong* argument is one in which the conclusion is probably true, but not guaranteed, given the premises. So, if the premises are true, then the conclusion is probably true as well. If the argument is not strong, it is weak. Note that strength and weakness come in degrees (unlike validity). Thus, an argument can be more or less strong, or more or less weak.

**KEY CONCEPT: STRONG ARGUMENT**
An argument is **strong** if and only if given true premises, the conclusion is probably true as well, but not guaranteed.

### Strength: Structure vs. Truth

As with validity, whether an argument is strong or weak has nothing to do with whether its premises are true or false. Rather, like validity, what matters is that *if the premises are true, then* the conclusion is probably true as well. So, like validity, it is possible to have the following scenarios with a *strong argument:*

### Scenario #1: Strong Arguments with True Premises and True Conclusion

In the first scenario, we find *strong* arguments that have all true statements, both premises and conclusion. Here are three examples:

#### Example #1 of a strong argument with all true statements

Premise: Most people who have lived in Wisconsin love the Green Bay Packers.

Premise: Brett Favre has lived in Wisconsin.

Conclusion: [Therefore,] Brett Favre loves the Green Bay Packers.

#### Example #2 of a strong argument with all true statements

Premise: Thousands of mature bull elk have been randomly observed in various places in the United States over several years, and most have antlers of at least 50".

Conclusion: [Therefore,] most mature bull elk have antlers of at least 50".

#### Example #3 of a strong argument with all true statements

Premise: The towing capacity of Chevy Silverado 1500 is comparable to the towing capacity of a Ford F-150.

Premise: A Chevy Silverado 1500 can easily pull a Forest River Aurora trailer.

Conclusion: [Therefore,] a Ford F-150 can easily pull a Forest River Aurora trailer.

There are a few points to be noted about these examples.

First, each has *true* statements throughout the argument.

Second, each is *strong*, since in each the conclusion is probably true, given the premises.

Third, a couple of the examples are *counterexamples* to the idea that inductive arguments have specific statements as premises and general statements as conclusions. While the second example has this format, the first and third do *not*. The first has a "general to specific" format, and the third has a "specific to specific" format. This helps to make the point that one should *not* define an inductive argument as one that is "specific to general,"

> **KEY CONCEPT: COGENT ARGUMENT**
> An argument is **cogent** if and only if it is *strong* and has *true* premises.

but instead one should define it as was done above, to capture the essence of inductive arguments.

The cases in the first type of scenario are *strong* arguments with *true* premises. An argument of this sort (strong with true premises) is a *cogent* argument.

### Scenario #2: Strong Arguments with False Premises and False Conclusion

In the second scenario, we find *strong* arguments that have all *false* statements, both premises and conclusion. Just as considering valid arguments with all false statements helped us see that validity is a matter of structure, so also considering *strong* arguments with all false statements can help one see that *strength* is a matter of *structure*, not true content. Let's have a look at some examples:

### Example #1 of a strong argument with all false statements

Premise: When comparing the Ptolemaic model of the universe to the Copernican model of the universe, one can see that the Ptolemaic model *far* better explains the data.

Conclusion: [Therefore,] the Ptolemaic model is the more rational theory to adopt.

### Example #2 of a strong argument with all false statements

Premise: Tens of thousands of mysterious aircraft have been seen at various times over several years flying over Las Vegas, and they have all been space alien spacecraft from other planets.

Conclusion: [Therefore,] most aircraft flying over Las Vegas are alien spacecraft from other planets.

We can make several points about each of these examples as well.

First, each has *false* statements throughout the argument.[2]

Second, and importantly, each is *strong*, since in both the conclusion is probably true, given the premises. Again, in order to help see that these are strong, despite having false statements, for the moment ignore the fact that the premises are false and assume that they are true—that is, imagine that we live in a world in which the premises in each are true. Given this, we can see that the conclusion in each case is *probably* true as well.

Third, given our definition of *cogency*, while these arguments are *strong*, they are *not cogent*.

### Scenario #3: Strong Arguments with False Premises and True Conclusion

In the third scenario, we find *strong* arguments that have *false* premises with a *true* conclusion. While, once again, this may be puzzling to some, with understanding that it is *structure* that matters, and not true content, this also becomes problem free. Here is an example:

Premise: Most plants are furry animals.

Premise: Grumpy Cat is a plant.

Conclusion: [Therefore,] Grumpy Cat is a furry animal.

To repeat *with emphasis*, what *cannot* occur is a *strong* argument that has *true* premises with a probably *false* conclusion, since a strong argument is one in which true premises make the conclusion *probably* true.

---

2.  The statements in the first example are false, since it is the opposite—the Copernican model is the better explanation and more rational to adopt.

### EXERCISE 5.4

The questions below are intended to help you review the important concepts about inductive arguments and the related concepts.

1. What is an inductive argument?
2. What does it mean for an argument to be *strong*?
3. Is the *strength* of an argument a matter of content, structure, or both?
4. True or false: All inductive arguments are strong arguments.
5. What is the term for an argument that is strong and has true premises?
6. Can a *strong* argument have false premises and a false conclusion?
7. Can a *strong* argument have false premises and a true conclusion?
8. Can a *strong* argument have true premises and a false conclusion?
9. True or false: If all the statements in an inductive argument are *true*, then the argument is definitely *strong*.
10. True or false: If all the statements in an inductive argument are *false*, then the argument is definitely *weak*.
11. True or false: All cogent arguments are strong arguments.
12. True or false: A cogent argument can have a false conclusion.
13. If the premises of a strong argument are true, what is the truth-value of its conclusion?

## Types of Inductive Arguments

There are at least five types of inductive arguments: *statistical syllogism, generalization, analogical argument, causal arguments,* and *abductive argument (inference to the best explanation).*

Not only is each of these inductive arguments different from the others, but each has different criteria for what makes the argument strong. Later chapters will look at these arguments and their criteria for strength in depth—chapter 8 will cover *statistical syllogism, generalization, analogical argument,* and *causal arguments,* and chapter 9 will cover *abductive arguments.* In each of these respective chapters, methods for determining whether the arguments under consideration are strong or weak will be discussed. As a result, methods for determining whether an inductive argument in general is strong or weak have *not* been considered in this chapter.

## Recap

In this chapter, we took a more extensive look at arguments by considering the two types of arguments—*deductive* and *inductive.* We defined each and learned the following important related concepts: *valid* argument, *sound* argument, *strong* argument, and *cogent* argument. We further discussed a couple of "everyday" methods for judging the validity of arguments—namely, the *thought experiment method* and the *abstraction and diagramming method.* Below are some important definitions that should have been learned:

- **Cogent Argument**: An argument is cogent if and only if it is *strong* and has *true premises*.

- **Deductive Argument**: An argument in which one is *attempting* to create a *valid* structure.

- **Inductive Argument**: An argument in which one is *attempting* to create a *strong* structure.

- **Sound Argument**: An argument is sound if and only if it is *valid* and has *true premises*.

- **Strong Argument**: An argument is strong if and only if, given true premises, the conclusion is probably true as well, though not guaranteed.

- **Thought Experiment**: A fictional scenario created using one's imagination to illustrate a point, explore a concept, hypothesize, entertain, test a theory, and provide conceptual analysis, and in particular to test an argument for validity.

- **Truth-Preserving**: An *argument* structure is truth-preserving if and only if it never has a false conclusion when its premises are true.

- **Valid Argument**: An argument is *valid* if and only if it is *impossible* for the conclusion to be false, if the premises are true.

# 6

# DEDUCTIVE LOGIC I
## *Categorical Logic*

In chapter 5, deductive arguments were introduced, and *deductive argument*, *valid argument*, and *sound argument* were defined. These concepts should be well in hand at this point, as they will be assumed in this chapter as we delve deeper into deductive arguments by taking an introductory look at what is called *categorical logic*. This deductive logic system is important to study for at least two reasons. First, it helps clarify our understanding of everyday concepts and statements by thinking about them in formal terms. Second, learning and studying this logic is useful as an exercise in precise, clear, and exact reasoning that yields definitive results. While we will use various symbols and diagrams in this chapter, it takes little effort to understand them.

In this chapter, we will learn the basics of categorical logic. This includes learning how to understand categorical statements, including equivalencies and entailments between them. We will also learn how to evaluate categorical syllogisms using Venn diagrams. And, as with previous chapters, one should be attentive to the following key terms as one works through this chapter:

## KEY WORDS

| | |
|---|---|
| Categorical Logic | Obversion |
| Categorical Statement | Predicate Term |
| Categorical Syllogism | Quality of Categorical Statement |
| Contradictory Statements | Quantifier |
| Contraposition | Square of Opposition |
| Contraries | Subalterns |
| Conversion | Subcontraries |
| Copula | Subject Term |
| Entailment | Venn Diagram |
| Equivalent Statements | |

## Introduction to Categorical Logic

*Logic* in general is the study of principles of good inferences and arguments. *Categorical* logic, dating back to the philosophy of Aristotle (384–322 BC), focuses in particular on statements about *classes* (or *categories*). "Class" is used synonymously with "collection," "category," "group," and the like. It refers to any actual or possible collection, including natural collections (such as the collection or class of *dogs*) and arbitrary collections (such as the collection of *red things in the room*), as well as collections that have no actual members but could have had members (such as the collection of *unicorns*).

**KEY CONCEPT: CATEGORICAL LOGIC**
**Categorical logic** is a deductive logic focusing on statements about *classes* (or *categories*) *and* the logical relationships between such statements derived from the components of the statements.

## Categorical Statements

Since categorical logic is the logic of classes, it makes sense that the *statements* involved in the inferences and arguments are *statements about classes*. Such statements are called *categorical statements*. Categorical statements are statements that say that the members of one class are either *included in* or *excluded from* another class. For example:

- Every dog is an animal.
- None of the people in this room are Democrats.
- Rattlesnakes are not nice.
- A few of the trees have died.
- Some of the universities have philosophy departments.

While there are all kinds of ways of expressing such statements, there are only *four types of categorical statements*—two expressing the *inclusion* relation between classes and two expressing the *exclusion* relation between classes. To be precise, we can say that:

- *every* member of one class is *included in* another class,
- *some* of the members of one class are *included in* another class,
- *every* member of one class is *excluded from* another class, or
- *some* of the members of one class are *excluded from* another class.

**KEY CONCEPT: CATEGORICAL STATEMENT**
**Categorical statements** are statements about classes, in which the members of one class are said to be *included in* another class or *excluded from* another class.

### Standard Form

To make our task of thinking about categorical statements simpler, we write them in *standard form*, which medieval philosophers labeled as A-, E-, I-, and O-statements. They derived these labels from the Latin words *Affirmo* (meaning I *affirm*) and *Nego* (meaning I *deny*). Two of the types of categorical statements use the *inclusion* relation—they *affirm* that members of one class are in another class. Thus, the medieval philosophers labeled the *affirmative* categorical statements with A and I, which are the first two vowels of *Affirmo*. The other two categorical statements use the *exclusion* relation—they *deny* that members of one class are in another class. Thus, the medieval philosophers labeled the *negative* categorical statements with E and O, which are the vowels of *Nego*. The *structure* of each type of statement can be put as follows:

### Standard Form of Categorical Statements

**(A)**  *All* _____ are _____.  (*Example:* All dogs are animals.)

**(E)**  *No* _____ are _____.  (*Example:* No rocks are trees.)

**(I)**  *Some* _____ are _____.  (*Example:* Some plants are trees.)

**(O)**  *Some* _____ are not _____.  (*Example:* Some students are not males.)

## Terminology

Let's familiarize ourselves with some terminology about categorical statements. First, what goes in the *blanks* of each categorical statement *structure* is called a *term*, which is the *content* of the categorical statement. The *subject term* goes in the first blank, and the *predicate term* goes in the second blank. In *standard* form, the terms are always *nouns* or *noun phrases* (e.g., *red things*). However, in *non-standard* form, the predicate term is often an adjective, as in *All trucks are red*. But since we are focusing on *standard form*, write the terms as nouns or noun phrases. Thus, using *S* and *P* for subject and predicate terms, respectively, the structure of standard form statements looks like this:

(A)  All *S* are *P*.

(E)  No *S* are *P*.

(I)  Some *S* are *P*.

(O)  Some *S* are not *P*.

The words *All*, *No*, and *Some* are called *quantifiers*. They are so-called because they indicated *how many* of the subject class are included in, or excluded from, the predicate class. The quantifiers *All* and *No* indicate that *every* member of the subject class is being referenced. For example, in the statement

*All dogs are animals,*

"all" references every dog. And, in

*No rocks are trees,*

"no" picks out every rock. As are result, 'All' and 'No' are *universal* quantifiers.

In contrast, 'Some' refers to at least one of the members of some class, but not to all the members, and thus it a *particular* quantifier. Thus, we have:

*All*—Universal Quantifier

*No*—Universal Quantifier

*Some*—Particular Quantifier

Moreover, if every member of a class is referenced by the quantifier, then we say that the *term* picking out that class is *distributed*. For example, in

*All dogs are animals,*

"all" picks out every dog, and thus "dog" is *distributed*. In fact, in all A-statements, the subject term is distributed. In an E-statement, *both* the subject and predicate terms are distributed. Consider the statement

*No rocks are trees.*

Every rock is *excluded* from the class of trees, and every tree is *excluded* from the class of rocks.

In I-statements, neither of the terms is distributed, since we are *not* saying something about every member of either class. For example, consider the statement

*Some plants are trees.*

In this statement, both the subject and predicate terms pick out at least one plant and tree, respectively, but do *not* reference every plant and tree, respectively. In contrast, consider the following O-statement:

*Some students are not males.*

While we are not picking out every student, we *are* referencing every male. We are saying that there is at least one student, such that the *entire* class of males *excludes* that student. Or, put differently, we are saying that *every* male is distinct from at least one student. Thus, the *predicate term* is distributed in the O-statement.

And, finally, "are" and "are not" in the standard form statements, or any conjugation of the verb "to be" in non-standard form statements, are called *copulas*. Putting the terminology all together, we get the following terminology for the structure of our categorical statements:

**Quantifier [subject term] copula [predicate term].**

Here is a summary of the terminology for standard form statements.

| Label | Structure | Quantity | Quality | Distribution | |
|-------|-----------|----------|---------|--------------|--------------|
| | | | | Subject Term | Predicate Term |
| A | All S are P | Universal | Affirmative | Distributed | Undistributed |
| E | No S are P | Universal | Negative | Distributed | Distributed |
| I | Some S are P | Particular | Affirmative | Undistributed | Undistributed |
| O | Some S are not P | Particular | Negative | Undistributed | Distributed |

**EXERCISE 6.1**

For each of the following categorical statements, identify: (a) the letter label (A, E, I, O) for the statement, (b) the quantity, (c) the quality, (d) the subject and predicate terms, and (e) which terms are distributed.

   *1. No computers are thinking things.
   2. Some critical thinkers are not philosophers.
   3. All people who love God are people who obey God.
   *4. Some fish that attack people are sharks.
   5. No people who love all equally are racists.
   6. Some people who criticize the ideas of others are not bigots.
   *7. All large bodies that orbit the earth are planets.
   8. Some creatures that crawl on the ground are creatures that bite.
   9. All cell phones that work well are iPhones.
   10. Some books containing philosophical statements are books that contain true statements.

## Translating into Standard Form

As mentioned, to simplify our task of evaluating the validity of arguments in categorical logic, we use *standard form* categorical statements. But in life we often encounter categorical statements that are not in standard form. So, to do the logic, we translate them into standard form to simplify our task. Not only will this make the logic easier, but translation will help our understand of various non-standard form categorical statements and thus help our critical thinking about them.

In translation, we translate a non-standard form categorical statement into an *equivalent* standard form categorical statement.

> Statements are equivalent if and only if they have the same truth value in all possible circumstances.

Thus, for any two *equivalent* statements $S_1$ and $S_2$, any possible situation in which $S_1$ is *true* will be a situation in which $S_2$ is *true*, and vice versa; and any possible situation in which $S_1$ is *false* will be a situation in which $S_2$ is *false*, and vice versa.

There are a few things to keep in mind to help translate non-standard form statements into a standard form—namely, whether it is in standard or non-standard form, it has the following:

1. A <u>quality</u>. Recall that the *quality* of a statement concerns whether it is an *affirmative* or *negative* statement, and thus whether the statement is an A- or I-statement, on the one hand, or an E- or O-statement, on the other hand. In many cases, the presence of the words "*no*," "*not*," or "*none*" indicate that it is negative.

2. A quantifier. In standard form, these are: *All, No,* and *Some.* In *non-standard* form, the quantifier can vary widely, but will always function exactly like one of *All, No,* or *Some.* For example, *"every"* functions exactly like *"All."* So, in translation, one must identify the *quantifier* in the non-standard form statement, which will indicate whether one is dealing with a universal statement or a particular statement.

3. Terms. Recall that a categorical statement is a statement about *collections,* or *classes,* of *things,* specifically about *two* different collections, where the statement says either that the members (some or all) of the one collection are *included* in the other collection, or that they are *excluded* from the other collection. Thus, when encountering the non-standard form statement, one should attempt to identify the two collections, and keep in mind that in translation these are to be referenced with a noun or noun phrase, which are the *terms.*

Translation can be straightforward in many cases, where the *quality, quantifier,* and *terms* in the non-standard form statement are fairly transparent. Consider the following for example:

> *Every citizen is a patriot.*
>
> *A few of the students are males.*
>
> *Not one snake is poisonous.*

We can easily identify the *quality, quantifier,* and *terms* in each of these.

In the first example, the *quality* is *affirmative* and so we know that our straightforward translation should be to an A- or I-statement. But since the *quantifier* "every" is a *universal* quantifier, we know that it should be translated as an A-statement. Further, "every" ranges over *citizens,* and thus we know that *"citizens"* is the *subject* term. Thus, the first translates to:

> *All citizens are patriots.*

In the second case, we can see that it is *affirmative* in quality, and thus that it is an A- or I-statement, but that the quantifier "a few" ranges over some, but not all, *students,* and thus that this is an I-statement. Thus, the second statement translates to:

> *Some students are males.*

And in the third case, we can see that it is *negative* in quality, and thus that it is an E- or O-statement, and that the quantifier "not one" ranges over all *snakes,* and thus this translates to an E-statement. Further, recall that the terms must be nouns or noun phrases, since they refer to collections. But, "poisonous" is not a noun. However, this can be re-written as "poisonous things," which *is* a noun phrase. Thus, the third example translates to:

> *No snakes are poisonous things.*

While there are these straightforward cases, there are other cases that can be a bit challenging. Five of these challenging cases are the following:

## Challenging Case #1: Translating Statements with Implicit Quantifiers

Occasionally a non-standard form statement does not have an explicit quantifier but leaves it implicit. Here are some examples:

> *Electrons are negatively charged particles.*

> *Apples are not vegetables.*

While the *quantifiers* in these examples are implicit, it should be fairly clear that both are *universal—all* electrons and apples are being referenced.

Since the first example is affirmative, it translates to an A-statement, and since the second is *negative*, it translates to an E-statement. Thus, we get:

> *All electrons are negatively charged particles.*

> *No apples are vegetables.*

We can generalize:

> *If a non-standard form statement with an <u>implicit</u> quantifier is affirmative, translate it as an A-statement; and if a non-standard form statement with an <u>implicit</u> quantifier is <u>negative</u>, translate it as an E-statement.*

## Challenging Case #2: Translating Statements with the Phrases "Not Every" or "Not All"

Consider such statements as:

> *Not every earthquake is deadly.*

> *Not all prisoners are guilty.*

If these are **true** (which they arguably are), then it must be that:

> *Some earthquakes are not deadly things.*

> *Some prisoners are not guilty people.*

Of course, it does not follow from this alone that *some earthquakes are deadly*, and that *some prisoners are guilty* (more on this below). Thus, we can generalize:

> *If a non-standard form statement starts with the phrase "Not every" or "Not all," translate it as an O-statement, in which the subject term is the term that follows the phrase "Not every" or "Not all" in the non-standard form statement.*

## Challenging Case #3: Translating Statements in which Quantifier Refers to Places or Times

In some of our statements, we refer primarily to a time or place that something occurs, and only secondarily to the thing that takes place at the time or place. Here are some examples:

> *The lamb went everywhere that Mary went.*
>
> *Freddy sometimes wears a suit to work.*

Notice that in these examples, the *quantifiers* range over *places* and *times*, respectively. Notice that the first references *"Everywhere ... ,"* and the answer to the second *"sometimes ... ."* Thus, these are primarily about *places* and *times*, respectively, and only secondarily about the lamb, Mary, Freddy, and his suit. So, we know that the *terms* in the first and second, respectively, are:

> *places* that Mary went, and *places* that the lamb went
>
> *times* that Freddy wears a suit, and *times* that Freddy goes to work

Further, we know that the first is an A-statement, since its quantifier is *"every."* And since the order of terms matters with A-statements, we need to determine which term is the subject and which is the predicate. Notice that it says

> *... everywhere that Mary went*

Thus, the subject term is *"places that Mary went."* Thus, the first statement gets translated as:

> *All places that Mary went are places that the lamb went.*

The second statement is an I-statement. As we will learn below, the order of the terms in an I-statement does not matter. Thus, our translation can be:

> *Some times that Freddy wears a suit are times that Freddy goes to work.*

However, we don't want to generalize and say that all statements about places and times are A- and I-statements. Consider that in first statement, *"everywhere"* could have been replaced with *"nowhere," "somewhere,"* or *"somewhere that Mary did not go,"* in which cases the standard form would be an E-, I-, and O-, respectively. And in the second statement, *"sometime"* could have been replaced with *"always," "never,"* or *"sometimes does not,"* in which cases the standard form would be an A-, E-, and O-, respectively.

## Challenging Case #4: Translating Statements with the Words "Only" and "the Only"

The next challenging cases involve statements that have either "only" by itself as a quantifier, or "the only" as the quantifier. Let's begin with statements that contain *"only"* by itself.

### "Only" Statements

One thing that makes these statements challenging is that often people confuse *"Only Fs are Gs"* with *"All Fs are Gs."* However, these do not mean the same thing. Consider two examples:

> *Only US citizens can legally vote in a US election.*
>
> *Only men are players in the NFL.*

Notice a couple of things about these examples.

- One, the *quality* is *affirmative*, and thus these translate to A- or I-statements. But since the *quantifier* "only" is *universal* (explained shortly), these translate to A-statements.
- Two, they're both *true*, since there are no *non-citizens* who can legally vote in the United States (in the first example) and no women in the NFL (in the second example).

Now suppose that we translated these into standard form as follows:

> All US citizens are legal voters in a US election.

> All men are players in the NFL.

While we correctly translated them as A-statements, these translations are *false* since there are US citizens who *cannot* legally vote in a US election (e.g., a three-year-old) and men who are not NFL players. Since the original non-standard form statements are *true*, and the translations just above are *false*, the translations are *not* equivalent to the originals, and thus are *not* the correct translations. Therefore, "*Only Fs are Gs*" does not mean that "*All Fs are Gs.*"

Instead, in any statement of the form "*Only Fs are Gs*," "only" indicates a restriction on things that are Gs—namely, that they (the Gs) are all Fs. Since it is saying something about every G (namely, that they are all Fs), "only" is a universal quantifier. And since "only" in "Only Fs are Gs" says something about all the Gs, the *correct* way to translate these is as follows. Consider again the original non-standard form statements with the terms following "*only*" underlined:

> Only <u>US citizens</u> can legally vote in a US election.

> Only <u>men</u> are players in the NFL.

Given the meaning of "*only*," the <u>correct</u> translation is as follows:

> All legal voters in a US election are <u>US citizens</u>.

> All NFL players are <u>men</u>.

Notice that the *term* that immediately follows "*only*" in the originals goes to the **predicate** place of the standard form translation. We can generalize and get a rule of thumb for "*only*" (by itself), namely:

> Statements of the form "*Only Fs are Gs*" translate to A-*statements*, in which the *predicate* is the term that immediately follows "only" in the non-standard form statement.

### Phrases that Function Like "Only"

There are various phrases that function like "only" by also introducing the predicate term of an A-statement, including "*only if*," "*except for*," "*unless*," and "*nothing but*." Consider the following example with the word "*only*":

> Only <u>animals</u> are dogs.

Note that this is *true*, since no non-animals are dogs (that is, *all* dogs are animals). We could express the same statement using other sentences with the expressions above. Consider:

> Something is a dog <u>only if</u> it's an animal.
>
> <u>Except</u> for animals, nothing is a dog.
>
> It's not a dog, <u>unless</u> it's an animal.
>
> <u>Nothing but</u> animals are dogs.

In each case, the underlined phrase puts a restriction on what counts as a dog—namely, that it be an animal—that is, each functions like "*only*." And, each gets translated as:

> All dogs are animals.

While there are other equivalent translations which can be given using equivalence rules (conversion, obversion, contraposition) to be discussed below, for now use the rule of thumb for "only" for these expressions.

### 'The Only' Statements

In contrast to statements with "*only*" by itself, is the phrase "*the only*" that occurs in some statements. For example:

> The only movies that George like are thrillers.
>
> Fish are the only living things in this tank.

Like "*only*" statements, "*the only*" statements are also *affirmative*, and "*the only*" is a *universal* quantifier. For instance, in the first example, "*the only*" picks out *every* movie that George likes. Thus, these are also translated as A-statements.

We learned that "*only*" introduces the *predicate* of an A-statement, but what about "*the only*"? Let's see what we learn from the two examples. In the first example, "*the only*" picks out *all the movies that George likes*, and says that they are thrillers, and in the second, "*the only*" refers to *all the living things in the tank* and says that they are *fish*. Thus, we can see that these get translated as follows:

> All movies that George like are thrillers.
>
> All living things in this tank are fish.

Notice that the *term* that immediately follows "*the only*" in the originals is put in the **subject** place of the standard form translation. We can generalize and get a rule of thumb for "*the only*," namely:

> Statements of the form "The only Fs are Gs" translate to <u>A-statements</u>, in which the <u>subject</u> is the term that immediately follows "<u>the only</u>" in the non-standard form statement.

## Challenging Case #5: Translating Statements with Individuals or Stuff as Subjects

Consider the following statements:

> Plato is a philosopher.
>
> Mary's friend is not the professor's wife.
>
> Water is transparent liquid.
>
> Juice is made from fruit.

The first two examples have a subject term that refers to an *individual*, while the third and fourth have a subject term that refers to a *stuff*. Words or phrases that refer to an individual are called *count nouns*, whereas words or phrases that refer to stuff are called *mass nouns*. So, "Plato," "Mary's friend," and "*the* professor's wife" are *count nouns*, whereas "water," "transparent liquid," and "juice" are *mass nouns*. One thing in common between count nouns and mass nouns is that neither refers to a *collection* of things. Thus, translating non-standard form statements that contain these into standard form can be challenging. Nevertheless, translation can be done, as will be shown below.

## Challenging Case #6: Translating Statements with Count Nouns—Reference to Individuals

Consider the statement:

> Plato is a philosopher.

This does not appear to be categorical statement, since categorical statements are statements about *classes*, and "Plato" does *not* pick out a class, but an individual. Nevertheless, it can be treated as a categorical statement.

However, translating such statements into standard form can be tricky, since we want to be sure to satisfy the following requirements:

1. Make sure that the terms in the standard form translations are nouns that refer to *classes*.
2. Make sure that the term that is supposed to pick out the individual picks out that individual and *only* that individual.
3. Make sure that the translation has the same truth-value as the original.

Because of these requirements, the following translations of the example won't work:

> All Platos are philosophers.
>
> All people named "Plato" are philosophers.
>
> Some people named "Plato" are philosophers.

The first of these translations won't work since "Platos" does not pick out anything, let alone a collection of things, contrary to requirement #1. The second and third translations will not work because "people named 'Plato'" refers to people additional to the Plato referenced in the original statement, contrary to requirement #2. And the second of the translations won't do for the additional reason that it is *false* (since not all people named "Plato" are philosophers), but our original statement is *true* (and thus the two are not equivalent), contrary to requirement #3.

The only way to translate such a statement into standard form and satisfy the requirements is to translate reference to the individual (e.g., Plato) as "*things*" *identical to that individual*. Thus, our original statement gets translated to

All <u>people identical to Plato</u> are philosophers.

There are a few points to make about this.

- "Identical to" here refers to numerical identity. So, to say that "x is identical to y" means that "x is numerically one and the same thing as y." For example, Spider-man is (numerically) identical to Peter Parker—"Spider-man" and "Peter Parker" name one and the same thing. Further, for each individual thing x, there is exactly one thing numerically identical to x—namely, x! Everything is self-identical, and not identical to anything else.

- Given the last point, the phrase "all things identical to x" refers to exactly one individual—namely, x. So, while the phrase refers to a collection, it refers to a collection of one.

- Since any collection picked out by the phrase "all things identical to ..." will always have exactly one member, the quantifier will also be a universal quantifier (since to refer to any member of the collection is to refer to all members of the collection—namely, the one member), and thus the standard form translations will always be an A-statement or E-statement, depending on whether it is affirmative or negative. Since "Plato is a philosopher" is affirmative, we translated it as an A-statement.

- Further, given the first two points, translating "Plato is a philosopher" to "All people identical to Plato are philosophers" satisfies the three requirements above:

  1. It satisfies requirement #1, since both "*people identical to Plato*" and "*philosophers*" refer to classes of things, even with the former referring to a class with one member.
  2. It satisfies requirement #2, since "*people identical to Plato*" refers to Plato and only to Plato.
  3. It satisfies requirement #3, since in every situation in which the original non-standard form statement is true (or false), the standard form translation will also be true (or false), and vice versa.

Note that if both the subject and predicate of a non-standard form statement contains a count noun, then the translation must use the phrase "*things identical to ...*" in *both* the subject and predicate, since both refer to individuals. Consider this example:

Mary's friend is not the professor's wife.

Both "Mary's friend" and "the professor's wife" refer to individuals, and thus must be treated the same. Thus, the translation would go something like this:

> No people identical to Mary's friend are people identical to the professor's wife.

### Challenging Case #7: Translating Statements with Mass Nouns—Reference to Stuff

Turning to *mass nouns*, consider:

> Water is a transparent liquid.

Translating statements such as these into standard form must meet similar requirements as when translating a count noun.

1. Make sure that the terms in the standard form translations are nouns that refer to *classes*.
2. Make sure that the term that is supposed to pick out the stuff picks out that stuff and *only* that stuff.
3. Make sure that the translation has the same truth-value as the original.

Because of these requirements, the following translations of the example won't work:

> All water are transparent.

> All stuff like water are transparent stuff.

These translations won't work since they fail to meet the requirements. The first doesn't work since it fails to satisfy requirement #1, because "water" does not pick out a collection. The second example will not work because it fails to meet requirements #2 and #3. It fails to meet criterion #2 since "stuff like water" refers to more stuff than just water, and it fails to meet criterion #3, since not all stuff like water is transparent, and thus the second statement is false, whereas the original is true.

The only way to translate such statements into standard form and satisfy the requirements is to translate reference to the stuff (e.g., "water") as *"examples of the stuff."* Thus, our original statement gets translated to:

> All examples of water are examples of transparent stuff.

This satisfies the requirements.

- Both "examples of water" and "examples of transparent stuff" refer to collections, thereby satisfying requirement #1.
- "Examples of water" refers to and only to water, and "examples of transparent stuff" refers to and only to transparent stuff. Thus, requirement #2 is met.
- It satisfies requirement #3, since in every situation in which the original non-standard form statement is true (or false), the standard form translation will also be true (or false), and vice versa.

## EXERCISE 6.2

Translate each of the following statements into standard form, recalling all the important points made about standard form and translation.

*1. Every BMD i8 is fast.
 2. Physicists are very intelligent.
 3. Not all protesters are peaceful.
*4. A person knows a statement only if the statement is true.
 5. No snakes have feet.
 6. The only fish that Fred likes is salmon.
 7. Where I go, you cannot come.
*8. Computers cannot think.
 9. You will receive your reward when your task is complete.
 10. Not every dog is an alligator.
 11. Only vehicles are Jeeps.
 12. Jesus is the savior of the world.
 13. You cannot legally drive unless you have a driver's license.
*14. If a tree falls in the forest, then it does make a sound.
 15. Only critical thinkers are good philosophers.
 16. Most Australian snakes are poisonous.
 17. No one can be saved except by trust in Jesus.
 18. Water is composed of $H_2O$.
*19. Only mammals are whales.
 20. Very few police officers misuse their power.
 21. A statement is true only if the structure of reality matches the statement.
 22. The stuff in my room is all that I care about.
 23. If it is raining, then the ground is slippery.
 24. Nobody can enter who has not been tested for Covid-19.
*25. My key is not your key.

## Equivalencies—Conversion, Obversion, Contraposition

Thinking further about categorical statements, it is useful to be familiar with a few equivalencies between the statements. To get started, you may have suspected that with at least two of our types of statements—namely, I- and O-statements—the order of the terms does not really matter. So, for example, whether we say

No rocks are trees, or

No trees are rocks

we are saying the same thing. Or, in other words, these statements are *equivalent*. So, in any circumstance in which a statement is true, a statement equivalent with it will also be true in that circumstance; and any circumstance in which one is false, then other is also false. There are three important *equivalences* between our statements. Being familiar with these is useful in thinking about categorical logic.

## Conversion

The first equivalence is called *conversion*. It allows us to switch the subject and predicate terms in two of our statements and end up with *equivalent* statements. Indeed, the *converse* of a statement occurs when the subject and predicate terms are switched. However, the equivalency here is *restricted* to E- and I-statements. It can be expressed as follows:

Conversion: E- and I-statements are *equivalent* to their converses.

Here are a couple of examples of equivalencies by conversion:

No dogs are cats—*is equivalent to*—No cats are dogs.

Some birds are males—*is equivalent to*—Some males are birds.

However, conversion on an A- and O-statement does *not* result equivalent expressions. Consider:

All dogs are animals—*is not equivalent to*—All animals are dogs.

Some animals are not dogs—*is not equivalent to*—Some dogs are not animals.

## Obversion

The next equivalence is *obversion*. Unlike conversion, obversion is *unrestricted*, applying to each type of statement. In order to obtain the obversion equivalency, *two* steps are required:

### Step 1—Change the Quality of the Statement

The first step in creating the obverse of a statement is to change the *quality* of the statement. The *quality*, recall, concerns whether it is affirmative or negative. So, one changes the quality of a universal affirmative (A-statement) by making it a universal negative (E-statement), *and vice versa*; and one changes the quality of a particular affirmative (I-statement) by making it a particular negative (O-statement), *and vice versa*.

### Step 2—Replace the Predicate with Its Compliment

The second step in creating the obverse of a statement is to *replace* the predicate term (only) with its compliment.

The compliment of any class is everything *outside* that class.

We often express the compliment of a class by prefixing the class name with *non-*. For example, "*non-dogs*" is the compliment of "*dogs*." The class of *non-dogs* contains literally everything that is not a dog. Note that by definition, not only is "*non-dogs*" the compliment of "*dogs*," but "*dogs*" is the compliment of "*non-dogs*," since everything outside the class of non-dogs just is in the class of dogs.

So, in the second step to create the obverse of a statement, replace whatever term is in the predicate (*P*) with its compliment (*non-P*), or replace *non-P* with its compliment *P*. When both steps are done, the two statements are equivalent. Here are some examples of equivalencies by obversion:

All men are sinners—*is equivalent to*—No men are *non-sinners*.

No circles are squares—*is equivalent to*—All circles are *non-squares*.

Some plants are trees—*is equivalent to*—Some plants are *not non-trees*.

Some rocks are not granites—*is equivalent to*—Some rocks *are non-granites*.

Note that when converting an I-statement to an O-statement using obversion, such as in the third example above, one *must* include "not" in the copula of the O-statement in order for it to be an *O-statement*, and thereby perform obversion correctly. So, while it sounds awkward to say "not non-," it *is* correct. To help see it, consider that a *rock* (for example) is a non-tree. Thus, in all possible situations in which there is a plant that is a tree, that very plant is not a rock (a non-tree). And vice versa—any situation is which there is tree that is not a rock (which is all situations), that very tree is a plant.

## Contraposition

The final equivalency is called *contraposition*. Like conversion, contraposition is *restricted* to two of our statements—namely, to A- and O-statements. And, like obversion, contraposition involves two steps.

### Step 1—Switch the Subject and the Predicate

First, switch the subject and predicate.

### Step 2—Replace Both Terms with Their Compliments

Second, *replace* both terms with their compliments. When both steps are done, the two statements are equivalent. Here are two examples:

All triangles are shapes—*is equivalent to*—All non-shapes are non-triangles.

Some cats are not males—*is equivalent to*—Some non-males are not non-cats.

These can be more challenging to "see" the equivalencies, so let's briefly discuss the example to help "pump the intuitions." Consider the A-statements. Remember that the compliment of a class $\alpha$ is *non-*$\alpha$, which includes *everything* outside of the class of $\alpha$, and vice versa. Therefore, if every triangle is a shape, which is true, then every non-shape (the color *red*, for example) must be a non-triangle (e.g., *red* is not a triangle), which is true. Further, if every non-shape (e.g., *red*) is a non-triangle, then it must be that every triangle is a shape.

Next consider the O-statement:

Some cats are not males—*is equivalent to*—Some non-males are not non-cats.

Obviously, *females* are *non-males*. So, in any situation in which there is a cat that is not a male (the cat is a female), that very cat (who is a female) is <u>not</u> a *non-cat*, since she is a *cat*. And the same is true in the other direction. In any situation in which there is a non-male (it is a female) that is <u>not</u> a non-cat (and thus it is a cat), is a situation in which that very non-male is a cat that is not male.

Let's take a look at the E- and I-statements, and why they are **not** equivalent with their contrapositive. Let's begin with an E-statement:

No dogs are birds—*is not equivalent to*—No non-birds are no-dogs.

It is true that *no dogs are birds* (obviously), but it is not true that *no non-birds are non-dogs*. A *tree* (for example) is a *non-bird*, and a *plant* (for example) is a *non-dog*. And it is false that *no trees (non-bird) are plants (non-dog)*.

Similarly, with I-statements. Consider:

Some plants are trees—*is not equivalent to*—Some non-trees are non-plants.

It is true that *some plants are trees* (obviously), but it is not true that *some non-trees are non-plants*. A *rock* (for example) is a *non-tree*, and a *dog* (for example) is a *non-plant*. It is false that *some rocks (non-tree) are dogs (non-plant)*.

You may be thinking that the examples (*no trees [non-bird] are plants [non-dog]*, and *some rocks [non-tree] are dogs [non-plant]*) turned out false only because of the examples chosen. However, consider:

(Left side) *No dogs are birds*, and (right side) *No non-birds are non-dogs*.

and

(Left side) *Some plants are trees*, and (right side) *Some non-trees are non-plants*.

If the left side were *equivalent* to the right side in each case, then *no matter what examples* are chosen for the right side, if the left side were true, the right side would be as well. Since there is *at least* the one case for each (the ones chosen) in which the left side is true but the right side false, that is enough to show that contraposition on E-statements and I-statements does not result in equivalent statements.

**EXERCISE 6.3**

For each of the following statements, (a) find the converse, obverse, and contrapositive of the statement, and (b) determine whether the two statements (the original and the statement after the operation) are equivalent.

*1. All quarks are particles.

2. Some philosophers are Greeks.

3. No elephants are giraffes.

*4. Some desks are not square things.

5. All colors are properties.

6. Some helicopters are blue things.

*7. No Americans are Germans.

8. Some birds are not animals.

9. All Christians are Baptists.

10. No apples are fruit.

*11. Some dancers are electrons.

12. Some squares are not shapes.

## Entailments—Square of Opposition

In addition to equivalencies (conversion, obversion, and contraposition) between the statements, there are also various *entailments* that hold between our statements.

> One statement *entails* another statement if and only if it's impossible for the second to be false, if the first is true.

For example, the following are entailments:

> *The table is square,* entails *the table has four sides.*
>
> *Sam is a bachelor,* entails *Sam is a male.*
>
> *Oso is a dog,* entails *Oso is an animal.*

Note that these entailments, unlike our equivalencies, go *one way*. For example, while *the table is square* entails *the table has four sides*, the entailment does *not* go the other way, since an object can have four sides but not be square. Moreover, note that one claim being *true* can entail that another is *false*, and one being false can entail that another is true. For example:

> The truth of *The table is square* entails that it is false that *the table is triangular.*
>
> The falsity of *Oso is an animal* entails that it is true that *Oso is not a dog.*

If one statement being *true* entails that another is *false, and vice versa*—the one being false entails that the other is true, then the statements are *contradictory*—that is,

> Contradictory statements have *opposite* truth-values in *all* possible circumstances.

With the concepts of *entailment* and *contradiction* in hand, we can understand *four entailment relationships* between our categorical statements: *contradictories, contraries, subcontraries,* and *subalterns.* These relationships can be represented in what is called *the square of opposition,* which is a diagram formed by drawing a square with the universal statements A- and E- in the top left and right corners, respectively, and the particular statements I- and O- in the bottom left and right corners, respectively. Figure 6.1 shows the square.

Let's see how the four relations can be represented in the square.

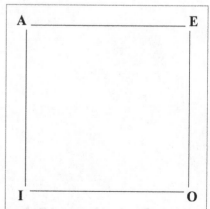

**FIGURE 6.1**

## Contradictories

Consider the following two standard form structures:

(A)  *All S are P*

(O)  *Some S are not P*

If we think about examples in which the subjects and predicates are the same (in which case the two statements *correspond* with each other—*corresponding* statements have *the same subjects and predicates*), we can see that these are *contradictory* to each other. Consider the following examples:

> *All tables are square things.*

> *Some tables are not square things.*

It should be clear that if the A-statement is *true*, then the corresponding O-statement must be *false*. But if the A-statement is *false*, then the corresponding O-statement must be *true*. Further, if the O-statement is *true*, then the corresponding A-statement must be *false*. But if the O-statement is *false*, then the corresponding A-statement must be *true*.

The same is the case for E- and I-statements. Consider these examples:

> *No Fords are red things.*

> *Some Fords are red things.*

Again, it should be clear that if the E-statement is *true*, then the corresponding I-statement must be *false*. But if the E-statement is *false*, then the corresponding I-statement must be *true*. Further, if the I-statement is *true*, then the corresponding E-statement must be *false*. But if the I-statement is *false*, then the corresponding E-statement must be *true*.

These contradictory relationships can be show in the *square of opposition*, as in figure 6.2:

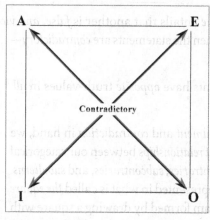

**FIGURE 6.2**

## Contraries and Subcontraries

The next two entailment relations are *contraries* and *subcontraries*. Let's begin with *contraries*, which concerns A- and E-statements.

## Contraries

Consider the follow corresponding statements:

> All frogs are green things.

> No frogs are green things.

It should be clear that if the A-statement is true, then the corresponding E-statement <u>must be</u> false. Alternatively, if the E-statement is true, then the corresponding A-statement <u>must be</u> false. It should be clear that this is true of *every* corresponding A- and E-statements—namely, that *they cannot both be true.*

Of course, it could be the case that both of the statements are *false*, as it could be that *some frogs are green things*, and *some frogs are not green things*. So, we can say that corresponding A- and E-statements <u>cannot</u> be *true* simultaneously, while they *can* be *false* simultaneously. (Given this, they are *not* contradictories.)

This *contrary* relationship between A- and E-statements can be expressed as follows:

> <u>Contraries</u>: An A- or E-statement being *true* <u>entails</u> that the corresponding other is *false*. (But, an A- or E-statement being *false* does *not* entail that the corresponding other is *true*.)

## Subcontraries

Let's turn to I- and O-statements, which are *subcontraries*. Consider:

> Some apples are red things.

> Some apples are not red things.

To understand the entailment relationships between these, let's be clear about what I- and O-statements are saying exactly. An I-statement, *Some S are P*, is saying that there is *at least one* object *x*, such that *x* is an *S* and *x* is a *P*. So, the statement

> Some apples are red things

means that there is *at least one* object *x*, such that *x* is an apple *and x* is a red thing. And an O-statement, *Some S are not P*, is saying that there is *at least one* object *x*, such that *x* is an *S*, but *x* is *not* a *P*. So, the statement

> Some apples are not red things

means that there is *at least one* object *x*, such that *x* is an apple, but *x* is *not* a red thing.

There tends to be some confusion about what exactly I- and O-statements *entail*, and what they *do not* entail. Let's begin by seeing what is *not* entailed by such a statement.

First, a *true* I- or O-statement does <u>not</u> entail that its corresponding I- and O-statement is also *true*. Suppose that John knows exactly one fact about apples—namely, that he is holding one and that it is red. Given this, he knows that the following statement is true:

> Some apples are red things.

If John does not know anything else about any other apples, he cannot validly infer from this alone that it's true that *some apples are not red things*. As far as he knows, all other apples in the world are also red. Thus, the statement *some apples are red things* being *true* does *not* entail that *some apples are not red things*. And, for similar reasons, the reverse entailment (from a *true* O-statement to a *true* I-statement) also does *not* hold.

Second, a *true* I- or O-statement does *not* entail that its corresponding I- and O-statement is *false*. Again, while John knows that *some apples are red things*, from the example above, he cannot validly infer from this alone that it is *false* that *some apples are not red things*, since there may be some non-red apples.

So, what do I- and O-statements entail? Assuming that there are some apples, any given apple is either red or not red. Thus, *at least one* of the following is true:

> *Some apples are red things.*

> *Some apples are not red things.*

Thus, if we know that one of these is *false*, then we know that the other must be *true*. For example, suppose that *Some apples are red things* is *false*. And, given that there are some apples, this *entails* that *Some apples are not red things* is *true*.

Thus, the *subcontrary* relationship between I- and O-statements can be expressed as follows:

> Subcontraries: An I- or O-statement being *false* entails that the corresponding other is *true*. (But, an I- or O-statement being *true* does *not* entail that the corresponding other is also *true*, and nor that the corresponding other is *false*).

We can add these *contrary* and *subcontrary* relationships to the square of opposition as follows in figure 6.3:

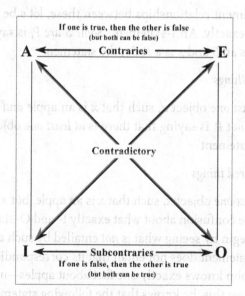

**FIGURE 6.3**

## Subalterns

The last entailment relation between our statements is called a *subaltern*. It is a *one-way* entailment relation that holds between a *universal* and a corresponding *particular* statement that have the same *quality* (affirmative or negative). That is, an A-statement stands in the subaltern relation with a corresponding I-statement, and an E-statement stands in the subaltern relation with a corresponding O-statement. More precisely, it is a "truth entailment" relation, such that if an A-statement is *true*, then the corresponding I-statement <u>must</u> also be *true*, and if an E-statement is *true*, then the corresponding O-statement <u>must</u> also be *true*.

Consider some examples. If it's *true* that *All men are mortal*, then it's also *true* that *Some men are mortal*, and if it's *true* that *No trees are rocks*, then it's also *true* that *Some trees are not rocks*.

However, *falsehood* is *not* entailed from the universal to the corresponding particular. Suppose that it is *false* that *All apples are red things*. From this it does not validly follow that it's *false* that *Some apples are red things*, and similarly entailment does *not* hold from a *false* E-statement to a *false* corresponding O-statement.

The *subaltern* relationship can be expressed as follows:

<u>Subalterns</u>: An A-statement being *true* <u>entails</u> that the corresponding I-statement is also *true*, and an E-statement being *true* <u>entails</u> that the corresponding O-statement is also *true*.

We can now complete the square of opposition by adding the *subaltern* entailment relations, as follows in figure 6.4:

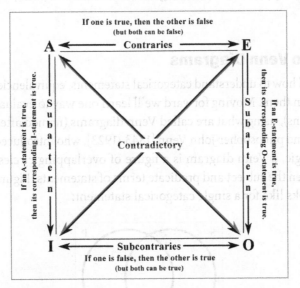

**FIGURE 6.4**

We can use the square of opposition to make valid inferences from one standard form statement to another corresponding statement. So, we can start with knowing that one of our A-, E-, I-, or O-statements is true (or false) and from this validly derive the truth-value of several other corresponding statements, using the entailment relations in the square. Sometimes if we know from the start that one of our statements is *true*, for example, we can use the entailment relations in the square to derive the truth-value of the other three corresponding statements. Other times, however, if we know the truth value of one of our statements (for example that it is *false*), we can only derive the truth-value of its contradictory statement.

**EXERCISE 6.4**

For each of the following categorical statements, (a) assume it has the truth-value given in the parentheses following the statement and then (b) identify the truth-values of all the corresponding statements using the square of opposition. If you cannot determine a truth-value from the square of opposition, write "undetermined" for that statement.

  **\*1.** No Muslims are Christians. (True)

  **2.** Some good books are ESP books. (False)

  **3.** Some owls are not white things. (True)

  **4.** All protesters are peaceful people. (False)

  **\*5.** Some pens are blue things. (True)

  **6.** No Jeeps are fast vehicles. (False)

  **7.** All Colombians are South Americans. (True)

  **8.** Some elementary particles are not things smaller than atoms. (False)

## Introduction to Venn Diagrams

So far, we've learned how to understand categorical statements, equivalencies between them, and entailments between them. Moving forward we'll learn one way to evaluate arguments (called categorical syllogisms), using what are called Venn diagrams (named after the English mathematician, logician, and philosopher John Venn [1843–1923], who introduced the Venn diagram).

In categorical logic, a Venn diagram is a figure of overlapping circles that represents the relationships between the subject and predicate terms of statements. Figure 6.5 illustrates what a Venn diagram looks like for a single categorical statement:

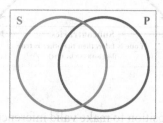

**FIGURE 6.5**

Notice that the circles are labeled S and P, where circle labeled S represents the *subject class*, and the circle labeled P represents the *predicate class*. There are three areas in the Venn diagram for a single categorical statement, as in figure 6.6:

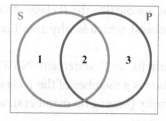

**FIGURE 6.6**

*Area 1* represents anything in the subject class (S) that is not also in the predicate class (P). *Area 3* represents anything in the predicate class (P) that is not also in the subject class (S). And *area 2* represents anything that is in both classes—it is an S and a P.

The diagram is completed to represent a categorical statement either by placing an X in an area or by shading an area, which indicates the following:

- An X in an area indicates that there is at least one object in that area.
- Shading in an area indicates that there is nothing in that area (it is empty).
- Note that if an area lacks an X or shading, nothing is indicated—it does not indicate that there is an object in that area nor that it is empty. It indicates that we know nothing about that area.

With these points in mind, the following (figure 6.7) are *always* the Venn diagrams for our four standard form statements:

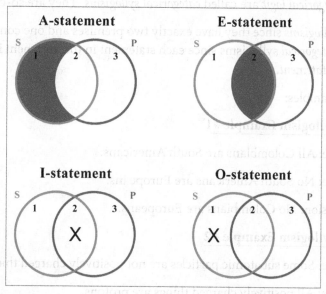

**FIGURE 6.7**

The diagrams can be understood as follows:

1. Regarding the Venn diagram for an A-statement: All *S* are *P*. An A-statement is saying that any member of the *S* class is also a member of the *P* class, and thus there are no members of the *S* class that are outside the *P* class—that is, in the Venn diagram, area 1 is empty (having no members), which is why area 1 is shaded in the diagram for the A-statement.

2. Regarding the Venn diagram for an E-statement: No *S* are *P*. An E-statement is saying that no member of the *S* class is a member of the *P* class, and vice versa—that is, in the Venn diagram, area 2 is empty (having no members), which is why area 2 is shaded in the diagram for the E-statement.

3. Regarding the Venn diagram for an I-statement: Some *S* are *P*. Remember that this means that there is at least one object X, such that X is an *S* and X is a *P*. So, in the Venn diagram for the I-statement, an X is placed in area 2, representing that there is at least one thing that is both an *S* and a *P*.

4. Regarding the Venn diagram for an O-statement: Some *S* are not *P*. Remember that this means that there is at least one object X, such that X is an *S*, but X is not a *P*. So, in the Venn diagram for the O-statement, an X is placed in area 1, representing that there is at least one thing that is an *S*, but not a *P*.

## Categorical Syllogisms

With the Venn diagram for individual statement understood, we can move on to understand how Venn diagrams can be used to evaluate categorical arguments—called *categorical syllogisms*.

### Categorical Syllogisms

Arguments in *categorical logic* are called *categorical syllogisms*. They are so-called because:

- They are *syllogisms* since they have exactly two premises and one conclusion.
- They are *categorical* syllogisms since each statement in the argument is a *categorical statement*.

Here are some examples:

### Categorical Syllogism Example #1

> Premise: All Colombians are South Americans.
>
> Premise: No South Americans are Europeans.
>
> Conclusion: No Colombians are Europeans.

### Categorical Syllogism Example #2

> Premise: Some subatomic particles are not positively charged things.
>
> Premise: All positively charged things are protons.

Conclusion: Some subatomic particles are not protons.

### Categorical Syllogism Example #3

Premise: Some robots are very small objects.

Premise: Some very small objects are black objects.

Conclusion: Some robots are black objects.

Notice that in a categorical syllogism there are *always* three terms, each of which occurs exactly twice in the argument, in two different statements. The three terms are labeled as follows:

- Major Term: This is the *predicate* term of the conclusion.
- Minor Term: This is the *subject* term of the conclusion.
- Middle Term: This is the term that's in the *premises*, but *not* in the conclusion.

So, for example, in Categorical Syllogism Example #1, the terms are as follows:

- Major Term: *Europeans*
- Minor Term: *Colombians*
- Middle Term: *South Americans*

## Testing the Validity of Categorical Syllogisms with Venn Diagrams

While there are various methods to test categorical syllogisms for validity, our focus will be on the Venn diagram method. Venn diagrams can be used to test an argument for validity in the following way:

### The Set-Up

First, we set up a Venn diagram (figure 6.8) with *three* overlapping circles, one for each of our terms, placing two overlapping circles on bottom, and one on top. Label the bottom *left* circle the *minor* term, the bottom *right* circle the *major* term, and the top circle the *middle* term, as follows:

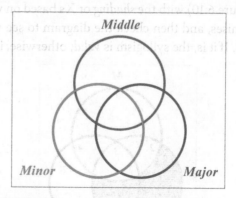

**FIGURE 6.8**

Notice that there are *seven* areas in the Venn diagram for syllogisms (figure 6.9).

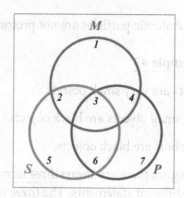

FIGURE 6.9

These represent the following:

- *Areas 1, 5, and 7* represent anything that is an M, S, or P, respectively, but are not in the other two classes.
- *Areas 2, 4, and 6* represent things in the respective overlapping classes, but are not in the third class.
- *Area 3* represents anything that is an M, P, and S.

### Example #1—All Universal Statements

In order to see the next steps, consider an example with all universal statements:

### Categorical Syllogism Example #4

Premise: All bats are mammals.

Premise: All mammals are warm-blooded things.

Conclusion: All bats are warm-blooded things.

### Step #1—Diagram the Premises

We fill in the diagram (figure 6.10) with the *shading* or Xs based on what's in the *premises*. But we diagram *only* the premises, and then check the diagram to see whether the conclusion is also thereby diagrammed. If it is, the syllogism is *valid*; otherwise, it is *invalid*.

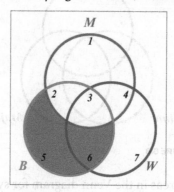

FIGURE 6.10

We'll begin with the first *premise*. Notice that the premise mentions only *bats* and *mammals*, and so we focus only on those circles in our diagram, and shade the *entire* area of the *bat* circle that does *not* overlap the *mammals* circle, according to the diagram for an A-statement:

Notice that we shaded *both* areas 5 and 6, since *both* are areas that include *bats* that are *not mammals*.

Next, we diagram the second premise (figure 6.11). Notice that it mentions only *mammals* and *warm-blooded things*, and so we focus only on those circles in our diagram, and shade the *entire* area of the *mammals* circle that does *not* overlap the *warm-blooded things* circle, according to the diagram for an A-statement:

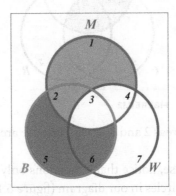

**FIGURE 6.11**

Notice that we shaded *both* areas 1 and 2, since *both* are areas that include *mammals* that are *not warm-blooded things*.

### Step #2—Observe and Determine Validity

At this point, *no more is added to the diagram*. Instead, we *obverse* the diagram and determine whether the conclusion is also diagrammed. Notice that the conclusion says that *All bats are warm-blooded things*. It is represented in the diagram if and only if the *entire* area of the *bats* that does *not* overlap the *warm-blooded things* circle is shaded—that is, it is represented if and only if areas 2 and 5 are shaded. Notice that those areas *are* shaded, and thus the conclusion *is* represented.

Therefore, Categorical Syllogism Example #4 is *valid*, since the premises being represented as true in the diagram *thereby* represent the conclusion as being true, which means that the premises *guarantee* the conclusion.

### Example #2—All Universal Statements

Consider another example with all universal statements:

#### Categorical Syllogism Example #5

Premise: No Christians are polytheists.

Premise: All polytheists are religious people.

Conclusion: No Christians are religious people.

*Step #1—Diagram the Premises*
Again, we'll begin with the first premise. Notice that the premise mentions only *Christians* and *polytheists,* and so we focus only on those circles in our diagram (figure 6.12), and shade the *entire* area where the two circles overlap, according to the diagram for an E-statement:

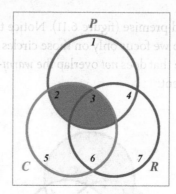

**FIGURE 6.12**

Notice that we shaded *both* areas 2 and 3, since those are areas where include the *Christians* and *polytheists* circles overlap.

Turning to the second premise, notice that it mentions only *polytheists* and *religious people,* and so we focus only on those circles in our diagram (figure 6.13), and shade the *entire* area of the *polytheists* circle that does *not* overlap the *religious people* circle, according to the diagram for an A-statement:

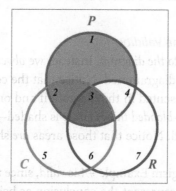

**FIGURE 6.13**

Notice that we shaded *both* areas 1 and 2, since *both* are areas that include *polytheists* that are *not religious people.*

*Step #2—Observe and Determine Validity*
Again, *no more is added to the diagram.* Instead, as before, we *obverse* the diagram and determine whether the conclusion is also diagrammed. Notice that the conclusion says that *No Christians are religious people.* It is represented in the diagram if and only if the *entire* area where *Christians* and *religious people* overlap is shaded, which includes areas 3 and 6. Notice that area 6 is *not* shaded, and thus the conclusion is *not* represented.

Therefore, Categorical Syllogism Example #5 is *invalid*, since the premises being represented as true in the diagram do *not thereby* represents the conclusion as being true, which means that these premises *do not* guarantee the conclusion.

### Example #3—All Particular Statements

Consider an example with all particular statements:

### Categorical Syllogism Example #6

> Premise: Some chilis are spicy things.
>
> Premise: Some spicy things are not red things.
>
> Conclusion: Some chilis are not red things.

*Step #1—Diagram the Premises*

Again, we'll begin with the first premise. Notice that this premise is a *particular* premise, and thus we are going to place an X somewhere, and *not* shading. In placing the X, we must satisfy the following criteria:

1.  Criterion #1: We can place only one X for each premise.
2.  Criterion #2: We can place an X in an area only if we know that the area in question has at least one member.

The premise mentions only *chilis* and *spicy things,* and so we focus only on those circles in our diagram. The first premise is an I-statement, and thus we will place an X where *chilis* and *spicy things* overlap, which includes areas 2 and 3. Suppose that we place the X in area 3, which is an area where *chilis* and *spicy things* overlap (figure 6.14).

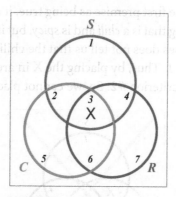

**FIGURE 6.14**

While this does represent the first premise as being true, it says *too much*. It not only indicates that there is something that is a *chili* and is *spicy*, but it also indicates that it is *red*. However, since the first premises does not tell us that the chili is red, we do *not know* that it is red, relative to the first premise. Thus, by placing the X in area 3, we are going beyond what we *know*, which violates criterion #2. So, we cannot place the X in area 3 (figure 6.15).

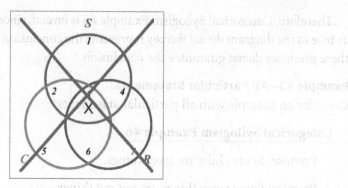

**FIGURE 6.15**

So, suppose that we place the X in area 2 (figure 6.16), which is another area where *chilis* and *spicy things* overlap.

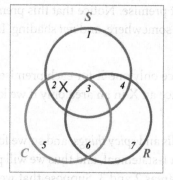

**FIGURE 6.16**

While this does represent the first premise as being true, it again says *too much*. It not only indicates that there is something that is a *chili* and is *spicy*, but it also indicates that it is *not* red. However, since the first premises does not tell us that the chili is *not* red, we do *not know* that it is *not* red, relative to premise 1. Thus, by placing the X in area 2, we are going beyond what we *know*, which again violates criterion #2. So, we cannot place the X in area 2 (figure 6.17).

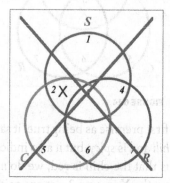

**FIGURE 6.17**

Well, if we cannot place the X in areas 2 or 3, where do we place it? We do not have the option of placing *two* Xs, one in area 2 and the other in area 3, since that violates criterion #1. The *answer* is that we place it *on the line* between areas 2 and 3 (figure 6.18).

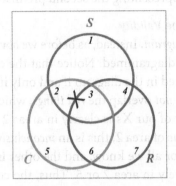

**FIGURE 6.18**

By placing it on the line, we are communicating that it is either in area 2, or in area 3, but we don't know which. However, the line between areas 2 and 3 is in the general area where *chilis* and *spicy things* overlap. Thus, we are still representing the premise as true, since the X is both a *chili* and a *spicy thing* where it is placed.

Next, we diagram the second premise. This is an O-statement, and thus we again place an X somewhere. The premise mentions only *spicy things* and *red things*, and so we focus only on those circles in our diagram. This time we place an X in the general area of *spicy things* that does not overlap the *red things*. As with the I-statement, this general area also has two subareas areas 1 and 2. But the same criteria apply—we have one X and we cannot indicate something that we do not know.

If we place it in area 1, we are again indicating something beyond what we know, as we are thereby saying that the spicy thing is *not* a chili, which we do not know from this premise. And, if we place the X in area 2, we are indicating something beyond what we know, as we are thereby saying that the spicy thing *is* a chili, which we do not know from this premise.

So, as we the other X, we place the X on the line between areas 1 and 2 (figure 6.19):

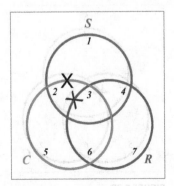

**FIGURE 6.19**

Again, by placing it on the line between areas 1 and 2, we are communicating that it is either in area 1 or in area 2, but we don't know which. However, the line between areas 1 and 2 is in the general area where *spicy things* do *not* overlap *red things*, so we know that this X is *spicy* but *not red*. Thus, we are still representing the second premise as true.

### Step #2—Observe and Determine Validity

Again, *no more is added to the diagram*. Instead, as before we *observe* the diagram and determine whether the conclusion is also diagrammed. Notice that the conclusion says that *Some chilis are not red things*. It is represented in the diagram if and only if there is an X *somewhere* in the general area where the *chilis* do *not* overlap the *red things*, which includes subareas 2 and 5.

However, notice that *neither* of our Xs is clearly in areas 2 or 5. Neither is even touching area 5. While both are <u>on the line</u> of area 2, this is an *inconclusive* indication that it *is* in area 2. The one X might be in area 3 for all we know, and the other in area 1 for all we know. Thus, no X is clearly and inconclusively in area 2 or 5. Thus, the conclusion is *not* represented as true in the diagram.

Therefore, Categorical Syllogism Example #6 is *invalid*, since the premises being represented as true in the diagram do *not thereby* represent the conclusion as being true, which means that these premises *do not* guarantee the conclusion.

### Example #4—Mix of Particular and Universal Statements

Consider an example with a mix of particular and universal statements:

### Categorical Syllogism Example #7

Premise: Some towels are soft things.

Premise: All soft things are things made of cotton.

Conclusion: Some towels are things made of cotton.

### Step #1—Diagram the Premises

It might be tempting to begin with the first premise, as we have with the last examples, and diagram it as follows (figure 6.20):

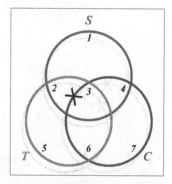

**FIGURE 6.20**

However, consider what happens when we then diagram premise 2 (figure 6.21):

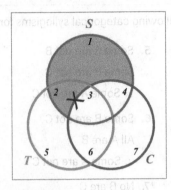

**FIGURE 6.21**

Notice that area 2 contains shading, which means that there is *definitely* nothing there—it is empty. In contrast, an X in an area means that something *is* in the area. Thus, the questionable placement of X on the line between areas 2 and 3, which we placed by diagraming it first, is *not* in question. Shading "forces any X out" of an area. Thus, we *know* that it is *not* in area 2. Thus, since it must be in either area 2 or area 3, it must be in area 3 (figure 6.22):

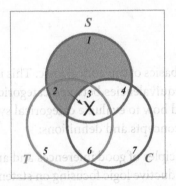

**FIGURE 6.22**

In order to avoid moving the X, when we encounter an argument with a particular and universal premise, we begin with the universal premise. Thus, we begin with the second premise.

### Step #2—Observe and Determine Validity

Again, *no more is added to the diagram.* Instead, as before, we *obverse* the diagram and determine whether the conclusion is also diagrammed. The conclusion says that *Some towels are things made of cotton.* It is represented in the diagram if and only if there is an X *somewhere* in the general area where the *towels* circle overlaps the *things made of cotton* circle, which includes subareas 3 and 6. Notice that the X is in area 3, and thus the conclusion *is* represented.

Therefore, Categorical Syllogism Example #7 is *valid*, since the premises being represented as true in the diagram *thereby* represent the conclusion as being true, which means that the premises *guarantee* the conclusion.

**EXERCISE 6.5**

Use Venn diagrams to test the following categorical syllogisms for validity.

**\*1.** All A are B
   All A are C
   ∴ All B are C

**2.** No A are B
   No B are C
   ∴ No A are C

**3.** All A are B
   No B are C
   ∴ No A are C

**\*4.** Some A are B
   Some A are C
   ∴ Some B are C

**5.** Some A are not B
   Some B are not C
   ∴ Some A are not C

**6.** Some B are not C
   All A are B
   ∴ Some A are not C

**\*7.** No B are C
   Some A are B
   ∴ Some A are not C

**8.** Some A are B
   No B are C
   ∴ Some A are not C

**9.** Some B are C
   All A are B
   ∴ Some A are C

**10.** No A are B
   All A are C
   ∴ No B are C

## Recap

In this chapter, we learned the basics of categorical logic. This included learning how to understand categorical statements, equivalencies between categorical statements, and entailments between them. We also learned how to evaluate categorical syllogisms using Venn diagrams.

Below are some important concepts and definitions:

- **Logic:** The study of principles of good inferences and arguments.
- **Categorical Logic:** A deductive logic focusing on statements about *classes* (or *categories*), dating back to the philosophy of *Aristotle* (384–322 BC).
- **Categorical Syllogism:** An argument with exactly two premises and one conclusion, in which all the statements are categorical statements.
- **Categorical Statement:** A statement about classes, in which the members of one class are said to be *included in* another class or *excluded from* another class. There are four types, two using the *inclusion relation* and two using the *exclusion relation*.
   - **Standard Form Categorical Statement:** A categorical statement in one of the following forms:

      (A) All *S* are *P*.

      (E) No *S* are *P*.

      (I) Some *S* are *P*.

      (O) Some *S* are not *P*.

- **Equivalent Statements**: Statements are *equivalent* if and only if they have the same truth-value in all possible circumstances.
- **Equivalence Relations**: Relations that hold between equivalent standard form categorical statements, including the following:
  - **Conversion**: E- and I-statements are equivalent to their converses, where the converse of a statement is obtained by switching the subject and predicate.
  - **Obversion**: A-, E-, I- and O-statements are equivalent to their obverses, where the obverse of a statement is obtained by (a) changing the statement from universal to particular or particular to universal, and (b) replacing the predicate term with its compliment.
  - **Contraposition**: A- and O-statements are equivalent to their contrapositives, where the contrapositive of a statement is obtained by (a) switching the subject and predicate, and (b) replacing both terms with their compliments.
- **Entailment**: One statement *entails* another statement if and only if it's impossible for the second to be false, if the first is true.
- **Contradictory Statements**: Statements that have opposite truth-values in all possible circumstances.
- **Square of Opposition**: A diagram that represents the logical relationships that hold between categorical statements in virtue of their form.
- **Venn Diagram**: A figure of overlapping circles that represents the relationships between the subject and predicate terms of categorical statements. In categorical logic, it is used to evaluate categorical syllogisms.

# 7

# DEDUCTIVE LOGIC II
## *Propositional Logic*

In this chapter, we will take an introductory look at another important deductive logic, called *propositional logic*. Since it is a deductive system, like categorical logic, the concepts of *deductive argument, valid argument,* and *sound argument* should be well in hand, as they will be assumed in this chapter. Like categorical logic, *propositional logic* is important to study for at least two reasons. First, it helps clarify our understanding of everyday concepts and statements, particularly the words "*not*," "*if*," "*and*," and "*or*." Second, studying this logic is useful as an exercise in precise, clear, and exact reasoning that yields definitive results. We will approach this logic by using symbolic language. While it may initially appear intimidating, it takes little effort to understand the symbolic language.

In this chapter, we will learn the basics of propositional logic. This includes learning how to "*symbolize*" English statements, understand the logic of "*not*," "*if*," "*and*," and "*or*," and how to use truth-tables to test arguments for validity. We will also learn a few basic logical rules, as well as some *invalid* mistakes associated with those rules. As with previous chapters, one should be attentive to the following key terms as one works through this chapter:

---

## KEY WORDS

Affirming the Consequent
Antecedent
Compound Statement
Conditional
Conjunction
Consequent
Denying the Antecedent
Disjunction
Disjunctive Syllogism
Erroneous Disjunctive Syllogism
Erroneous Hypothetical Syllogism
Hypothetical Syllogism

Logical Constant
Modus Ponens
Modus Tollens
Negation
Propositional Logic
Simple Statement
Truth Table
Variable
Well-Formed Formula

## Introduction to Propositional Logic

*Propositional* logic (also known as sentential logic) dates to ancient philosophy. Among other things, the logic studies ways of joining statements (or sentences) to form more complicated statements *and* the logical relationships between such statements derived from the combinations.

An important aspect of this logic is the study of the logic of "*not*," "*if*," "*and*," and "*or*," which are combined with simpler statements to create more complex statements, whose truth-value depends entirely upon the truth-value of the simpler statements it contains as components, along with the meaning of "*not*," "*if*," "*and*," and "*or*."

Further, *truth tables* are used to show the possible truth-values of a statement, as well as to test arguments for validity. In this chapter, we will unpack the details of these basic aspects of the logic.

**KEY CONCEPT: PROPOSITIONAL LOGIC**
A deductive logic that studies ways of joining statements to form more complicated statements *and* the logical relationships between such statements derived from the combinations.

## Language of Propositional Logic: Symbolized Language

In propositional logic, the focus is on the *structure* or *syntax* of sentences, and the logical relationships between statements based on their *structure*. To facilitate focusing on the structure (or *form*) of the statements, *symbolic language* is used, which may initially appear intimidating, but is fairly easy to grasp. In this section, this *symbolic language* will be introduced.

### Well-Formed Formulas (WFFs)

In natural languages, such as English, we communicate with natural language sentences (e.g., *English sentences*), among other things. In mathematics, we use *numbers*, among other things. In the *symbolic language* of propositional logic, we use *well-formed formulas*. A well-formed formula ("wff" for short) is a string of symbols, like a sentence, that represents a statement and satisfies the syntactic rules of the symbolic language, which will be specified below.

### Vocabulary

There are three components to the vocabulary of the language: *variables*, *logical constants*, and *parentheses*. These are expressed with symbols, to be introduced below, to make up the wffs.

### Variables

In propositional logic, the smallest, indivisible unit is a <u>whole</u> *simple* statement (unlike categorical logic which considers the components of a statement—the subject and predicate). To define a *simple statement*, first consider a *logical constant*.[1] A *logical constant* is, in a *natural* language (as opposed to the symbolic language of propositional logic), a word that either modifies a statement or connects two other statements. The logical constants that we will focus on are *not, and, or,* and *if*. We can define a *simple statement*, then, as follows:

---

1.  These are sometimes called "logical *connectives*." "Logical *constant*" is preferable, however, since "*connective*" in "logical *connectives*" connotes *connecting* two or more things. Indeed, one often sees definitions of "logical connective" as intending a word that *connects* statements. While this is true of *many* logical constants, there is one of which it is not true—namely, *negation*. Negation does *not* connect anything, but instead *modifies* a statement. Hence, "logical *constant*" is the preferred label.

Simple Statement: A *simple statement* is a statement in which there are *no* logical constants.

In contrast, there are *compound statements*. These are statements that contain at least one of the logical constants, along with at least one simple statement. The following are some examples of *simple* statements:

*God exists.*

*Telling the truth is morally right.*

*Las Vegas is located in Nevada.*

*The Green Bay Packers are the greatest NFL team ever.*

In propositional logic, each of the above statements is treated as a basic *simple* statement. Even though the last example is a much longer statement than the first example, they are equally simple, as simplicity does *not* come in degrees. What makes these *simple* statements is that none contains a logical constant (*not, and, or,* and *if*).

To facilitate our focus on *structure* and not the content of statements, we *symbolize* simple statements. Since simple statements are the basic, indivisible components, we use a *variable* to stand for them. A *variable* is any letter, often in lower case ($a, b, c, ..., x, y, z$), which can be subscripted for more options ($a_0, a_1, a_2, b_0, b_1, b_2$, etc.). So, the first component of the vocabulary is a *variable*.

For example, we could symbolize the statements above as follows:

$g$ = God exists.

$m$ = Telling the truth is morally right.

$l$ = Las Vegas is in Nevada.

$p$ = The Green Bay Packers are the greatest NFL team ever.

Note that *any* variable could have been used for our statements. So, instead of using $g, m, l$, and $p$, respectively, we could have used $p, q, r$, and $s$, respectively, or we could have used $a, b, c$, and $d$, respectively, or any other combination of letters.

## Logical Constants

The next component of the vocabulary is the use of *logical constants*. We defined a logical constant as a word that either modifies a statement or connects two other statements. Again, for this chapter, the logical constants are *not, and, or,* and *if.* Let's discuss the basic idea of these, how they modify or connect statements, and introduce their symbols.

### Not

"*Not*" is our first logical constant. It is a statement *modifier*, such that when added to a statement, the result is the *negation* of the original. For example, consider our statement:

*God exists.*

If we add "*not*" to the statement, the result is the *negation* of the original. Thus, the statement

> God does not exist.

is the *negation* of *God exists*.

And any expression synonymous with *not* (such as *it is false that, it is not the case that*) functions in the same way. So, for example, the following is also the negation of *God exists*:

> It is false that God exists.

Note that *not* (as well as any of its synonyms) *always* modifies *exactly one* statement. We can express *negation* as follows:

> <u>Negation</u>: For *any* statement ϕ, not-ϕ is the *negation* of ϕ.

(Note that ϕ does *not necessarily* stand for a variable. Rather, it represents *any* statement, including a variable, or one of the compound expressions below [e.g., "*p* and *q*"].)

In propositional logic, we symbolize not just simple sentences, but also logical constants. The symbol for "*not*" varies depending on the textbook, but we will use the standard *tilde* (pronounced TIL-duh): ~. So, we can state negation this way, in partial symbolic language:

> <u>Negation</u>: For *any* statement ϕ, ~ ϕ is the *negation* of ϕ.

For example, having stipulated that *g* stands "God exists," and that ~ stands for "not," then we would symbolize "God does *not* exist" as: ~ *g*.

### And

The next logical constant is "*and*." In propositional logic, *and* is used to *connect* statements into a compound statement. Any compound statement with *and* as its *main* logical constant is a conjunction. For example, the following is a conjunction:

> God exists *and* Las Vegas is in Nevada.

Further, any expression synonymous with *and* (such as *but, moreover, however*) functions in the same way.

Note that "*and*" (as well as any of its synonyms) *always* connects *exactly two* statements. We can express *conjunction* as follows:

> <u>Conjunction</u>: For *any* statements ϕ, ψ, "ϕ and ψ" is a *conjunction*.

(Note that ψ, like ϕ, does *not necessarily* stand for a variable. Rather, it represents *any* expression, including a variable, or one of the compound expressions below [e.g., "*p* or *q*"].)

The symbol for "*and*" also varies from textbook to textbook, but we will use the *ampersand* symbol: &. So, we could state conjunction this way, in partial symbolic language:

> <u>Conjunction</u>: For *any* statements ϕ, ψ, "ϕ & ψ" is a *conjunction*.

For example, having stipulated the *g* stands for "God exists," that *l* stands for "Las Vegas is in Nevada," and that & stands for "*and*," we would symbolize "God exists *and* Las Vegas is in Nevada" as: *g* & *l*.

*Or*

The next logical constant is "*or*." Like "*and*," "*or*" is used in propositional logic to *connect* statements into a longer compound statement. Any compound statement with "*or*" as its *main* logical constant is a disjunction. For example, the following is a disjunction:

Telling the truth is morally right **or** Las Vegas is in Nevada.

Further, any expression synonymous with "*or*" (such as *unless*) functions in the same way.

Note that "*or*" (as well as any of its synonyms) *always* connects *exactly two* statements.

We can express *disjunction* as follows:

Disjunction: For *any* statements φ, ψ, "φ *or* ψ" is a *disjunction*.

The symbol we use for "*or*" is the wedge: ∨. So, we could state disjunction this way, in partial symbolic language:

Disjunction: For *any* statements φ, ψ, "φ ∨ ψ" is a *disjunction*.

For example, having stipulated the *m* stands for "Telling the truth is morally right," that *l* stands for "Las Vegas is in Nevada," and that ∨ stands for "*or*," we would symbolize "Telling the truth is morally right or Las Vegas is in Nevada" as: *m* ∨ *l*.

*If*

Our last logical constant is "*if*." This is also used to *connect* two statements into a longer compound statement. Any compound statement with "*if*" as its *main* logical constant is a conditional. For example, the following is a conditional:

*If God exists, then the Green Bay Packers are the greatest NFL team ever.*

There are *many* ways to express a conditional in English, which we will consider shortly. But, for now, any expression synonymous with "*if*" functions in the same way.

Note that "*if*," like "*and*" and "*or*," *always* connects *exactly two* statements. We can express a *conditional* as follows:

Conditional: For *any* statements φ, ψ, "If φ then ψ" is a *conditional*.

The symbol for "*if*" is the arrow: →. So, we could state a conditional this way, in partial symbolic language:

Conditional: For *any* statements φ, ψ, "φ → ψ" is a *conditional*.

For example, having stipulated the *g* stands "God exists," that **p** stands for "The Green Bay Packers are the greatest NFL team ever," and that → stands for "*if*," we would symbolize "If God exists, then the Green Bay Packers are the greatest NFL team ever" as: *g* → *p*.

Figure 7.1 below summarizes the four logical constants and their basic function in a statement.

| Logical Constant | Symbol | Basic Structure of WFF with Constant | Name of Statement with Constant as Main Constant | Basic Example in English | Example Symbolized |
|---|---|---|---|---|---|
| *not* | ~ | ~ __ | Negation | Paul did *not* walk. | *~ p* |
| *and* | & | __ & __ | Conjunction | Paul walked *and* Quinn ran. | *p & q* |
| *or* | ∨ | __ ∨ __ | Disjunction | Paul walked *or* Quinn ran. | *p ∨ q* |
| *if* | → | __ → __ | Conditional | *If* Paul walked, then Quinn ran. | *p → q* |

**FIGURE 7.1**

## Parentheses and Main Logical Constant

The final component of the vocabulary is the use of *parentheses*. In addition to the *basic compound logical expressions*, or wffs (~ p, p & q, p ∨ q, and p → q, where "*p*" and "*q*" are variables), there are lengthier compound statements that contain multiple constants and simpler statements. For these lengthier compound statements, parentheses are needed in order to clarify the structure of the statement, which would otherwise be ambiguous (and fail to express a wff). Consider the following expression:

p & q ∨ r

Recall that "&" and "∨" *always* connect *exactly two* statements. So, which *two* statements are being connected by &, and which *two* by ∨? In order to clarify the intended meaning, parentheses are used. So, we can disambiguate the expression in one of the following two ways:

p & (q ∨ r)

(p & q) ∨ r

In the first of these, & connects p and (q ∨ r), and ∨ connects q and r. Notice that & has the widest *scope*, since it ranges over the entire wff, whereas ∨ has narrower scope, ranging only over what is inside the parentheses. Any constant that has the *widest* scope is the *main constant* and defines the statement. Thus, the first wff is a *conjunction*, since & is the *main constant*.

In the second, ∨ connects (p & q) and r, and & connects p and q. Notice that with this one, ∨ has the widest *scope*, since it ranges over the entire wff, whereas & has narrower scope, ranging only over what is inside the parentheses. As a result, ∨ is the *main* constant, and the second wff is a *disjunction*.

If parentheses were not used, the statement would be ambiguous (and thus not a wff), and we would not know whether it is intended to be a conjunction or disjunction. Therefore, we use parentheses to clarify lengthier compound statements.

## Summary of the Vocabulary of Symbolic Language of Propositional Logic

In summary, the basic vocabulary of the symbolic language of propositional logic is:

Variables: *Variables* (*a, b, c, ..., x, y, z*) stand for *simple* statements.

Logical Constants: The symbols ~, &, ∨, and → stand for logical constants, where ~ *always* modifies *exactly one* wff, and &, ∨, → *always* connect *exactly two* wffs.

Parentheses: ( ) are used to clarify the structure of a complex wff.

## Rules Governing WFFs

As we saw above, not just *any* string of symbols is a wff. For example, "*p* & *q* ∨ *r*" is *not* a wff since it lacks parentheses. Fortunately, there are four simple rules governing wffs, which will help us to formulate them and recognize where something may have gone wrong in formulation.

### Rules Governing WFFs:

1. Any *variable* (*a, b, c, …, x, y, z*) is a wff.
2. For *any* expression ϕ, if ϕ is a wff, then ~ ϕ is a wff.
3. For *any* expressions ϕ, ψ, if ϕ and ψ are wffs, (ϕ & ψ), (ϕ ∨ ψ), (ϕ → ψ) are wffs.
4. Nothing else is a wff.

Note once again that ϕ and ψ represent either a variable or a compound expression. Thus, rule 2 allows us to form such expressions as:

~ p

~ (p ∨ q)

~ (p & (q ∨ r))

And, rule 3 allows us to form such expressions as:

p & (q ∨ r)

p → (q ∨ ~ r)

p → ~ (q ∨ r)

p & (p → (q ∨ ~ r))

And, of course we can have much more complex (potentially infinitely long) statements.

### EXERCISE 7.1

For each string of symbols below, indicate whether it is a wff, or not a wff.

| | | |
|---|---|---|
| *1.  ~ *p q* | 6.  *p → q* | 11.  *p* & ~ (*q → r*) |
| 2.  ~ *p* ∨ *q* | *7.  *p* ~ & *q* | *12.  (*p* & ~ (*q → r*) |
| 3.  & *q r* | 8.  ~ *p* & *q* | 13.  ~ (*p*) → *q* |
| *4.  *q* & *r* | 9.  (*p* ∨ *q* & *r*) | *14.  *p* ∨ & ~ *q* |
| 5.  *p q* → | *10.  *p* ∨ (*q* & *r*) | 15.  *p* ∨ ~ *q* & *r* |

## How to Symbolize

In this section, we will learn how to re-write an English sentence in the *symbolic language* of propositional logic—that is, we will learn how to *symbolize* an English sentence. Let's begin by considering the various synonyms of *"not," "and," "or,"* and *"if."*

### Negation

Any statement with *"not"* in it is a *negation*. But we saw that there are words and phrases that are synonymous with *"not,"* such as *"it is false that"* and *"it is not the case that."* Thus, any statement that has one of these expressions is also a negation. Consider again the statement:

> *God exists.*

Each of the following express its *negation*:

> God does *not* exist.
>
> *It's false that* God exists.
>
> *It is not the case that* God exists.

If we stipulate that *g* stands for "God exists," then we would symbolize each of the above in the same way, as: ~ *g*

Further, if the statement that is being negated is a compound statement, then we need parentheses. So, consider the following sentence for example:

> *It is false that* both Bob and Fred ran.

The scope of *"it is false that"* ranges over the entire sentence, and thus we need parentheses around the conjunction. Let's stipulate that *b* stands for "Bob ran" and that *f* stands for "Fred ran." Then we'd symbolize the statement this way:

> ~ (b & f)

Compare this to a different statement, namely:

> Bob did *not* run, and Fred did run.

Notice that the scope of "not" in that state is narrower than *"it is false that"* in the statement above. Whereas *"it is false that"* covered the entire statement in the first example, *"not"* only covers part of the statement in the second case—namely, the simple sentence "Bob ran." Thus, we symbolize the second statement as ~ *b* & *f*.

We don't need parentheses here since it is clear and unambiguous that the scope of ~ ranges just over *b* alone.

### Conjunction

"And" is the basic way we express a *conjunction* in English. However, sometimes we introduce it with *"both."* So, we say "Both *this* and *that*." For example, "Both Bob and Fred ran." However, *"both"* is *not* an additional logical constant, but is merely a way of introducing the conjunction.

Further, if we want to contrast two things, we sometimes use the word "*but*" instead of "*and.*" For example, we might say, "Bob didn't run but Fred did." This is still a conjunction. Other words that function the same are "*however,*" "*moreover,*" "*furthermore,*" and other synonyms. So, each of the following are conjunctions:

> *Bob ran and Fred ran.*
>
> *Both Bob and Fred ran.*
>
> *Bob ran but Fred also ran.*
>
> *Bob ran however Fred also ran.*
>
> *Bob ran moreover Fred also ran.*
>
> *Bob ran furthermore Fred also ran.*

If we stipulate that **b** stands for "Bob ran" and that *f* stands for "Fred ran," then we'd symbolize each statement this way: b & f.

## Disjunction

The basic way that we express a disjunction is with the word "or." Sometimes we introduce it with "*either.*" So, we say "Either *this* or *that.*" For example, "Either Bob ran or Fred ran." However, "*either*" is *not* an additional logical constant, but is merely a way of introducing the disjunction.

Further, if we want to contrast two things, we sometimes use the word "*unless.*" For example, we might say "Bob ran unless Fred ran." This is still a disjunction, but in this case we are saying that one or the other, but not both. So, each of the following are disjunctions:

> *Bob ran or Fred ran.*
>
> *Either Bob ran or Fred ran.*
>
> *Bob ran unless Fred also ran.*

Again, if we stipulate that *b* stands for "Bob ran" and that *f* stands for "Fred ran," then we'd symbolize each statement this way: b ∨ f.

## Conditional

There is a *lot* to say about conditional statements. Let's begin with terminology. *All* conditionals have two parts—the *antecedent* and the *consequent*. Furthermore, we often express a conditional with an "if" statement. When we do, "if" *always* introduces the *antecedent*. Thus, we have:

> If *antecedent*, then *consequent*.

So, consider the sentence:

> If *it is raining*, then *the ground is wet*.

Here, "*it is raining*" is the antecedent, and "*the ground is wet*" is the consequent. The "if" and "then" introduce, but are *not* part of, the antecedent and consequent, respectively.

In our symbolization of the conditional, the *antecedent* <u>always</u> comes in front of →. Thus, using "*a*" for "antecedent" and "*c*" for "consequent," we express this idea this way:

$$a \rightarrow c$$

Note that in English, we don't always introduce the consequent with "then." Sometimes we leave it unstated. For example:

> If *it is raining, the ground is wet.*

Additionally, we sometimes use other words or phrases in English to express "if." For example, instead of saying "If *a*, then *c*," we could say "Provided that *a*, then *c*," or "Given that *a*, then *c*." And, of course, there may be other ways as well.

Further, we <u>always</u> introduce the antecedent with "if" (or one its equivalent expressions—such as *given that*), even if in English we introduce it mid-sentence. In other words, while we can write a conditional in English beginning with "if," as in "If *it is raining*, then *the ground is wet*," we can also write it in English by beginning with our consequent. For example, we could have written our conditional this way:

> *The ground is wet*, if *it is raining.*

Here "*it is raining*" is still the *antecedent*, even though it occurs in the second half of the *English* statement. We know this because "if" <u>always</u> introduces the antecedent. So, using *r* for "*it is raining*," and *g* for "*the ground is wet*," we symbolize the statement just above as: $r \rightarrow g$.

In contrast, we introduce the *consequent* with the phrase "only if." So, we could have written our conditional this way:

> *It is raining* <u>only if</u> *the ground is wet.*

Symbolically, we write this the same way—namely, as: $r \rightarrow g$.

In order to really understand a conditional, it is important to understand that it expresses two logical relationships between the antecedent and the consequent. The first logical relationship goes *from* antecedent *to* the consequent. It is a relationship of sufficiency. That is, in a conditional, what is being said is that the antecedent is a *sufficient condition for* the consequent. Recall from chapter 3 that to say that one statement is a sufficient condition for another means that the former being true *guarantees* that the latter is true. For example, the truth of "The desk is square" is a sufficient condition for "The desk has four sides." The truth of the former *guarantees* the truth of the latter. So, we could have written our conditional about rain and the wet ground this way:

> *Rain falling* <u>is a sufficient condition for</u> *the ground being wet.*

Or, this way:

> *Rain falling* <u>guarantees</u> that *the ground is wet.*

In both cases, the symbolization is the same—namely, $r \rightarrow g$.

The other relationship between the antecedent and the consequent goes from consequent *to* the antecedent. So, in a conditional, another thing being said is that the consequent is a *necessary condition for* the antecedent. Recall from chapter 3 that to say that one statement is a necessary condition for another means that the former being true is *required for* the latter to be true. For example, the truth of "The desk has four sides" is a necessary condition for "The desk is square." The truth of the former is *required* for the truth of the latter. So, we could have written our conditional about rain and the wet ground this way:

> *The ground being wet* is a necessary condition for *rain falling.*

Or, this way:

> *The ground being wet* is required for *rain falling.*

In both cases, the symbolization is the same—namely, $r \rightarrow g$.

In summary, we have the following ways of expressing the conditional (which is *not* an exhaustive list):

> *If* it is raining, *then* the ground is wet.
>
> *If* it is raining, the ground is wet.
>
> *Provided that* it is raining, the ground is wet.
> *Given that* it is raining, the ground is wet.
>
> The ground is wet, *if* it is raining.
>
> It is raining *only if* the ground is wet.
>
> Rain falling *is a sufficient condition for* the ground being wet.
>
> Rain falling *guarantees that* the ground is wet.
>
> The ground being wet *is a necessary condition for* rain falling.
>
> The ground being wet *is required for* rain falling.

Using *r* for "*it is raining*" and *g* for "*the ground is wet*," we symbolize each of these *the same* way: $r \rightarrow g$.

## Steps for Symbolizing

Symbolizing an English sentence may *appear* difficult, but it is actually rather easy, if one symbolizes in steps and practices with a few exercises. Let's look at an example. Consider the statement:

> *If Paul didn't break the vase, then either Sam broke it or Dave broke it.*

Let's symbolize this in steps.

### Step 1

The first step of symbolizing is to identify the *simple* statements in the compound statement and then assign a variable to each. So, in the statement above, the *simple* statements within it are the following, preceded by the variable that will be assigned to represent each:

p = Paul broke the vase.

s = Sam broke the vase.

d = Dave broke the vase.

Notice that the antecedent of the compound statement is "Paul *didn't* break the vase." But "*not*" is a logical constant making "Paul *didn't* break the vase" a compound statement, and not a simple statement. The simple statement is "Paul broke the vase."

### Step 2

In the second step, *replace* each simple sentence with its assigned variable. But, do *not* add, remove, or change anything else in the statement. Thus, consider the statement again:

*If Paul didn't break the vase, then either Sam broke it or Dave broke it.*

Step 2 urges us to partially symbolize it as follows:

If not p, then either s or d.

Notice that all that we did was *replace* each simple sentence with its assigned variable and drew out the "*not*" in the antecedent.

### Step 3

In the third step, we identify each logical constant, as well as the scope of each. For the statement above, the logical constants are "*if*" ($\rightarrow$), "*not*" ($\sim$), and "*or*" ($\vee$):

If <u>not</u> p, then either s <u>or</u> d.

Next, we identify the *scope* of each statement, keeping in mind the following:

The scope of "*not*" ($\sim$) is *always* over *exactly one* statement ($\sim$ __ ).

The scope of "*if*" ($\rightarrow$) is *always* over *exactly two* statements—the antecedent and the consequent ($a \rightarrow c$).

The scope of "*or*" ($\vee$) is *always* over *exactly two* statements ( __ $\vee$ __ ).

Notice that the scope of "*not*" ($\sim$) is p. Thus, somewhere in the symbolized version of our statement, we will have $\sim p$.

Further, the scope of ($\vee$) is s and d. Thus, somewhere in the symbolized version of our statement, we will have $s \vee d$.

Finally, given that "*if*" always introduces the antecedent of the conditional, somewhere in the symbolized version of our statement, we will have $\sim p \rightarrow$ __. The consequent goes in the blank, completing our conditional.

To find the consequent, simply ask, "If ~ p, then what?" The answer is the disjunction (s ∨ d). So, it might be tempting to think that the completed symbolization is:

~ p → s ∨ d

However, recalling the rules for wffs, we can see that the above expression is not a wff. It is lacking parentheses around the consequent. Thus, we move to step 4.

### Step 4

In the fourth and final step, parentheses are added if needed. Thus, to complete the symbolization of the statement above, we add (), to get ~ p → (s ∨ d).

Note that parentheses are not always needed, and if they are not, then step 3 will be the final step. For example, consider the following statement, followed by the three first steps:

*If Paul goes to the movies, then Quinn will not go to the movies.*

Step 1 results:

*p* = Paul goes to the movies.

*q* = Quinn goes (will go) to the movies.

Step 2 results:

If *p*, then not *q*.

Step 3 results:

p → ~ q

Notice that there is no ambiguity in that expression, and thus it is a wff. Further, it exactly represents the statement. Thus, the symbolization is complete after step 3 in this case.

### EXERCISE 7.2

Below are 20 English compound sentences. Your task is to symbolize each. Recall that step 1 is to identify the simple statement in the compound statement and then assign a variable to it. This first step is done for you. Here are the simple sentences, and assigned variables for the first 10:

*p* = Peter enters (entered, will enter) the empty tomb.

*j* = John remains (remained, will remain) outside.

*m* = Mary sits (sat, will sit) crying.

Complete the symbolization for each of the following, recalling the steps.

1. Peter entered the empty tomb, but John remained outside and Mary sat crying.

2. Peter did not enter the empty tomb, and John did not remain outside.

*3. If Peter entered the empty tomb then John remained outside, and Mary sat crying.

*4. If Peter entered the empty tomb, then John remained outside and Mary sat crying.

5. Mary sat crying and if Peter entered the empty tomb John remained outside.

6. If Mary sat crying and John remained outside, then Peter entered the empty tomb.

7. Either Peter will enter the empty tomb or John will remain outside, and Mary will not sit crying.

8. Mary will sit crying if Peter will enter the empty tomb and John will remain outside.

*9. If Peter entered the empty tomb then if John remained outside Mary sat crying.

10. If Peter entered the empty tomb John remained outside, and if Peter entered the empty tomb Mary sat crying.

Here are the simple sentences, and assigned variables for the last ten:

$l$ = The Lord appears (appeared, will appear) to the disciples.

$d$ = The disciples are (being, were, will be) overjoyed.

$t$ = Thomas believes.

11. If either the disciples were overjoyed or Thomas believed then the Lord appeared to the disciples.

12. If the Lord appears to the disciples then either the disciples will be overjoyed or Thomas will believe.

*13. It is false that if the disciples are overjoyed and Thomas does believe, then the Lord did not appear to the disciples.

*14. If the Lord didn't appear to the disciples, then the disciples are not overjoyed and Thomas does not believe.

15. The Lord appearing to the disciples is a necessary condition for Thomas believing or the disciples being overjoyed.

16. The Lord appearing to the disciples is a sufficient condition for the disciples being overjoyed and Thomas believing.

17. Thomas will believe and the disciples will be overjoyed only if the Lord appears to the disciples.

*18. Neither Thomas believing nor the disciples being overjoyed is a necessary condition for the Lord appearing to the disciples.

19. Thomas will not believe and the disciples will not be overjoyed unless the Lord appears to the disciples.

20. Given that the Lord appeared to the disciples, Thomas believed and the disciples were overjoyed.

## Introduction to Truth Tables

Now that we understand the symbolic language of propositional logic, we move on to study methods for determining whether an argument (specifically one represented with wffs) is valid or invalid. One general method is the use of *truth tables*. More specifically, there is a *long truth table method* and a *short truth table* method for testing arguments for validity. We will learn each. But first we need an introduction to truth tables for our basic statements.

A truth table is a table that shows *all possible truth-values* for a statement, as well as how the truth-value of a compound statement depends upon the truth-values of the simpler statements composing it along with the meaning of the logical constant within it.

## Truth Table for Variable

Let's begin with the truth table for a variable—representing a simple statement. Consider the statement:

> *God exists.*

There are *only two* possible truth-values for this statement (indeed for *any* statement)—namely, *true* or *false*. If God exists in reality, then the statement is true. If not, then the statement is false. (Recall the discussion of truth in chapter 2.) A truth table does not settle which is *true*. Rather it simply represents both possibilities. So, if we stipulate that *p* stands for the simple statement "God exists," then its truth table is shown in table 7.1:

**TABLE 7.1**

| *p* |
|:---:|
| T |
| F |

Indeed, that is the truth table for *any* simple statement (or for *any* variable).

## Truth Tables for Compound Statements

As is now clear, compound statements are composed of simpler statements plus logical constants, and in more complex cases, parentheses. In the simplest cases, there is only one constant and the appropriate number of variables. Thus, in the most basic cases we have the following: ~ *p*, *p* & *q*, *p* ∨ *q*, and *p* → *q*.

A compound statement is true or false based upon the truth-value of the simpler statements composing it along with the meaning of the logical constant within it. Below are the truth-tables for the basic cases.

### Truth Table for Negation

A negation (e.g., ~ *p*) and the statement negated (e.g., *p*) *always* have opposite truth-values, given the meaning of "not" (or, ~). So, consider the statement

> *God exists,*

and its negation,

> *God does not exist.*

These have opposite truth-values, given the meaning of "*not.*" If the first is true, the second is false, and if the first is false, the second is true, and vice versa. Given this, we construct the truth table to include the possible truth-values for the negated statement, and then show the results when "*not*" (~) is applied. So, in the basic case in which we have just a single variable (*p*), there are again two possibilities: *p* is true, or it is false. Thus, we have table 7.2.

**TABLE 7.2**

| *p* | ~*p* |
|-----|------|
| T   |      |
| F   |      |

Since ~ *p* always has the truth-value opposite that of *p*, then when "~" is applied, we get the following results (table 7.3), which is the truth-table for negation:

**TABLE 7.3**

| *p* | ~*p* |
|-----|------|
| T   | F    |
| F   | T    |

Notice that in possible scenario 1 in which *p* is true, ~ *p* is false, and in possible scenario 2 in which *p* is false, ~ *p* is true.

That is the truth table for negation—it *never* changes.

### Truth Table for Conjunction

Imagine that you are presented with a box, the contents of which you cannot see, and that you are told the following *conjunction*:

*There is a red object inside the box and there is a square object inside the box.*

Given the meaning of "and," under what conditions is the conjunction true?

If you open the box and *fail* to find a red object, then the statement is false, and if you open the box and *fail* to find a square object, then the statement is false. Clearly, it is true if and only if *both* "there is a red object in the box" and "there is a square object in the box" are true. Generalizing, a conjunction (no matter what the contents) is true if and only if *both* conjuncts (the statements flanking "and" [or synonyms]) are true. Thus, table 7.4 is *always* the truth table for a conjunction:

**TABLE 7.4**

| $p$ | $q$ | $p \& q$ |
|:---:|:---:|:---:|
| T | T | T |
| T | F | F |
| F | T | F |
| F | F | F |

### Truth Table for Disjunction

Now imagine that you are presented with a box, the contents of which you cannot see, and that you are told the following *disjunction*:

> *There is a red object inside the box or there is a square object inside the box.*

Given the meaning of "or," under what conditions is the disjunction true?

If you open the box and *fail* to find a red object, <u>and</u> *fail* to find a square object, then the statement is *false*. But suppose you *do* find a red object, but *fail* to find a square object, then the disjunction is *true*. Or, if you find a square object, but *fail* to find a red object, then the disjunction is *true*.

But what if you find *both* a red object and a square object (indeed what if you find a red square)? To answer this, consider two uses of the word "or"—an *inclusive* use and an *exclusive* use:

*Exclusive "or"*

Sometimes when we utter a disjunction, we intend to communicate that one of the disjuncts (the statements flanking "or") is true, *and* only one is true—that is, we intend to express that at least one, and at most one, of the disjuncts is true. In this case, we are intending the "or" in the disjunction to be an *exclusive* "or."

Often, we make this exclusive use explicit by choosing disjuncts that are contradictory, as in:

> *Either it is raining, or it is not raining.*

However, we can intend an exclusive "or" even if the disjuncts are not contradictory, such as:

> *Either you clean your room, or you cannot go to the movie.*

While those disjuncts are not contradictory, still when one (typically a parent) utters such a disjunction, one intends the disjuncts to be exclusive—one and only one disjunct is true.

*Inclusive "or"*

In contrast, sometimes we utter a disjunction and intend to express that *at least* one of the disjuncts is true, but also <u>permit</u> *both* to be true. For example, in some restaurants you may be given the option to have soup or salad with your dinner—that is, you are told the following:

> *You can have soup with your dinner, or you can have salad with your dinner.*

However, in typical cases, you *can* have both, though you may have to pay a little more. In such a case, the disjunction is still *true*. This is because the disjunction is using an *inclusive* "or," which means that *at least* one is true, period. This is compatible with both being true.

Here is another example to think about for *inclusive* "or." Suppose you are standing outside your house at night and see light coming from a single window. You know that there are two lamps that could produce light from that window—the lamp positioned to the right of the couch and the lamp positioned to the left of the couch. Thus, you know that the following disjunction is true:

> The light is coming from the right lamp, or it's coming from the left lamp.

While either the left or right could be producing the light that you see, it could also be that *both* lamps are on. If so, the disjunction is still *true*, since the "or" is an *inclusive* "or."

### Back to Truth Table for Disjunction

In basic propositional logic, the logic we are studying in this chapter, "or" is treated as an *inclusive* "or." Thus, consider again the original disjunction example:

> There is a red object inside the box or there is a square object inside the box.

We already established that if both disjuncts are false, the disjunction is false (indeed this is the case whether one is working with an inclusive "or" or an exclusive "or"), and that if one but not the other of these is true, then the disjunction is true. Further, since we treat this as an *inclusive* "or" in basic propositional logic, it is also true if both disjuncts are true.

Thus, for basic propositional logic, table 7.5 is *always* the truth table for a disjunction:

**TABLE 7.5**

| $p$ | $q$ | $p \vee q$ |
|:---:|:---:|:---:|
| T | T | T |
| T | F | T |
| F | T | T |
| F | F | F |

### Truth Table for Conditional

To better understand the truth table for conditional, recall the two relationships expressed—the *sufficient condition* relation going from the antecedent to the consequent, and the *necessary condition* relation going from the consequent to the antecedent. That is, what is being expressed in a conditional is that the antecedent being true is a sufficient condition for the consequent to be true, and the consequent being true is a necessary condition for the antecedent to be true. So, consider the following conditional:

> *If the table is square, then the table has four sides.*

In this conditional, one is *not* saying that the table *is* square, nor that it *has* four sides. Rather, one is saying that *the table being square* guarantees that *it has four sides*, and that *it being four-sided* is required for *it to be square*.

So, under what conditions is a conditional true, and under what conditions is it false? The answer is simple—it is true under any possible scenario in which the antecedent really does guarantee the consequent, and the consequent really is required for the antecedent. It is false otherwise. Let's consider some examples, beginning with the example from above:

> *If the table is square, then the table has four sides.*

Since in every possible scenario in which there is a square table, that table has four sides, we know that being square guarantees having four sides, and in every possible scenario, being four-sided is required for being square.

On the other hand, consider the following conditional:

> *If I own an animal, then I own a dog.*

In this case, while "I own an animal" and "I own a dog" *can both be* true, it can also be the case that I own an animal, but I do *not* own a dog. Thus, owning an animal does not *guarantee* owning a dog. Further, owning a dog is not *necessary* for owning an animal. Thus, that conditional is *false*.

What if the *antecedent* is *false*? Consider the following example:

> *If Mr. Gates is US president in 2019, then the United States has a male president in 2019.*

Notice that this conditional is *true*, since *Mr.* Gates being the US president *guarantees* that the United States has a *male* president, and *the* United States *having a male president* is *required* for *Mr.* Gates to be the US president. Further, it is true even though the antecedent is actually *false*—Mr. Gates is *not* US president in 2019. The *necessary* and *sufficient* relationships hold even though the antecedent is false.

Similar points can be made if *both* antecedent and consequent are actually false. Consider this example:

> *If Ms. Smith is US president in 2019, then the United States has a female president in 2019.*

This conditional is also *true*, since *Ms.* Smith being the US president *guarantees* that the United States has a *female* president, and *the United States having a female president* is *required* for *Ms.* Smith to be the US president. Further, it is true even though both the antecedent and consequent are actually *false*.

In short, what makes a conditional true or false is *not* the actual truth value of the antecedent and consequent, but rather the relationship between the two. It is false if and only if the antecedent does not guarantee the consequent, and the consequent is *not* necessary for the antecedent. Thus, table 7.6 is *always* the truth table for a conditional:

**TABLE 7.6**

| p | q | p → q |
|---|---|---|
| T | T | T |
| T | F | F |
| F | T | T |
| F | F | T |

Table 7.7 provides an overview of the truth tables for the four basic types of statements—negation, conjunction, disjunction, and conditional.

**TABLE 7.7**

| Variable | | Negation | |
|---|---|---|---|
| p | | p | ~p |
| T | | T | F |
| F | | F | T |

| Conjunction | | | Disjunction | | | Conditional | | |
|---|---|---|---|---|---|---|---|---|
| p | q | p & q | p | q | p ∨ q | p | q | p → q |
| T | T | T | T | T | T | T | T | T |
| T | F | F | T | F | T | T | F | F |
| F | T | F | F | T | T | F | T | T |
| F | F | F | F | F | F | F | F | T |

## Truth Tables for Longer Well-Formed Formulas (WFFs)

So far, we have learned the truth tables for the basic compound statements (wffs). We can now build upon that and use the basic truth tables to construct truth tables for longer statements (wffs). In this section, we will learn how to construct such tables.

As you have seen, a truth table consists in a number of *rows* (horizontal) representing each possible scenario, a number of *columns* (vertical) representing a wff, and a T or an F in a cell ($row_n$, $column_n$) representing the truth-value of the wff in that specific possible scenario. As a result, to correctly fill out the truth table, one must have the following:

- The correct number of rows to represent all possible scenarios,
- The correct number of columns to represent all the given wffs,

- T and F in all the correct places.

In order to get the correct number of *rows*, use the following:

*The number of rows is equal to 2n, where n is equal to the number of variables.*

For example, recall that for the truth table for a variable, or for a negated variable, there is exactly one variable, and thus the number of rows is $2^1 = 2$ rows. And that there are two variables in the basic truth tables for conjunction, disjunction, and conditional, and thus the number of rows is $2^2 = 4$ rows. If there are three variables in a statement (or argument), then the number of rows is $2^3 = 8$ rows, et cetera. So, we have:

Two variables = $2^1$ = 2 rows

Two variables = $2^2$ = 4 rows

Two variables = $2^3$ = 8 rows

Two variables = $2^4$ = 16 rows

Two variables = $2^5$ = 32 rows

Et cetera.

Further, each row represents a different possible scenario of truth-value combinations, with the entire table representing *all possible* combinations. In order to ensure that *all possible* combinations of truth-values are represented, follow the patterns shown in table 7.8:

**TABLE 7.8**

| $p$ | $p$ | $q$ | $p$ | $q$ | $r$ | $p$ | $q$ | $r$ | $s$ | Etc. |
|---|---|---|---|---|---|---|---|---|---|---|
| T | T | T | T | T | T | T | T | T | T | |
| F | T | F | T | T | F | T | T | T | F | |
| | F | T | T | F | T | T | T | F | T | |
| | F | F | T | F | F | T | T | F | F | |
| | | | F | T | T | T | F | T | T | |
| | | | F | T | F | T | F | T | F | |
| | | | F | F | T | T | F | F | T | |
| | | | F | F | F | T | F | F | F | |
| | | | | | | F | T | T | T | |
| | | | | | | F | T | T | F | |
| | | | | | | F | T | F | T | |
| | | | | | | F | T | F | F | |
| | | | | | | F | F | T | T | |
| | | | | | | F | F | T | F | |
| | | | | | | F | F | F | T | |
| | | | | | | F | F | F | F | |

Notice that if there is one variable, we alternate T / F starting with T. With two variables, we alternate T T / F F with the first variable, and then T / F with the second. With three variables, we alternate T T T / F F F with the first variable, followed by T T / F F with the second, and T / F with the third, et cetera. This ensures that we have *all possible* truth-value combinations represented.

For the *columns*, each wff in the given statement gets its own column, from the variables to the whole wff, beginning with the variable and filling right in the order of complexity, ending with the whole wff. Consider the following example:

$\sim p \rightarrow (q \,\&\sim r)$

The sub-wffs in this wff include the variables, the negated variables, and the conjunction. Each is placed in its own column, followed by the whole wff, as follows:

$p \mid q \mid r \mid \sim p \mid \sim r \mid q \,\&\sim r \mid \sim p \rightarrow (q \,\&\sim r)$

Finally, to *correctly place T or F in cell* ($\text{row}_n$, $\text{column}_n$) use the basic truth tables for negation, conjunction, disjunction, and conditional.

Putting this all together, let's fill out a truth table for the statement, step by step, Again, our statement is $\sim p \rightarrow (q \,\&\sim r)$. Table 7.9 shows the set-up.

**TABLE 7.9**

|   | $p$ | $q$ | $r$ | $\sim p$ | $\sim r$ | $q \,\&\sim r$ | $\sim p \rightarrow (q \,\&\sim r)$ |
|---|---|---|---|---|---|---|---|
| 1 | T | T | T |  |  |  |  |
| 2 | T | T | F |  |  |  |  |
| 3 | T | F | T |  |  |  |  |
| 4 | T | F | F |  |  |  |  |
| 5 | F | T | T |  |  |  |  |
| 6 | F | T | F |  |  |  |  |
| 7 | F | F | T |  |  |  |  |
| 8 | F | F | F |  |  |  |  |

Table 7.10 shows the correct placement of T or F in the $\sim p$ column, which is determined by (a) using the basic truth table for negation and (b) using the $p$ column as input.

**TABLE 7.10**

|   | $p$ | $q$ | $r$ | $\sim p$ | $\sim r$ | $q \,\&\sim r$ | $\sim p \rightarrow (q \,\&\sim r)$ |
|---|---|---|---|---|---|---|---|
| 1 | T | T | T | F |  |  |  |
| 2 | T | T | F | F |  |  |  |
| 3 | T | F | T | F |  |  |  |
| 4 | T | F | F | F |  |  |  |
| 5 | F | T | T | T |  |  |  |
| 6 | F | T | F | T |  |  |  |
| 7 | F | F | T | T |  |  |  |
| 8 | F | F | F | T |  |  |  |

Table 7.11 shows the correct placement of T or F in the ~ r column, which is determined by (a) using the basic truth table for negation and (b) using the r column as input.

**TABLE 7.11**

|   | p | q | r | ~p | ~r | q & ~r | ~p → (q & ~r) |
|---|---|---|---|---|---|---|---|
| 1 | T | T | T | F | F | | |
| 2 | T | T | F | F | T | | |
| 3 | T | F | T | F | F | | |
| 4 | T | F | F | F | T | | |
| 5 | F | T | T | T | F | | |
| 6 | F | T | F | T | T | | |
| 7 | F | F | T | T | F | | |
| 8 | F | F | F | T | T | | |

Table 7.12 shows the correct placement of T or F in the q & ~ r column, which is determined by (a) using the basic truth table for conjunction and (b) using the q and ~ r columns as input.

**TABLE 7.12**

|   | p | q | r | ~p | ~r | q & ~r | ~p → (q & ~r) |
|---|---|---|---|---|---|---|---|
| 1 | T | T | T | F | F | F | |
| 2 | T | T | F | F | T | T | |
| 3 | T | F | T | F | F | F | |
| 4 | T | F | F | F | T | F | |
| 5 | F | T | T | T | F | F | |
| 6 | F | T | F | T | T | T | |
| 7 | F | F | T | T | F | F | |
| 8 | F | F | F | T | T | F | |

Finally, table 7.13 shows the correct placement of T or F in the ~ p → (q & ~ r) column, determined by (a) using the basic truth table for conditional and (b) using the ~ p and (q & ~ r) column as input.

**TABLE 7.13**

|   | p | q | r | ~p | ~r | q & ~r | ~p → (q & ~r) |
|---|---|---|---|---|---|---|---|
| 1 | T | T | T | F | F | F | T |
| 2 | T | T | F | F | T | T | T |
| 3 | T | F | T | F | F | F | T |
| 4 | T | F | F | F | T | F | T |
| 5 | F | T | T | T | F | F | F |
| 6 | F | T | F | T | T | T | T |
| 7 | F | F | T | T | F | F | F |
| 8 | F | F | F | T | T | F | F |

Table 7.14 shows the completed and correct truth table for $\sim p \rightarrow (q \& \sim r)$:

**TABLE 7.14**

|   | $p$ | $q$ | $r$ | $\sim p$ | $\sim r$ | $q \& \sim r$ | $\sim p \rightarrow (q \& \sim r)$ |
|---|---|---|---|---|---|---|---|
| 1 | T | T | T | F | F | F | T |
| 2 | T | T | F | F | T | T | T |
| 3 | T | F | T | F | F | F | T |
| 4 | T | F | F | F | T | F | T |
| 5 | F | T | T | T | F | F | F |
| 6 | F | T | F | T | T | T | T |
| 7 | F | F | T | T | F | F | F |
| 8 | F | F | F | T | T | F | F |

**EXERCISE 7.3**

Write out truth tables for each wff below:

1. $\sim p \& \sim q$
2. $p \rightarrow (p \vee q)$
3. $p \rightarrow (q \& r)$
4. $(p \vee q) \& \sim r$
5. $\sim ((p \rightarrow \sim q) \& (\sim p \& r))$

## Using Truth Tables to Test for Validity

Truth tables are an excellent method for testing deductive arguments for validity. In this section, we will learn how to do this, and the precision and definiteness of the method. There are two truth table methods to test an argument for validity—a long method and a short method. Let's begin with the long method.

### Long Truth Table Method

Consider the following simple argument:

Premise: Mr. Johnson's truck is not red, and it is does not have a lift kit.

Conclusion: Therefore, it does not have a lift kit.

Symbolized, the argument would look like the following:

$\sim r \& \sim k$

$\therefore \sim k$

Note that the symbol $\therefore$ is the conclusion symbol, indicating that what follows it is the conclusion.

We can test this argument for validity using a truth table. First, create a truth table for it, labeling the premise and conclusion columns, as shown in table 7.15:

**TABLE 7.15**

|   | k | r | ~k | ~r | ~r & ~k |
|---|---|---|----|----|---------|
|   |   |   | **C** |  | **P** |
| 1 | T | T | F | F | F |
| 2 | T | F | F | T | F |
| 3 | F | T | T | F | F |
| 4 | F | F | T | T | T |

Next, focus on the premise(s) and conclusion columns only, and use the following information to determine the validity of the argument:

1. Ignore any row that has at least one false premise, and instead focus on rows that have all true premises.
2. If the conclusion is true in every row in which the premises are true, then the argument is valid.
3. If *any* row has true premises and a false conclusion, then the argument is invalid.

The explanation for points 2 and 3 is this. The truth table shows *all possibilities*. So, for point 2, if the table shows that in all possible scenarios in which the premises are true, the conclusion is also true, we know that true premises *guarantee* a true conclusion, which means that the argument is valid. And, for point 3, if the table shows that there *can be* true premises with a false conclusion, then we know that this is possible, and thus that the argument is invalid.

So, consider table 7.16, and notice that in every row in which the premise is true, which is just row 4, the conclusion is also true. Since these are all the possibilities, we know that in all possible scenarios in which the premise is true for this argument, the conclusion is also true. Thus, the argument is valid.

**TABLE 7.16**

|   | k | r | ~k | ~r | ~r & ~k |
|---|---|---|----|----|---------|
|   |   |   | **C** |  | **P** |
| 1 | T | T | F | F | F |
| 2 | T | F | F | T | F |
| 3 | F | T | T | F | F |
| 4 | F | F | T | T | T |

Let's consider a bit more complicated argument:

Premise: If Pauline goes to the store, then Holly will go to the store.

Premise: If Pauline goes to the store, then Sarah will go to the store.

Conclusion: Therefore, if Holly goes to the store, then Sarah will go to the store.

Symbolized, the argument would look like the following:

$p \rightarrow h$

$p \rightarrow s$

$\therefore h \rightarrow s$

Again, we create a truth table for this, as is shown in table 7.17:

**TABLE 7.17**

|   | | | | **P1** | **P2** | **C** |
|---|---|---|---|---|---|---|
|   | **h** | **p** | **s** | $p \rightarrow h$ | $p \rightarrow s$ | $h \rightarrow s$ |
| 1 | T | T | T | T | T | T |
| 2 | T | T | F | T | F | F |
| 3 | T | F | T | T | T | T |
| 4 | T | F | F | T | T | F |
| 5 | F | T | T | F | T | T |
| 6 | F | T | F | F | F | T |
| 7 | F | F | T | T | T | T |
| 8 | F | F | F | T | T | T |

Next, we check it for validity, using the 3-point guideline. Rows 1, 3, 4, 7, and 8 have true premises. And, while rows 1, 3, 7, and 8 have true conclusions, row 4 has a *false* conclusion, which shows that it's *possible* to have true premises with a false conclusion with this argument, and thus that it is invalid—see the table 7.18.

**TABLE 7.18**

|   | | | | **P1** | **P2** | **C** |
|---|---|---|---|---|---|---|
|   | **h** | **p** | **s** | $p \rightarrow h$ | $p \rightarrow s$ | $h \rightarrow s$ |
| 1 | T | T | T | T | T | T |
| 2 | T | T | F | T | F | F |
| 3 | T | F | T | T | T | T |
| 4 | T | F | F | T | T | F |
| 5 | F | T | T | F | T | T |
| 6 | F | T | F | F | F | T |
| 7 | F | F | T | T | T | T |
| 8 | F | F | F | T | T | T |

Note that it is *incorrect* to think of this argument as being valid in rows 1, 3, 7, and 8, but invalid in row 4. Rather, all the rows show are the *possibilities*. Since row 4 has true premises with a false conclusion, the *entire table* shows that the argument is invalid.

Compare that argument to this one:

Premise: Either Kyle will buy a cat, or he will buy a fish and a bird.

Premise: He will not buy a fish and a bird.

Conclusion: Therefore, he will buy a cat.

Symbolized, the argument would look like the following:

$c \lor (f \& b)$

$\sim (f \& b)$

$\therefore c$

We create a truth table for this, as is shown in table7.19:

**TABLE 7.19**

|   |   | **C** |   |   | **P1** | **P2** |
|---|---|---|---|---|---|---|
|   | *b* | *c* | *f* | *f & b* | *c* ∨ (*f & b*) | ~(*f & b*) |
| 1 | T | T | T | T | T | F |
| 2 | T | T | F | F | T | T |
| 3 | T | F | T | T | T | F |
| 4 | T | F | F | F | F | T |
| 5 | F | T | T | F | T | T |
| 6 | F | T | F | F | T | T |
| 7 | F | F | T | F | F | T |
| 8 | F | F | F | F | F | T |

Again, we check it for validity using the three-point guideline. Notice that rows 2, 5, and 6 each have true premises. And, the conclusion is also true in *each* of these rows. Therefore, the argument is valid, since true premises *guarantee* a true conclusion in this argument—see table 7.20.

**TABLE 7.20**

|   |   | **C** |   |   | **P1** | **P2** |
|---|---|---|---|---|---|---|
|   | *b* | *c* | *f* | *f & b* | *c* ∨ (*f & b*) | ~(*f & b*) |
| 1 | T | T | T | T | T | F |
| 2 | T | T | F | F | T | T |
| 3 | T | F | T | T | T | F |
| 4 | T | F | F | F | F | T |
| 5 | F | T | T | F | T | T |
| 6 | F | T | F | F | T | T |
| 7 | F | F | T | F | F | T |
| 8 | F | F | F | F | F | T |

**EXERCISE 7.4**

Construct long truth tables for the following arguments and determine whether the argument is valid or invalid.

**\*1.** $p$

∴ $p \lor q$

**2.** $\sim p \& \sim q$

∴ $\sim p$

**3.** $\sim p \lor \sim q$

$\sim p$

∴ $\sim q$

**\*4.** $p \to (p \lor q)$

$\sim p$

∴ $\sim (p \lor q)$

**5.** $(p \lor q) \to p$

$\sim p$

∴ $\sim (p \lor q)$

**6.** $\sim (p \lor q)$

$r \to p$

∴ $\sim r$

**\*7.** $(p \lor r) \to q$

$q \& \sim r$

∴ $\sim p$

**8.** $p \lor \sim r$

$q \to r$

∴ $p \to \sim q$

**9.** $p \to q$

$q \to r$

∴ $(q \& r) \to (p \& q)$

**\*10.** $p \to q$

$\sim (q \lor r)$

∴ $\sim p$

**11.** $(p \& r) \to q$

$\sim q$

∴ $\sim p$

**12.** $p \to (r \to q)$

$\sim (p \to r)$

∴ $\sim q$

**13.** $p \to q$

$\sim (q \lor r)$

∴ $\sim p$

**14.** $(p \to q) \to r$

$r \to (p \lor q)$

∴ $(p \lor q) \to (p \to q)$

**15.** $(p \& r) \to (r \lor q)$

$\sim (r \lor q)$

∴ $\sim (p \& r)$

## Short Truth Table Method

As you probably noticed, filling out long truth tables can be quite tedious, and we've only been dealing with three variables. Imagine the headache with four or more variables. Further, it is rather easy to make careless errors in filling out all the Ts and Fs, even with good understanding of the basic truth tables. Fortunately, there is a short truth table method for dealing with arguments with many variables, which helps to minimizes careless errors. It is introduced second as understanding of the long truth table is required for understanding the short truth table method. In this section, we will learn the short truth table method.

### The Concept of the Short Method

Let's approach the short truth table method this way. Think about an *invalid* argument and a *long* truth table with its many rows showing it to be invalid. For example, consider the argument from above:

$p \to h$

$p \to s$

∴ $h \to s$

We saw that in the long truth table for this argument there are *five* rows with true premises, four of which also have a true conclusion. However, the one row (row 4) has a *false* conclusion, which is sufficient to show us that the argument is invalid. Here again is truth table 7.18:

**TABLE 7.18 (REPEATED)**

|   | h | p | s | P1<br>$p \to h$ | P2<br>$p \to s$ | C<br>$h \to s$ |
|---|---|---|---|---|---|---|
| 1 | T | T | T | T | T | T |
| 2 | T | T | F | T | F | F |
| 3 | T | F | T | T | T | T |
| 4 | T | F | F | T | T | F |
| 5 | F | T | T | F | T | T |
| 6 | F | T | F | F | F | T |
| 7 | F | F | T | T | T | T |
| 8 | F | F | F | T | T | T |

We can approach the short truth table method as a game of trying to find a row like row 4, without having to fill out all the other rows. That is, for any argument under investigation, we are attempting to find a row which has true premises and a false conclusion. Put differently, we are attempting to prove that the argument is *invalid*. If successful, then we have proven that the row exists, and that the argument is *invalid*. If we fail, and we cannot prove that the row exists, then the argument is *valid*, and there is no row with true premises and a false conclusion. Two points to note:

Success = Invalid.

That is, *succeeding* in the goal to find a row with true premises and a false conclusion means that the row exists, and thus that the argument is invalid.

Failure = Valid.

That is, *failing* in the goal to find a row with true premises and a false conclusion means that the row does *not* exist, and thus that the argument is valid.

## How to Implement the Short Method

To implement the short truth table to test an argument for validity, follow these steps for the game.

*Step 1—Create Columns*

We begin by creating columns consisting of and only of the premises and conclusion, and label them accordingly. We do *not* have any other columns. For example, consider the argument from just above. We set up the columns as seen in table 7.21:

**TABLE 7.21**

| P1<br>$p \to h$ | P2<br>$p \to s$ | C<br>$h \to s$ |
|---|---|---|
|   |   |   |

*Step 2—Set Goal*

For any argument under consideration, the goal is *always* the same—namely, to try to prove that the premises can be true and the conclusion false simultaneously. Thus, we set the *goal* of trying to make each premise true, and the conclusion false. Note that this is *merely* a goal and does *not* mean that the premises are already true and the conclusion already false from the beginning. Rather, this is merely what we are trying to prove. We will either succeed or fail. So, as seen in table 7.22, our goal looks like this:

**TABLE 7.22**

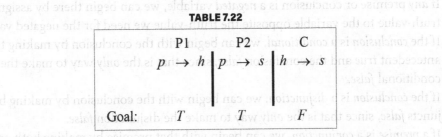

*Step 3—Create Variable Box*

We will attempt to accomplish each goal by assigning truth-values to the variables. To keep track of what truth-value is assigned to each variable, we set up a *"variable box"* to the side of the table, as seen in table 7.23:

**TABLE 7.23**

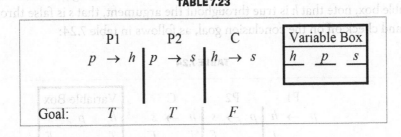

*Step 4—Attempt to Achieve Goal*

Finally, we begin filling in the short table by creating a truth-value tree from the variables to the goal. However, we do not begin randomly, as we may lengthen our task and steps. For example, we may attempt one option of achieving a goal (e.g., making premise 1 true) and fail. But we cannot stop and conclude that the argument is valid, since there may be other ways to succeed in proving that wff true or false. We'd have to explore all options before concluding that we cannot prove the goal. So, we begin by assigning the truth-values to variables that we *must* assign in order to accomplish our goal. To do this, we use the information in our basic truth tables.

Any variable (e.g., $p$) and its negation ($\sim p$) have *opposite* truth-values.

A conjunction (e.g., $p \,\&\, q$) is *true* when and *only* when both conjuncts ($p$, $q$) are *true*.

A disjunction (e.g., $p \lor q$) is *false* when and *only* when both disjuncts ($p$, $q$) are *false*.

A conditional (e.g., $p \rightarrow q$) is *false* when and *only* when its *antecedent* ($p$) is *true* and its *consequent* ($q$) is *false*, simultaneously.

That information helps us to know where to begin filling out the table in the shortest way possible. So, we can begin filling out the table using any of the following rules:

1. If *any* premise or conclusion is a variable, we can begin with that variable, since there is only one way to make that variable true or false.
2. If *any* premise or conclusion is a *negated* variable, we can begin there by assigning a truth-value to the variable opposite the truth-value we need for the negated variable.
3. If the *conclusion* is a *conditional*, we can begin with the conclusion by making the antecedent *true* and the conclusion *false*, since that is the *only* way to make the conditional *false*.
4. If the *conclusion* is a *disjunction*, we can begin with the conclusion by making both disjuncts *false*, since that is the *only* way to make the disjunction *false*.
5. If a *premise* is a *conjunction*, we can begin with that premise by making both conjuncts *true*, since that is the *only* way to make the conjunction *true*.

Let's consider a few examples, beginning with the argument that we have already set up.

Notice that the conclusion is a conditional, and that we want it to be false for our goal. So, using rule 3, we begin with the conclusion. Note that the *only* way to make it false (for our goal) is to make *h* true and *s* false. Thus, we record those truth-value assignments to the variables in the variable box, note that *h* is true throughout the argument, that *s* is false throughout the argument, and check off on the conclusion goal, as follows in table 7.24:

**TABLE 7.24**

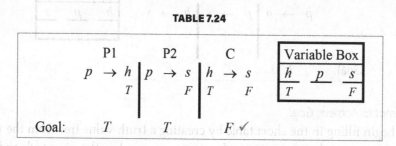

Having succeeded in the conclusion goal, we move to the premises. Notice that premise 1 is a conditional, and that its consequent *h* is *true*. Since a conditional is *false* only if it has a *false* consequent, we know that premise 1 is *true*, and thus we can check off on that goal as well, as seen in table 7.25:

**TABLE 7.25**

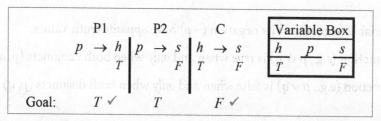

This leaves premise 2. It is a conditional, and it has a false consequent (*s*). Thus, in order to make premise 2 *true*, we need to make the antecedent *false*, since if we make the antecedent true, the results would be a true antecedent with a false consequent, resulting in a *false* premise. So, we record *p* as *false* in our variable box, note that *p* is false throughout the argument, and we can check off on that goal, as seen in table 7.26:

**TABLE 7.26**

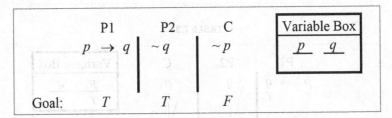

Since we have checked off on each goal, indicating that we have *succeeded* in proving each goal, we know that we have found the row that shows that this argument can have true premises and a false conclusion. Thus, we know that this argument is *invalid*.

Let's next consider a *valid* example, to compare. Consider the following argument (already set up) in table 7.27:

**TABLE 7.27**

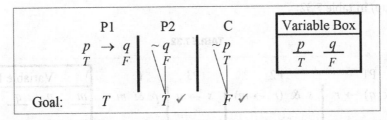

Since both premise 2 and the conclusion are negated variables, rule 2 allows us to begin with either one. Let's do them in one step. Thus, we make *p* true, so that ~ *p* is *false* for the conclusion, and *q* false, so that ~ *q* is *true* for premise 2. As illustrated in table 7.28, we record that in the variable box and note those truth-values throughout the argument.

**TABLE 7.28**

This brings us to premise 1. Notice that, as table 7.29 shows, it is a conditional, and that it has a *true* antecedent (because of what we were *forced* to do to make the conclusion false), and a *false* consequent (because of what we were *forced* to do to make premise 2 true). This means that premise 1 is *false* (not true), contrary to our goal.

**TABLE 7.29**

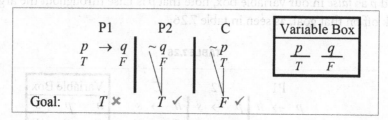

And, if we were to make an adjustment to it, by either making the antecedent false or the consequent true, the results would be failure to achieve either making premise 2 true, or the conclusion false. See tables 7.30 and 7.31, respectively, for this.

**TABLE 7.30**

**TABLE 7.31**

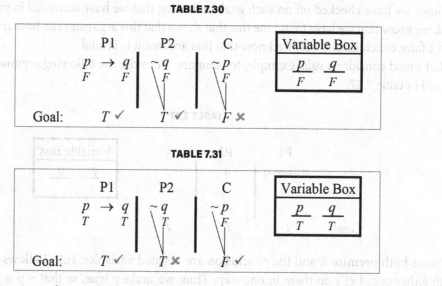

Since we *cannot* achieve our goal of making the premises true and the conclusion false, we know that this row does not exist on the long truth table, and thus that this argument is *valid*.

Let's consider one more example in which we encounter a scenario in which we are not *forced* to assign a particular truth-value to a variable. So, consider the following argument (already set up) in table 7.32:

**TABLE 7.32**

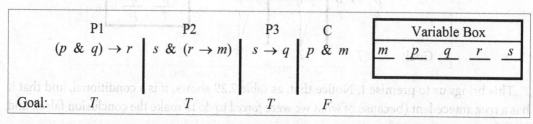

With this argument, we begin with premise 2, since it is a conjunction, and there is only one way to make a conjunction true—namely, by making both conjuncts true. So, we make *s* true, and note that $r \to m$ has to be true as well, though at this point we do not assign a truth-value to *r* or *m* since we are not forced to assign a particular truth-value to either. We will come back to those later in the process. So, as seen in table 7.33, we record that *s* is true in the variable box and note this throughout the argument.

**TABLE 7.33**

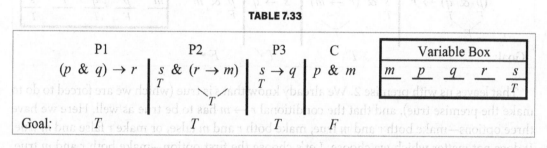

Next, we turn to premise 3, since we know that *s* is true (because of premise 2). Since premise 3 is a conditional, and since it has a true antecedent, the consequent also has to be *true*, if the conditional is to be true (which is our goal). Thus, we make *q* true. As table 7.34 shows, we record this in the variable box, check off on goal 3 as achieved, and note throughout the argument that *q* is true.

**TABLE 7.34**

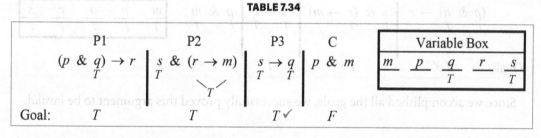

At this point, we are not *forced* to assign any particular truth-value to any other variable, but we have options. This is *typically* (though not always) an indication that the argument is invalid and that there are multiple rows in the long truth table with true premises and a false conclusion. We just have to find *one* of these rows to prove that the argument is invalid. So, we move forward to find one.

If we look over the whole argument, note that *p* is in both premise 1 and in the conclusion. Notice that if we make *p* false, it makes the conclusion false, since the conclusion is a conjunction and if either conjunct is false, the conjunction is false. Thus, by making *p* false, we thereby accomplish our goal of making the conclusion false. Turning our attention back to premise 1, we notice two things. First, it is a conditional, and second, its antecedent is a conjunction, with *p* as a conjunct. So, by making *p* false, we make the conjunction false, which makes the antecedent false, which makes the conditional *true*. So, by making *p* false, we thereby accomplish two goals—making the conclusion false and premise 1 true. We record this in the variable box, note this throughout the argument, and check off on goal 1 and goal 4 as achieved, as shown in table 7.35:

**TABLE 7.35**

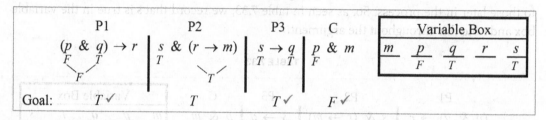

That leaves us with premise 2. We already know that *s* is true (which we are forced to do to make the premise true), and that the conditional *r* → *m* has to be true as well. Here we have three options—make both *r* and *m* true, make both *r* and *m* false, or make *r* false and *m* true. It does not matter which we choose. Let's choose the first option—make both *r* and *m* true. We record this in the variable box, note this throughout the argument, and check off on goal 2 as achieved, as shown in table 7.36:

**TABLE 7.36**

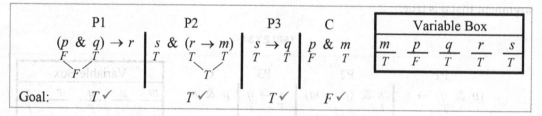

Since we accomplished all the goals, we successfully proved this argument to be *invalid*.

**EXERCISE 7.5**

Construct *short* truth tables for the following arguments and determine whether the argument is valid or invalid.

*1. $p \rightarrow (q \,\&\, m)$

$(q \,\&\, m) \rightarrow r$

~ *r*

∴ ~ *p*

2. $(s \,\&\, q) \vee p$

$p \rightarrow w$

$r \rightarrow s$

∴ $(r \,\&\, q) \rightarrow w$

3. $p \rightarrow (q \vee r)$

~ $(q \vee r) \,\&\, s$

∴ ~ *p* & *s*

*4. ~ $(q \rightarrow m) \rightarrow s$

~ *s* ∨ ~ *p*

$r \rightarrow p$

∴ $(q \rightarrow m) \vee r$

5. ~ $p \rightarrow (q \vee r)$

$r \rightarrow (s \,\&\, w)$

~ *q*

∴ ~ $p \rightarrow$ ~ *w*

6. $p \rightarrow (q \,\&\, r)$

$(q \,\&\, r) \rightarrow (s \vee w)$

∴ $p \rightarrow (s \vee w)$

**\*7.** $p \to q$          **9.** $(p \& q) \to (r \vee \sim s)$          **10.** $p \& (q \& n)$

    $r \to s$              $(n \vee q) \& (s \to p)$              $m \to p$

    $\sim r \vee \sim p$              $\sim n \& p$              $r \to \sim q$

    $\therefore \sim s \vee \sim q$              $s \to m$              $s \vee r$

**8.** $\sim p \to q$              $\therefore s \to r$              $\therefore m \& n$

    $s \vee \sim r$

    $p \vee (q \to r)$

    $\therefore s \vee p$

## Important Deductive Patterns

We will finish this chapter by considering four **valid** patterns that are important for all critical thinkers to know well. Additionally, there are four *invalid* patterns that can be mistaken for the four valid patterns, but are actually formal fallacies.

### Valid Patterns

The *valid* patterns are:

> Modus Ponens (also called *Affirming the Antecedent*)
>
> Modus Tollens (also called *Denying the Consequent*)
>
> Hypothetical Syllogism
>
> Disjunctive Syllogism

We'll consider each in turn, beginning with *modus ponens*.

### Modus Ponens

The first pattern is *modus ponens*, or *affirming the antecedent*. "Modus ponens" is Latin for *mode of affirming*. It has the following form:

> Premise: If *p*, then *q*
>
> Premise: *p*
>
> Conclusion: *q*

Or, symbolized:

> $p \to q$
>
> $p$
>
> $\therefore q$

Notice that the first premise is a conditional, and the second is the *affirmation* of its *antecedent*.[2] This is why its pattern is named *affirming the antecedent* (or, *modus ponens*—way of *affirming*).

It is *valid* since the first premise states that p guarantees q, and the second affirms that p is true, which thereby *guarantees* the conclusion—namely, that q is true. Further, a modus ponens argument is valid in every possible scenario, whether the *content* contains true statements or false statements. Consider the following example:

Premise: If Mexico is part of the United States, then Mexico is in Europe.

Premise: Mexico *is* part of the United States.

Conclusion: [Therefore,] Mexico is in Europe.

This argument is valid since it exhibits the *modus ponens* pattern. This is the case even though all the statements are false.

## Modus Tollens

The second pattern is *modus tollens*, or *denying the consequent*. "Modus tollens" is Latin for *mode of denying*. It has the following form:

Premise: If p, then q

Premise: *not q*

Conclusion: *not p*

Or, symbolized:

$p \rightarrow q$

$\sim q$

$\therefore \sim p$

Notice that the first premise is also a conditional. But, with this pattern, the *consequent* (q) is *denied* (or negated) in the second premise. This is why it is called *denying the consequent* (or, *modus tollens*—way of *denying*).

It is *valid* since the first premise states that q is required for p, and the second *denies* that q is true, which thereby *guarantees* the conclusion—namely, that p is *false*. Further, just like modus ponens, a *modus tollens* argument is valid in every possible scenario, whether the *content* contains true statements or false statements. Consider the following example:

Premise: If Donald Trump is human, then Donald Trump is a man.

Premise: Donald Trump is not a man.

Conclusion: [Therefore,] Donald Trump is *not* human.

---

2. While the condition is listed as the first premise, and the affirmation of the antecedent the second, in this standard form presentation the conditional does *not* have to be the first premise.

This argument is valid since it exhibits the *modus tollens* pattern. This is the case even though all the statements are false.

## Hypothetical Syllogism

The third pattern is *hypothetical syllogism*. It has the following form:

Premise: If *p*, then *q*

Premise: If *q*, then *r*

Conclusion: If *p*, then *r*

Or, symbolized:

$p \rightarrow q$

$q \rightarrow r$

$\therefore p \rightarrow r$

Another name for a conditional statement is "*hypothetical* statement," and since the argument is a *syllogism*, we get the name *hypothetical syllogism*. It is *valid* since if *p* guarantees *q*, and *q* guarantees *r*, it follows by transitivity that *p* guarantees *r*, which is the conclusion.

Further, just like the first two patterns, *hypothetical syllogism* is valid in every possible scenario, whether the *content* contains true statements or false statements. Consider the following example:

Premise: If Las Vegas is in Asia, then Las Vegas is in the Indian Ocean.

Premise: If Las Vegas is in the Indian Ocean, then Las Vegas is on the moon.

Conclusion: [Therefore,] if Las Vegas is in Asia, then Las Vegas is on the moon.

This argument is valid since it exhibits the *hypothetical syllogism* pattern. This is the case even though all the statements are false.

## Disjunctive Syllogism

The final pattern is *disjunctive syllogism*. It has the following form:

Premise: *p* or *q*

Premise: *not p*

Conclusion: *q*

Or, symbolized:

$p \vee q$

$\sim p$

$\therefore q$

This name derives from the fact that the first premise is a *disjunction,* and the argument is a *syllogism*—hence, it is called a *disjunctive syllogism.*

As with the other patterns, *disjunctive syllogism* is valid in every possible scenario, whether the *content* contains true statements or false statements. Consider the following example:

Premise: Either that dog is a cat, or that dog is a bird.

Premise: It is not a cat.

Conclusion: [Therefore,] that dog is a bird.

This argument is valid since it exhibits the *disjunctive syllogism* pattern. This is the case even though all the statements are false.

Each of these arguments can be proven valid by truth tables, which we will leave as an exercise for you.

## Invalid Patterns

In contrast to the four valid patterns just given, there are four *invalid* patterns, which may *appear* to be valid, but are not. They may *appear* to be valid given that in each case they resemble one of the valid patterns. These invalid patterns are actually formal fallacies—they are *fallacies* because they are bad arguments, and *formal* because the fallacy is based on the form or structure of the argument. Let's have a look at these:

Affirming the Consequent

Denying the Antecedent

Erroneous Hypothetical Syllogism

Erroneous Disjunctive Syllogism

### Affirming the Consequent

Let's begin with *Affirming the Consequent.* It has the following pattern:

Premise: If *p*, then *q*

Premise: *q*

Conclusion: *p*

Or, symbolized:

$p \rightarrow q$

$q$

$\therefore p$

Notice that it *resembles* modus ponens. However, there is an important difference. With modus ponens one affirms the *antecedent* in premise 2. However, in *affirming the consequent*, one affirms the *consequent* of the conditional in premise 2. Hence, the name "affirming the consequent."

This is *invalid* because while the antecedent of a conditional guarantees the consequent, it does *not* follow from this that the consequent guarantees the antecedent. Hence, affirming the consequent does not, by itself, guarantee the antecedent. Here's an example:

Premise: If the earth has two moons, the earth has at least one moon.

Premise: The earth has at least one moon.

Conclusion: [Therefore,] the earth has two moons.

Clearly both premises are true, while the conclusion is false. Thus, this argument is invalid.

### Denying the Antecedent

Next consider *Denying the Antecedent*. It has this pattern:

Premise: If *p*, then *q*

Premise: *not p*

Conclusion: *not q*

Or, symbolized:

$p \rightarrow q$

$\sim p$

$\therefore \sim q$

Notice that it *resembles* modus tollens, but is importantly different in that unlike modus tollens, in the second premise of *denying the antecedent* one is *denying* the *antecedent* of the conditional of the first premise. This is invalid because while the consequent is necessary for the antecedent, in the conditional, it does not follow from this that the antecedent is necessary for the consequent. Hence, denying the antecedent does not, by itself, guarantee the falsity of the consequent. Here's an example:

Premise: If the Pentagon is square, the Pentagon has more than two sides.

Premise: It's false that the Pentagon is square.

Conclusion: [So,] it's false that the Pentagon has more than two sides.

Clearly both premises are true, while the conclusion is false. Thus, this argument is *invalid* as well.

### Erroneous Hypothetical Syllogism

There is not an official name for the next pattern, and thus we are calling it "*erroneous hypothetical syllogism*." The pattern is:

Premise: If *p*, then *q*

Premise: If *p*, then *r*

Conclusion: If *q*, then *r*

Or, symbolized:

$p \rightarrow q$

$p \rightarrow r$

$\therefore q \rightarrow r$

Notice that it *resembles* hypothetical syllogism, but is importantly different in that the second premise and conclusion are swapped in *erroneous hypothetical syllogism*. This is invalid because *p* can guarantee both *q* and *r*, without *q* guaranteeing *r*. Here is an example:

Premise: If that object is square, then that object has at least two sides.

Premise: If that object is square, then that object has four sides.

Conclusion: [So,] if that object has at least two sides, then that object has four sides.

Again, both premises are true, while the conclusion is false. Thus, this argument is *invalid*.

## Erroneous Disjunctive Syllogism

There is not an official name for the next pattern, and thus we are calling it "*Erroneous Disjunctive Syllogism*." The pattern is:

Premise: Either *p* or *q*

Premise: *p*

Conclusion: not *q*

Or, symbolized:

$p \vee q$

$p$

$\therefore \sim q$

Notice that it *resembles* disjunctive syllogism, but is importantly different in that the second premise and conclusion are swapped in *erroneous disjunctive syllogism*. However, this pattern is invalid *only with* inclusive "or." The pattern is valid with *exclusive* "or." Since we are working with an *inclusive* "or" in basic propositional logic, the given mere fact that one of the disjuncts is true, as stated in the second premise, it does not follow that the other is false, as stated in the conclusion. So, the pattern is invalid with an *inclusive* "or." Here's an example:

Premise: Either Las Vegas is in Nevada, or Los Angeles is in California.

Premise: Las Vegas is in Nevada.

Conclusion: [So,] it's false that Los Angeles is in California.

Both premises are true, while the conclusion is false. Thus, this argument is invalid.

Each of these arguments can be proven invalid by truth tables, which we will leave as an exercise for you. Figure 7.2 shows a summary of the eight patterns:

## Deductive Patterns

| Valid Patterns | Invalid Patterns |
|---|---|
| **Modus Ponens**<br>(Affirming the Antecedent)<br><br>$p \rightarrow q$<br><br>$p$<br><br>$\therefore q$ | **Affirming the Consequent**<br><br>$p \rightarrow q$<br><br>$q$<br><br>$\therefore p$ |
| **Modus Tollens**<br>(Denying the Consequent)<br><br>$p \rightarrow q$<br><br>$\sim q$<br><br>$\therefore \sim p$ | **Denying the Antecedent**<br><br>$p \rightarrow q$<br><br>$\sim p$<br><br>$\therefore \sim q$ |
| **Hypothetical Syllogism**<br><br>$p \rightarrow q$<br><br>$q \rightarrow r$<br><br>$\therefore p \rightarrow r$ | **Erroneous Hypothetical Syllogism**<br><br>$p \rightarrow q$<br><br>$p \rightarrow r$<br><br>$\therefore q \rightarrow r$ |
| **Disjunctive Syllogism**<br><br>$p \vee q$<br><br>$\sim p$<br><br>$\therefore q$ | **Erroneous Disjunctive Syllogism**<br><br>$p \vee q$<br><br>$p$<br><br>$\therefore \sim q$ |

**FIGURE 7.2**

It is important to be familiar with these patterns as we use them all the time, and knowing which is valid and which is invalid is important for ensuring that we are using good reasoning. Further, if one encounters an argument that exhibits one of the patterns, one can very quickly identify it as valid or invalid, since the patterns have already been proven to be valid in four of the cases and invalid in the other four, and thus one is less likely to be tripped up by content.

**EXERCISE 7.6**

Identify the pattern of each of the following arguments and whether it is valid or invalid.

**\*1.** If a wave hits that bridge, the bridge will collapse.
A wave hit the bridge.
So, the bridge will collapse.

**2.** If Matthew goes without water, then he will become dehydrated.
If Matthew becomes dehydrated, he will get muscle cramps.
So, if Matthew goes without water, he will get muscle cramps.

**3.** If the egg was placed on the hot pan, the egg was fried.
The egg was fried.
Thus, the egg was placed on the hot pan.

**\*4.** Either the virus came from a lab in China or it came from a wet market in China.
The virus did not come from a wet market in China.
Therefore, the virus came from a lab in China.

**5.** If the lights in the sky were from space aliens, then the lights moved in a circular motion.
The lights did not move in circular motion.
Hence, the lights in the sky were not from space aliens.

**6.** If that vehicle is a Wrangler, then it is a Jeep.
If that vehicle is a Wrangler, then it has four wheels.
So, if that vehicle is a Jeep, then it has four wheels.

**\*7.** If objects persist over time, then time exists.
Objects don't persist over time.
Therefore, times does not exist.

**8.** If the universe is contingent and fine-tuned for life, then God exists.
The universe is contingent and fine-tuned for life.
Thus, God exists.

**9.** Either the book came from the library or it came from the university.
The book came from the library.
So, the book did not come from the university.

10. If a person has mental states, then a person is conscious.

    If a person is conscious, then a person has an immaterial soul.

    Therefore, if a person has mental states, then a person has an immaterial soul.

11. If Saul drinks coffee before bed, he will not be able to sleep.

    Saul is able to sleep.

    Therefore, Saul did not drink coffee before bed.

12. Either the radio is powered by electricity from the wall or it is battery powered.

    The radio is battery powered.

    Thus, the radio is not powered by electricity from the wall.

13. If the temperature outside is below 30°F, then the sidewalk is frozen.

    The sidewalk is frozen.

    Therefore, the temperature outside is below 30°F.

14. Either I am going to Colombia for my vacation or I am going to Switzerland for my vacation.

    I am not going to Switzerland for my vacation.

    Thus, I am going to Colombia for my vacation.

15. If your pet is warm-blooded, your pet is a bird or a mammal.

    If your pet is warm-blooded, your pet tries to maintain a constant body temperature.

    Therefore, if your pet is a bird or a mammal, then your pet tries to maintain a constant body temperature.

16. If Kyle eats healthy, he is unlikely to be overweight.

    Kyle does not eat healthy.

    So, Kyle likely to be overweight.

## Recap

In this chapter, we learned the basics of propositional logic. This included learning how to "symbolize" English statements; increasing our understanding of the logic of "not," "if," "and," and "or," and learning how to use truth-tables to test arguments for validity. We also learned a few basic logical rules, as well as some *invalid* mistakes that may be confused with those rules. Below are some important concepts and definitions:

- **Antecedent**: The antecedent is a statement in natural language or wff in symbolic logic that is part of a conditional statement, often introduced with "if" in English or coming before → in a wff, and (in a true conditional) is a sufficient condition for the consequent.
- **Compound Statement**: A compound statement is a statement that contains at least one logical constant and at least one simple statement.
  - **Negation**: For *any* statement $\phi$, not-$\phi$ is the negation of $\phi$ ($\sim \phi$ is the negation of $\phi$).
  - **Conjunction**: For *any* statements $\phi$, $\psi$, "$\phi$ and $\psi$" is a *conjunction* ($\phi$ & $\psi$ is a conjunction).

- **Disjunction**: For *any* statements φ, ψ, "φ or ψ" is a *disjunction* (φ ∨ ψ is a disjunction).
- **Conditional**: For *any* statements φ, ψ, "*if* φ, then ψ" is a *conditional* (φ → ψ is a conditional).

■ **Conjunct**: Any statement connected to another statement with "and" (&) is a conjunct.

■ **Consequent**: The consequent is a statement in natural language or wff in symbolic logic that is part of a conditional statement, often following "then" in English or coming after → in a wff, and (in a true conditional) is a necessary condition for the antecedent.

■ **Disjunct**: Any statement connected to another statement with "or" (∨) is a disjunct.

■ **Logical Constant**: Logical constants in propositional logic include *not*, *and*, *or*, and *if* in English, and are used to either modify a statement or connect two other statements. These are symbolized as ~, &, ∨, and →, respectively.

■ **Propositional Logic**: A deductive logic that studies ways of joining statements (or sentences) to form more complicated statements, *and* the logical relationships between such statements derived from the combinations.

■ **Simple Statement**: A simple statement is a statement in which there are no logical constants.

■ **Symbolic Language**: Our approach to propositional logic is with symbolic language, in which well-formed formulas are used.

- **The vocabulary** of the symbolic language of propositional logic is:
  - ▲ **Variable**: Variables (*a, b, c, ..., x, y, z*) stand for *simple* statements.
  - ▲ **Logical Constant**: The symbols ~, &, ∨, and → stand for logical constants, where ~ *always* modifies *exactly one* wff, and &, ∨, and → *always* connect *exactly two* wffs.
  - ▲ **Parentheses**: ( ) are used to clarify a complex wff.
- **Well-Formed Formula (WFF)**: A well-formed formula (wff) is a string of symbols that represents a statement using variables, logical constants, and parentheses, and satisfies the syntactic rules of the symbolic language.
- **Rules Governing WFFs**:
  1. Any *variable* (*a, b, c, ..., x, y, z*) is a well-formed formula (wff).
  2. For *any* expression φ, if φ is a wff, then ~ φ is a wff.
  3. For *any* expressions φ, ψ, if φ and ψ are wffs, (φ & ψ), (φ ∨ ψ), (φ → ψ) are wffs.
  4. Nothing else is a wff.

■ **Truth Table**: A truth table is a table that shows all possible truth-values for a statement, as well as how the truth-value of a compound statement depends upon the truth-value of the simpler statements composing it, along with the meaning of the logical constant within it.

# INDUCTIVE LOGIC I

## Statistical Syllogisms, Generalizations, Analogical Arguments, Causal Arguments

**8**

While we often use precise, exact deductive arguments in which the conclusion is already contained in the premises (and thus, we are not concluding anything beyond what is already in the premises), we also often create and evaluate arguments in which we are drawing a conclusion that goes beyond the information given in the premises—that is, we often create and evaluate *inductive arguments*.

For example, we frequently make generalized statements about a large group based only on a sample of that group. One example of this is a political poll, in which pollsters investigate what voters think about the candidates. In the poll, not every voter is interviewed, but only some, as it is neither practical nor necessary to interview every voter to draw a reasonable conclusion. Further, while the conclusion "reaches beyond" the premises, this is perfectly acceptable *if done correctly*. In this chapter, we will study how to create and evaluate such inductive arguments.

More precisely, in this chapter, we will look at four types of inductive arguments—statistical syllogisms, generalizations, analogical arguments, and causal arguments. We will study the structures of each, criteria for strength of each, and mistakes associated with each. Here are some key terms to master as we work through this chapter:

## KEY WORDS

Analogical Argument
Analogy
Causal Argument
Causal Hypothesis
Causal Statement
Faulty Analogy
Generalization
Hasty Generalization
Post Hoc Fallacy
Random Sample

Relevant Property
Representative Sample
Sample
Source Analog
Statistical Syllogism
Target Analog
Target Group
Unbiased Sample

## Statistical Syllogism

Analogical arguments, generalizations, and statistical syllogisms are somewhat similar in structure, and can be confused with each other when one is first learning to identify these arguments. We will carefully study each and the difference between them. In this section, we will look at *statistical syllogisms*. A statistical syllogism is an argument in which one applies a general statement, or statistical data, to a particular scenario. It has the following basic structure:

> Premise: A percentage of Fs are Gs.
>
> Premise: x is an F.
>
> Conclusion: x is a G.

Here is an example:

> Premise: Most German shepherds are excellent watch dogs.
>
> Premise: My dog is a German shepherd.
>
> Conclusion: My dog is an excellent watch dog.

**KEY CONCEPT:
STATISTICAL SYLLOGISM**
A **statistical syllogism** is an argument in which one applies a general statement, or statistical data, to a particular scenario.

It is called "statistical syllogism" since it is a syllogism, and the main premise is a general statistical statement, applied to a particular case.

While the general structure is as noted above, one can be more specific in one's main general, statistical premise, such as in the following example:

> Premise: 98.5% of people who get Covid-19 recover.
>
> Premise: Charlie was just diagnosed with Covid-19.
>
> Conclusion: [Thus,] probably Charlie will recover from his illness.

Statistical syllogism is a simple, straightforward argument. The strength is fixed by the percentage specified in the main statistical premise. To understand this, let's digress a bit and recall the discussion of strength from chapter 5.

Recall that for an inductive argument to be strong, the conclusion must be probably true, given the premises. This comes in degrees. Technically, an inductive argument is strong if the probability that the conclusion is true, given that the premises are true, is greater than 50% but less than 100%. In probabilistic notation, we could write it this way:

$$P\left(C_T \mid P_T\right) > 0.5 < 1.0$$

(Read: The probability that C is true, given that P is true, is greater than 0.5 [50%], but less than 1.0 [100%]).

Of course, if the probability that the conclusion is true, given the premises, is close to 50% but greater than 50%, one might want to be cautious in judging that the conclusion really is true. And, the closer that the probability that the conclusion is true (given the premises) is to

100%, the more confidence one can have that the conclusion is true, assuming one is confident that the premises are true.

Turning back to statistical syllogisms, the higher the percentage in the main, statistical statement, the higher the probability will be that the conclusion is true, given that the premises are true. For example, consider the following argument:

Premise: Sixty percent of the fish from this pond are over 10 inches in length.

Premise: I am fishing in this pond.

Conclusion: [Thus,] probably I will catch a fish that is over 10 inches in length.

It is technically a strong argument (structurally), since 60% is greater than 50%. However, a stronger argument would be:

Premise: Seventy-five percent of the fish from this pond are over 10 inches in length.

Premise: I am fishing in this pond.

Conclusion: [Thus,] probably I will catch a fish that is over 10 inches in length.

And, an even stronger argument would be:

Premise: Ninety-nine percent of the fish from this pond are over 10 inches in length.

Premise: I am fishing in this pond.

Conclusion: [Thus,] probably I will catch a fish that is over 10 inches in length.

Of course, if one says that *all the fish in the pond are over 10 inches in length*, one then will *not* be offering an inductive argument, but a (valid) deductive argument. So, in short, if the percentage given in the main, statistical premise is greater than 50% but less than 100%, then one has a strong statistical syllogism, with the strength being greater the closer it is to 100%.

---

**EXERCISE 8.1**

Identify the premises and conclusion, and the strength of the following statistical syllogisms:

1. Ben is highly likely to survive Covid-19 since he is under 44 years old, and 99.2% of people under 44 years of age survive Covid-19.

2. While only 5% of keno players win, Liam is going to win in his keno game today.

3. The Green Bay Packers win over the Chicago Bears 66% of the time, and thus the Packers are likely to beat the Bears this coming Sunday.

4. I am betting on Penny to win the dog race today, in spite of her winning percentage being only 30%.

5. Ninety-five percent of flies die within five hours after their birth, and thus we need not worry about that fly in our house, as it will be dead in less than five hours.

## Generalization

In the introduction to this chapter, we consider an example of a political poll, in which pollsters investigate what voters think about candidates in an upcoming election. In the poll, the pollsters draw a conclusion about what voters think about the candidates based on the voters interviewed. This is an example of a *generalization* argument. In a generalization, one draws a conclusion about a population (of any objects—it need not be people) from an observation of a portion of that population. The structure of a generalization is:

Premise: The *observed* xs have feature F.

Conclusion: [So,] probably all the xs have F.

> **KEY CONCEPT: GENERALIZATION**
>
> A **generalization** is an argument in which one draws a conclusion about a population from an observation of a portion of that population.

In order to assist in specifying the components of generalization arguments, let's get some terminology down. The population over which one is generalizing is the *target group* (*target* for short). The observed portion of the target is the *sample*. And the feature F is the *relevant property*. Here is an example:

Premise: All the people that I have met from Colombia have been very friendly.

Conclusion: So, probably Colombians are very friendly people.

In this example, the *sample* is *the people that I have met from Colombia*, the *target* is *Colombians*, and the *relevant property* is *very friendly*:

Sample: *the people that I have met from Colombia*

Target: *Colombians*

Relevant Property: *very friendly*

Or, consider the following example:

All the leaves on the trees in the city are green, since the leaves on the trees in my neighborhood are green.

Can *you* identify the *sample*, the *target*, and the *relevant property*?

### Note a Few Points

In order to help identify the components of a generalization, note the following. First, the *sample* and the *target* are the *same kinds of objects* (e.g., Colombians), since *the sample has been drawn from* the population.

Second, the *sample* and *target* are each collections of things. Hence, *always* identify them with a noun or *noun phrase* (NOT with a complete sentence). It will *always* be the *subject* of the sentence.

Third, the *relevant property* is a *property*. Hence, *always* identify it with a phrase like *"being F,"*—for example, *being green*; or with a phrase like "does A,"—for example, *runs fast*. Further, note that we do *not* include the subject when labeling the relevant property. For example, in the first example above, one would *not* write the relevant property as *Colombians are very friendly*, since the property is not just a property of the target but also a property of the sample. And the sample in the first example (for instance) does *not* have the property *Colombians are very friendly*. Instead, we would label it as a *property—being very friendly*, or simply *very friendly*.

### Steps to Identify Analogs, Similarities, Relevant Property

An important aspect of evaluating generalizations is to first identify the sample, the target, and the relevant property. To facilitate this identification, one can proceed in steps. To illustrate the steps, consider the following generalization:

> *I don't want to have children, because they are noisy. Every time I go to the mall or store, I see children crying. Face it, children just cry!*

### Step 1

The first step is to identify the generalization in the passage in question. Sometimes the generalization is the *entire* passage in question. However, often a generalization is not the whole passage but is embedded within a broader context, and sometimes embedded in an argument. That is the case with the example above—the generalization is embedded in a larger argument. In the example, the first sentence is *not* part of the generalization, but is the broader context. So, the first step is to clearly identify the generalization. In the passage above, the generalization is:

> *Every time I go to the mall or store, I see children crying. Face it, children just cry!*

There are four more steps in the process of identifying the components of the generalization. The order in which one does these steps ultimately does not matter and may vary depending on the generalization one is evaluating. However, in general, the following order is recommended.

### Step 2

The second step is to identify the *conclusion* of the generalization. The reason for this is that the *target* is *always* found in the conclusion—it is the subject of the conclusion. So, by identifying the conclusion, we have helped to focus in on the target, which we will identify in the next step. In the generalization we are considering, the conclusion is:

> *children just cry!*

(The phrase "face it" is simply an expression of the confidence level that the arguer has in the conclusion but is not part of the conclusion.)

### Step 3

In the third step, we identify the *target*. Remember that the target is a *collection* of things, picked out by a *noun* or *noun phrase*. It will *always* be the *subject term* of the conclusion. Thus, we identify the *subject term* of the conclusion, and we have thereby identified the *target*. In the conclusion above, the subject term (collection) is *children*.

> Target: *children*

## Step 4

The fourth step is to identify the *sample*. Remember that the *sample* is drawn from the target—that is, the sample is just a sub-collection of the target group. Thus, if the target consists in As, the sample **must** also be As, but just a smaller portion of the As. We have already identified the target to be *children*. Thus, the sample **must** also be *children*, but just a smaller portion of the children. Which smaller portion?

To answer this, we turn our attention to the premise(s). The *sample* is *always* in the premise(s). Further, remember that the sample is also a collection of things just like the target and is picked out by a *noun* or *noun phrase*. It will *always* be the *subject* of the premise(s). In the premise in the example, the subject term is *children I see in the mall or store*. Since we have identified the subject, we have *thereby* identified our *sample*. So, the sample is:

> Sample: *children I see in the mall or store*

## Step 5

The final step is to identify the *relevant property*. Remember that the relevant property is the *property* had by *both* the sample and target. It is usually mentioned in both the premise and conclusion, and if it is, it is found in the *predicate* of the premise and conclusion. It is *what is being said of* the sample and target. So, what is said of the *children I see in the mall or store* and the *children* in general? They *cry*! Thus, the relevant property is **cry** or *is a crying thing*:

> Relevant Property: *cry* or *is a crying thing*

So, consider again the generalization:

> *Every time I go to the mall or store, I see children crying. Face it, children just cry!*

We have (correctly) identified the *sample, target,* and *relevant property* as:

> Sample: *children I see in the mall or store*
> Target: *children*
> Relevant Property: *cry* or *is a crying thing*

## Assessing the Strength of Generalizations

The first step in evaluating a generalization is to identify its components, which we have already learned how to do. Next, we want to evaluate the *structure* of the generalization—that is, we want to identify its strength. Remember that an inductive argument is strong if and only if given true premises, the conclusion is probably true as well (though not guaranteed). So, a generalization has a *strong* structure if and only if its premises make the conclusion probably true. There are three features of a *generalization* that contribute to its strength.

- Sample Size
- Representativeness of the Sample
- Unbiased Sample

We will consider each of these in turn.

### Sample Size

It is probably somewhat obvious that if one generalizes over a population, one needs a sufficiently large sample if the generalization is to be strong.

*How large does the sample need to be?*

The answer is that the appropriate size of the sample is relative to each generalization. If one is generalizing over a population of 50, then what counts as a large enough sample will be different than if one is generalizing over a population of 10 million.

Further, the more *diverse* the target, the larger the sample will have to be (up to a point) in order for the sample to represent the target. If one is generalizing over the American population, then given its diversity, one would need a fairly large sample to represent that diversity. But if one is generalizing over all the coffee in a large vat, then one would not need that large of a sample because the coffee is homogenous. A few cups may be a good enough sample size.

The strength criterion can be expressed as follows:

Sample Size Criterion: Up to a point, the larger the sample, relative to the target group, the stronger the argument.

The reason for the clause "up to a point" is that the law of large numbers informs us (roughly) that when the sample is large enough to achieve representativeness, increasing the sample size beyond that point does not substantially increase representativeness. Thus, the sample size only needs to reach a certain point.

If the sample size of a generalization is too small relative to the target, then the argument commits the *logical fallacy* called hasty *generalization*—that is, one is guilty of committing a hasty generalization. Here is an example:

*I don't want to go to that restaurant. The staff is very rude, which I know because the hostess that sat us in our previous visit was quite rude.*

Notice that in this generalization, the arguer is generalizing over many (diverse) staff members based on a sample of **one**! Clearly, that is not nearly large enough, and the arguer is guilty of committing a hasty generalization.

### Representativeness of the Sample

There appears to be some confusion about the next two criteria for an argument to be strong—namely, *representativeness* and *unbiased sample*. These are *different* criteria, which will be shown. In this section, we will discuss *representative sample*.

Any mass of stuff or collection of things will either be completely homogenous or contain some diversity. For example, the coffee in a pot is pretty homogenous, whereas the population of people on earth is quite diverse.

The point of drawing a sample from the population is that the sample is supposed to *represent* the population. If indeed the sample *does* represent the target group, then the sample is representative. To achieve this representation, the sample must have the same sort of diversity as the target population. For example, if the population is red, green, and blue marbles in a bag, then the sample must have red, green, and blue marbles in order to represent the diversity. The representativeness criterion can be expressed as follows:

>  Representative Sample Criterion: The more that the diversity of the sample reflects the diversity of the target, the stronger the argument.

If the sample of a generalization is not representative, then the argument commits the *logical fallacy* called *unrepresentative sample*. This can occur even if the sample is large enough. Here is an example:

>  *Ten thousand people participated in a poll in Manhattan. Ninety percent of those polled said that they favor a tuition decrease for college students. Thus, probably most US citizens favor a tuition decrease for college students.*

The sample size is indeed large enough to represent the population of the United States. However, people who live in New York City simply do *not* represent all US citizens. For example, they do not represent farmers, folk from small cities, people living in the south, et cetera. Therefore, this argument is weak, as it has an unrepresentative sample.

## Unbiased Sample

The final criterion that must be met in order for a generalization to be strong is that it must have an *unbiased* sample. This criterion is different than being representative, as a sample can be more or less representative but still biased, as we will see.

Note that this criterion concerns having an unbiased *sample* and is *not* that the *person* making the generalization must be unbiased, which is very difficult to achieve, since we all have biases. An unbiased *sample* is defined as follows:

>  Unbiased Sample: A *sample* is *unbiased* if and only if *every member* of the target population has an *equal chance* of being a member of the sample.

Notice that this, like the other criteria, also comes in degrees, since some members may have a greater chance of being a part of the sample than other members. Thus, we can state the *unbiased* criterion this way:

>  Unbiased Sample Criterion: The more that the sample is unbiased, the stronger the argument.

One is more likely to achieve an unbiased sample by engaging in **random sampling**. This is simply a process of picking the desired sample from a population in such a way that each member of the population has an equal chance of being selected until the desired sample size is achieved.

If the sample of a generalization fails to meet this criterion, then the argument commits the *logical fallacy* called *biased sample*. It was stated that a sample can meet the other two criteria, and yet still be biased. Here is an example.

*Over 8,000 college students were interviewed from campuses across the United States, including major universities, and private and state institutions, as well as midsize and smaller institutions and community colleges, from coast to coast, north and south, and the Midwest. Male and female students, students from each class (freshman, sophomore, junior, senior), students from all the age groups, including returning older adults, and students from every major were interviewed. Most said that they did not believe in God. So, most college students do not believe in God.*

This generalization satisfies the first two criteria—it has a large enough sample, and it is representative. But, is it strong? That is, is the conclusion justified given the premises? It depends on whether the sample is biased or unbiased. Suppose that *all* the interviews took place on a Sunday morning on the college campus. If so, the sample is **biased**. The reason is that not every college student had an equal chance of being part of the sample, even though every group was represented. Specifically, theists who are religious were probably in church when the interviews occurred, and thus could not have been interviewed.

Therefore, a generalization *can* have a large enough sample, be representative, but yet fail to be unbiased. So, one must check all three criteria in judging a generalization to be strong or weak. One thing to note is that failure trickles down from sample size to representativeness to bias—that is, if the generalization has too small of a sample, then it is also unrepresentative and biased. And, if it is unrepresentative, then it is also biased. However, failure does not trickle in the other direction, as was shown. So, one must be sure to check all criteria in judging generalizations.

## Dealing with Percentages

Sometimes in a generalization, arguers will specify that only a certain *percentage* of the sample and target have the relevant property. Consider the following two examples:

Premise: Most of the white Dodge Neons that I have seen had peeling paint.

Conclusion: So, probably most white Dodge Neons have peeling paint.

and,

Premise: Seventy percent of the fish that I have caught in this lake were at least 10 feet long.

Conclusion: So, probably 70% of the fish in this lake were at least 10 feet long.

Notice the phrases "most of" in the first example, and "70% of" in the second. How does this change how we label the sample and target? <u>Answer</u>: It doesn't change a thing! In fact, ignore it *when identifying sample and target*! The percentages are *not* part of the sample and target. Instead, the percentages only indicate how much of the sample and target have the property.

So, for example, in the first example above, we have the following components:

<u>Sample</u>: *white Dodge Neons that I have seen*

<u>Target</u>: *white Dodge Neons*

Relevant Property: *have peeling paint*

The phrase "most of" simply indicates that of *all* that the Neons that "I have seen" (sample), most have peeling paint, and of *all* Neons (target), most have peeling paint. So, exclude "most of" from sample and target.

We can see the same thing in the second argument. The components are:

Sample: *fish that I have caught in this lake*

Target: *fish in this lake*

Relevant Property: *being longer than 10 inches*

The phrase "70% of" simply indicates that of *all* the fish that I have caught, 70% are longer than 10 inches long, and of *all* the fish in the lake (target), 70% are longer than 10 inches long. So, exclude "70% of" from sample and target.

On the other hand, if the percentages are included in the sample and target, it actually *misrepresents* the sample and target. For example, suppose that someone drinks from 10 cups of water taken from various places on a college campus and then presents the following argument:

> *Eight of 10 of these cups contain terrible tasting water. So, most of the water on this campus tastes terrible.*

What is the sample? Well, from how many cups of water did the person drink? Answer: *10 cups*! So, the sample is the water in the *10 cups*. And over what is the person generalizing? Answer: *All the water on campus*. If we were to have said that the sample was eight cups of water, we would have misrepresented what the sample is, and similarly for the target. So, in short, exclude percentages from sample and target.

### EXERCISE 8.2

For the generalizations below, (a) identify the sample, target, and the relevant property; (b) determine whether the argument is strong or weak; and (c) if the argument is weak, state whether its sample is too small, not representative, biased, or some combination of these.

*1. Parents try to make life better for their children, since my parents tried to make life better for me, and my friends' parents did the same.

2. A random poll of 10,000 students was taken at Southwest University over the course of a semester at various days and times, and included students from each class and each major, in which students were asked if they prefer online classes or in-person classes. Seventy percent of those polled said that they prefer in-person classes. Thus, most students at Southwest University prefer in-person classes.

3. It is clear that writers and directors of TV shows don't think accurately about husbands. They all depict husbands as idiots barely capable of tying their own shoes, which is clear from the last three TV shows I have watched that depicted husbands in this way.

**\*4.** Max loves to observe pigeons—everything about them. Every pigeon he has observed in Las Vegas and Los Angeles over the past 10 years has a beak that is shorter than one inch. Therefore, it is probably the case that all pigeons on earth have beaks shorter than one inch.

**5.** There is no doubt that Polycycline kills mice, because over the past two years, in laboratories around the world, a total of 5,500 randomly selected mice were given Polycycline, and over 80% die from this drug.

**6.** Jack and John are guitarists, and they feel pain in their fingers after playing two hours straight. Jill is also a guitarist, and she feels the same pain after playing the guitar for two hours. Therefore, guitarists feel pain in their fingers after playing two hours straight.

**\*7.** Over 1,500 bull elk were observed in various places in the United States. Ninety-eight percent of these had antlers over 36 inches long. So, probably most bull elk in the United States have antlers over 36 inches long.

**8.** It is clear that all success is entirely the result of good luck, which can be seen from the fact that Barry became manager of the store simply because he was present in the store when promotions were being given, and Josey's invention turned out to be successful only because she made a lucky guess on the base of her model.

**9.** Los Angeles is colder than Bogota. Charlie lives in Los Angeles, and has visited Bogota on three occasions, in different months. Each visit, Bogota was warmer than Los Angeles.

**10.** Sophie, Ava, Isabella, and Amelia all said that they want to have large families, and they each said that their mothers also wanted to have large families. Therefore, all women want to have large families.

**11.** Police officers are corrupt, which is clear from the Minneapolis police officer who killed George Floyd by kneeling on his neck for five minutes, from the Chicago police officer who was caught dealing drugs, and from the Los Angeles police officer who was convicted of accepting a bribe.

**12.** Philosophers are arrogant, cocky people. My last two philosophy professors were clearly arrogant and cocky, and I watched a philosophy YouTube video (required by one of my philosophy professors) in which the philosopher in the video was even more arrogant and cocky than my professors.

## Analogical Argument

The next inductive argument that we will consider is an *analogical argument*. With this type of argument, one relies upon an *analogy* between two (or more) things. An *analogy* is a comparison between two (or more) things, in which one focuses on what one takes to be similarities between the things compared. In an *analogical argument*, there is an analogy in the premises that mentions various similarities between things compared, supporting the conclusion that there is further similarity between the things compared. The *basic* structure can be expressed this way:

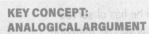

**KEY CONCEPT: ANALOGICAL ARGUMENT**
An **analogical argument** is an argument in which one draws an analogy between two things based on supposed similarities between them, supporting the conclusion that there is further similarity between them.

Premise: $S$ and $T$ are (known to be) similar in various ways.

Premise: $S$ has additional property $F$.

Conclusion: [Therefore,] probably $T$ has $F$.

Here is a concrete example:

Premise: Crest whitening toothpaste is similar to Colgate whitening toothpaste.

Premise: Crest whitened my teeth.

Conclusion: Probably, Colgate will whiten my teeth.

Similar to generalizations, in order to assist in specifying the components of an analogical argument, let's establish our terminology. In an analogy, the things being compared are *analogs*. In a basic analogical argument, we will call the analog in the premise (that is known to have the relevant property) the *source analog*. The analog referenced in the conclusion is the *target analog*. Let's call the known similarities between the analogs, *similarities*. And finally, we will call the property known to be had by the source analog and said to be had be the target analog in the conclusion the *relevant property*.

Consider another example:

*I think that wolves would make great pets—after all, they are similar to dogs in that they descend from a common ancestor, they share almost 99% of the same DNA, and can interbreed. Further, dogs make great pets.*

In this example, the *source analog* is *dogs*; the *target analog* is *wolves*; the *similarities* are *descend from common ancestor, share almost 99% of the same DNA, and can interbreed*; and the *relevant property* is *make great pets*:

Source Analog: *dogs*

Target Analog: *wolves*

Similarities: *descend from common ancestor, share almost 99% of the same DNA, can interbreed.*

Relevant Property: *make great pets*

## Note a Few Points

As with generalizations, there are a few points to note to help identify the components of an analogical argument. First, the *analogs* are *distinct* things, stuffs, events, properties, et cetera. Thus, they are *always* identified with a *noun* or *noun phrase* (NOT with a complete sentence). It will *always* be the *subject* of the sentence.

Second, the *relevant property* is *not* one of the similarities. The similarities are *known* to be properties of both analogs, whereas while we know that the relevant property is had by the source analog, we do not know that it is had by the target analog, but instead one is concluding that it is.

Third, the *similarities* and *relevant property* are *properties*. Hence, *always* identify them with a phrase like "being F,"—for example, *being green*; or with a phrase like "does A,"—for example, *runs fast*. Further, note that we do *not* include the analogs when labeling the similarities or relevant property. Consider that, in the example above, one would *not* write the similarities, for example, as *wolves descend from common ancestor, share almost 99% of the same DNA, can interbreed* since the property is not just a property of wolves, but also of dogs, and the dogs do not have the property *wolves descend from common ancestor, share almost 99% of the same DNA, can interbreed*. Similar points apply to the relevant property. Instead, we would label it as a *property—make great pets*.

## Steps to Identify Analogs, Similarities, Relevant Property

Just as we take steps to identify the components of a generalization, we can also take steps to identify the components of an analogical argument. Let's consider the following example adapted from James 1 in the New Testament of the Bible:

> The Word of God is like a mirror, in that when one looks carefully into either, facts about oneself are reflected. One fixes one's appearance when looking in a mirror based on what one sees reflected about oneself, and therefore one should fix one's character when studying the Word of God based on what one sees reflected about oneself.

### Step 1

The first step is to identify the *analogs*, and identify which is the *source analog* and which is the *target analog*. To identify the analogs, ask

What things are being compared?

If we ask this question about the argument above, the answer is:

A *mirror* and *the Word of God*

Those are the analogs. One way (the way recommended) to identify which is the *source analog* and which is the *target analog* is to first identify the conclusion of the argument. The *target analog* is the analog found there. In the example, the conclusion is:

> [O]ne should fix one's character when studying the Word of God based on what one sees reflected about oneself.

Given that *a mirror* and *the Word of God* are the analogs, and *the Word of God* is the analog found in the conclusion, the latter is the *target analog*. So, the target analog is:

Target Analog: *the Word of God*

That leaves the other analog as the *source analog*. Thus, the source analog is:

Source Analog: *a mirror*

The next two steps can be done in any order, perhaps determined by the case in question. So, while we will proceed as we do below, the order is not essential.

### Step 2

Next, we identify the *relevant property*. Remember that the relevant property is the *property* had by *both* analogs, and thus will be mentioned in both the premise and conclusion. It is *what is being said of* the analogs. The best way to identify it, and not confuse it with the similarities between the analogs, is to once again look in the conclusion. It is what is said of the target analog in the conclusion. So, what is said of the *Word of God* in the conclusion? <u>Answer:</u> *One should fix oneself based on what is reflected about oneself.* Thus:

> <u>Relevant Property:</u> *One should fix oneself based on what is reflected about oneself*

### Step 3

Finally, we identify the *similarities*, which are properties that we know are had by both analogs. Remember that the similarities do *not* include the relevant property. To identify the *similarities*, we look to the *premises* and identify what the analogs have in common, excluding the relevant property. So, what do a *mirror* and the *Word of God* have in common? <u>Answer:</u> *They reflect facts about oneself when one looks into it.* Thus, the similarities are:

> <u>Similarities:</u> *Reflect facts about oneself when one looks in it.*

So, we have (correctly) identified the *analogs*, *similarities*, and *relevant property* as:

> <u>Source Analog:</u> *A mirror*
>
> <u>Target Analog:</u> *The Word of God*
>
> <u>Similarities:</u> *Reflect facts about oneself when one looks in it*
>
> <u>Relevant Property:</u> *One should fix oneself based on what is reflected about oneself*

## Assessing the Strength of Analogical Arguments

Logicians and philosophers have noted several criteria that play a role in making an analogical argument strong. We will consider three of these criteria that are particularly important:

- Similarities between analogs
- Dissimilarities between analogs
- Multiple analogs

We will consider each of these in turn.

### Similarities Between Analogs

In an analogical argument, one is making an analogy between things believed to be similar, and drawing a conclusion based on the analogy. Thus, roughly, the more similarities there are between the things compared, the stronger the analogy, and thus the stronger the argument.

While the rough idea is correct, there are more details that we need to consider. First, the similarities between the analogs are *not* equal, in the sense that some are more *relevant* to the relevant property than are others. Consider the following analogical argument.

> *Aaron's upcoming logic class is similar to the math class he took last semester, in that both use symbolic language, deductive reasoning, and axioms and rules of inference, and have instructors that Aaron likes. Aaron did well in the math class, and thus, he will do well in the logic class.*

Notice that there are the following similarities mentioned between the analogs (the math class and the logic class):

Use symbolic language

Use deductive reasoning

Use of axioms and inference rules

Have instructors that Aaron likes

It should be obvious that the first three similarities are more relevant to the relevant property than is the fourth similarity. Indeed, the fourth similarity is barely relevant, except that having an instructor that one likes can make a difference to one's learning. But the point is that these four similarities are not all equal. We can generalize as follows:

Relevancy of Similarities Criterion: The more *relevant* that the similarities are to the relevant property, the stronger the argument.

Second, obviously the arguer can list more or fewer similarities between the analogs as they see fit. It is no doubt clear that the *more* relevant similarities the arguer lists, the stronger the argument. For example, compare the argument just above to the following, in which fewer similarities are mentioned:

> *Aaron's upcoming logic class is similar to the math class he took last semester, in that both use symbolic language and have instructors that Aaron likes. Aaron did well in the math class, and thus, he will do well in the logic class.*

The first argument listed four similarities, as noted, whereas this argument has only two of those similarities. Clearly the first is stronger by virtue of containing more similarities. Again, we can generalize:

Number of Relevant Similarities Criterion: The *more numerous* relevant similarities that are included in the argument, the stronger the argument.

Third, similarities between things can be alike or quite diverse. For example, suppose one is comparing two brothers, by suggesting that they both like thriller movies, horror movies, and drama movies. The similarities are alike, in that they all involve *movies*. On the other hand, if one compares the brothers by saying that they both like thriller movies, they both like to ride dirt bikes, and they both like fine dining, then one has listed a more *diverse* set of similarities. To the degree that the diverse similarities are each relevant to the relevant property in question, the stronger the argument, which gives us our third and final similarity criterion:

> Diversity of Relevant Similarities Criterion: The *more diverse* the relevant similarities are, the stronger the argument.

Putting this altogether, we get the following *similarity criterion*:

> Similarities Criterion: The more *relevant, numerous, and diverse* the *similarities* are between the analogs, the stronger the argument.

## Dissimilarities Between Analogs

Analogs in an analogy not only have similarities, which is often why they are being compared, but they also have *dissimilarities*. Whereas similarities between analogs in an analogical argument strengthen the argument, dissimilarities between the analogs *weaken* the argument.

To be more precise, like similarities, dissimilarities can also be more or less *relevant* to the relevant property, more or less *numerous*, and more or less *diverse*. The general dissimilarities criterion can thus be put as follows:

> Dissimilarities Criterion: The more *relevant, numerous, and diverse* the *dissimilarities* are between the analogs, the weaker the argument.

One way to evaluate analogical arguments is to compare the similarities and dissimilarities between the analogs in terms of these criteria. The general idea is that if there are more similarities than dissimilarities, the stronger the argument. However, it may be that it is not a matter simply of how *numerous* the similarities are compared to the dissimilarities, but how *relevant* each is to the relevant property.

Consider the following argument:

> *Dogs and wolves share much of the same genetics, have very similar physical attributes, need social interaction to thrive, use vocal communications (such as barking or howling) to express their needs, and have similar behaviors, such as traveling in packs. Dogs make great house pets, and thus wolves would make great house pets.*

There are five similarities mentioned in this argument. However, even assuming that they are somewhat relevant to the relevant property (making great house pets), one can list just three relevant *dissimilarities* to substantially weaken this argument—namely, that wolves, unlike dogs, are distrustful of humans, are elusive, and are difficult to train. Even though the *number* of dissimilarities is less than the *number* of similarities (if the dissimilarities were added to the argument), the dissimilarities are far more **relevant** to the relevant property (making great house pets), and thus render the argument weaker than stronger.

In short, when evaluating an analogical argument, one must be mindful of similarities compared to dissimilarities between the analogs, and especially be mindful of the *relevancy of* these to the relevant property. And if the dissimilarities outweigh the similarities in relevancy if not in number, then the argument commits the *logical fallacy* called *faulty analogy*.

## Multiple Analogs

In all the examples of analogical arguments that we have considered, there have been only two analogs—one source analog and one target analog. Such arguments can be strong. However, one increases the strength of an analogical argument by including more *source analogs*. For example, compare the following two arguments:

> Argument A:
>
> *Mr. Smith bought his truck at Baron's Chevy dealership on a Saturday afternoon in June and encountered a very friendly staff and an easy-to-work-with finance manager. Since I am buying my truck at Baron's Chevy dealership on a Saturday afternoon in June, probably I will also encounter a very friendly staff and an easy-to-work-with finance manager.*
>
> Argument B:
>
> *Mr. Smith bought his truck at Baron's Chevy dealership on a Saturday afternoon in June and encountered a very friendly staff and an easy-to-work-with finance manager. Ms. Jones also purchased her car at Baron's Chevy dealership on a Saturday afternoon in June and encountered a very friendly staff and an easy-to-work-with finance manager. Since I am buying my truck at Baron's Chevy dealership on a Saturday afternoon in June, probably I will also encounter a very friendly staff and an easy-to-work-with finance manager.*

Whatever the strength level of Argument A, it should be clear that Argument B is stronger (even if ultimately weak).

The reason for this is that the more scenarios in which there are things that have both the (relevant) similarities mentioned and also the relevant property, the greater our justification in thinking that there is a connection between having the (relevant) mentioned similarities and the relevant property. While we could of course be mistaken that there is such a connection, and of course there are exceptions, the more scenarios in which there are the connections, the more we are justified in believing that there is a connection, and thus the more we are justified in judging the analogical argument to be strong. Thus, we have the following criterion:

> **Multiple Analogs Criterion:** The more source analogs there are in which the analogs have both the relevant similarities and the relevant property, the stronger the argument.

## EXERCISE 8.3

For the analogical arguments below, (a) identify the source and target analogs, the similarities between the analogs, and the relevant property; and (b) determine whether the argument is strong or weak, and why (*excluding* the statement in parentheses). Finally, suppose the statement in parentheses were included in the argument, would it strengthen the argument, weaken the argument, or be irrelevant to the argument?

**\*1.** Abortion is similar to capital punishment in that both involve killing a person. Since abortion is morally wrong, so is capital punishment.

(*A fetus is an innocent person, but people on death row are not.*)

**2.** I loved Vince Flynn's previous three books about terrorist assassin Mitch Rapp. I cannot wait for the next book in the Mitch Rapp series. I know I will love it too!

(*In each novel that I read, Flynn got better and better at developing the story.*)

**3.** Sam and his brother Arnold are both practicing attorneys, raised in a conservative house. Since Sam is a Republican, I bet Arnold is too!

(*Sam and Arnold both love classical music.*)

**\*4.** You should hire my dog sitter Beth as your babysitter! She loves babies just as much as dogs. She is excellent at taking care of my dog. No doubt she would also be excellent at taking care of your baby.

(*Beth babysat for my friend Phil one night and was excellent.*)

**5.** George has loved the three Chevrolets that he has owned in the past 15 years, each of which were white, and had leather seats, and power doors and windows. So, he will probably love the Chevrolet he bought yesterday, since it also is white, and has leather seats, and power doors and windows.

(*He bought all his previous Chevrolets in Iowa, but he bought yesterday's in Nevada.*)

**6.** Spiders are arachnids that have two body segments with eight legs; develop in stages, beginning from eggs; and are predatory. Further, spiders have fangs that they use to inject venom. Scorpions, like spiders, have two body segments with eight legs; develop in stages, beginning from eggs; and are predatory. Therefore, scorpions also have fangs that they use to inject venom.

(*Scorpions have a stinger located at the end of their tail to inject venom.*)

**\*7.** The body builders that I follow on YouTube have managed to gain lean muscle mass and lose fat while maintaining a caloric deficit and working out regularly. So, I will place myself on a caloric deficit and work out regularly. I'm sure I can also lose body fat while gaining muscle mass.

(*The body builders I follow on YouTube have many years experiencing lifting weights, whereas I am just beginning.*)

**8.** Alcohol prohibition is like marijuana prohibition. When alcohol was prohibited, there was organized crime in the United States, and there is organized crime in Mexico, resulting from marijuana prohibition there. Legalization of alcohol eliminated organized crime in the United States. Therefore, legalization of marijuana will eliminate organized crime in Mexico.

(*When marijuana was legalized in the Netherlands, organized crime there was eliminated.*)

**9.** The universe is a complex system with the appearance of design, just like a watch. We wouldn't think that a watch can come about by accident, since something so complicated and seemingly designed must have been created by an intelligent designer. The universe is a lot more complex and bears the marks of design much more than does a watch, and so it also must have been created by an intelligent designer.

(*The universe and a watch are both incredibly fine-tuned for some end (universe fine-tuned for life, and watch fine-tuned for keeping time.*)

**10.** Unwanted pregnancy is like the following scenario: You wake up one day to find that an unconscious violinist is attached to your body, brought about by the Society of Music Lovers kidnapping you, and plugging the violinist's circulatory system into yours, so that your kidneys can be used to extract poisons from his blood as well as your own. If he is unplugged now, he will die, but in nine months he will have recovered, and can safely be unplugged from you. Just as you are not morally obligated to remain plugged into the violinist, so, too, you are not morally obligated to carry a baby to term if you do not wish to be pregnant.[1]

(*Most unwanted pregnancies result from consensual sex.*)

---

1. Example borrowed and modified from Judith J. Thomson's article "A Defense of Abortion," *Philosophy and Public Affairs* 1, no. 1 (Autumn 1971): 47–66.

## Causal Arguments

The idea that the occurrence of one event is the cause of another event permeates our thinking about the world. Consider:

> The blowing wind stirred up pollens into the air *causing* me to have itchy watery eyes, stuffed-up nose, sneezing, and, in general, misery!
>
> The earthquake was *caused* by the tectonic plates rubbing together.
>
> The lack of water *is the cause of* my leg cramps.
>
> The bleach with hydrogen peroxide mixture *caused* the explosion.
>
> His fear of heights *caused* his legs to go numb.

Not only do we make such claims *daily*, but we make them throughout the day. Let's set aside the philosophical questions of just what causation is and what it consists in (whether it consists in events, things, sets of conditions, etc.) and instead assume there really is a causal relation and that it occurs between events. For our purposes, we'll define an *event* as an object having a property (e.g., a rock being solid) or objects standing in various relationships (e.g., tectonic plates rubbing together). Our question is:

> How should we justify our causal statements?

*One* general way to do so is to use a *causal argument*, which is a type of *inductive* argument in which one concludes with a causal statement, thought to be justified by the premises of the argument. In this section, we will discuss such arguments, beginning with a closer look at *causal statements*.

**KEY CONCEPT: CAUSAL ARGUMENT**

A **causal argument** is an argument in which one concludes with a causal statement, where such a statement may be taken to be true, or as a hypothesis.

## Causal Statements

The list of statements above are *causal statements*, in which there is the expression of a relationship between one event as *cause* and another as *effect*. The statements above all use the words *cause* or *caused* to express the relationship. However, other words or phrases can be used in place of these, such as *because, as a result of, due to, brought about, is explained by,* and others. Consider:

> I have itchy watery eyes, stuffed-up nose, sneezing, and, in general, misery *due to* the blowing wind stirring up pollens into the air.

> The earthquake was *a result of* the tectonic plates rubbing together.

> My legs cramped *because* of lack of water.

> The bleach with hydrogen peroxide mixture *brought about* the explosion.

> His legs going numb *is explained by* his fear of heights.

Note that some of these words and phrases can also be premise indicators (such as *because, as a result of, due to*), and thus it is important to recognize the context in which the word or phrase is occurring and be able to identify whether one is dealing with an argument or an explanation.

## Necessary and Sufficient Condition

In chapter 3 we learned that we can define a concept in terms of necessary and sufficient conditions. Additionally, *causes* can be necessary, sufficient, or both, and we can go deeper in our thinking about causes by thinking about them in this way. First, let's be reminded of what necessary and sufficient condition are.

Recall that a *necessary condition* is a condition that *must* be met; it is *required*. In chapter 3, we talked about necessary conditions in general, not limited to causation, and gave examples such as:

> Something is square only if it has four sides.

> Something is a dog only if it is an animal.

The conditions to the right of "only if" are necessary, not in a causal sense, but in a *definition* sense. It is part of the essence of squares that they are four-sided and part of the essence of canines that they are animals.

However, *causes* can also be necessary. When an event is a necessary *as a cause*, it is because of the laws of nature—because of the way things are in reality. In the causal sense, the necessary event *must* occur in order for the effect in question to occur. For example,

> A necessary causal condition for a piece of wood to burn is that heat is applied to it.

This is a result of the structure of reality, given the laws of nature.

Notice, however, the mere fact that heat is applied to the wood, while necessary, is not sufficient. Other events *must* also occur in conjunction with the applied heat in order to bring about the wood burning, such as the presence of oxygen. This brings us to *cause* as a *sufficient condition*.

Recall that a *sufficient condition* is a condition that *guarantees*. In chapter 3, we also talked about sufficient conditions in general, not limited to causation, and gave examples such as:

*If something is a truck, then it is an automobile.*

*If something is a snake, then it is a reptile.*

The conditions immediately following "If" are sufficient, not in a causal sense, but in a *definition* sense. It is part of the essence of trucks that they are automobiles and part of the essence of snakes that they are reptiles.

But just as *events* can be necessary *causes, events* can be sufficient as causes. When an event is a sufficient *as a cause*, then its occurrence *guarantees* the occurrence of another event as its effect. For example,

The combination of the events of *rain falling* and *the ground being uncovered* are sufficient for the event *the ground is wet.*

While the combination of the first events (rain plus uncovered ground) are sufficient to *cause* the third event (wet ground), neither of the first two events is necessary for the occurrence of the third event. The ground can be caused to be wet by events other than falling rain and can be caused to be wet even if covered, by water rising from below.

So, in nature we find that the occurrence of some events that are necessary but not sufficient for the occurrence of other events, and that some events are sufficient but not necessary for the occurrence of other events. Further, we find that the occurrence of some events is both necessary and sufficient for the occurrence of other events. For example,

The event of sufficient amount of heat being applied to a piece of wood together with the event of the wood being in an oxygenated environment is necessary and sufficient for the event of the wood burning.

In summary, sometimes causal statements specify a necessary causal condition, other times a sufficient causal condition, and other times both. When judging such statements to be true or false, we as critical thinkers need to be mindful of this and be able to recognize which sort of causal statement it is, or at least recognize that we need to inquire further which it may be.

## Mistakes in Causal Reasoning

Having looked in some detail about the nature of causal statements, we return to our question:

How should we justify our causal statements?

Before considering some rational, legitimate ways of justifying our causal statements, let's first see why it matters, given the possible mistakes that we can make. For our discussion, we will make a simplifying assumption. While it is typically the case that there is not a single event that causes another, but rather a collection of events occurring that causes another, to simplify our discussion, let's suppose that causation involves a relation between two single events, in which the first brings about (is the cause of) the second.

## Confusing Correlation with Causation

Sometimes we judge that one event caused another event simply because the events are *correlated*, and we confuse correlation with causation. Consider a superstition. Suppose that every time you do well on an exam, you are wearing your favorite gray sweatshirt. In this case, the two events of *you wearing a gray sweatshirt* and *you doing well on the exam* are correlated; they show up together. This has too often lead some to conclude that one of the events (in this case, the *wearing of the gray sweatshirt*) is the cause of the other (*doing well on the exam*).

The problem is that correlation is *not* causation, and mere correlation is simply not enough to establish causation. While many examples can be used to show that reasoning from correlation to causation is bad, consider the following example, in case it is not obvious:

> Every day when the noon bell rings at a factory in New York, a 9:00 a.m. buzzer goes off in a factory in Los Angeles informing the workers that it is time to begin work.[1]

The two events—noon bell ringing in New York and 9:00 a.m. buzzer in Los Angeles—are correlated. But clearly neither is the cause of the other nor do they have any underlying common cause; rather they are simply two completely (causally) unrelated but correlated events.

The point is that it is a mistake to conclude that event A is the cause of event B *merely because* the two events are correlated. We need more justification than correlation to justify the inference.

## Confusing Temporal Order with Causation

A closely related mistake that we make is when we judge that one event caused another event simply because one of the events came before another in time. This can be even more deceptive if the temporal ordering occurs regularly. For example, perhaps you had a headache and then drank a coke, after which your headache ceased. It would be a mistake to conclude that drinking the coke caused the headache to cease simply because the drinking came before the cessation of the headache. After all, many things could have been occurring simultaneous with the drinking, and which could be the real causes of the cessation.

It is a mistake *even if* the temporal ordering of the events is a regularity. Consider the following example:

> Every day the rooster crows, which is always followed by the sun rising.

Clearly, the rooster crowing is *not* the cause of the sun rising (or more exactly, the cause of earth rotating on its axis). However, there is the regular temporal ordering of the events, in which the one regularly follows the other. Thus, the mere fact that one event comes before another does *not* justify the judgment that the first is the cause of the second. To reason in this way is to commit the logical fallacy called *post hoc ergo propter hoc* (which is Latin for "after this, therefore because of this"—let's call the fallacy *post hoc* for short).

In order to help avoid these mistakes and make rational judgments about the truth-value of causal statements, we can practice various methods for formulating our causal hypotheses and

---

1. This example was adapted from a similar example given by A. C. Ewing in his book *The Fundamental Questions of Philosophy* (Routledge: 1951), ch. 8.

then ultimately forming a judgments about what is the cause of some phenomenon in question. It is to *some of* these methods that we now turn.

## Mill's Methods

Once again, we return to our question:

How should we justify our causal statements?

Clearly, one very important way to justify causal statements is by the scientific method, which is done (more or less) by developing a hypothesis (which is a provisional and testable explanation) from observed data and then conducting experiments to test the hypothesis. Aside from this, there are ways to form rational causal judgments, or at least hypotheses (which we can perform in our everyday lives), without conducting experiments. Among these ways of formulating rational causal statements are *inference to the best explanation,* and four methods proposed by the nineteenth century English philosopher John Stuart Mill. We will set aside inference to the best explanation for now, since chapter 9 is devoted to it. Here we will consider Mill's methods, which are useful for everyday critical thinkers in making judgments about causal statements, as well as by scientists in formulating their causal hypotheses for experimentation.

The methods are:

Method of Agreement

Method of Difference

Method of Concomitant Variation

Method of Residues

We will consider each in turn.

## Method of Agreement

In the *method of agreement*, one judges a causal statement to be true, or forms a causal hypothesis, based on multiple instances of some event, each instance of which has different factors, except for a common factor, which is postulated to be the cause of the event. Its structure can be put this way:

Premise: There are multiple instances of event *E*—namely, instances X, Y, Z, etc.

Premise: X, Y, Z, etc. each contain different factors, except that they all contain factor C (instances X, Y, Z all *agree* in containing C).

Conclusion: [Therefore,] probably, C is the cause of *E*.

Here is an example:

Adam, Bob, and Carl went to dinner together, after which they each had a stomachache. Adam, Bob, and Carl each ate something different for dinner, except they all had apple pie for dessert. Therefore, it is probably the apple pie that caused the stomachache.

The argument can be put in standard form as follows:

> Premise: Adam, Bob, and Carl each ate something for dinner, and then each got a stomachache (three instances of an event E).
>
> Premise: Adam, Bob, and Carl each ate something *different* for dinner (different factors), but they all had apple pie for dessert (the *one* common factor).
>
> Conclusion: [Therefore,] probably, the apple pie is the cause of the stomachache.

### Method of Difference

In the *method of difference*, one judges a causal statement to be true, or forms a causal hypothesis, based on the fact that some event is present in one scenario but *not* present in a similar scenario, and that there is only one other relevant *difference* between the scenarios, which is postulated to be the cause of the event. Its structure can be put this way:

> Premise: An event E is present in scenarios X, but is *not* present in similar scenario Y.
>
> Premise: Scenarios X and Y have various similarities, but only one other relevant *difference*—namely, that scenario X contains factor C, but scenario Y does *not* contain C.
>
> Conclusion: [Therefore,] probably, C is the cause of E.

Here is an example:

> *Adam and Bob went to dinner together, after which Adam had a stomachache, but Bob did not. Adam and Bob each ate the same thing for dinner, but Adam ate apple pie for dessert, whereas Bob did not. Therefore, it is probably the apple pie that caused the stomachache.*

The argument can be put in standard form as follows:

> Premise: Adam and Bob each ate something for dinner (two "scenarios"), after which Adam got a stomachache (presence of event E), but Bob did not (absence of event E).
>
> Premise: Adam and Bob each ate the same thing for dinner (similarities), but Adam ate apple pie for dessert, whereas Bob did not (the *one* difference).
>
> Conclusion: [Therefore,] probably, the apple pie is the cause of Adam's stomachache.

While the method of agreement and the method of difference are good methods for formulating reasonable causal statements or hypotheses independently, combined we get an even more powerful method. When combined, one derives a causal statement, or forms a causal hypothesis, based on combining the methods of agreement and difference. However, we will focus on the methods individually.

### Method of Concomitant Variation

The third method is the *method of concomitant variation*. In this method, one judges a causal statement to be true, or forms a causal hypothesis, as a result of observing that the occurrence of instances of an event varies based on the variation of some other factor associated with the instances. Its structure can be put this way:

Premise: Instances of event E are each correlated with factor C.

Premise: When instances of C increase (or decrease), the instances E increase (or decrease), correlatively.

Conclusion: [Therefore,] probably, C is the cause of E.

Here is an example:

*Higher GPAs are correlated with online instruction. The more online classes that run at a university, the higher the GPAs are at that university. So, probably, online instruction is a contributing cause of higher GPAs.*

The argument can be put in standard form as follows:

Premise: Higher GPAs at universities are correlated with online instruction.

Premise: The more online classes that run at a university (increase in the instances of factor C), the higher the GPAs are at that university (increase in the GPAs).

Conclusion: [Therefore,] probably, online instruction is a contributing cause of higher GPAs.

Note that the correlative relationship between the instances of the factor and the instances of the event in question need not be increase-to-increase but can be increase-to-decrease (e.g., eating more vegetables decreases chance of getting cancer), decrease-to-decrease (e.g., fewer drunk drivers decreases automobile accidents), or decrease-to-increase (e.g., fewer days exercising can increase body fat).

### Method of Residues

The final method is the *method of residues*. In this method, one judges a causal statement to be true, or forms a causal hypothesis, by a process of elimination. The process proceeds as follows: There is set of events needing explanation and a set of events that are the potential causes. In the simple and straightforward cases, all but one of the potential causes are known to be causally linked to all but one of events needing explanation. The conclusion is that the remaining potential cause is the cause of the remaining event needing explanation. Its structure can be put this way:

Premise: Events A, B, and C are the potential causes of events E, F, G.

Premise: We know that A is the cause of F and that B is the cause of G.

Conclusion: [Therefore,] probably, C is the cause of E.

Here is an example:

*Adam had a steak with red wine for dinner, followed by a piece of apple pie for dessert. After dinner, he had a headache, his jaw hurt, and he had a stomachache. He knows that eating steak causes his jaw to hurt, and thus knows that the eating of the steak is the probable cause of his present jaw ache. And, he knows that drinking red wine frequently gives him headaches, and thus he knows that it was the red wine that is the probable cause of his headache. That leaves the apple pie and the stomachache to be linked. Adam concludes that it was probably the apple pie that caused the stomachache.*

The argument can be put in standard form as follows:

> Premise: Eating steak and drinking red wine for dinner, and having apple pie for dessert are the potential causes of Adam's headache, aching jaw, and stomachache.

> Premise: It is known that chewing steak causes his jaw to hurt and drinking red wine causes him to have headaches.

> Conclusion: [Therefore,] probably, the apple pie is the cause of the stomachache.

## Limits of Mill's Methods

While Mill's methods are good ways to make rational judgments that causal statements are true, or to formulate reasonable hypotheses, they don't settle the matter, and allow for potential errors. Thus, ultimately, the causal conclusion drawn is only probably true at best and may require scientific testing to confirm it. So, depending on the situation, take the causal statement with a grain of salt. Let's conclude by discussing four possible errors that can be made with the methods.

### Focusing on Irrelevant Factors

While the Mill's methods are good, one error that can occur is *focusing on an irrelevant factor* (whether that be an irrelevant common factor, difference, or other that appears to be relevant). For example, in the example of *method of agreement, perhaps* the cause of each of Adam's, Bob's, and Carl's stomachache is *not* the apple pie, despite appearance. Maybe, unknown to all in the scenario, the apple pie was perfectly fine, and the stomachache was caused by some ingredient common to each entre, or perhaps a result of each person overeating. So, while the hypothesis that the apple pie is the cause *is reasonable*, one must exercise caution that one is not focusing on an irrelevant common factor here until one can conduct further tests (perhaps scientific testing).

### Overlooking Additional Relevant Factors

Second, even if the proposed cause in the reasoning (e.g., the apple pie) is *a* contributing factor in causing the event in question (e.g., the stomachache), there may be *more than one common factor* that is relevant. For example, consider the *method of difference* argument above. While the apple pie may be *one relevant* difference between Adam and Bob, and may even be *a* contributing factor in causing Adam's stomachache, there may be *more than one common factor* that is relevant. For example, perhaps eating the apple pie contributed to Adam's stomachache, but that was in combination with Adam overeating, such that *overeating* dessert, which happened to be *apple pie*, caused Adam's stomachache. So, while the apple pie played a role in the cause, it was not the only relevant factor. Thus, one must be mindful that one is not overlooking additional relevant factors. And if there are multiple common factors, one might have to conclude with a disjunction, such as:

> [Therefore,] probably, C1 is the cause of E, or C2 is the cause of E, or C1 plus C2 is the cause of E. etc.

Again, further testing is required (perhaps scientific testing) to settle the matter.

### Confusing Cause and Effect

A third error that can occur with the methods is *confusing cause and effect*. This one occurs when one concludes that:

> Something X is the cause of something Y.

However, in *reality*,

> Y is the cause of X.

This mistake probably will not occur if one knows that X came before Y in time, as backward temporal causation is impossible. Rather, this error potentially occurs when one is not sure about the temporal order—that is, one does not know which came first in time, X or Y.

For example, suppose someone engages in the following method of concomitant variation reasoning (though this mistake could occur in any of the methods):

> *I have observed a correlation between Mary coming over to John's house and John's house being clean. The more she is at his house, the cleaner the house is. Probably, it is the fact that John cleans his house that is the cause of Mary coming over.*

The conclusion of this argument is that the event of *John cleaning his house* is the cause of *Mary coming over*. This conclusion is not irrational, given the reasoning. However, it could also be, instead, that the causal order is reversed—that the event of *Mary coming over* is the cause of *John cleaning his house*.

Thus, one must also be mindful of this possible error, particularly in cases in which the temporal order is not known. Again, scientific testing may be required to settle the matter.

### Overlooking Underlying Common Cause

The fourth error that can occur with the methods is *overlooking an underlying common cause*. This one occurs when one concludes that:

> Something X is the cause of something Y.

However, in *reality*,

> There is some underlying factor Z, such that Z is the cause of both X and Y.

This mistake is made as a result of the *appearance* of X causing Y since they are showing up together in a causal way, since they have an underlying common cause.

For example, suppose someone engages in the following method of difference reasoning (though this mistake could occur in any of the methods):

> *Helen and Susan have gone out to eat together each month for the past six months. This month, Susan (who is now pregnant) ate a large hamburger, with a pickle and mushrooms, followed by ice cream sundae for dessert. After eating, she rushed off to the bathroom and vomited. Helen reasoned as follows: In the last several months, Susan did not vomit after eating her lunch, but this month she did vomit. In past months, Susan never ate such a large hamburger with such toppings, followed by dessert, but this month she did. Probably, eating what she did caused her to vomit.*

Helen's conclusion in her method of difference reasoning is that the event of *Susan eating what she did for lunch* is the cause of *Susan vomiting after lunch*. This conclusion is not irrational, given the reasoning. However, it could also be, instead, that Helen is overlooking an underlying common cause of the two events—namely, the event of *Susan being pregnant*. If so, then what is really occurring is that the fact that Susan is pregnant caused her cravings, which caused her to eat as she did, and (independently) her being pregnant caused her to vomit (which she would have done no matter what she ate). So, while there is not the causal link that there *appears* to be (namely, that the eating caused the vomiting), there is a causal link—namely, that the event of *Susan being pregnant* is the underlying cause of *Susan eating what she did for lunch* and the cause of *Susan vomiting after lunch*.

**EXERCISE 8.4**

For the causal arguments below, (a) identify the conclusion, which is a causal statement; (b) identify which of Mill's methods was used to arrive at that conclusion; and (c) discuss possible weaknesses in each argument, including a discussion of possible mistakes being made.

**\*1.** For the past several days, cicadas have been buzzing loudly late in the afternoon. Some of the days were hotter than others, and each afternoon the buzzing began at different times. However, each day before the buzzing a large storm was about to arise. Thus, it must be the storms that cause the cicadas to buzz loudly.

**2.** Violent protests are linked to large, angry crowds. The larger the crowd and the angrier the protesters, the more violent the protests become. Clearly, it follows that large, angry crowds cause violent protests.

**3.** When David ate the soup, he began to sweat, his tongue swelled up, and his throat hurt. When he asked the waitress what was in the soup, she reported that it contains vinegar, spicy red peppers, and peanuts. He knows that spicy red peppers cause him to sweat, which explains the sweating, and that vinegar tends to burn his throat. Thus, he concludes that the peanuts are causing his tongue to swell, and that he is allergic to peanuts.

**\*4.** Up to yesterday, Dr. Garber and Dr. Smith were having a nice debate about the best explanation of the empty tomb. Dr. Garber was making the case that Jesus rising from the dead is the best explanation for the facts surrounding the empty tomb, including the historical and religious context. But today Dr. Smith won't even look at Dr. Garber, let alone talk to him. The only relevant factor that I can think of that would make the difference between the pleasant discussion yesterday and today's coldness is that fact that Dr. Garber laughed at Dr. Smith's theory that the empty tomb is explained by Jesus mysterious lost twin brother.

**5.** Every morning, Jack leaves for work at 7:15 a.m. and arrives at work five minutes early. Today, however, Jack left the house at 7:10 a.m. and arrived at work 15 minutes early. The five minutes made a huge difference, since leaving just five minutes earlier got him to work 15 minutes early. From now on, Jack will leave at 7:10 a.m., since he likes to arrive earlier to work.

**6.** Listening to classical music helps one to focus on and learn the material. Elizabeth often studies for tests under different circumstances—sometimes at home, sometimes in the library, sometimes while snacking, and other times while fasting. But she always listens to classical music, and she does well on the tests.

**\*7.** Yesterday Victoria rescued a dog from the streets that had swollen paws, a potbelly, itching, and malnourishment, as well as fleas, splinters in its paws, and worms in its stool. Clearly the malnourishment is a result of lack of food, which Victoria fixed by feeding the dog nourishing food. The itching is caused by the fleas, which she treated with special shampoo. The swollen paws were caused by the splinters, which Victoria removed, and she treated the paws with ointment. Thus, it must be that the worms are causing the potbelly.

**8.** Last week, Emma, who lives in Miami, had a cough, sore throat, congestion, fatigue, and body aches. James and Lucas showed the exact same symptoms, but James lives in Los Angeles, and Lucas lives in Chicago. However, these three people have one thing in common—namely, they each recently traveled to China. Thus, there is no doubt that someone in China is the cause of the disease.

**9.** There is a clear connection between George sleeping on his side and his back hurting. The more frequently he sleeps on his side, as opposed to on his back or stomach, the more his back hurts in the morning. So, probably, George's back pain is caused by his side sleeping. My recommendation, then, is that he learn to get comfortable sleeping on his back or get a new mattress that can support his side sleeping.

**10.** The launch of NASA and SpaceX rocket Falcon 9 was scheduled to launch for the first time on Wednesday, May 27, at 4:33 p.m. but was scrubbed in the last few minutes. However, on Saturday, May 30, at 3:22 p.m., Falcon 9 successfully launched. The weather in Cape Canaveral, Florida, on both days was hot and humid, with rain and inclement weather in the area, but the difference is that on Wednesday, unlike Saturday, there was lightning within 10 miles of the launch site. It must be that the lightning caused the scrubbing of the first launch.

**11.** There seems to be a correlation between driving the car fast, and the car and steering wheel shaking. The faster we go in the car, approaching 75 miles per hour, the more the car and steering wheel shakes. As we approach 80 miles per hour, the car shakes really badly. It must be that driving too fast causes the car to shake.

# Recap

In this chapter, we studied four types of inductive arguments—statistical syllogisms, generalizations, analogical arguments, and causal arguments. We learned the structures of each, criteria for the strength of each, and mistakes associated with each. Below are some important definitions that should have been learned:

- **Analog**: In an analogy, the things being compared are *analogs*.
  - **Source Analog**: The *source analog* is the analog mentioned in the premise(s) of an analogical argument, but *not* in the conclusion.
  - **Target Analog**: The *target analog* is the analog mentioned in the conclusion of an analogical argument (and also in the premise[s]).
- **Analogical Argument**: An argument in which one draws an analogy between two things based on supposed similarities between them to support the conclusion that there is further similarity between them.
  - **Faulty Analogy**: A faulty analogy is a logical fallacy committed with analogical argument. It occurs when the dissimilarities of the analogs outweigh the similarities in relevancy if not in number.
- **Analogy**: An analogy is a comparison between two (or more) things, in which one focuses on what one takes to be similarities between the things compared.
- **Causal Argument**: An argument in which one concludes with a causal statement, where such a statement may be taken to be true, or as a hypothesis.
  - **Post Hoc Fallacy**: Post hoc (short for the Latin phrase *post hoc ergo propter hoc*) is a logical fallacy committed with causal reasoning, in which one reasons that some event C is the cause of another event E simply because C came before E in time.
- **Causal Hypothesis**: A *causal* hypothesis is a provisional and testable causal statement derived from observation and potentially tested with experiments.
- **Causal Statement**: A causal statement is one that asserts that one event is the cause of another event.
- **Generalization**: An argument in which one draws a conclusion about a population from an observation of a portion of that population.
  - **Hasty Generalization**: A hasty generalization is a logical fallacy committed with generalizations. It occurs when the sample size of a generalization is too small relative to the target.
- **Mill's Methods**: Four methods proposed by the nineteenth-century English philosopher John Stuart Mill. The methods are used to derive rational causal statements or hypotheses.
  - **Method of Agreement**: In the *method of agreement*, one judges a causal statement to be true, or adopts a causal hypothesis, based on multiple instances of some event, each instance of which has different factors, except for a common factor, which is postulated to be the cause of the event.
  - **Method of Difference**: In the *method of difference*, one judges a causal statement to be true, or adopts a causal hypothesis, based on the fact that some event is

present in one scenario but not present in a similar scenario, and that there is only one other relevant difference between the scenarios, which is postulated to be the cause of the event.

- **Method of Concomitant Variation**: In the *method of concomitant variation*, one derives a causal statement, or forms a causal hypothesis, as a result of observing that the occurrence of instances of an event vary based on the variation of some other factor associated with the instances.

- **Method of Residues**: In the *method of residues*, one judges a causal statement to be true, or forms a causal hypothesis, by a process of elimination, in which one proceeds by observing that there is a set of events associated with a set of the potential causes. One knows that all but one of the potential causes are causally linked to all but one of events needing explanation. The conclusion is that the remaining potential cause is the cause of the remaining event needing explanation.

- **Relevant Property**: In generalizations and analogical arguments, the relevant feature is a property said to be had by the target (based on the fact that it is had by the sample or source).

- **Sample**: In a generalization, the observed portion of the target is the *sample*.
  - **Large Sample Criterion**: Up to a point, the larger the sample in a generalization, relative to the target group, the stronger the argument.
  - **Representative Sample Criterion**: The more that the diversity of the sample reflects the diversity of the target in a generalization, the stronger the argument.
  - **Unbiased Sample**: In a generalization, a sample is unbiased if and only if every member of the target population has an equal chance of being a member of the sample.
  - **Unbiased Sample Criterion**: In a generalization, the more that the sample is unbiased, the stronger the argument.
    - ▲ **Random Sampling**: *Random sampling* is a process of picking the desired sample from a population in such a way that each member of the population has an equal chance of being selected until the desired sample size is achieved.

- **Statistical Syllogism**: An argument in which one applies a general statement, or statistical data, to a particular scenario.

- **Target**: In a generalization, population over which one is generalizing is the target (short for *target group or population*).

---

**EXERCISE 8.5**

Identify each argument below as statistical syllogism, generalization, analogical argument, or causal argument.

*1. My energy bill last July was very high, since I was running my A/C all day to keep my house cool from the heat. I bet this July's energy bill will be even higher, since it has been an even hotter month.

2. *Gerald*: I just bought a Harley motorcycle.

   *Henry*: Bad idea! It's going to leak oil a lot, since most Harleys leak oil a lot.

*3. Scorpions and crabs are basically the same, or at least very similar. So, no doubt crabs are poisonous, since scorpions are.

4. *Jill*: I don't want to go to that store! The employees there are very rude!

   *Sophie*: Why do you think that they are rude?

   *Jill*: Well, because the last two times I was in there the employee helping me each time was rude to me.

5. The past several times that the Atlanta Falcons have played the Buffalo Bills, the Falcons have won. However, the Falcons lost last Sunday. It must be because Matt Ryan did not play quarterback for the Falcons last Sunday, which resulted in their loss.

*6. M. Night Shyamalan movies are scary, judging from the one I watched last night.

7. A majority of Democrats favor universal health care, and since Senator Smith is a Democrat, he favors universal health care.

8. Target gives refunds on returns, no questions asked. I found this out yesterday when I returned a shirt I did not like. They refunded my money without any questions.

9. I love the Trader Joe's brand of coffee. So, I'm sure I'll love the Trader Joe's brand of oatmeal.

10. Mental states are correlated with physical brain states. Whenever the brain is stimulated in various ways, a person experiences various mental states. Thus, brain states cause mental states.

# INDUCTIVE LOGIC II
## Inference to the Best Explanation

# 9

In chapter 8, we took a brief look at *causal* explanations, and considered Mills' Methods for choosing which explanation to adopt (at least as a hypothesis) based on those methods. In this chapter, we will take a closer look at explanations, not just causal explanations, and focus on what is called *inference to the best explanation* as a method for choosing which explanation to adopt. Let's begin by thinking about a couple of cases involving competing explanations.

After putting out the forest fire, investigators determine that the fire was started by lightning striking the dry forest. Or course, they *could* be wrong. It could be that evil spirits started the fire. However, probably the *better* explanation in this case is that the fire was caused by lightning striking a dry tree.

You are rock climbing up a cliff and as you reach the top, you look down to the ground floor below and see *Amy Smith* clearly spelled out with rocks. You conclude that someone (probably named *Amy Smith*) was there previously and spelled out the name with rocks. Of course, you *could* be mistaken, and perhaps the rocks formed that way by a combination of erosion, falling rocks, and other natural events. But the *better* explanation for the formation of rocks is your explanation that a person was there and *intended* to spell out the name with rocks.

We encounter phenomena in need of explanation every day, and daily offer explanations for such phenomena. Further, we frequently seek for, or believe that we are offering, the *best* explanation for the various phenomena. But how do we decide which is the *best* explanation? In this chapter we will explore this issue. More specifically, we will take a closer look at explanations, criteria for determining the best explanation, and how to apply the criteria relative to the type of explanations under investigation. Here are some key terms to master when working through the chapter.

## KEY WORDS

Epistemically Good Explanations
Explanandum
Explanans
Explanation
Explanatory Power
Explanatory Scope
Independent Support for Explanans

Inference to the Best Explanation
Metaphysically Good Explanations
Non-Causal Explanation
Nonrepeatable Causal Explanation
Problems with Explanans
Repeatable Causal Explanation
Teleological Explanation

**KEY CONCEPT:
EXPLANATION**

An **explanation** is a collection of statements in which one
states *how* or *why* something is
the case.

# A Closer Look at Explanations

In chapter 4, we stated that an explanation is stating *why* or *how*
something is the case. Let's elaborate. In this section, we will take
a closer look at explanations by doing the following: making a distinction between explanatory acts and explanations; focusing our
attention on *why* explanations; discussing the relata of explanations
and establishing some terminology; stating the difference between
true and false explanations, and distinguishing between two types of causal explanations; and
considering non-causal explanations.

## Explanatory Acts vs. Explanations

In thinking about explanations, it is important to distinguish between an *act* of offering an
explanation (an explanatory act) and the *product* of the explanatory act, which is the *explanation*.
An explanatory *act* is just what it sounds like—it is an act of a person offering an explanation
to someone; it is a social interaction. In such an interaction, a person offers an *explanation* to
another. The explanation is the product of the act.

In contrast, an explanation is *not* a social interaction. Indeed, it is *not* an act at all. Rather, it
is a collection of statements, which involves a relationship between two (or more) statements—
more on this below. Our focus is on explanations, and *not* on explanatory acts.

## Why vs. How Explanations

Explanations state *how* or *why* something is the case. *How* explanations include such explanations as *how to ride a bike, how to get from point A to point B*, et cetera. While some of these
are interesting and certainly worth thinking about, such as *how did life on earth appear*, often
they do not involve serious critical thinking, such as in the case of *how to boil an egg* or *how to
get from point A to point B.*

In contrast, *why* explanations answer the question of *why* something is the case:

- Why does the earth revolve around the sun and not fly off into space?
- Why do the rocks spell out *Amy Smith* down below?
- Why do bodybuilders eat bananas?
- Why does a good God allow evil?
- Why is the universe fine-tuned for intelligent life?

These often require much more critical thinking, especially when it comes to determining the *best* answer. Thus, our focus will be on explanations saying *why* various things are the case, though occasional examples will be *how* explanations.

## The Relata

An explanation expresses a relation between at least two things. But what things does the explanation relation relate—that is, what are its *relata*? There is not agreement on this among philosophers. Some suggest that the relata are *facts*, others that they are *events*, others treat the relata as *phenomena*, and others as *statements*. It could be that all of these are correct, as perhaps the explanation relation relates a variety of things. However, for our purposes, which we choose will not matter. Thus, to simplify, we will treat the relata as *statements*. More specifically, in a *correct* explanation, one statement being true is being explained by another statement being true. Here are some examples, using *because* or *in virtue of* to express the explanation relation:

1.  *There was a forest fire because lightning struck a dry tree.*
2.  *The rocks spell out "Amy Smith" in virtue of a person arranging the rocks to spell "Amy Smith."*
3.  *The ball is red because it is crimson.*

Following convention, we will call the statement that is being *explained* the *explanandum*, and we will call the statement that contains the explanation the *explanans*. So, in 1–3 above, the statement that comes before *because* or *in virtue of* is the *explanandum* and the statement that comes after *because* or *in virtue of* is the *explanans*. So, in an explanation, the explanans is offered as the *why* (or *how*) the explanandum is true.

## Correct and Incorrect Explanations

Just above, it was stated that in a **correct** explanation, one statement being true is being explained by another being true. Let's elaborate.

First, *correct* explanations are *objectively* correct (see chapter 2 on objectivity). The explanation relation is a *real* relation holding between true statements in objective reality. What we are trying to *discover* with our critical thinking is the *correct* (objective) explanation *in the particular case under investigation*.

Second, there are *incorrect* explanations. These are presented with the same form: *statement P is true because statement Q is true.*

So, what is the (objective) difference between correct and incorrect explanations? *Correct* explanations have two features: (a) *both* the explanandum and explanans are true, *and* (b) the explanation relation really does hold between the explanandum and the explanans. In contrast, in an incorrect explanation (of the form *P is true because Q is true*), either (a) the explanans (Q) *is true* but the explanation relation fails to hold between the explanans (Q) and explanandum (P)—that is, the incorrect explanation notwithstanding, it is not the case that *P is true because Q is true*, even if both P and Q are true, or (b) the explanans (Q) is *false*, which of course entails that the explanation relation fails to hold between the explanans and explanandum.

Determining whether an explanation is correct or incorrect can be easy or difficult, depending on the case. And, some we may simply never know. Often the best we can do is choose the best among alternatives and hope that we have the correct one. Later in the chapter we will consider criteria for what makes an explanation a good one, and thus what we should look for to determine which is the best explanation.

## Repeatable Causal, Nonrepeatable Causal, and Non-Causal Explanations

All explanations involve expressing *a relation* between the explanans and the explanandum, which we often express with *because* or *in virtue of*. Again, consider the examples from above:

1. *There was a forest fire* because *lightning struck a dry tree.*
3. *The ball is red* in virtue of *the fact that it is crimson.*

However, not all the relations expressed by *because* or *in virtue of* express the same relations, even though one often reads in the literature that all such relations are *causal*.

Indeed, *some* of these relations are *causal*. They express that the explanans is the *cause of* the explanandum—or perhaps better, that the phenomena referenced in the explanandum are caused by the phenomena referenced in the explanans. This is clearly the explanatory relation being expressed in (1). It can be expressed this way:

1a. Lightning striking a dry tree *is the cause of* the forest fire.

Among causal explanations, we can further distinguish between *repeatable* causal explanations and *nonrepeatable* causal explanation. While the explanatory relation in both is a *causal* relation, the difference is that with *repeatable* causal explanations, the causal relationship has, will, or at least can obtain between similar explanans and explananda many times throughout history—such as lightning strikes causing fires. In contrast, *nonrepeatable* causal explanations are such that the causal relationship obtains *only once* since the explanandum and explanans are unique, one-time events. We will elaborate on this below.

However, *other* relations in the explanation are clearly *not* causal. Consider (3), for example. It makes no sense to say:

3a. The ball being crimson *is the cause of* the ball being red.

(3a) is false, since the sort of relationship between the general property *red* (called a *determinable*) and the specific property *crimson* (called a *determinate*) is *not* a causal one.

Rather, we can say that it involves a *metaphysical grounding* relation (however this is analyzed or not analyzed). Thus, a correct way to state (3) in other terms is:

3b. The ball being crimson *grounds* the ball being red.

And, for emphasis, *ground* here is *not* causation.

## Teleological Explanations

One kind of non-causal relationship worth mentioning is what is called a *teleological* explanation. Teleological explanations appeal to the *purpose, end, goal,* or *function* of something—more exactly, the *explanans* refers the *purpose, end, goal,* or *function* of the phenomena referenced in the explanandum. These explanations are called *teleological* explanations, from the Greek words *telos* (which translates as "end") and *logos* (which translates as "reason"). Many of these refer to the intentions of a person.

The reason we are treating these as *non-causal* explanations is because the explanans does *not* reference phenomena that *cause* the phenomena referenced in the explanandum. Rather the phenomena referenced in the explanandum occur (whatever their cause) *for the sake of* the phenomena referenced in the explanans. We often express the explanatory relation in these with the phrase *in order to*. Here are some examples:

4. The cat's heart beats *in order to* circulate blood through its body.
5. The German shepherd barked at the pit bull *in order to* warn the pit bull to stay away.
6. The police officer pulled his gun *in order to* stop the criminal.
7. God allows evil *in order to* allow humans to have freedom of will.

### Distinguishing Repeatable Causal, Nonrepeatable Causal, and Non-Causal Explanations

It is not always clear whether the explanatory relation is *repeatable* causal, *nonrepeatable* causal, or *non-causal*. However, in many cases we *can* distinguish these, which is important because it affects how we apply the criteria for what makes an explanation a good explanation, and thus what makes one the *best* explanation. So, we should have some idea of how to do so. One way to distinguish these is to ask whether it makes sense to treat the phenomena referenced in the explanans as a *cause* of the phenomena referenced in the explanandum. And, if it makes sense to treat it as *causal*, we should ask whether the explanans and explanandum are *repeatable* (i.e., there have been, will be, or can be similar explanandum and explanans), or whether they are unique, one-time events. Often the answer will be clear. Here are some examples in which we can treat the explanatory relation (expressed with *because*) as *repeatable* causal:

8. The car tire pressure is low because there was a drastic temperature drop overnight.
9. The earth revolves around the sun because the mass of the sun curves the space around it (generating the gravitational force), causing the earth to spiral around the curvature.
10. The deep-sea fish died when it was brought to the surface because the pressure decreased dramatically as it was raised, rapidly increasing the volume of gases in its blood and swim bladder.
11. The leaves turn from green to red or yellow in the fall because as the temperature gets colder, the leaves stop making chlorophyll (which absorbs all sunlight colors except green, which is reflected back), but instead breaks down chlorophyll into smaller molecules, leading to other pigments in the leaf (carotenoids, anthocyanins, tannins) becoming visible.

In each of these, it makes sense to treat the explanans as the *cause* of the explanandum, and notice that each involves repeatable phenomena, which means that we can use empirical, scientific methods for applying the criteria for determining a good, and the best, explanation.

In contrast, there are cases in which the explanatory relation is clearly causal, but is also clearly *nonrepeatable*, involving unique, one-time events. Here are some examples:

12. The universe is fine-tuned for life because God designed and created it to be fine-tuned.
13. The dinosaurs all died because a meteor struck the earth, killing them.
14. The tomb was found empty because Jesus rose from the dead and left the tomb.
15. World War I started because the Serbian terrorist Gavrilo Princip assassinated Archduke of Austria, Franz Ferdinand.

Clearly, the *because* in each of these indicates a *causal* relationship between the explanans and explanandum. However, none of these events are repeatable. Thus, how we apply our criteria for testing good explanations *cannot* be by way of trying to repeat the events by experiment, nor by looking at how frequently such events have occurred, nor by predictions they make. They each involve unique, one-time causal relationships. Thus, we must apply our criteria to test them in different ways, which will be illustrated below.

Finally, in other explanations, it simply makes no sense to treat the explanatory relation (expressed with *because*) to be *causal*. Here are some examples:

16. The morning star is the evening star because the morning star is numerically identical to Venus and the evening star is numerically identical to Venus.
17. Mental states are not brain states because brain states and mental states have entirely different properties.
18. John Smith freely chose to eat the chicken because he wanted chicken.
19. The act is wrong because it treats the person as a means merely.

Each of these expresses a different explanatory relation, but importantly, none expresses a *causal* relationship. Thus, like nonrepeatable causal, we *cannot* apply our criteria for testing good explanations by way of trying to repeat the events by experiment, by looking at how frequently such events have occurred, or by predictions they make, since the explanatory relationship is *non-causal*. Thus, we must apply our criteria to test them in different ways, which will be illustrated below.

Being able to determine the difference between these three types of explanations is important, once again, because it affects how we apply the criteria for determining the best explanation.

**EXERCISE 9.1**

Review Questions

1. What is an explanation?
2. True or false: Explanatory acts and explanations are the same thing.
3. What do we call the part of the explanation that is being explained?
4. What do we call the part of the explanation that is doing the explaining?

5. True or false: Whether an explanation is correct or incorrect is subjective.

6. What are the two features of all (and only) correct explanations?

7. What is a repeatable causal explanation?

8. What is a nonrepeatable causal explanation?

9. True or False: The explanation relation in *non-causal* explanations is *not* a causal relation.

10. What is a teleological explanation?

## EXERCISE 9.2

For each explanation below, state which part is the explanans and explanandum.

**\*1.** The lack of water is what caused the tree to die.

**2.** Arnold took steroids in order to get larger muscles.

**3.** Tom does not wear shoes because all shoes hurt his feet.

**\*4.** There appears to be a table there in virtue of simple particles being arranged in a "table-wise" way.

**5.** The fact that humans have free will explains the fact that we cannot predict perfectly how a human will act in some environment in the future.

**6.** Why is there so much crime in New York City? It is, in large part, a result of Mayor de Blasio's actions, including, but not limited to, bail reform, releasing prisoners, being weak on pursuing criminals, and actually defunding the police!

**\*7.** Your extra belly fat as of late is caused by your excessive alcohol use.

**8.** I'll tell you why the remote suddenly stopped working: You banged it on the coffee table!

**9.** God declaring that murder is wrong is the ground of murder being wrong.

**10.** There was an explosion in the garage because of the leaking propane tank being ignited by a spark from the faulty wiring.

## EXERCISE 9.3

For each explanation below, state whether it is a *repeatable causal*, a *nonrepeatable causal*, or a *non-causal explanation*, and if it is a non-causal *teleological explanation*, indicate this.

**\*1.** There is water on the kitchen floor because someone dropped an ice cube and it melted.

**2.** The hypotenuse of a right triangle is the longest side because its square is equal to the *sum* of the squares of the other two sides of the triangle.

**3.** The Israelites were finally able to leave Egypt because Pharaoh ordered them to leave after all the Egyptian first-born male babies died, including Pharaoh's son.

**\*4.** Paul wrote his letter to the Romans, in part, because he wanted to explain the gospel of grace to them.

**5.** The printer put out a blank page because it is out of ink.

**6.** There are universal human rights because all humans share the same nature.

**\*7.** Japan surrendered in 1945 because the United States dropped atomic bombs on Hiroshima and Nagasaki.

**8.** The air here is toxic because of the chemicals being released from the factory.

**9.** Jared took the longer route home in order to avoid the traffic on the shorter route.

**10.** The water pipes cracked because the water in them froze, expanded.

## Inference to the Best Explanation

Our goal as critical thinkers, obviously, is to adopt the *correct* explanation—the one in which both the explanandum and explanans are true, and in which the explanation relation really does hold between the explanandum and explanans. However, often the best we can do is choose the *best* explanation among alternatives and hope that our *reasonable* choice based on our critical thinking is the correct choice. As critical thinkers, one way of getting at the best explanation is to is create an *inference to the best explanation* argument or engage in *inference to the best explanation* reasoning. An inference to the best explanation can be expressed this way:

> Inference to the Best Explanation: An inference to the best explanation is an *inference* in which one concludes that one explanation among competing explanations is the *best* explanation based on *correct-indicating* features of explanations.

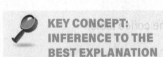

**KEY CONCEPT: INFERENCE TO THE BEST EXPLANATION**

An **inference to the best explanation** is an inference in which one concludes that one explanation among competing explanations is the *best* explanation based on *correct-indicating* features of explanations.

Below we will unpack this.

Sometimes an inference to the best explanation is rather easy, such as explaining rocks spelling out *Amy Smith* on the mountain floor in terms of a *person* forming them that way over explaining the formation in terms of *erosion and rockslides,* if these are the only options. Other examples are much more difficult, such as explaining why an electron sometimes behaves as a wave and sometimes as a particle. So, to help us think about the more difficult cases, and even be more confident in the easier cases, we should think about the *correct-indicating* criteria for determining what makes an explanation a *good* explanation, and in turn what we are appealing to in our inference to the *best* explanation.

## What Is a Good Explanation?

In order to answer that question, we need to make an important distinction—between an explanation being *metaphysically* good and an explanation being *epistemically* good.

*Metaphysics* is the branch of philosophy that studies the fundamental structure of reality; it has to do with *being*. Thus, an explanation is *metaphysically* good if and only if it is the *correct* explanation (objectively), based on the structure of reality.

In contrast, *epistemology* is the study of knowledge, and includes whether a belief is rational or irrational. Thus, an explanation is *epistemically* good if and only if it has features that indicate it is correct, which give us reason to believe that it is correct.

It should be clear that epistemologically good explanations vary in degrees of goodness. Some are better than others. Explanation A is better than an explanation B if and only if the *overall* correct-indicating features of A are more indicative of correctness than the *overall* correct-indicating features of B.

Our ultimate concern is to arrive at a metaphysically good explanation in every case. However, often the best we can do is arrive at an epistemically good explanation, and if there are competing explanations, choose the epistemically best explanation. So, our focus will be on criteria for *epistemically good explanations*, and in turn *epistemically best explanations* (hereafter, we'll just say *good explanation* or *best explanation* rather than qualifying these with *epistemically*, but we will intend the epistemic sense—though occasionally we will add the qualification for emphasis).

Note that the best explanation is defined in terms of the good explanation—that is, the best explanation is the one, among alternatives, that has the *overall* greater correct-indicating features. So, we'll consider some correct-indicating features of a good explanation.

To help us think about the criteria for an *epistemically* good explanation, let's recall what makes an explanation *metaphysically* good. A metaphysically good explanation is the *correct* explanation—which means that (i) both the explanandum *and* explanans are true, and (ii) the explanation relation really does hold between the explanans and explanandum (or to be more precise, it holds between the phenomena referenced in these). Thus, it makes sense to think that what makes an explanation *epistemically* good is that the explanation has features which indicate both (i) and (ii) of the metaphysical explanation. While philosophers have cited various features that make an explanation good, we'll focus on the following four:

- *Power of the explanation*
- *Scope of the explanation*
- *Support for the explanans*
- *Problems with the explanans*

The first of these criteria concern feature (ii) of a metaphysically good explanation—the *explanatory relation* between explanans and explanandum. The second also concerns the relationship between the explanans and explanandum, but also between the explanans and additional explananda. The last two concern feature (i) of a metaphysically good explanation—the *truth* of the explanans.

## Misguided Criteria

Before turning to our four criteria, which are acceptable criteria for *all* explanations, let's consider two criteria that have been, or may be, suggested, and show why we are *not* including them in our list of criteria for testing explanations.

These misguided criteria are being mentioned, and then set aside, for the following reason. Some (many) have been misled into thinking that *all* explanations must satisfy these (misguided) criteria in order to be good explanations, and thus are among the criteria for determining the best explanation, and as a result have ruled out some (good and even correct) explanations as bad, or not the best, by virtue of failing to meet these (misguided) criteria. The problem is that such (misguided) criteria have no application to the explanation being rejected, as such criteria are limited to only a small subcollection of explanations and don't apply to the explanation under investigation. It is like trying to find a plank of wood with a metal detector. It is instructive to consider them, and see how they are limited and why we are *not* including them in are list of criteria.

### Testable

Some have suggested that in order for an explanation to be a good explanation, it must be *testable* in a particular way. What such thinkers mean is that there must be some experiment or procedure that we can follow to test the explanation, where the sort of experiment or procedure is some sort of *empirical* test, often taken to be a *scientific* test. The problem with this is that it is limited to *causal* explanations, and in fact even further limited to *repeatable* causal explanations.

First, the testability criterion does not apply to non-causal explanations, which are perfectly acceptable, and often *correct*, explanations. For example, consider again (17) and (19) from above:

17. Mental states are not brain states because brain states and mental states have entirely different properties.
19. The act is wrong because it treats the person as a means merely.

There are good (philosophical) reasons for thinking that not only is each of these a *good* explanation, but that each is the *correct* explanation. However, there is no experiment, nor any *empirical* procedure, for testing these. Of course, we could engage in *thought* experiments, but these are not the sorts of procedures that testability criterion requires. Thus, since (17) and (19) are perfectly *good* explanations, and arguably *correct*, but they are not testable in the *way* that the testability criterion requires, we must reject the testability criterion *as a general criterion* for good theories.

Second, the testability criterion does not apply to *nonrepeatable* causal explanations. For example, it does not apply to unique events in history. Consider (12) and (14) from above:

12. The universe if fine-tuned for life because God designed and created it to be fine-tuned.
14. The tomb was found empty because Jesus rose from the dead and left the tomb.

These are both *causal* explanations. Jesus rising from the dead and leaving the tomb would *cause* it to be empty, and God designing the universe to be fine-tuned for life would *cause* it to be so. However, both of these events (Jesus rising from the dead and leaving the tomb, and God designing the universe) are *unique* events. Because they were one-time, unique events in history (let's assume for the moment), there is no test or procedure that we could do to confirm them, at least not in the *way* that this criterion requires. Nevertheless, not only are these perfectly good explanations, they are arguably the *correct* explanations. And, of course, unique historical events are not limited to religious examples, but include a host of examples from many areas. For example, *The Library of Alexandria was destroyed by fire because Julius Caesar set fire to the Egyptian ships, and the fire spread to the rest of the city, including the library.* Once again, the testability criterion simply does not apply.

Therefore, because the *testability* criterion does not apply to many causal explanations (but applies only to a limited subcollection of causal explanations), and because it does not apply at all to non-causal explanations, we will not include the testability criterion in our list of criteria for what makes an explanation a good one.

### Predictive Power

Some have suggested that in order for an explanation to be a good explanation, it must have *predictive power*—*it* must allow us to more or less accurately predict some *new*, previously *unknown*, feature of the universe. This is different from the *testability* criterion in that an explanation can be testable by experiment (e.g., we can mix chemicals in a lab to test an explanation about chemical compounds) without predicting some *new*, previously *unknown*, feature of the universe. But, the problem with this criterion is exactly the same as the last criterion—namely, that it is limited to only a subcollection of *causal* explanations.

Again, consider unique historical events—such as Jesus rising from the dead (explaining the empty tomb and the eyewitness accounts, etc.). Since this was a miraculous event, if it occurred, and a unique one at that, it does not allow us to make any successful predictions about other dead people. Nevertheless, it is a *causal* explanation, and a *good* explanation, and arguably the *correct* explanation.

And, as with the testability criterion, the *predictive power* criterion does not apply to non-causal explanations. Consider the *good*, and plausibly *correct*, explanation in (18):

18. John Smith freely chose to eat the chicken because he wanted chicken.

This does not lend itself to future predictions, since in the future John may want chicken but choose to not have chicken, since it is a *free will* act.

Thus, as with the testability criterion, since the *predictive power* criterion does not apply to many causal explanations (but applies only to limited subcollection of causal explanations), and because it does not apply at all to non-causal explanations, we will not include the predictive power criterion in our list of criterions for what makes an explanation a good one.

### Correct Criteria

Having considered and set aside some misguided criteria for what makes an explanation a good one, let's consider some good criteria. We are calling these the *good* criteria for three reasons.

First, the criteria are related directly to the structure of what makes a *metaphysical* explanation a good one—namely, in a good *metaphysical* explanation, the explanans is true, and there really is an explanatory relationship between the explanans and explanandum. As will be shown, the criteria that we will consider are related directly to these features.

Second, the criteria are universal—that is, the criteria apply to *all* explanations, to both types of causal explanations and to non-causal explanations.

Third, the criteria are objective. Whether one explanation is a good explanation, and whether one is better than another, is an *objective* issue and not simply a matter of which the chooser prefers. To help see this, compare two explanations:

20. The glass of water spilled because the cat jumped onto the counter and knocked it over while trying to drink from it.
21. The glass of water spilled because the glass was tired of standing upright and decided to fall over.

Clearly, (20) is the better explanation (objectively) even if someone prefers (21) because they like the idea of a glass choosing to fall over. What a person prefers is irrelevant to whether an explanation is a good one, and whether it is the *best* among alternatives.

Also, above it was stated that we are considering *some* good criteria. Perhaps there are additional good criteria that we are not considering. But if there are additional criteria, still the criteria we are considering are central and are important and will do for everyday purposes of helping us to choose the best explanation.

## Explanatory Power

To begin our discussion of this criterion, let's note that it is *different* from the *predictive power* criterion above. The *explanatory power* of an explanation concerns the explanatory relationship between the explanans and explanandum—in other words—how well the explanans explains the explanandum. Let's be more specific. Something E is evidence for something H if E makes it more likely that H is true. Given this, we can state the explanatory power criterion this way:

> *Explanatory Power*: The greater the evidential support that the explanans gives to the explanandum, the greater the explanatory power of the explanation.

This leads us to our first criterion for choosing between competing explanations:

> Explanatory Power Criterion: All else being equal, an explanation that has the greatest explanatory power (among the available explanations) is the epistemically best explanation (among the available explanations)—that is, is more likely true (among the available explanations).

In the statement of this criterion, it was noted three times that its application is relative to *available explanations*. Let's look a bit further into this. There are three levels, which give us three levels of confidence that we can have in our conclusion. The first level involves a comparison of explanations immediately known to the thinker. So, for example, at a given moment you may be attempting to choose whether the best explanation for your car not starting is that it is out of gas or it has a clogged fuel filter. You are choosing between these, *in this moment*, because that is all *you* know about. You may decide that *given your knowledge* the best explanation is the clogged fuel filter. However, this conclusion is relative to your knowledge at the time. You should be open to being corrected by your mechanic after they inspect your engine.

At that time, the mechanic may add other options to your (and their) options and may see an explanation with even greater explanatory power.

At the second level, there is comparison of available options that we *humans* have in our available explanations, given the history of thought. So, for example, we may be evaluating philosophical explanations for a particular philosophical puzzle, where the explanations we are considering are *all* those available *since the beginning of recorded human thought*. We then apply the explanatory power criteria to these, and draw a conclusion about which is the best. In these cases, we can have more confidence in our conclusions, since we are expanding the available options to all known to humans up to that time. Of course, even these are subject to being overturned as we learn more.

At the third level, there is comparison of all *possible* explanations. In some cases, we may be able to know all the possible explanations because they are logically limited to just a small few, which we can see. But, with many others, we will not be able to know all the possible options, as we are simply limited as humans. We strive for this third level but are typically limited to the first two levels.

The point here is that we should understand that the application of the explanatory power criterion should be understood to be *relative to available options*, and conclusions should be accepted with the appropriate level of confidence, with an awareness that we may discover new explanations that could replace the old as better explanations. This happens in science all the time.

Each of the criteria that we will discuss below has the same relativity to available criteria—that is, each applies to the available explanations. Having elaborated here on this relativity, we will not do so in the criteria below, but the same elaboration applies to each criterion.

The relativity of the application of this criterion is in place no matter what kind of explanations (i.e., repeatable causal, to nonrepeatable causal, or to non-causal explanations causal) that we are considering. However, there is a difference in *how* we apply the criterion, depending on whether it is applied to repeatable causal, to nonrepeatable causal, or to non-causal explanations. We will explore these differences later in this chapter. However, it will be instructive to consider one example here. Consider the example above about the rocks spelling *Amy Smith*, and compare two explanations of this:

22. The rocks spell *Amy Smith* because a person arranged the rocks to spell *Amy Smith*.
23. The rocks spell *Amy Smith* because over time through erosion, falling rocks, and other natural phenomena the rocks came to be so arranged.

Regarding the relativity of available options, we can stipulate that these are the only known (viable) options and compare the two. Furthermore, among these two, there is a very low probability that the rocks would come to be arranged to spell *Amy Smith* by the natural phenomena referenced in the explanans in (23). Thus, the explanans in (23) does not make it very likely that explanandum would be true. However, the explanans in (22) would make it highly likely that the explanandum would be true. Hence, (22) has greater explanatory power than does (23). Thus, all else being equal, (22) is the better explanation because it has greater explanatory power, *among these options*. If these are the only two we know about, then we should adopt

(22), but with an appropriate level of adherence, realizing that it could be overthrown by a better explanation. And if these are the only two *possible* explanations, then (22) is the *best* explanation, period, and we should adopt it with great confidence.

### Explanatory Scope

The *explanatory scope* of an explanation concerns the relationship between the explanans and explanandum in a given explanation, *and* between the explanans and additional explananda. Let's elaborate.

The scope of the explanans includes any explanandum that it explains. If we were to assign a numeric value to the scope of an explanans, and if an explanans explains exactly one explanandum, then the explanans has a scope of 1. If it explains two explananda, it has a scope of 2, et cetera. Here is an example of an explanans having a scope of at least 2:

20. The grass is wet (here and now) because it is raining (here and now).
21. The car is wet (here and now) because it is raining (here and now).

Here the explanans (*it is raining [here and now]*) explains the *two* explananda (and no doubt many more)—namely, *the grass is wet* and *the car is wet*. So, we have:

> *Explanatory Scope*: The more explananda that the explanans explains, the greater the scope of the explanans.

This leads us to accept our second criterion for choosing between competing explanations:

> Explanatory Scope Criterion: All else being equal, an explanation that has the greatest explanatory scope (among the available explanations) is the epistemically best explanation (among the available explanations)—that is, is more likely true (among the available explanations).

Let consider another example, using the rocks spelling *Amy Smith*. Again, we have:

22. The rocks spell *Amy Smith* because a person arranged the rocks to spell *Amy Smith*.
23. The rocks spell *Amy Smith* because over time through erosion, falling rocks, and other natural phenomena the rocks came to be so arranged.

Set aside explanatory power for a moment, and let's focus on scope. Suppose that in addition to the rock arrangement (spelling *Amy Smith*) there are shoeprints all around the rock arrangement. The explanans in (22)—there was a person present who arranged the rocks—explains the shoe prints. However, the explanans in (23)—the rocks became so arranged from erosion, falling rocks, and other natural phenomena—provides *no* explanation for the shoe prints. Therefore, (22) has greater explanatory scope than does (23), relative to the factors we are considering. Thus, explanatory power aside, and all else being equal, (22) is the better explanation (among our available explanations) because it has greater explanatory scope (in this case), and if these are the only two *possible* explanations, then (22) is the *best* explanation, and we should adopt it.

### Independent Support for the Explanans

Recall that what makes a *metaphysical* explanation a good one is, in part, that its explanans is *true*. This third criterion tells us that we increase the *epistemic* value of an explanation by providing independent support for its explanans—that is, support for its truth independent of the explanation in question.

Before stating the criterion explicitly, let's consider an example. We'll again use the rock arrangement example:

22. The rocks spell *Amy Smith* because a person arranged the rocks to spell *Amy Smith*.
23. The rocks spell *Amy Smith* because over time through erosion, falling rocks, and other natural phenomena the rocks came to be so arranged.

Suppose we add that we know that Amy Smith reported a week ago that she would be going rock climbing in the very location where the rocks are so arranged. This provides independent support for the explanans in (22), since we now have independent reason to believe not only that a person was in the spot, but that it was *Amy Smith*! But suppose that we have no independent support for rocks naturally being arranged to spell anything, let alone *Amy Smith*. In this case, if the two explanations are otherwise equal, we have greater reason to prefer (22). Thus, we have our third criterion for choosing between competing explanations:

> Independent Support for the Explanans Criterion: All else being equal, an explanation whose explanans has the most independent support (among the available explanations) is the epistemically best explanation (among the available explanations)—that is, is more likely true (among the available explanations).

Here's another example: Suppose that Fred and Wilma enter the kitchen to find the milk glass knocked over with the milk spilling out. They offer the following explanations:

> *Fred*: The milk glass is knocked over because a strong wind blew through the open window and knocked over the glass.

> *Wilma*: The milk glass is knocked over because the cat was attempting to drink from the glass and knocked it over.

Let's suppose, for the moment, that these are equal in power and scope. How do we decide which is the better explanation—that is, more likely the correct one? Well, suppose that as they are debating the issue, Betty enters and says that when she was looking through the *closed* window a few minutes ago on her way to the door, she saw the cat sitting on the counter next to the glass of milk. This provides support to Wilma's explanans, since we have independent reason to accept that there was a cat present and that it was sitting on the counter near the glass of milk. In contrast, notice that Betty included the detail that the kitchen window was *closed*. This means that Fred lacks similar independent support for his explanans. Thus, if the two explanations are otherwise equal, Wilma's is the better explanation.

Let's be clear about the difference between explanatory scope of the explanans and independent support for the explanans. Something is in the *scope* of the explanans if the explanans explains it, otherwise not. In contrast, something can provide evidential support to the explanans but fail to be in its scope. Let's consider a couple of examples to make this point clear.

Think about the rock arrangement cases once again. Compare Amy's report (that she would be rock climbing) to the shoeprints (around the rocks). The explanans (*that there was a person who arranged the rocks*) *does explain* the shoeprints since a person arranging rocks would tend to leave shoeprints *but does not explain her report from a week prior. Thus, the shoeprints are in the scope of the explanans, but the report is not. However, the report does offer independent support to the explanans since it does give us some reason to accept that there would be a person present.*

Likewise, in the spilled milk cases, Betty's report is not in the scope of the explanans *that the cat knocked over the glass* since that statement does not *explain* Betty's observation that there was a cat sitting near the glass. In contrast, Betty's report does give us reason to believe that there was a cat and that it was near the glass, and thus supports the explanans. So, explanatory scope of the explanans and independent support for the explanans are two different criteria.

**Fewer Problems than Rivals**

This last criterion also concerns the explanans. Broadly, there are two ways that an explanans can be problematic. First, the explanans may be *incompatible* with something we know to be true or have good reason to accept as true. Second, it may presuppose (or assume) a statement that is unsupported in a problematic way or is unreasonable. Let's consider each of these.

*Incompatibility Problem*

Two statements are incompatible if and only if they contradict each other—they necessarily have opposite truth-values, or they are contraries, such that if one is true, the other must be false, though both could be false (see chapter 6 for more on contradictories and contraries). Both of these entail that incompatible statements cannot both be true simultaneously.

Relating this to an explanation, an explanation can be problematic by virtue of its explanans being *incompatible* with other things we know or have good reason to believe. If this is the case, then either we should outright reject the explanans, and thus the explanation that contains it, or at least be slow to accept it until we engage in further critical thought about the issues. Let's consider an example.

Consider our Fred and Wilma explanations, together with Betty's report. Their explanations were:

> *Fred*: The milk glass is knocked over because a strong wind blew through the open window and knocked over the glass.

> *Wilma*: The milk glass is knocked over because the cat was attempting to drink from the glass and knocked it over.

And, Betty reported that she was looking through the *closed* window when she saw the cat. If we assume that we have good reason to accept that Betty's report is true, then there is a *problem* with Fred's explanans. It is *incompatible* with something else we know, or have good reason to believe, about reality—namely, the window was *closed*, which would prevent the wind from blowing in.

There are a few points worth noting about this potential problem. First, before rejecting an explanans as false on the grounds that it conflicts with an apparent truth, we need to be sure that there really is a conflict. Here is an example. Consider again (22).

22. The rocks spell *Amy Smith* because a person arranged the rocks to spell *Amy Smith*.

Now suppose that someone points out that a reputable and very watchful park ranger has been carefully monitoring the area for years via a satellite and has reported that until your recent arrival to climb the rock, there has been no person there. One may take the explanans in (22) to conflict with something we have very good reason to believe—namely, the ranger's report—and thus that the explanans is to be rejected as false, and thus that the explanation fails.

The problem is that there is not really an incompatibility here. There are a number of ways in which both the ranger's report and the explanans in (22) can be true. For example, perhaps in spite of his usual careful attentiveness, the ranger fell asleep while Amy Smith was there arranging the rocks. Or perhaps the usually reliable satellite stopped relaying information while Amy Smith was there. The point is that we need to be sure there really is a conflict before we reject that explanans, and thus reject the explanation.

Second, the degree of confidence we should place in the explanans being *false* as a result of a *real* conflict is proportional to the amount of or type of reasons we have for the conflicting statement. After all, not all statements share the same degree of, or same type of, support. For example, our reasons for accepting that there is intelligent life on earth (us) is far greater than our reasons for thinking that there is other intelligent life in the universe *even if* we assume that we have *some* evidence for the latter. And, the type of evidence we have that 2 + 2 = 4 is not only different from but much stronger than the evidence we have that the expansion of the universe began with a big bang.

So, if the explanans conflicts with a statement that we have *very* good reason to accept, then we have that much reason to reject the explanans, and thus the explanation that contains it. In contrast, if the explanans conflicts with a statement that we have *only some* good reason to accept, but far less than conclusive reason to accept, then we have that much less reason to reject the explanans.

This brings us to our third point—if the explanans conflicts with a statement that we have less confidence in, because it simply does not enjoy a great deal of support, then perhaps the problem is not with the explanans but with the conflicting statement. Here is an example.

Suppose that someone offers the following explanation:

26. The vast array of life on earth is a result of an intelligent designer who created it.

Someone (e.g., Richard Dawkins) might suggest (indeed, Dawkins flat-out stated) that (26) conflicts with our well-established theory of evolution, according to which all life is a result of *blind, unguided* processes. That is, the claim is that the explanans of (26) is incompatible with:

27. All life is a result of blind, unguided processes.

But, someone (e.g., Alvin Plantinga) may point out that while there is indeed an incompatibility between the explanans of (26) and (27), the fact is that (27) is *not* an aspect of the theory of evolution, and in fact is not a statement of biology at all, nor a statement of any science. Indeed, it *cannot* be supported by science, since no experiment can verify or falsify it. Rather, (27) is a philosophical statement. The aspects of evolutionary theory for which we have *scientific* evidence (i.e., what really is included in our biological theory of evolution) *excludes* (27). Indeed, *scientific* evolutionary theory is perfectly compatible with an intelligent designer guiding the evolutionary processes.

Our defender of (26)—for example, Alvin Plantinga—may further point out that not only is (27) not a scientific thesis, it has no support at all, not even philosophical support. Thus, while there is indeed an incompatibility between the explanans of (26) and (27), this does not amount to a conflict between the explanans of (26) and science, but rather amounts to a conflict between the explanans of (26) and an unsupported philosophical thesis. Thus, one— for example, Alvin Plantinga—may suggest that since the explanans of (26) does explain the diversity of life, and since we have independent support for the explanans of (26), we should reject (27) and not the explanans of (26).

The third point here, illustrated with this rather lengthy example, is that sometimes when there is a conflict between an explanans and some other accepted statement, the statement to be rejected is not the explanans but the statement with which it conflicts.

There is an important general point to be made summing up these three notes. We have to be careful in rejecting an explanation because its explanans apparently conflicts with an apparent truth. We must take great care to ensure that (a) there really is a conflict between the explanans and some other accepting statement (point 1), (b) the conflicting statement really is well supported (point 2), and (c) the reasons we have for accepting the conflicting statement outweigh the reasons we have for accepting the explanans (point 3).

*Unsupported or Unreasonable Assumptions*

Alternatively, an explanans may be problematic because it presupposes an unreasonable or problematically unsupported statement. Often when we make a statement, we are presupposing other statements (i.e., making background assumptions that must be the case in order for our statement to be true). For example, if one makes the statement, *The Green Bay Packers defeated the Chicago Bears*, one is presupposing that the two teams played each other, that there is a way for one team to defeat another, and that there was someone or something that applied the rules to determine that one team defeated the other. Often such presuppositions are reasonable or supported in appropriate ways—in short, the assumptions are above reproach. Occasionally, however, such assumptions are problematically unsupported or unreasonable in some way.

A presupposition is problematically unsupported or unreasonable if it lacks sufficient rational support and is such that most rational people (or perhaps all rational persons) would reject it without sufficient rational support. This is to be distinguished from an intuitive truth, which is rational to accept without support (see chapter 3 for more on intuitive truths).

Note that a problematically unsupported or unreasonable statement is not *incompatible* with something we have good reason to accept, but rather it is such that at best few rational people would accept it as true without sufficient rational support. For example, consider the statement:

28. *God has assembled a five-feet-diameter Death Star made entirely of Legos and set it in orbit around Mars.*

Statement (28) is not *incompatible* with anything we know or have good reason to believe, since, *for all we know,* both (28) and all that we know or have good reason to accept could be true, simultaneously. However, (28) is simply problematically unsupported or unreasonable; most rational people would not accept it.

Here is an example applied to explanations. Suppose that Keith and Scott are standing in a conference room on a university campus in California and are wondering how a five-hundred-pound table that was on one side of the room in the morning was moved to the other side of the room in the afternoon. They offer the following explanations:

*Keith:* The table was moved by virtue of strongman Hafþór Júlíus Björnsson (a strong man who recently deadlifted over 1,100 pounds) moving the table.

*Scott:* The table was moved by virtue of six campus custodians moving the table.

To help focus on the issue here, let assume that Keith's and Scott's explanations are equal in all other criteria.

Still, Keith's explanation is problematic in having an explanans that makes problematically unsupported assumptions. It assumes, without support, that Björnsson (an *Icelandic* strongman) would even be in California at the time, that he would be *on this campus* at the time, that he would have a reason for moving the table, et cetera. While these assumptions are not incompatible with other things we know (assume we do not know where Björnsson was), they are assumptions that *need* rational support. In contrast, Scott's explanation makes no problematic assumptions. The *campus* custodians are expected to be on campus, and since it is a campus *in California,* they would be expected to be in California. Further, the custodial staff would have reason to move the table—for cleaning, for example. Thus, Scott's explanation is the better explanation, all other things being equal.

We thus arrive at our fourth criterion:

Fewer Problems with the Explanans Criterion: All else being equal, an explanation whose explanans has the fewest problems (among the available explanations) is the epistemically best explanation (among the available explanations)—that is, is more likely true (among the available explanations).

## What About Simplicity?

We cannot talk about inference to the best explanation without at least addressing simplicity—after all, nearly everyone is familiar with Occam's Razor. However, it is often *misstated* as *the simplest explanation is usually the best explanation.* This is incorrect. Rather, a better statement of the razor, though perhaps still not quite right, is: *All else equal, the simpler theory is the better theory.* That is, if two theories or explanations are *equal* on *all* other criteria, *then* simplicity kicks in.

But, simpler how? After all, there are at least three conceptions of simplicity. There is simplicity in basic principles (or axioms) of a theory, which we can call *elegance*. The fewer the basic principles, the more elegant a theory is. Thus, one way of approaching it is that, *all else equal*, the more elegant theory is the better theory.

And, there is simplicity in the number of basic kinds of entities entailed by a theory or explanation. The idea is that the fewer *fundamental* kinds or types of entities that must exist in order for the theory or explanation to be true, the simpler the theory or explanation. Let's call this sort of simplicity, *parsimony*. Thus, another way of approaching simplicity is to say that, *all else equal*, the more parsimonious theory is the better theory.

And, there is simplicity in the basic *concepts* that are employed by the theory or explanation. We can call this *ideological simplicity*. The fewer the basic concepts employed by a theory or explanation, the more ideologically simple the theory or explanation. And, thus, another way of approaching simplicity is to say that, *all else equal*, the more ideologically simple theory is the better theory.

However, this is just a first pass. Each of these need further discussion. Questions such as the following must be answered:

- How exactly should we define simplicity?
- What exactly is the role of simplicity in evaluating explanations?
- Why should we think that simplicity matters or that it is a criterion of choosing the best explanation? In other words, what is its rational justification?

It should be noted that there is *not* agreement among philosophers on the answers to these questions.

Furthermore, simplicity kicks in when *and only when* two theories or explanations are otherwise equal on all previous criteria. We would not want to begin with it. Suppose that two explanations are being compared, one of which is simpler than the other. However, suppose that the more complex explanation has far greater explanatory power, scope, and independent support, and fewer problems than the simpler explanation. If so, the simpler one is *not* the better explanation. The first four criteria trump simplicity. So, simplicity comes in only to break the tie. But, how often are two explanation *really* tied (or equal) on *all* the other criteria? The suspicion is that this is rare.

Therefore, because there are several conceptions of simplicity, each of which needs exploration that would take us far beyond the scope of this chapter, and because there is controversy about how to answer the three questions, and because simplicity rarely comes into play, we will not consider it for our purposes in this chapter. The first four criteria are sufficient to decide on a vast majority of explanations, and especially everyday explanations that we are more likely to encounter.

## How to Apply the Criteria

Above it was stated that how we apply our criteria varies across the different types of explanations. This will be illustrated with the three types of cases—*repeatable causal explanations*, *nonrepeatable causal explanations*, and *non-causal explanations*.

## Repeatable Causal Cases

The kind of explanations referenced here are first *causal*. That is, the explanatory relation is a causal one, such that the explanans is to be understood as *causing* the explanandum. Second, the causal relationship is *not* a unique event but has or will (or can) occur multiple times in reality. In short, the causal relationship is repeatable in reality. These two features of the explanation—that it is *causal* and *repeatable*—determine *how* we apply our criteria. We can test both its explanatory power and its scope by way of (i) the occurrence of previous similar explanations, (ii) some empirical experiment or procedure, or (iii) by the predictions that it makes. The *independent support for the explanans* and *problems with the explanans* will consist in observations of various empirical phenomena. Let's consider an example to illustrate these points.

Suppose that Roger and Jessica are debating why the computer suddenly shut off. They offer the following explanations:

> *Roger:* The computer shut off because it got over heated.

> *Jessica:* The computer shut off because the house power shut off.

While these are not incompatible explanations, let's suppose that at most one of them is correct (though both could be wrong), for the purposes of illustrating application of the criteria. In order to test the *explanatory power* of these explanations, they must assess how probable each explanans makes the explanandum. Obviously, Jessica's has *great* explanatory power. If its power supply was cut off, then it would shut off. Of course, they *could* always look at past examples of the power supply being severed from a computer and note that in each case the computer shut off, or even run a test in which they cut off the power to a running computer to see whether it shuts off, to further test its explanatory power. But, in short, it has great explanatory power.

It is not as obvious that Roger's explanation has the same explanatory power. Perhaps a computer can get overheated but remain running, even if in so doing damage is being done to it. Again, they *could* always look at past examples of computers being overheated and note whether it caused the computer to shut off, or even run a test by purposely overheating the computer to see whether it shuts off. If past overheated computers do not automatically shut off, or the test does not result is the computer shutting off immediately, then Jessica's has greater explanatory power.

However, does that mean that Jessica's is the best explanation? Not necessarily, since Roger's explanation may be superior to Jessica's in the other criteria. We will see how this *could* happen. So, let's turn to the other criteria to compare Roger's and Jessica's explanations.

Let's turn to explanatory scope next (not that we have to consider them in any particular order). The explanatory scope of an explanation, you will recall, has to do with how many explananda the explanans explains. So, let imagine a couple of possible scenarios.

*Scenario 1:* Suppose that there is smoke and a burnt-wire scent coming from the computer. If so, then Roger's explanans has greater explanatory scope, since his overheating explanans explains not only the computer shutting off, but the smoke and burnt-wire scent, whereas Jessica's explanans does not explain these phenomena.

*Scenario 2*: Suppose that there is no smoke or burnt-wire scent. And, suppose that the computer is powered by the house electricity and has no other source of power (e.g., battery, generator). Further, suppose that when the computer shut off, the house lights shut off simultaneously. In this case, Jessica's explanans has greater explanatory power, since her explanans can explain the lights going out as well as the computer shutting off, but Roger's explanans cannot.

So, if we suppose that *scenario 1* obtains, but not scenario 2, then Roger's explanation has greater explanatory scope, even though Jessica's has greater explanatory power *relative* to the computer shutting off. If these were the only criteria, then scope here seems to trump power, and we would adopt Roger's explanation. And clearly if scenario 2 obtained, then Jessica's wins on both power and scope, and thus should be the explanation that we adopt.

But we do have additional criteria, so let's bring them in, beginning with *independent support for the explanans* criterion. Recall that independent support for an explanans consists in reasons to think that the explanans is true, *independent of its role in the explanation*. And, with repeatable causal explanations, the reasons will consist in *empirical* evidence.

In order to illustrate how this criterion may play a role, let's again make some assumptions about the situation. Let's suppose that Roger and Jessica had no other electrically powered appliance or lights running—only the computer. Further, suppose that there is no smoke coming from the computer but that there *is* a burnt-wire scent. Given these assumptions, Jessica's has the greater explanatory power, but Roger's has the greater explanatory scope (explaining both the computer shut off and the burnt-wire scent). However, the scope does not necessarily defeat the power in this case, especially if we bring in the additional criterion. Let's suppose that the neighbor calls Jessica (on a *cell* phone) and says this:

> Hey, my power is out! I looked outside and it looks like the whole neighborhood is without power. I assume yours is also out. Do you know anything about this?

This provides *independent support* for Jessica's explanans—that the house power shut off. Let's assume that Roger has no independent support for his explanans. Given this scenario, while Roger's has the greater explanatory scope, Jessica's has the greater explanatory power *and* independent support. In *this* case, we should adopt Jessica's explanation as the better explanation. However, it is *not* because Jessica's wins on more of the criteria, but because *overall* Jessica's satisfies the criteria better. But this is not necessarily because one satisfies *more* of the criteria. One theory can win on three of the criteria, but lose on only one, but that loss outweighs the wins, rendering it a bad explanation, and thus not the best.

Let's continue comparing Roger's and Jessica's explanations by bringing in our final criterion –*problems with the explanans*. Recall that *problems with an explanans* ranges from the explanans relying on problematically unsupported or unreasonable assumptions to being incompatible with other things we have reason to accept.

To apply this criterion to our Roger versus Jessica explanation comparison, let's again make some assumptions. First, initially we assumed that Jessica's has the greater explanatory power (which seems clear), since lack of power supply would indeed shut it off, but overheating will not *obviously* do so. Let's continue to make the assumptions that Roger and Jessica had no other electrically powered appliance or lights running—only the computer, and that there is a burnt-wire scent coming from the computer. Thus, it looks like Roger's has greater explanatory power. And, assume the neighbor called but gave a slightly different report, saying:

*Hey, my power is out! Is yours out?*

This gives *some*, though not as strong, independent support for Jessica's explanans. And, assume that Roger has no independent support for his explanans. Thus, so far it again looks like Roger's has the greater explanatory scope, and Jessica's has the greater explanatory power *and* independent support. But now let's make one more assumption. Suppose that immediately after the computer shut off and before the neighbor's phone call, Roger walks into the bathroom, flicks the light switch up, which *turns on the lights* (powered by the house power), and then plugs in his electric razor, which immediately turns on, and begins shaving. The result is a serious problem for Jessica's explanans.

Suppose to counter the problem, Jessica suggests that it must have just been a very short power outage. This would appear to remove the problem. But, suppose that Roger has a battery-run house electricity meter that very accurately detects when the house is powered and when it is not, and the meter shows *no* power outage in the past several weeks. Then the problem with Jessica's explanans remains, especially if the neighbor is still reporting an outage at his house, since then the independent support for her explanans no longer counts as evidence for her explanans. Given this, Roger's explanation is the best.

We considered the details of the various scenarios to make this point. *How* the criteria apply, and the weight given to the various criterion, various from explanation to explanation and is relative to what else we know, or have reason to believe, about reality. Thus, as was emphasized above, the best explanation is the explanation that *overall* satisfies the criteria better than rivals. Let's now turn to see how the criteria can be applied to *nonrepeatable* causal explanations.

## Nonrepeatable Causal Cases
The kind of explanations referenced here, like the first kind of explanations, are *causal*. That is, the explanatory relation is a causal one, such that the explanans is to be understood as *causing* the explanandum. However, *unlike* the first kind of explanation, these involve events or phenomena that are *not* repeatable. They involve a causal relationship that is a one-time, *unique* event. As a result, we *cannot* test the explanatory power or scope by way of (i) the occurrence of previous similar explanations, (ii) some empirical experiment or procedure, or (iii) the predictions that it makes. Nevertheless, we *can* still apply the power and scope criteria, which will be illustrated. And *independent support for the explanans* and *problems with the explanans* may consist in observations of various empirical phenomena but will also consist in other facts and reasons. Let's consider a very familiar (to many) example to illustrate this—namely, by comparing two explanations (actually one is not really an explanation at all) of the fact that the universe is fine-tuned for life. We will go through the explanation comparison, and then wrap-up by once again showing that *how* the criteria were applied was different from how they were applied to *repeatable* causal explanations.

The Set-Up: First, let's get clear on what it means for the universe to be *fine-tuned for life*. Recently, physicists have discovered that certain conditions in the universe are very tightly constrained, such that even slight variations in these conditions would have resulted in a universe that would not be life-permitting. For example, very roughly, if the universe were slightly hotter or colder, or the right sort of chemicals did not exist, or the forces of nature were slightly stronger or weaker, there would be no life. The various conditions that are tightly constrained include the initial conditions of the universe (including the amount of entropy and initial explosion); the existence of forces of nature (gravity, electromagnetism, and the weak and strong nuclear forces); the strength of these forces; the mass of subatomic particles; and higher-level laws of nature—for example, laws in chemistry. If there were even a slight variation in any of these, the universe would simply not be life-permitting. While much more detail can and has been given, that will do for our purposes.[1] The question: *Why is the universe fine-tuned for life?*

Two competing explanations: While there are other explanations, let's consider just two explanations to illustrate how to apply our criteria to nonrepeatable causal explanations:

> *God Explanation*: The universe is fine-tuned for life because God designed and created it to be fine-tuned for life.

> *Chance Explanation*: The universe is fine-tuned for life because the various conditions just *happened* to come to be arranged in a fine-tuned way.

Before applying our criteria, let's note a few things about these explanations. First, technically, the "chance explanation" is no explanation at all. It amounts to saying that the universe is fine-tuned, and there is no explanation. However, let's set this aside for now and treat it as an explanation for the sake of illustrating our criteria.

Second, these are *causal* explanations (again, treating our so-called *chance explanation* as an explanation). This is clearly seen in the *God explanation*. The explanation amounts to saying that God *caused* the fine-tuned universe. And, if we may put it this way, the *chance explanans* says that *chance* "caused" the fine-tuning.

Third, these explanations involve an explanandum that is a one-time, unique fact—namely, the one-time (though, for all time) unique fact that our universe is fine-tuned. And, the explanans in each involve one-time unique events—namely, the *one time* that God created the universe (in the one explanation), and the one time that chance did so (in the other). This happened only *once*, and will *not* happen again, *at least not in our human experience*. Therefore, for applying explanatory power and scope, we cannot appeal to other similar cases in the past, or to experiments, or to predictions about universes. Let's turn to the application of our criteria.

Applying the Criteria to the Explanations: Let's begin by applying the *explanatory power* criterion. To apply this, you will recall, we ask how probable the explanandum, is given the explanans. Let's begin with the *God explanation*. If God exists, and wants a universe with life, then the probability that the universe *that he creates* will be fine-tuned is extremely probable (even *guaranteed*, assuming he is omnipotent and can bring about anything that he wants). In contrast, since the array of possible conditions of the universe that would *prevent* life far

---

1. For more details, as well as an elaborate presentation and defense of the *fine-tuning argument*, see Robin Collins' article "God, Design, and Fine-Tuning." An updated version is available at http://home.messiah.edu/~rcollins/Fine-tuning/FT.HTM.

outnumber (to put it very mildly) the array of possible conditions of the universe that would allow for life, the probability that the universe would be fine-tuned for life *by chance* is astronomically low. Thus, in terms of the explanatory power, the *God explanation* wins without question!

Note that *how* we applied the explanatory power criteria was by way of *thought-experiments*, and *not* by empirical experiments, unlike we do with the *repeatable* causal explanations. Indeed, there is no experiment that we could do to see how God would behave when starting from scratch with creating a universe. Nor could we appeal to previous cases of this. It was a one-time event in the past. Instead, for our *God* and *chance* explanations, we created a thought experiment, imagining how things would be *if*:

a. God existed and wanted a life-permitting universe, based on what we know about God—e.g., that he is omnipotent.
b. The conditions of the universe were randomly arranged based on what we know about the conditions, and chance.

The point being emphasized is that *how* we apply the criterion varies based on the type of explanation under investigation.

Let's move on to explanatory scope. The *chance explanation* has no broader scope, as it merely says that the array of conditions in the universe are randomly arranged. In contrast, the *God explanation* has much broader scope. Here are just three more things it plays a role in explaining: The worldwide, and in every generation, belief in God; the various reported miracles; and the various religious experience people have had. While there are alternative explanations for each of these, that is irrelevant to the fact that the *God explanation* does also (at least partially) explain these things. Thus, the *God explanation* has broader scope than the *chance explanation*.

Before moving on to the remaining criteria, note that *how* we apply the scope of the explanans of the *God explanation* to religious belief, religious experience, and miracles, once again, is *not* by way of empirical tests or procedures but instead by thought experiments and reason.

Our next criterion is *independent support for the explanans*. Again, it is difficult, at best, to see how there could be any independent support for explanans of the *chance explanation*. Any "support" would probably amount to arguing that the alternatives are highly problematic. In contrast, the *God explanans* has an abundance of independent support—there are the various versions of the big three types of arguments for God's existence, including the cosmological argument, the ontological argument, and the teleological argument. And, there are versions of the moral argument and the argument from religious experience, each of which provides independent support for the explanans of the *God explanation*.

Note, once again, that these arguments do *not* rely on repeatable experiments or procedures, but instead on rational means—though several do rely on observation of our universe. Still, the *way* that we apply this criterion is different than *the way* we apply the criteria to *repeatable causal* explanations.

So far, the *God explanation* satisfies the first three criteria far better than the *chance explanation*, and we saw that in each case, *how* we showed this is different than *how* we show that a repeatable causal explanation satisfies the criteria. Let's turn to our final criterion.

The final criterion is the *problems with the explanans* criterion. Here the *chance theorist* may point out that a big problem with the *God explanation* is the *problem of evil*. The chance theorist may point to all the various evils, natural and moral, and suggest that such evils are incompatible with the existence of God. But the God theorist will reply, first, that at best it is only incompatible with a *good* God, and the *God explanation* to explain the fine-tuned universe does not suggest that God must be good. But, second, the God theorist will point out that *all* attempts to date to show that evil and a *good* God are incompatible have failed, and such thinkers have gone on to show that there is perfect compatibility between God and evil. So, it is not clear that this really is a problem for the God explanans.

In contrast, there does seem to be a problem with the chance explanans—namely, that it is just *so* very improbable that it would result in such a beautiful, elegant, and fine-tuned universe. Thus, the God explanation satisfies each criterion far better than the chance explanation.

While these explanations need, and have had, much more discussion, the point has been that the way that we apply the criteria to nonrepeatable causal explanations is different from how we apply the criteria to repeatable causal explanations. For example, with the Roger and Jessica repeatable causal explanations, we can engage in experiments and procedures to test the power and scope of the explanans (power outage and overheating) relative to the computer shutting off (as well as their relations to other possible explananda). And, we can engage in experiments or empirical procedures to test how well each explanans is independently supported or problematic. In contrast, we cannot conduct experiments or engage in empirical procedures to test how well the *nonrepeatable* causal explanations satisfy the criteria.

## Non-Causal Cases

The kind of explanations referenced here are entirely *non-causal*; the relationship involved between the explanans and the explanandum is *not* one of causation—the explanans does not cause the explanandum, though it does still explain it. Thus, even more than nonrepeatable causal explanation, we cannot test how well non-causal explanations satisfy the criteria by empirical experiments or by empirical procedures. Instead, we must rely on other ways of testing how well the explanations satisfy the criteria, including thought experiments, appeals to rational intuition, and arguments from other things we have good reason to accept. Let's see how this works by considering a familiar (to many) philosophical example. We will compare two explanations (even though there are more) of the fact that persons persist over time and through change, known as the *problem of personal identity*.

The Set-Up: Let's set up the background. Consider the familiar case of an adult showing a baby picture of themselves and saying, "This is a picture of me when I was a baby." Interestingly, the baby looks nothing like the adult showing the picture. Indeed, we know from our background knowledge that not only do they not look alike, they really have nothing physical in common. Not only do they have different masses, shapes, and looks, but all the matter that made up that baby's body is now scattered throughout the biosphere and beyond, and (most likely) none of the matter in the adult was also in the baby. Further, they have different thoughts, beliefs, desires, hopes, dreams, et cetera. In short, their mental lives are radically different.

One way of putting the above point is by saying that the baby and the adult are *qualitatively different*—they are *not* qualitatively identical (i.e., they do not share all their parts and properties). On the other hand, none of us has any difficulty accepting that that baby and the adult are the same person—that is, the baby and the adult are *numerically* identical.

While much more detail can and has been said, that will do for our purposes. Our question: Why (or perhaps how would be better) are the baby and the adult the same person (numerically identical)?

Two competing explanations: While there are other explanations, let's consider just two explanations in order to illustrate how to apply our criteria to non-causal explanations:

> *Soul Explanation*: The baby is the same person as (numerically identical to) the adult because there is a single soul that was part of (of identical to) the baby, which is also part of (of identical to) the adult.

> *Materialist Explanation*: The baby is the same person as (numerically identical to) the adult because there is spatiotemporal continuity between the baby and the adult.

We need brief elaboration on the explanans of each, beginning with the *soul explanans*. By *soul* we mean to refer to an immaterial substance that is either part of or identical to a human person. It is a partless, simple substance and is an immaterial aspect of us that is conscious and "contains" the various mental states—thoughts, beliefs, desires, pains, pleasure, sensory experiences, et cetera. It remains that same in substance, even with changes in its mental contents and through changes in the material body with which it interacts.

In the *materialist* explanans, there is reference to *spatiotemporal continuity. Spatiotemporal*, obviously, refers to space and time (or to spacetime). We can say that what it is for there to be spatiotemporal *continuity* between objects existing at distant times in terms of what it is for there to be spatiotemporal *continuity* between objects existing at back-to-back times. So,

> *Back-to-Back Spatiotemporal Continuity*: There is back-to-back spatiotemporal continuity between an object A at one time and an object B *an instant later* just in case (i) there is no temporal gap between A and B, (ii) there are many similarities in parts and properties between A and B, (iii) the physical changes or differences between A and B are not so large that B is a different kind of thing (i.e., both A and B are both of the same kind—e.g., humans), and (iv) certain facts about the existence of A play a role in causing the existence of B.

We can then say what it is for there to be spatiotemporal *continuity* between objects existing at *distant* times in terms of this. So, for example, there is spatiotemporal continuity between an object A and a temporally distant object Z just in case there are material objects existing at each instance between A and Z, and there is back-to-back continuity between each consecutive member, beginning with A and ending with Z.

Applying the Criteria to the Explanations: Again, we will apply the criteria to show that *the way* we test the explanations with the criteria is *not* in terms of empirical experiments or procedures, but rather by philosophical methods—thought experiments, rational intuition, and reasoning based on other things we have good reason to accept.

Let's begin by applying the *explanatory power* criterion. Again, apply this criterion by asking how probable the explanandum is given the explanans. Let's begin with the *soul explanation*. If there are souls, such things are certainly a component of the essence of what we as humans are. Thus, our soul certainly plays a role in our continued existence. My soul cannot be removed and replaced, and I still exist; it is essential to me. So, if the baby and the adult have (are) the same soul, that certainly explains why they are the same person. Thus, the soul explanation does have good explanatory power in explaining personal identity over time.

Note that reflection on souls and essences here is based on philosophical methods, and not on empirical experiments or procedures, like we would do with repeatable causal explanations. Nevertheless, we can "see" that the soul explanans has explanatory power in explaining the explanandum.

How does the *materialist explanation* come out on explanatory power? How probable is it that the baby is the same person as the adult based solely on spatiotemporal continuity? It does seem fairly probable. After all, we do use spatiotemporal continuity as an *epistemic* method (as *evidence*) for determining one material object being the same as another over time. So, it does have some explanatory power.

How the explanatory power of the materialist explanation compares to the power of the soul explanation is not obvious. Perhaps soul theory has a slight edge here since the probability that two different people would have the same soul is 0%, but the probability that two *distinct* people would be spatiotemporal comparison is > 0%, since we can certainly form a coherent thought experiment in which this occurs, which gives us some reason to think that it is possible.

While the comparison ultimately requires more detail and elaboration, the point of emphasis here is that in both applying the explanatory power criterion and comparing two explanations vis-à-vis the criterion is done by *philosophical* methods, and *not* empirical scientific methods. Nevertheless, we can be every bit as confident in our explanations, and sometimes even more so.

Let's turn to *explanatory scope*. At the very least, the *materialist* explanans has a scope of two—it explains *metaphysical* personal identity over time (e.g., why the baby and the adult *are* the same person) and our *epistemological* method of *identifying* an object over time (i.e., how we *know* that the baby and the adult are the same person). Whether the spatiotemporal continuity between two objects explains more is not obvious.

In contrast, the soul explanans has a scope of at least three. First, like the materialist explanans, the soul explanans explains *metaphysical* personal identity over time (e.g., why the baby and the adult *are* the same person).

Second, many (perhaps most) of us have an intuition that two people can swap bodies (think of the movies *Freaky Friday*, *Change Up*, and *Nine Lives*, to name just a few of *many*). We can at least create thought experiments, write books, and create movies in which this *believably* occurs. Assuming that it is possible, the soul explanans can explain it, roughly, in terms of two humans swapping bodies, such that the soul of one person goes into the body of the other. In contrast, the materialist cannot explain this intuition (possibility?).

Third, many of us have the belief, and certainly the intuition, that we can (do) survive the death and destruction of our bodies. Again, we have created thought experiments, written books, and made movies about this, and many religious people believe that it is true. The soul explanans, but not the materialist explanans, can explain this. Thus, it *appears* at this point that the soul explanans has greater explanatory scope.

Let's pause once again to emphasize the point that in thinking about the scope of each explanans, we did *not* use empirical experiments or procedures (though we did appeal to the empirical fact that we *judge* material object identity over time in terms of spatiotemporal continuity). In short, we did *not* use scientific methods, but rather we used *philosophical* methods, which are every bit as good at judging philosophical explanations as are scientific methods for judging repeatable causal explanations.

Turning to *independent support for the explanans*, we encounter the jungle of philosophy of mind and all the arguments about the relationship between mind and body and the nature of a person. Getting into the details will take us far beyond the scope of this chapter and this book. But let's at least mention a few arguments and make a point about these. As independent support for the existence of the soul, and thus for the explanans of the soul explanation, we find such arguments as (i) Descartes' *modal argument* (or its contemporary variation in Gertler's *disembodiment argument*), (ii) Gertler's *property differences arguments* based on the radical differences in properties between a person, their mental life, and the body and brain states, and (iii) Plantinga's *replacement argument* and *Can a material object think? argument*, to name just a few.[2]

And while support of materialism (the view that we humans are entirely material things) does not directly support the explanans of the materialist explanation above, support from the view that we are material things does give some support to the idea that what makes us the same over time is in terms of *material facts*. A main argument in favor of materialism is based on the acceptance that mental states cause material states, and that the material world is causally closed.[3]

As far as which satisfies the *independent support for explanans* criterion, it strongly appears that the support for soul is much stronger. But we will not settle this here. The details of all this do not matter for our purposes. The point to be emphasized is that *all* of these arguments are *philosophical*, and *not* scientific—that is, we do not use scientific methods for settling the issues, and indeed we *cannot* use scientific methods for settling the issues.[4] They are to be decided on *philosophical* grounds alone. Nevertheless, we *can* support our explanans on such grounds.

2. René Descartes, *Meditations on First Philosophy: With Selections from the Objections and Replies, trans.* Mike Moriarty (Oxford: Oxford University Press, 2008); Brie Gertler, "In Defense of Mind-Body Dualism," in *Reason and Responsibility: Readings in Some Basic Problems of Philosophy,* ed. Joel Feinberg and Russ Shafer-Landau, 13th ed. Belmont, CA: Thomson Wadsworth, 2007); and Alvin Plantinga, "Materialism and Christian Belief," in *Persons: Human and Divine,* ed. Peter van Inwagen and Dean Zimmerman (Oxford: Oxford University Press, 2007) and "Against Materialism," *Faith and Philosophy* 23, no. 1 (2006): 3–32.
3. To say that the world is causally closed means, roughly, that all physical events that have a cause have a physical cause.
4. One might think that the issues can be solved by neuroscience, but, as is explained below, this is mistaken, and neuroscience *cannot* solve the philosophical issues.

The point is that with *philosophical* explanations, we apply the same criteria, but in *different ways* than we do so with repeatable causal explanans.

Our fourth criterion is *problem with the explanans*. Very similar points can be made here that were made regarding the previous criterion—namely, that there are too many things that have been said to mention here, but importantly *all* the problems are *philosophical* and *not* scientific. Let's have a glimpse.

The materialist suggests that soul explanans has the following problem. The more we learn about the brain, the more we see a correlation between brain activity, brain damage, and mental activity or lack of activity. This suggests, the materialist thinks, that mentality resides in the brain. They then think this is a problem for the soul explanans since the soul explanans loses one reason for thinking there are souls—namely, to explain mentality.

The soul theorist will reply that this is no problem for soul theory since all that is established by the materialist is that there is a tight *correlation* between the mental and the brain, the very thing the soul theorist has embraced all along. Thus, there is no incompatibility between the brain being *associated* with mentality and soul theory.

In contrast, the soul theorist will point out that the materialist explanation has the problem that it would imply the wrong results in body swap cases or survival of death cases. Again, it seems broadly possible that two humans can swap bodies, and that a human can survive the death and destruction of their body. The materialist account implies that both of these scenarios are impossible. To the degree that we have confidence that these cases are possible, we have reason to reject the materialist explanation.

While both soul theorist and materialist have pointed out additional problems, which comes out "winner" on this criterion is controversial. It would appear that soul theory satisfies it better, having fewer and less severe problems. However, the point to emphasize, once again, is that *all* these objections and arguments are *philosophical*, and *not* scientific—that is, we do not use scientific methods for determining what the problems are, or the severity of the problems, and indeed we *cannot* use scientific methods for settling these issues. They are to be decided on *philosophical* grounds alone. Nevertheless, we *can* show problems with the various philosophical explanans on philosophical grounds. The point is that with *philosophical* explanations, we apply the same criteria, but in *different ways* than we do so with repeatable causal explanans.

### Summary of the Steps of Inference to the Best Explanation

Above, we went into detail about the criteria used to determine whether an explanation is a good one and how to use the criteria to tell whether an explanation is the *best* explanation among alternatives. We saw how we test how well an explanation satisfies these criteria differently based whether we are dealing with a repeatable causal explanation, a nonrepeatable causal explanation, or a non-causal explanation. Here are the steps:

- First, clearly identify the explanations in question, as well as the explanans and explananda in each explanation.
- Second, identify whether the explanation is a repeatable causal explanation, a nonrepeatable causal explanation, or a non-causal explanation.

- Third, using appropriate methods (e.g., scientific, historical, philosophical), determine how well each explanation satisfies the criteria.
- Fourth, to the best of your ability, determine which satisfies the criteria the best.

From this, one creates an inference to the best explanation argument, which, once again, goes as follows:

Premise: Among explanations E1, ... , En, one (e.g., E1) satisfies the criteria better than the others.

Conclusion: Therefore, the one explanation (e.g., E1) is the best explanation.

### EXERCISE 9.4

Each passage below expresses some phenomenon (phenomena) in need of explanation, followed by two competing explanans to explain the phenomenon (phenomena). Based on the criteria in this chapter (explanatory power, explanatory scope, independent support for the explanans, problems with the explanans), (i) determine which explanation is the better explanation, and (ii) state which criterion (criteria) is most in play to make the one the better explanation.

(Note 1: Some of these leave room for debate.)

(Note 2: While some of the phenomena may have other or more complex explanations, limit your consideration and comparison to just the two explanans given; so, which *of the two explanans given* is the better explanation).

**\*1.** Phenomenon: The dog is constantly biting and scratching itself.

Explanans 1: The dog has fleas.

Explanans 2: The dog is trying to communicate that it wants it to be pet by its owner.

**2.** Phenomena: The lights went out and the TV shut off, simultaneously.

Explanans 1: My friend accidentally sat on the TV remote.

Explanans 2: The house power shut off.

**3.** Phenomenon: There were more votes cast in the presidential election than there are eligible, legal voters.

Explanans 1: Some voters illegally voted multiple times.

Explanans 2: The Chinese Communist Party forged thousands of mail-in ballots and mailed them in.

**\*4.** Phenomena: The rock wall toppled, and there is a large crack in the street out front.

Explanans 1: The wall was poorly constructed.

Explanans 2: There was an earthquake.

5. Phenomenon: There is a golf-ball sized bump on my elbow.

   Explanans 1: I banged my elbow when I fell down.

   Explanans 2: My neighbor put a curse on me after I called the police on her for practicing her witchcraft in her front yard.

6. Phenomenon: There has been a substantial increase of violent crimes in New York City over the past three months.

   Explanans 1: The mayor defunded the police.

   Explanans 2: The people are frustrated from being quarantined for so long.

7. Phenomenon: The child was jumping up and down and screaming loudly.

   Explanans 1: The child's mom told him that he could not have ice cream.

   Explanans 2: The child was trying to create an earthquake.

8. Phenomenon: Whereas I was completely blind from birth, suddenly I can now see perfectly.

   Explanans 1: God healed me.

   Explanans 2: I was running and ran face-first into a wall.

**EXERCISE 9.5**

Each passage below expresses a phenomenon in need of explanation (it will be the explanandum in an explanation). For each passage, (i) come up with two incompatible explanations (explanans) to explain the phenomenon, where one of the explanations is clearly better than the other (based on one or more of the criteria discussed in the chapter), and then (ii) state which one is better, and why—citing explanatory power, explanatory scope, independent support for the explanans, problems with the explanans, or some combination of these.

   (Note: Be creative and try to appeal to different criteria each time.)

   1. Recently, Kyle started behaving bizarrely and dangerously.
   2. The airplane suddenly fell from the sky.
   3. Marsha won the last six rounds of the poker game by having the strongest poker hand each time.
   4. Mary dreamed that there was an 8.6 earthquake on the San Andres fault shaking Los Angeles, killing thousands. Exactly one week later, an 8.6 earthquake hit Los Angeles just as Mary had dreamed.
   5. Not a single person who has entered this enchanted forest has ever been heard from or seen again.

# Recap

In this chapter, we took a closer look at explanations, including making a distinction between explanatory acts and explanations, establishing the terminology of *explanans* and *explanandum*, considering what makes an explanation true, and distinguishing a *metaphysically* and *epistemically* good explanation. We went on to study the criteria for what makes an explanation a good one, and how to use the criteria for determining the *best* explanation. Finally, we made an important distinction between repeatable causal, a nonrepeatable causal, and non-causal explanations, and saw that how we *apply* the criteria differs based on which type of explanation we are considering. Below are some important concept and definitions:

- **Explanation**: An explanation is a collection of statements (or a complex statement) in which one states *how* or *why* something is the case.
  - **Explanandum**: The part of the explanation (e.g., a statement) that is being explained.
  - **Explanans**: The part of the explanation (e.g., a statement) that contains the explanation.
- Three Types of Explanations:
  - **Repeatable Causal Explanation**: An explanation in which the explanans is the *cause* of the explanandum, and such that the causal relationship has, will, or at least can obtain between similar explanans and explananda many times throughout history—it is a repeatable causal relationship.
  - **Nonrepeatable Causal Explanation**: An explanation in which the explanans is the *cause* of the explanandum, but is such that the causal relationship obtains *only once* since the explanandum and explanans are unique, one-time events.
  - **Non-Causal Explanation**: An explanation in which the relationship between the explanans and the explanandum is *not* causal, but some other explanatory relationship, such as *grounding*.

- **Teleological Explanation**: A type of *non-causal* explanation in which the *explanans* refers to the *purpose, end, goal,* or *function* of the phenomena referenced in the explanandum. Many of these refer to the intentions of a person.

- **Metaphysically Good Explanation**: An explanation that is *the* objectively *correct* explanation, based on the structure of reality, and thus the explanandum and explanans are true, and the explanatory relationship really does hold between the explanans and the explanandum.

- **Epistemologically Good Explanation**: An explanation that has features (i.e., satisfies the criteria for good explanation) that *indicate* that it is the metaphysically correct explanation, which give us *reason to believe* that it is correct. And, one explanation is *better* than another if and only if the *overall* correct indicating features of it are more indicative of correctness than the *overall* correct indicating features of its rival.

- **Criteria for Epistemically Good Explanation**: Criteria that indicate that it is the metaphysically correct explanation. There are at least the following four criteria:
  - **Explanatory Power**: The explanatory power of an explanation concerns how probable the explanans makes the explanandum. The greater the evidential support that the explanans gives to the explanandum, the greater the explanatory power of the explanation.
  - **Explanatory Scope**: The explanatory scope of an explanation concerns how many explananda the explanans explains. The more explananda that the explanans explains, the greater the scope of the explanans.
  - **Independent Support for Explanans**: This criterion concerns reasons we have for accepting that the explanans is true, *independent* of the explanation. The more independent support that it has, the more reason we have for accepting the explanans as true, which is one aspect of a metaphysically good explanation (namely, that its explanans is true).
  - **Problems with Explanans**: This criterion concerns reasons we may have for *rejecting* the explanans as *false*. Problems can range from the explanans presupposing a statement that is unreasonable or problematically unsupported, to the explanans being outright incompatible with other things we know or have good reason to believe.
- **Inference to the Best Explanation**: An inference to the best explanation is an *inference* in which one concludes that one explanation among competing explanations is the *best* explanation based on *correct-indicating* features of explanations.

# LOGICAL FALLACIES

# 10

We all want to be able to persuade someone of something at least some-times. Perhaps it is something as trivial as going to a certain movie that we want to see, or something a bit more important, such as that they should purchase a particular house, and even extremely important, such as that they should accept that God exists. However, while we do want to persuade others at various times, we want to do so with good reasoning. Occasionally, however, we slip up and use bad reasoning in the attempt to persuade, perhaps appealing to the emotions of someone, or assuming too much about our premises, or misrepresenting a point of view.

In several chapters of this book we have seen various good ways of reasoning. In this chapter, we focus on the bad! We do so, however, in order to help *avoid* the bad.

To be more precise, in this chapter we will look at what are called *logical fallacies*. Being familiar with some common fallacies not only will help us to avoid offering bad arguments, it will also aid in providing us with an efficient way to communicate criticisms of other's bad reasoning. So, in this chapter, we will study some common fallacies. The following are the key words / fallacies to master as we work through this chapter:

**CHAPTER OVERVIEW**

*In this chapter we will cover the following:*

- Introduction to Fallacies
- Irrelevant Premises Fallacies
- Insufficient / Unacceptable Premises Fallacies

## KEY WORDS

| | |
|---|---|
| Abusive Ad Hominem | False Dilemma |
| Appeal to Emotion | Formal Fallacy |
| Appeal to Ignorance | Gambler's Fallacy |
| Appeal to Popularity | Genetic Fallacy |
| Appeal to Unqualified Authority | Guilt by Association |
| Begging the Question | Inconsistency Ad Hominem |
| Circumstantial Ad Hominem | Informal Fallacy |
| Composition | Perfectionist Fallacy |
| Decision-Point Fallacy | Poisoning the Well |
| Division | Slippery Slope |
| Equivocation | Straw Man |
| Fallacy | Subjectivist Fallacy |

A *fallacy* is an error in reasoning. Therefore, in order to commit a
fallacy, one *must* be presenting an *argument* or engaging in *reasoning*.
Merely making a false, unacceptable, or irrational *statement* is *not* a
fallacy. Rather, a fallacy occurs when one draws a *conclusion* from
some supposed premises, but the inference is a bad one. Thus, it is a
mistake to accuse someone of committing a fallacy simply because
they make a false, unacceptable, or irrational statement.

Further, saying that someone has committed a fallacy does *not* mean that the statements in
the argument are false. Indeed, each statement in the argument might be *true* and rational, but
still there is a fallacy in the *inference*. So, saying that an argument is fallacious does not entail that
the conclusion is false. Rather, there is simply a mistake in *reasoning*, which we want to avoid.

Fallacies are typically divided into *formal* and *informal*. Formal fallacies are fallacious strictly
because of their logical *form*. We saw examples of these in chapter 7—such as *affirming the
consequent* and *denying the antecedent*. An informal fallacy is fallacious because of its form *and*
its content. In this chapter, we are focusing exclusively on *informal fallacies*.

We have already encountered several formal and informal fallacies in previous chapters—for
example, as noted, we looked at a few formal fallacies in chapter 7. And, in chapter 8 we saw at
least three informal fallacies, including *hasty generalization*, *faulty analogy*, and *post hoc*. Since
we already examined those in the previous chapters, we will not cover them in this chapter.
Instead, in this chapter we will focus on informal fallacies that we have not previously examined.

Further, the purpose here is to introduce you to some common informal fallacies, but not
to provide an exhaustive look at all fallacies. Indeed, that task would take a large book on its
own, as there are hundreds of informal fallacies. Instead, the goal here is to introduce you to
a handful of common fallacies, with the intention that being familiar with these, and knowing
how to spot them and how to avoid them, will enable you to identify other fallacies you may
encounter, even if you have no name for them.

There are a variety of competing and overlapping ways to classify informal fallacies, and no
clear *right* way to do so. However, for the sake of providing some ordering to the fallacies we
will consider, which will perhaps facilitate learning them more efficiently, the fallacies will be
divided into two categories—*insufficient / unacceptable premises fallacies* and *irrelevant premises
fallacies*. We will consider each group in turn, beginning with irrelevant premises fallacies.

## Irrelevant Premises Fallacies

*Irrelevant premises fallacies* are fallacies that occur when one uses premises in one's argument that are entirely *irrelevant* to the conclusion. We will learn 10 general fallacies falling into
this category.

### Subjectivist Fallacy

Before discussing the subjectivist fallacy, let's be reminded of our discussion of what a subjective *statement* is from chapter 2. Recall that a statement is *subjective* if and only if the mere
act of believing it makes it *true*. Thus, the truth-value (true or false) of a subjective statement

is *dependent* on what someone believes. In chapter 2, we saw reasons for denying that there are any subjective statements. But even if there are subjective statements, the following way of arguing is still fallacious. Thus, to repeat the point from above, the following argument form is not fallacious because the conclusion is false (assuming that it is), but because the conclusion simply does not follow from the premise. Let's turn to the subjectivist fallacy.

The *subjectivist fallacy* occurs when one concludes that some statement is subjective simply because people have conflicting beliefs about the truth of the proposition. It has the following form:

Premise: People have conflicting beliefs about the truth of statement *p*.

Conclusion: Therefore, the truth of *p* is subjective.

Typically, it is offered in moral or religious contexts, though it is not limited to these contexts. Here are two examples:

*The statement that abortion is morally wrong is a matter of opinion and subjective, since people have different and conflicting beliefs about it.*

And:

*People disagree about whether God exists, and thus the statement that God exists is subjective.*

These are fallacious since the mere fact that people have conflicting beliefs *in no way* implies that everyone is correct. Some may be *wrong*. The premise is entirely *irrelevant* to the conclusion. To see that it is fallacious, consider the following example:

Premise: People have conflicting beliefs about the age of the earth.

Conclusion: Therefore, a statement that the earth is a particular age is subjective.

Clearly, that conclusion in no way follows from the premise. The earth is a particular age, period, *entirely* independent of what anyone believes—our beliefs are entirely *irrelevant* to the age of the earth. If Martha believes that the earth is 4.5 billion years old, and it is 4.5 billion years old, then Martha has a true belief, otherwise her belief is *false*. Her belief does not create truth. *The same applies to all arguments with the same structure*—because beliefs do not create truth and, certainly, conflicting beliefs do not imply that everyone is right. So, if one reasons in this way, one is committing the *subjectivist fallacy*.

## Appeal to Emotion

Emotions are an important aspect of our lives, and can be a guide to us—for example, in having empathy toward others, feeling remorse for wrong behavior, expressing anger at injustice, et cetera. However, they can also mislead us and be misused. One such misuse is when one uses appeals to emotion in place of reasons in the attempt to support a statement. When one does this, one is committing the fallacy of *appeal to emotion*. That is, *appeal to emotion* occurs when someone uses emotional appeals (such as pride, anger, pity, fear, and joy) in place of relevant facts to support a statement. It has the following form:

Premise: *Emotional expression E is evoked.*

Conclusion: Statement *S* is then asserted as if supported by the emotional expression.

Appeal to emotion is a general fallacy, under which fall more specific instances, in which a *particular* emotion is evoked. Let's consider a few examples. One instance of appeal to emotion is **appeal to anger**, in which one is angry, uses angry language, and attempts to get one's audience angry in order to attempt to persuade them to accept a statement as true. Here's an example:

> *The face masks from China are no good! The Chinese Communist Party covered up the deadliness of Covid-19 and allowed Chinese citizens to fly out of the country to other countries, spreading of the virus to the world, which ultimately resulted in tens of thousands of people dying and the world economies shutting down!*

Notice that the arguer here is attempting to persuade the audience that the face masks are not good, since they are from China, about which the arguer is clearly angry. But such anger, justified or not, is simply irrelevant to whether the *masks* are good or bad.

Another example of appeal to emotion is *appeal to pity*. This occurs when one tries to get one's audience to pity oneself or others in order to attempt to persuade them to accept a statement as true. For example:

> *Ladies and gentlemen of the jury, I urge you to find my client not guilty of the charge of murder, as his wife and children will be heartbroken if he is found guilty and sent to jail.*

Here, the defense attorney is attempting to persuade the jury that his client is not guilty, since his loving family would be heartbroken without him (pity the family). But such pity is simply irrelevant to whether he is guilty.

And for one more example, there is *appeal to fear*. This occurs when one tries to get one's audience to fear something in order to attempt to persuade them to accept a statement as true. For example:

> *If you don't vote for me in this upcoming election, be prepared for the economy to collapse, and for many to lose their jobs, including possibly you! Clearly, I am the best candidate.*

In this case, the politician is attempting to persuade his audience that he is the *best candidate*, since they should *fear* what would happen if they don't vote for him. But, as with the other examples, such emotional appeal (in this case to *fear*) is simply irrelevant to whether he is the *best candidate*.

And, of course, there are many other specific appeals to emotion, differing in which emotion is evoked—such as *appeal to envy*, *appeal to pride*, *appeal to joy*, *appeal to hatred*, and more. In each case, the emotional appeal is simply irrelevant to the truth-value of the statement one is trying to defend.

## Ad Hominem Fallacies

Our next fallacy type is *ad hominem,* which is Latin for "to the man." The general idea of this type of fallacy is that it involves rejecting a statement based on something about the person making the statement rather than refuting the statement itself. There are at least five more specific variations of ad hominem—*abusive ad hominem, inconsistency ad hominem, guilt by association, circumstantial ad hominem,* and *poisoning the well.* We'll consider each of these in turn.

### Abusive Ad Hominem

Perhaps the most common ad hominem fallacy is *abusive ad hominem.* This fallacy involves attempting to refute a person's statement by pointing out irrelevant bad characteristics of the person making the statement. The form can be put this way:

Premise: Person P asserts statement S.

Premise: P has bad feature F.

Conclusion: [Therefore,] statement S is false.

Here are two examples:

> Barry's claim that the United States should have open borders is clearly wrong—after all, Barry's an idiot.

And,

> Mr. Johnson suggests that the fine-tuning of the universe resulted from mere chance. However, Mr. Johnson was caught stealing money from the university and often lies about his past meth addiction.

Notice two things about these examples. First, the statement of the person in question (e.g., *the United States should have open borders* and *the fine-tuning of the universe is by chance*) is being rejected in each case by pointing out a bad feature of the person—this is the "abusive" aspect of the fallacy. Second, that bad feature of the person (whether it really is a feature of the person or not) is *irrelevant* to whether the statement in question is true or false—which makes it a *fallacy.*

### Inconsistency Ad Hominem

Closely related to abusive ad hominem is *inconsistency ad hominem* (also called *tu quoque,* which is Latin for "you too"). In this fallacy, one rejects a person's statement based on accusing the person making the statement of being inconsistent or hypocritical in making the statement. It is different from abusive ad hominem in that the hypocrisy referenced need not be considered a bad feature of the person in question—such as in the second example below. Its form can be stated as follows:

Premise: Person P asserts statement S.

Premise: P is being inconsistent (behaviorally or otherwise) in asserting S.

Conclusion: [Therefore,] statement S is false.

Consider the following two examples:

> *Reverend Paul's claim that sex outside of marriage is immoral is clearly false, as he has had several sexual encounters with prostitutes.*

And,

> *Raj constantly eats hamburgers, and thus his claim that animals are sacred is clearly absurd.*

Again, notice the two features of the fallacy. One, the statement of the person in question (e.g., *sex outside of marriage is wrong* and *animals are sacred*) is being rejected by pointing out that the person making the statement is being a hypocrite in making the statement. Typically, one points out that the *behavior* of the person making the statement is inconsistent with the person's statement in question. Two, note that the hypocrisy mentioned (whether correct or not) is entirely *irrelevant* to whether the statement in question is true or false—which makes it a *fallacy*.

### Guilt by Association

Also related to abusive ad hominem is *guilt by association*. In this fallacy, a person's statement is rejected because the person making the statement is accused of being associated with a person or group that is thought to be bad. It has the following form:

Premise: Person *P* asserts statement *S*.

Premise: *P* is associated with bad person *Q* or with bad group *G*.

Conclusion: [Therefore,] statement *S* is false.

Here are a couple of examples:

> *Melissa says that a fetus is a human life that is precious and should be protected, but Melissa is friends with Vanessa, who has had an abortion, and thus we can dismiss her statement.*

And,

> *Ryan believes that immigration laws should be stricter. However, Ryan is known to associate with Republicans, and specifically supports of Donald Trump. So, it is clear that Ryan's belief is absurd and should be rejected.*

Similar features can be seen here. First, the statement of the person in question (e.g., *a fetus is a human life to be protected* and *immigration laws should be stricter*) is being rejected by pointing out that the person making the statement is associated with someone or a group thought to be bad. Second, the association (whether correct or not) is entirely *irrelevant* to whether the statement in question is true or false—making it a *fallacy*.

**Circumstantial Ad Hominem**

A slightly different sort of ad hominem involves the rejection of a person's statement solely based on the person's circumstances, whether those circumstances are good or bad. This fallacy is *circumstantial ad hominem*. Put differently, the fallacy occurs when one suggests that a person's circumstances discredit the person's statement, when the circumstances are *irrelevant* to the truth-value of the statement. It has the following form:

Premise: Person *P* asserts statement *S*.

Premise: *P* is in circumstance *C*.

Conclusion: [Therefore,] statement *S* is false.

Here's an example:

> *We shouldn't accept Professor Zweir's claim that professors should be paid more—after all, he is only saying that because he is a professor.*

This is different from abusive ad hominem in two respects. First, one is not pointing out a *feature* of the person in question, and second, the circumstance which is cited to refute the statement need not be bad—after all, being a professor is *not* a bad thing. Still it is a fallacy since the circumstance of the person making the statement is entirely *irrelevant* to whether the statement is true or false. What does Professor Zweir being a professor have to do with whether professors should be paid more? *Nothing!*

A variation of this fallacy occurs when it is suggested that a person's *lack* of experience or failure to be in a circumstance refutes their statement. Here's an example:

> *Your marital advice is worthless, since you have never been married yourself.*

Notice that here it is pointed out that because the person in question is *not*, or has not been, in a particular circumstance (never been married), that lack of being in a circumstance refutes their statement. However, this is also a fallacy because such failure to be in a circumstance is *irrelevant* to the truth or falsity of the person's statement—for example, the marital advice may still be spot on!

**Poisoning the Well**

The final ad hominem is *poisoning the well*. This fallacy differs from the other ad hominem fallacies solely in virtue of *when* it is committed. All the other ad hominem fallacies are committed against the person in question *after* the person has made their statement. In contrast, *poisoning the well* is committed *before* the person in question has made their statement(s)—that is, poisoning the well occurs when one attempts to discredit a person *in advance* before they have made their statement. The fallacy is an *ad hominem* because the person committing the fallacy uses one of the other ad hominem fallacies (*abusive ad hominem, inconsistency ad hominem, guilt by association,* or *circumstantial ad hominem*) in the attempt to discredit. Its form can be put roughly as follows:

Premise: Person *P* is *about to* assert statement *S*.

Premise: *P* has bad feature *F* / is associated with bad person *Q* / is being inconsistent with what is about to be asserted / is in circumstance *C*.

Conclusion: [Therefore,] *P* statement *S* will be false.

Here's an example in which the poisoning of the well involves an *abusive ad hominem*:

> *Before turning the floor over to my opponent, I ask you to remember that she is a liar, an adulterer, and self-absorbed, which you should keep in mind as she claims that there should be term limits in Congress.*

Notice two things in the example. First, the person is using *abusive ad hominem* by calling her a liar, an adulterer, and self-absorbed in the attempt to refute her statement. Second, the ad hominem is committed *before* the person has had a chance to speak—making it a *poisoning the well*.

Here's another example involving circumstantial ad hominem:

> *Malorie is about to come tell you that the Jeep Wrangler Willys is better to purchase than the Rubicon, but you might want to take her claim with a grain of salt, since she is a salesperson at the local Jeep dealership.*

Again, notice the two features here—one is that the ad hominem is a *circumstantial* ad hominem, since the person is attempting to refute Malorie's statement by pointing out her circumstances, and two, that since it was done *in advance* before Malorie spoke, it is *poisoning the well*.

## Genetic Fallacy

A fallacy that is occasionally mistaken for ad hominem, but is *not* ad hominem, is the *genetic fallacy*. The fallacy is committed when one cites the origin of a statement as reason to reject the statement. More exactly, it occurs when one specifies *how, when,* or *where* a statement originated as the reason to reject it. Note that with genetic fallacy, unlike ad hominem fallacies, one is *not* rejecting a statement based on facts about the *person* making the statement but based on the origin of the *statement*. Below are examples, in terms of *how, when,* or *where* a statement originated, respectively. It has the following form:

Premise: Person *P* asserts statement *S*.

Premise: *S* came about in a particular way / time / or place.

Conclusion: [Therefore,] statement *S* is false.

Here is one in terms of *how* the statement arose:

> *Your idea that appealing to endurantism is a good way to support substance dualism is absurd, since you came up with that idea in a dream.*

Notice that in the example, the statement *that appealing to endurantism is a good way to support substance dualism* is rejected based on *how* the idea came about—namely, *by way of a dream*.

But note that *how* one arrives at an idea or statement is entirely *irrelevant* to whether the idea is good or bad, or the statement is true or false. After all, there had to be some *way* in which a statement arose, and *how* it did has nothing to do with whether it is true or false.

Alternatively, here is an example in terms of *when* the statement arose:

> *I reject the idea that there is an omnipotent, omniscient God, because the idea that there is such a being arose before the Enlightenment, at a time when humans were more superstitious.*

In this example, the statement *that there is an omnipotent, omniscient God* is rejected based on *when* the idea came about—namely, *before the Enlightenment*. But note that *when* an idea or statement comes to be is entirely *irrelevant* to whether the idea is good or bad, or the statement is true or false. After all, there had to be some *time* at which a statement arose, and *when* it did provides *no* rational support for it being true or false.

And, here is an example in terms of *where* the statement arose:

> *The notion that we should give stimulus relief checks to non-US citizens was proposed at the liberal, Socialist, Democrat meeting. Thus, we can safely reject it as a ridiculous idea.*

In this example, the statement *that we should give stimulus relief checks to non-US citizens* is rejected based on *where* it arose—namely, at the meeting of the Democrats (whether they really are liberal and Socialist is irrelevant). But as with the other examples, *where* an idea or statement arises is entirely *irrelevant* to whether the idea is good or bad, or the statement is true or false. After all, there had to be some*where* that the statement arose, and *where* it did provides *no* rational support for it being true or false.

## Appeal to Popularity

We humans are quite susceptible to the influence of others, even if we don't want to admit it. We care what others think of the way we dress, how we act, what we think, et cetera. This can be a good thing or a bad thing depending on the circumstances. One thing that is *always* bad, however, is believing that some statement is *true* (or false) *solely because* many believe it. To think in this way is to commit the fallacy of *appeal to popularity*. This fallacy is straightforward, having the following form:

> Premise: Many believe statement S.

> Conclusion: [Therefore,] statement S is true.

Here's an example:

> *Millions of Texans can't be wrong—the attorneys at Meyers, Hall, and Smith are the best!*

That statement is no doubt something like you'd see in an advertisement for the firm. Notice that in it, the advertisers (i.e., the attorneys at the firm) are suggesting that the attorneys are the best based solely on the fact that many believe it. But recall what has been emphasized a lot in this book—namely, that beliefs do not cause statements to be true, and the many can be *wrong*. Thus, the mere fact that many believe something is *irrelevant* to whether what they believe is true.

Here's another example:

> It is well recognized by most that humans are the result of millions of years of evolution. Since this is so widely held, there can be little doubt of its accuracy.

Whether it is true or not that humans evolved, it simply does *not* follow from the fact that many *believe* it. Again, many could believe it (indeed, everyone could believe it) and it still be false. Thus, again, the mere fact that many believe it is *irrelevant* to whether what they believe is true.

## Appeal to Unqualified Authority

One of our main sources of knowledge about the world is by way of personal testimony, in which a person(s) reports to another that something is (was, will be) the case. Many of our beliefs about history, science, weather, the condition of our bodies, and definitely about what others are thinking and feeling comes by way of such personal testimony. One goes to the medical doctor, who reports that one has high blood pressure, which in turn affects one belief about one's physical condition. So goes personal testimony.

Beliefs formed by way of personal testimony can be and often are rational and justified. However, occasionally they can be irrational. One way in which this can occur is if one person appeals to the testimony of another as an authority on the issue under investigation in order to justify a statement, but the person appealed to is *not* an authority on that issue (even if they are an authority on *something*). When this occurs, one has committed the fallacy of *appeal to unqualified authority*. The structure of this sort of argument goes more or less as follows:

> Premise: Authority person *P* says (said) that statement *S* is true.
>
> Conclusion: [Therefore,] statement *S* is true.

Note that this is a fallacy when *and only when* the person appealed to is *not* an authority on the issue in question. If the person is an authority on the issue, then there is no fallacy, such as appealing to one's dermatologist to justify one's belief that one has skin cancer. But let's consider an example of *appeal to unqualified authority*.

> Of course there is no God! I recently heard a talk by microbiologist Richard Dawkins, and he informed his audience that there is no such person as God.

While Dawkins is certainly an authority on issues in microbiology, as a microbiologist he is **not** an authority on whether God exists. Thus, what he asserted in this case is simply *irrelevant* to whether the statement that *God exists* is true or false.

## Straw Man

In order to evaluate a statement or an argument, one must "re-create the statement or argument" either mentally or in some public way, such as in writing or in a speech. When the "re-creation" is done appropriately, one re-creates the statement or argument *exactly* as the author of the statement or argument intended (or at least very close to it). However, occasionally we (accidentally or intentionally) *misrepresent, distort,* or *exaggerate* the statement or argument. Typically, when we do this, the result is a much weaker argument or an obviously false statement, which is, of course, much easier to refute. When this occurs, one is guilty of committing a *straw man fallacy.* It is so named because one is not refuting the real statement or argument, but instead is refuting a "straw revision." The structure can be put as follows:

Person₁ asserts *S* (where *S* can be a statement or an argument).

Person₂ misrepresents, distorts, or exaggerates *S*, resulting in *S\**

Person₂ proceeds to argue against, or note the obvious falsity of, *S\**, concluding that the original *S* has been refuted.

Here is an example:

Sheldon suggested that teens should be taught about contraception methods in school so they can practice safe sex should they choose to have intercourse. However, it is clearly absurd to maintain that kids should have license to have sex with no consequences!

Note that Sheldon's *actual* position is simply that kids should be *taught* various contraceptive methods *for the sake of safe sex should they choose to have sex,* whereas the arguer attempted to refute that, not by showing it to be wrong but by completely misrepresenting Sheldon's position to be that kids should have license to have consequence free sex. Since the latter is *not* Sheldon's position, it is a "straw revision" of it, and in fact completely *irrelevant* to the truth of Sheldon's statement. Thus, the arguer has *not* refuted Sheldon at all.

Here's another example:

Sal: I believe that the Untied States should have open borders.

Merl: Oh, so you want all the criminals and terrorists to just waltz into our country and commit all sorts of criminal and terrorist acts! That is absurd. Clearly the Untied States should not have open borders.

The straw man is probably clear here. Sal's position is merely that the US borders should be open. He did *not* express or imply that he *wants* criminals and terrorists to waltz right in. While Merl *could have* argued that a consequence of open borders is more easy access for criminals and terrorists, he did not. Instead, he *misrepresented* Sal's position to be one of *wanting* that. Thus, Merl committed a straw man fallacy, as what he presented as Sal's position is simply *not* Sal's position, and is in fact *irrelevant* to Sal's position.

## Appeal to Ignorance

Sometimes we can be lazy, not merely in failing to engage in activities when we should be so engaged, but also in failing to engage in reasoning when we should. Occasionally a person does the latter because they think that it is not their job to support a statement, but instead the burden is on others to prove them wrong. This can lead to the fallacy of *appeal to ignorance*. The form of this fallacy is roughly as follows:

Premise: No one has proven statement S to be false (true).

Conclusion: [Therefore,] statement S is true (false).

It can take either form—the non-parenthetical form or the parenthetical form. Let's see examples of each:

*I think that some people have psychic powers—after all, no one has proven that they don't.*

This is an example of arguing that since the statement hasn't been proven *false*, it therefore must be *true*. But, obviously, the mere fact that no one has proven it false is *irrelevant* to whether it is actually true. No one has proven that there is no Death Star made of Legos floating around the moon, but clearly it is not true that there is.

Or, it can be reversed, where one reasons that a statement is false since it hasn't been proven true. For example:

*Humans don't have souls, since we haven't proven it with our science.*

The mere fact we have not proven a statement to be true with science is *irrelevant* to whether the statement is true or false. Perhaps we have not yet tried, or perhaps we have not yet succeeded, or in this case, perhaps it is beyond the purview of science.

In short, the mere fact that a statement has not been *proven* true (false) is *irrelevant* to whether the statement is true or false, and thus to argue in this way is fallacious.

## Gambler's Fallacy

Our next fallacy is the **gambler's fallacy**, so named because it is frequently committed by gamblers, though it is not limited to them. It occurs when one argues that because there was a series of similar events $E_1$, $E_2$, $E_3$, et cetera, it follows that it is more probable that another similar event $E_4$ will (will not) occur, where the probability of each event in the series is independent of the others. To say that the probabilities are *independent* means that the occurrence of one of the events does not causally affect the occurrence of the other events. It has the following form:

Premise: Similar events $E_1$, $E_2$, $E_3$, etc., have occurred.

Premise: An event $E_4$ is similar to $E_1$, $E_2$, $E_3$.

Conclusion: [Therefore,] there is a greater probability that $E_4$ will (will not) occur.

The fallacy can occur in variations. Here is one variation:

*The past 10 times that I have flipped this (fair) coin, it has come up heads. Therefore, the next time I flip it, it will probably come up tails.*

In this example, one is arguing that the coin coming up heads the last 10 times makes it less likely that it will be heads on the eleventh flip (or alternatively, more likely that it will be tails). The thinking here is that the series of the coin landing on heads has "played itself out." However, since the probability that the coin will land on heads *each flip* is 0.5, the fact that it has come up heads 10 times in a row is simple *irrelevant* to the probability of the next flip.

Here's another example,

> For the past week, I have driven through the intersection of Fifth and Main at different times of the day, and each time I arrive at the intersection the light is green. So, I think I will take the route home that takes me through that intersection, as it will probably be green again when I arrive.

Again, here we have an example in which one thinks that the previous events of the light being green at the intersection affect the probability of the next event of the light being green, when in fact they are independent events. The occurrence of the previous events is *irrelevant* to the probability of the next event of the light being green.

## Equivocation

The last fallacy that we will consider in the *irrelevant premises fallacies* category is *equivocation*. This fallacy is often categorized differently than it is categorized here (it is typically categorized under the *fallacy of ambiguity* category). However, since we are dividing the fallacies into *irrelevant premises fallacies* and *insufficient / unacceptable premises fallacies*, it fits best into this category, as will be explained.

The fallacy of *equivocation* is based on the fact that terms can be ambiguous. Or put differently, it is based on one equivocating on a term in an argument. To better understand this, let's digress and compare *univocal* terms to *equivocal* terms. Some terms have only one meaning in all contexts (except for perhaps secret code contexts). For example, the temporal word *past* has only one meaning—"prior to the present." Words that have only one meaning like this are *univocal*.

In contrast, other words or phrases are *equivocal*, meaning that they have different meanings based on the context. Consider a few examples:

- The pencil is *left* of the paper.
- The maid *left* the room.
- The rabid *bat* flew out of the cave.
- The baseball player swung at the ball with the wooden *bat*.
- The *crane* lifted its long beautiful neck to look over the fence.
- The construction operator lifted the blocks to the top of the building with the *crane*.

The words in these examples are *equivocal* since they have different meanings in different contexts. Further, one *equivocates* on a word or phrase when one uses it more than once in a context but shifts its meaning in each use. Here is a famous example from Lewis Carroll's *Through the Looking Glass*:

> "Who did you pass on the road?" the King went on, holding his hand out to the messenger for some hay. "Nobody," said the messenger. "Quite right," said the King; "this young lady saw him too. So of course Nobody walks slower than you."

In this passage, Carroll beautifully exploits the ambiguity of *nobody*, equivocating upon it intentionally.

This brings us to the <u>*fallacy*</u> of *equivocation*, which occurs when one equivocates on a word or phrase *in an argument*. It can be formulated as follows:

Premise with word or phrase *W1* is used [where *W1* is one of the meanings of *W*].

Premise with word or phrase *W2* is used [where *W2* is a different meaning of *W*].
Conclusion drawn as if *W* was used univocally.

Here are a couple of silly examples:

Tom is deathly afraid of bats, and thus he will be terrified at the baseball games, since the players will be swinging their bats at the baseball throughout the game.

And:

Marty says he's not coming to the party because he's going to play with his rock band, but since he's 25 years old, he shouldn't be playing with rocks anymore.

While those are two silly examples, they illustrate the fallacy nicely. In the first, *bat* is used equivocally to mean the flying mammal in the one use (i.e., Tom is deathly afraid of the flying mammals, not the wooden club), and *bat refers to* the wooden club in the other use (i.e., player will be swinging the wooden club). And in the second example, *rock* is being equivocated upon, meaning a type of musical band in one use, and the mass of minerals and matter in the other.

These are *fallacious* since the conclusion simply does not follow, given the equivocal use of the terms. Consider the first argument, but with the ambiguity of *bat* clarified:

Premise: Tom is deathly afraid of flying mammals called "bats."

Premise: Players at the baseball game will be swinging wooden clubs (bats) throughout the game.

Premise: [Therefore,] Tom will be terrified at the baseball game.

When the argument is stated in that way, it is clear that the conclusion does not follow. Further, this *can* be treated as an *irrelevant premises fallacy* because the premises *independently*, as well as *taken jointly*, are simply *irrelevant* to the conclusion.

**EXERCISE 10.1**

For the following passages, identify which of the *irrelevant premises fallacies* is occurring (including *subjectivist fallacy, appeal to emotion, abusive ad hominem, inconsistency ad hominem, guilt by association, circumstantial ad hominem, poisoning the well, genetic fallacy, appeal to popularity, appeal to unqualified authority, straw man, appeal to ignorance, gambler's fallacy,* and *equivocation*).

**\*1.** Since more and more philosophers are adopting materialism and rejecting substance dualism, materialism must be the correct view.

2. Look, Christians have their opinions about religion and Muslims have their opinions. Let's just let everyone be—after all, there is no right answer, since we have all these religions.

3. Sam Smith is anti-America—after all, he used to attend a church run by Reverend David Barber, who often criticized the United States.

*4. Philosopher Thomas Aquinas gave us several arguments for God's existence, but we cannot trust those argument since Aquinas lived the thirteenth century.

5. Professor, I know that you made it clear in the syllabus and in class that no late work is accepted, but I deserve more time since my grandmother recently died and I was not able to submit my work on time.

6. Don't listen to Professor Terry's argument against the proposal for professors to have an increased teaching load this fall—after all, he's a professor.

*7. Zoey has a broken heart after her boyfriend dumped her. So, she needs to do some cardio, since cardio is good for the heart.

8. We cannot accept the Catholic priest's claim that God is good—after all, he is a pedophile.

9. I know that Nature's Way vitamins are the best, since Will Smith said that they are the best.

*10. You're a hypocrite! You claim that cows are sacred, but just last week I saw you eating a beef hamburger.

11. *Natalie*: Will you please take out the trash?

    *Ethan*: Oh my gosh, you want me to do *everything* around here.

12. Your claim that Christianity is the one true religion can't be right. The reason is that you believe it only because you were brought up as a Christian. If you were brought up in the Islam religion, you would think that Islam is the one true religion.

13. You know that scientists can't prove that we don't have free will, and thus I know that we do have free will.

14. The Garcias have had three girls in a row, and Ms. Garcia is pregnant again. I bet this one will be a boy, since the last three were girls.

15. Professor Johnson is often unfair in his class, frequently giving grades for wrong reasons. Therefore, I am simply not going to trust his statements about quantum physics.

## Insufficient / Unacceptable Premises Fallacies

*Insufficient / unacceptable premise fallacies* are fallacies that occur when one uses premises in one's argument that are either insufficient to support the conclusion, or they are in some way unacceptable. We will investigate four main fallacies in this category.

### Begging the Question

One frequently hears reporters use the phrase *this begs the question*, which they follow with a question. For example:

The Green Bay Packers selected a quarterback in the first round of the 2020 draft. And *this begs the question*: Is Aaron Rodgers planning to retire soon?

This is technically a *misuse* of the phrase *begs the question*. Instead, the reporters ought to say, *this begs for the question*, followed by their question.

Used properly, the phrases *begs the question*, *question begging*, and *begging the question* refer to a logical fallacy. To be precise, *begging the question* is a fallacy in which a premise in the argument presupposes the truth of the conclusion it is intended to support, rather than supporting it. To say that it *presupposes* the conclusion means that the only way that the premise can be true is if the conclusion is already true. Thus, the premise is not supporting the conclusion, but relying on it.

Begging the question comes in various degrees of explicitness. In an extreme case, the arguer uses the conclusion as the premise. For example,

> *German shepherds are the best guard dogs because German shepherds are the best guard dogs.*

In this case, the premise presupposes the truth of the conclusion because *the premise itself is the conclusion!*

In less, though still fairly, explicit cases, one also uses the conclusion as the premise, but rephrases it. For example:

> German shepherds are the best guard dogs because no dog breed is as good of a guard dog as is a *German shepherd.*

Notice that the premise (*no dog breed is as good of a guard dog as is a German shepherd*) is just the conclusion stated differently. Here's another example of how this sort of question begging might go:

> *The statement is true since it is not false.*

Just like the previous example, the premise itself restates the conclusion differently. Notice that *not false* is just another way of saying *true*.

An argument also begs the question in less explicit ways. Here is a famous example:

> *There is no doubt that God exists, since the Bible says that God exists, and the Bible is the word of God, which means that it is true.*

None of the premises explicitly repeat the conclusion (*God exists*). But, one of the premises can be true only if it is true that God exists, in which case the premise relies upon the conclusion rather than supporting it. Consider the argument in standard form to see this:

Premise: The Bible says that God exists.

Premise: The Bible is the Word of God, which means that it is true.

Conclusion: [Therefore,] God exists.

Notice that neither premise says that God exists. The first only says that there is a book that *says* it. And the second premise does not mention the existence of God. However, one of the premises presupposes that God exists, since the premise cannot be true unless God does exist. It is not the first premise, since the Bible can say that even if there is no God. However, it can be true that the Bible is the *Word of God* only if God exists to give the word! Thus, the argument begs the question.

Begging the question is categorized as an insufficient / unacceptable premise fallacy because the premise *does* have *something* to do with the conclusion, and thus it is *not* irrelevant. However, it is unacceptable, since it does not support the conclusion, but presupposes it.

## False Dichotomy Fallacies

A *dichotomy* is a division between two things. For example, there is a dichotomy between whales and fish, in that whales are mammals, but fish are not. We reason with dichotomies all the time, and already encountered one use in chapter 7—disjunctive syllogisms. However, we can make mistakes with dichotomy reasoning. We will examine three cases—*false dilemma*, *perfectionist fallacy*, and *line-drawing fallacy*.

### False Dilemma

We sometimes use the word *dilemma* to refer to a difficult choice. However, in this context, a dilemma is a choice between two or more alternatives, whether difficult or not. So, a disjunction (*either A or B*) is a type of dilemma. In the basic case, one commits the fallacy of *false dilemma* when one argues that there is a dilemma between two options, one of which is false, concluding that the other is true, when in fact there are more options. The structure may appear to be a disjunctive syllogism, but it is not since there are more options than what are presented. So, more or less it goes as follows:

Premise: Either *p* or *q* [though in reality there are more options].

Premise: *p* is false

Conclusion: [Therefore,] *q* is true.

Here is an example:

*Either we build a wall at our southern border, or we are inviting all the criminals and terrorists to march right into our country from the south. We clearly do not want criminals and terrorists running amok in our country. Thus, we need to build a wall on our southern border.*

That is a *false dilemma*, since there are other options. For example, we can increase drone patrols to catch people crossing the border illegally, increase manpower at the border, and more. Even if these may not be as effective, the point is that there are more options than were presented in the argument, and thus it is a *false dilemma*.

While the basic case involves a *false* choice between only two options, one also creates a false dilemma if one argues with a false choice between only three options, or only four, et cetera. Consider the following example, in which three options are presented, when in fact there are more.

*That must be an eastern brown snake, since it's not an inland taipan or a coastal taipan.*

While the dilemma is subtle here, the arguer has presented us with one—namely, that the snake in question is either an eastern brown, an inland taipan, or a coastal taipan. But this is a *false* dilemma since the snake could also be a *western brown snake*, a *mulga*, a *lowlands copperhead*, a *small-eyed snake*, or some other species of Australian snake. Of course, the argument above could have been given in a context in which all these others have been ruled out, but if not, then the argument is a *false dilemma*.

This fallacy (along with perfectionist fallacy and decision-point fallacy) is categorized as an insufficient / unacceptable premise fallacy because the premise *does* have *something* to do with the conclusion, and thus it is *not* irrelevant. After all, the options given in the false dilemma are relevant. It is just that ruling out all but one of the options listed in the argument is insufficient to draw the conclusion since there are more options.

## Perfectionist Fallacy

There are two more specific versions of false dichotomy—*perfectionist fallacy* and *decision-point fallacy*. We'll cover the former in this section and the latter in the next. *Perfectionist fallacy* occurs when one creates a false dichotomy specifically with the two options of *perfect* or *worthless*. It has the following form:

Premise: Either *x* is perfect, or it is worthless.

Premise: *x* is not perfect.

Conclusion: So, *x* is worthless.

This is a false dichotomy because there are many options in between perfect and worthless. Here is an example:

*Either the book is completely error free, or it is worthy of the flames. But I found a typo on page 36, and thus we need to burn it!*

It does not always come in this form, however. Often it comes in the form of rejecting a policy, proposal, or statement because the policy, proposal, or statement doesn't solve some problem *perfectly*. Here's an example:

*Congressman Mac's new policy is not going to completely eliminate homelessness, and therefore, it is a waste of time to implement it.*

This is a *perfectionist fallacy* since there is a lot of space between the policy being perfect and worthless. While the policy may not completely eliminate homelessness, it may help substantially reduce it, and thus may be worth implementing.

Or perfectionist fallacy can be more subtle, as in the following example:

*I thought you cleaned this room, but you didn't clean it at all—there is crumb right here!*

Notice that the person is reasoning that if there is just one crumb, and thus not perfect, the room wasn't cleaned at all! But clearly that is wrong.

## Decision-Point Fallacy

The last specific version of false dichotomy is *decision-point fallacy* (also called *line-drawing fallacy, argument to the beard,* among other names). It occurs when one rejects a statement involving a *vague* term because we cannot specify the exact point between when the vague term applies and when it does not. Or, put differently, it occurs when one creates a false dichotomy between the options: *specifying the exact point at which something x occurs,* and *the failure of x to occur.* Its form can be put as follows:

Premise: Either we can identify the exact point at which *x* occurs, or *x* does not occur.

Premise: We *cannot* identify the exact point at which *x* occurs.

Conclusion: So, x does not occur.

Here is an example:

*No, I am not bald! After all, either you specify the exact point of hair loss (the exact hair lost) at which baldness begins, or there is no baldness, and clearly you cannot specify that exact hair lost that is the line between non-bald and bald.*

This is the decision-point fallacy since even though one cannot specify the exact applications of the term *bald,* it does not follow that we cannot identify a bald person. Thus, the choices of *specifying the exact point at which baldness occurs* and *there is no baldness* is a false dichotomy.

The fallacy can occur with any vague term, as all vague terms are such that there are scenarios in which we don't know whether the term applies, and thus we cannot identify the exact point between when it applies and when it does not. Here is one more example:

*Either you can identify the exact dollar amount at which someone goes from non-rich to rich, or no one is rich. But you cannot identify the exact dollar amount at which someone goes from non-rich to rich. Therefore, Bill Gates is simply not rich!*

This is of course absurd, as we do know that the term *rich* applies to Bill Gates, even if we cannot specify the exact dollar amount that made him rich.

In short, in decision-point fallacy, one argues that there are only the two options specified, when in fact there are more options—namely, being able to identify when a vague term applies even if we cannot identify the exact line between its application and non-application.

## Fallacies in Reasoning About Parts and Wholes

The world is filled with wholes composed of parts, and a *lot* of philosophical reflection has transpired about the relationship between a whole and its parts. We think about parts and wholes all the time, drawing inferences about a whole based on its parts (such as that the whole has a certain mass because its parts have some mass), or about the parts based on the whole (such as that the parts are a certain color since the whole is a certain color). However, we can make mistakes in our thinking about parts and wholes. Two such mistakes are *composition* and *division.*

## Composition

The fallacy of *composition* occurs when one concludes that a whole has a particular property based on the premise that *all* its parts have that property. Its structure can be put this way:

Premise: Each of the parts of a whole $W$ have a property $P$.

Conclusion: Therefore, $W$ has $P$.

Here is a silly example to illustrate the fallacy.

> *Each of the clay bricks in that wall weighs about five pounds, and therefore the wall weighs about five pounds.*

Of course, we would not commit composition in *that* way. But some might be tripped up by it in a way like the following:

> *Of course I understand that sentence—after all, I understand each word of it.*

The conclusion does not follow. One may understand each word of a sentence but fail to understand the sentence.

Another way in which we sometimes commit composition is when reasoning about groups or our favorite team. Consider the following example:

> *My team has the best quarterback, the best running back, the best receiver, and so on for each position. Therefore, my team is the best!*

But, once again, the premises are insufficient to support the conclusion, as each individual player may be the best at their position, but they each fail to work with each other as a team and thus fail to be the best team collectively.

## Division

The fallacy of *division* is reasoning in the opposite direction from composition—namely, from the whole to the parts. It occurs when one concludes that *each part* of some whole has a particular property based on the premise that the whole has that property. Its structure can be put this way:

Premise: A whole $W$ has a property $P$.

Conclusion: Therefore, each part of $W$ has $P$.

Here is a silly example to illustrate this one:

> *The ball is spherical and thus each of its halves is spherical.*

Again, while we would not commit division in *that* way, we still get tripped up by it occasionally. For example, someone might commit it in an example like the following:

> *Johnny's bike is half the size of Mikey's bike. Thus, the tires on Johnny's bike must be half the size of the tires on Mikey's bike.*

But, of course, the conclusion does not follow, since the bike may be half the size without the tires also being half the size.

And, just like composition, one can commit division fallacy about groups. For example:

> The Green Bay Packers are the best team in the NFL. Therefore, the Green Bay Packers have the best running back in the NFL.

Obviously, the premises are insufficient to support the conclusion, since the team as a whole may be the best team, even if their running back is not all that great.

One way to tell the difference between composition and division is given by the names.

Composition: Reasoning from parts to whole.

Division: Reasoning from whole to parts.

When we put together many things to form a whole, we are *composing* the whole from the parts. And, we can break apart a whole by *dividing* its parts from the whole.

### Slippery Slope

The last fallacy that we will cover is *slippery slope*. The name is descriptive of the fallacy. In this fallacy, one reasons that the occurrence of one event will inevitably lead to the occurrence of another undesired event. It is a fallacy because there is no clear connection between the events, and thus the occurrence of the first is insufficient evidence to draw the conclusion that it will lead to the second event. We can state its form as follows:

Premise: If event $E_1$ occurs, the next thing you know event $E_2$ will occur.

Premise: $E_2$ is bad.

Conclusion: Therefore, we need to prevent $E_1$ from occurring.

Here is silly example to illustrate:

> If marijuana is legalized, it won't be long until we are all addicted to meth. Clearly, we don't want a meth pandemic (meth addiction is already bad enough). Thus, we need to vote against the legalization of marijuana!

Obviously, there is no clear connection between the legalization of marijuana and *everyone* being addicted to meth! Even if it can be shown that marijuana is a "gateway drug," the conclusion in the argument simply does not follow.

Slippery slope can also occur with a chain argument. DIRECTV deliberately exploited the fallacy for their advertising recently. The reasoning went more or less as follows:

> If your cable company puts you on hold, you get angry. If you get angry, then you go blow off steam. If you go blow off steam, an accident happens, and if an accident happens, then you get an eye patch from the doctor. If you get an eye patch, then people think you are tough. If people think you are tough, they want to fight you. And if people want to fight you, then you get hurt. You will end up in a roadside ditch. Don't end up in a roadside ditch. Switch to DIRECTV!

While DIRECTV purposely committed slippery slope here, it nicely illustrates the fallacy.

However, we have to be careful in accusing someone of committing slippery slope just because the person is engaged in chain reasoning. After all, such reasoning can be *good*. Here is an example:

> If you corner and anger or scare that inland taipan snake, you are likely to get bit, since they bite under such conditions. And, if you get bit by that snake, you will die if you do not get to a hospital quickly to receive the anti-venom (because it is an incredibly venomous snake). So, if you don't want to end up in the hospital and perhaps die, stay away from that snake!

Clearly *that* chain argument is justified, and the conclusion follows from the premises.

Nevertheless, we do occasionally make the mistake of *slippery slope*, and being aware of it may help us avoid it.

**EXERCISE 10.2**

For the following passages, identify which of the *insufficient / unacceptable premises fallacies* is occurring (including *begging the question, false dilemma, perfectionist fallacy, decision-point fallacy, composition, division,* and s*lippery slope*).

**\*1.** No, Paul, you cannot come with us to the new Star Wars movie, because you won't like it. The reason is that you love Star Trek, and either you love Star Trek and hate Star Wars or you love Star Wars and hate Star Trek.

**2.** I hear you telling me to exercise and eat healthy, but I don't see the point of that. After all, it is not going to prevent my death—we're all going to die no matter what.

**3.** There is no doubt that predestination is real, given that everything that happens has already been predetermined from the beginning.

**\*4.** I don't know why you all are making a big deal about me calling Morgan Freeman a boy. It is no big deal that I call him a boy, really, since he was a boy when he was three years old, and he was a boy when he was 10 years old, as well as when he was 14. Since you cannot tell me exactly when he stopped being a boy, you have no grounds for telling me that I cannot call him a boy now.

**5.** We must keep marriage defined as holding solely between man and woman, because it is a dangerous road to change it. If, for example, we change the definition to include same sex couples, before you know it we'll have to change it to include allow marriage between adult and child, and then between humans and animals, plants, and non-living things.

**6.** No, I don't want to buy that car. It's cheap, which I know because I know that each of its parts is cheap.

**\*7.** Pleasure is the greatest good for humans, since all other values are inferior to it.

**8.** *Pelosi*: Every protester was peaceful and legal.

   *Baier*: But they clearly were not! Why think they were?

   *Pelosi*: I know that each protester was peaceful and legal because the protest was peaceful and legal.

9. Max, you say that you believe in women's rights, but I don't think you do—after all, either you vote for Ms. Miller or you don't believe in women's rights, and I see that you didn't vote for Ms. Miller.

10. I think I'm going to buy a house this summer in Las Vegas, because prices will be down since they are down in the United States.

## Recap

In this chapter, we studied 20 informal fallacies, and divided them into those with *irrelevant premises* and those with *insufficient or unacceptable premises*. While there are many more informal fallacies, being familiar with the ones we studied will help you not only avoid them and know when others are committing them, but may also enable you to identify other fallacies you may encounter, even if you have no name for them. Below are short definitions of each of the fallacies that we covered:

- **Fallacy**: Mistake in reasoning.
  - **Formal Fallacy**: Fallacy resulting strictly from logical *form*.
  - **Informal Fallacy**: Fallacy resulting from logical form and content.
- *Irrelevant Premises Fallacies*: Fallacies that occur when one uses premises in one's argument that are *entirely irrelevant* to the conclusion.
  - **Subjectivist Fallacy**: Arguing that some statement is subjective simply because people have conflicting beliefs about the truth of the proposition.
  - **Appeal to Emotion**: Appeal to emotion occurs when someone uses emotional appeals (such as pride, anger, pity, fear, and joy) in place of relevant facts to support a statement.
  - **Ad Hominem Fallacies**: Ad hominem fallacies involve rejecting a statement based on something about the person making the statement rather than refuting the statement itself.
    - ▲ **Abusive Ad Hominem**: Attempting to refute a person's statement by pointing out irrelevant bad characteristics of the person making the statement.
    - ▲ **Inconsistency Ad Hominem**: Rejecting a person's statement based on accusing the person making the statement of being inconsistent or hypocritical in making the statement.
    - ▲ **Guilt by Association**: Rejecting a person's statement because the person making the statement is accused of being associated with a person or group that is thought to be bad.
    - ▲ **Circumstantial Ad Hominem**: Arguing that a person's circumstances discredit the person's statement, when the circumstances are *irrelevant* to the truth-value of the statement.
    - ▲ **Poisoning the Well**: Attempting to discredit a person *in advance* before they have made their statement, and committing one of the other ad hominem

fallacies (*abusive ad hominem, inconsistency ad hominem, guilt by association,* or *circumstantial ad hominem*) in the attempt to discredit.

- **Genetic Fallacy**: Arguing that a statement is false based on the origin of a statement (*how, when,* or *where* it originated).
- **Appeal to Popularity**: Arguing that some statement is *true* (or false) *solely because* many believe it.
- **Appeal to Unqualified Authority**: Attempting to justify a statement by appealing to the testimony of another as an authority on the statement, but the person appealed to is *not* an authority on that statement.
- **Straw Man**: Rejecting a person's statement or argument based on a (accidental or intentional) *misrepresentation, distortion,* or *exaggeration* of the statement or argument.
- **Appeal to Ignorance**: Arguing that some statement is true (or false) because no one has proven that it is false (or true).
- **Gambler's Fallacy**: Arguing that because there was a series of similar events $E_1$, $E_2$, $E_3$, etc., it follows that it is more probable that another similar event $E_4$ will (will not) occur, where the probability of each event in the series is independent of the others.
- **Equivocation**: Equivocation occurs when one equivocates on a word or phrase *in an argument*.

- **Insufficient / Unacceptable Premises Fallacies**: Fallacies that occur when one uses premises in one's argument that are either insufficient to support the conclusion, or they are in some way unacceptable.
  - **Begging the Question**: Begging the question is a fallacy in which a premise in the argument presupposes the truth of the conclusion it is intended to support, rather than supporting it.
  - **False Dichotomy Fallacies**: False dichotomy fallacies involve reasoning as if there are only two options (or *n* options), when there are in fact more options (*n*+ options).
    - ▲ **False Dilemma**: Arguing that there is a dilemma between two (or more) options, all but one of which are false, concluding that the remaining statement is true, when in fact there are more options.
    - ▲ **Perfectionist Fallacy**: This fallacy occurs when one argues that something is worthless since it is not perfect.
    - ▲ **Decision-Point Fallacy**: This fallacy is based on vague concepts and occurs when one rejects a statement involving a *vague* term because we cannot specify the exact point between when the vague term applies and when it does not.
  - **Fallacies in Part / Whole Reasoning**: These fallacies involve reasoning either from facts about the whole to facts about the parts of the whole, or from facts about the parts to facts about the whole of which they are parts.

▲ **Composition**: Arguing that a whole has a particular property because each of its parts has that property.

▲ **Division**: Arguing that *each part* of some whole has a particular property because the whole has that property.

• **Slippery Slope**: Arguing, without justification, that one event will inevitably lead to some other undesirable event.

---

**EXERCISE 10.3**

For the following passages, identify which of the fallacies from the chapter is occurring.

**\*1.** I'm not going to accept your statement that we must be tolerant of *everyone* and of *all* beliefs, while you simultaneously criticize Christians for saying that homosexual behavior is morally wrong.

**2.** Your argument concludes that humans have a soul, but I can tell you that many people don't accept that. While it is fine for you, it is not true for many. So, ultimately, there is no right answer regarding whether we have a soul.

**3.** *Child*: Mommy, you have to buy me this toy truck.

*Mom*: No, Timmy, I do not have to buy it.

*Child*: Well, you say you love me, and either you buy me the toy truck or you don't love me.

**\*4.** Let's have tacos for dinner, and not pizza, because tacos are obviously better than pizza, since tacos are better than nothing, and nothing is better than pizza.

**5.** The idea that we have a soul is just silly and laughable. Surely you don't believe it, do you?!

**6.** I know that it appears that you can see the rock, but it is mere appearance and not reality. The reason you cannot really see it is that it is invisible to the naked eye, which we know because it is composed of atoms, each of which is invisible to the naked eye.

**\*7.** Why are you talking to and hanging out with Rob? He is a jock and on the football team. But many of the football players are idiots and bullies.

**8.** I didn't try too hard on this paper because I know that no matter how much time and effort I put into it, it won't be perfect. So, why bother trying?

**9.** Some people think that rioting and looting is the best way to express anger in protest, and others think that peaceful demonstration is the right way to go about it. Given this disagreement, the governor's claim that we should have peaceful demonstrations cannot be right.

**\*10.** *Sister*: Mom, I told you why I should not be grounded for not doing my chores. Now Luke will try to tell you I should be grounded rather than him, but he'll just be feeding you some pathetic argument to weasel out of his guilt, and you know he's not very bright.

**11.** I'm opposed to lowering the legal drinking age, because if we do, the next thing you know we'll be lowering the age we send our kids to war, and lowering the voting age and the driving age. Before you know it, kids will be legally able to do everything we adults now do.

12. *Salesman*: The Bose speaker has the brightest and most bold dynamic sound among all our speakers.

    *Frank*: I seriously doubt that. You're just saying that because you work here.

13. So many dentists cannot be wrong; this toothpaste is surely the best.

*14. I overheard Gary say that he is opposed to homosexual behavior, but Gary's hatred of all homosexuals cannot be tolerated. Do not vote for him.

15. I don't want to take the class because the textbook is very lengthy, and thus I know that all the assigned readings from the text will be lengthy, and I simply don't have time to do all that reading.

16. Governor Newsom thinks the state needs to raise the minimum wage, but how can we believe that since he is not even smart enough to run a successful business—he has had two failed businesses.

17. Of course my experiences reflect reality as it is in itself—after all, I can see, hear, touch, smell, and taste things in the world.

18. The idea that we need to control and dominate the rioters was invented by the fascists, and thus we need to reject that idea and just let them destroy and loot.

*19. *Alice*: Would you like some of this soup?

    *Lydia*: No, I won't like it, since it is made from potatoes, carrots, peas, dill, and chicken stock, and I don't like any of those individual ingredients. Thus, I know I won't like the soup.

20. I was struggling whether to purchase a Chevy Silverado or a Ford F-150, but ever since my dentist told me that the Silverado is clearly the better truck, I decided to buy the Chevy. I'm happy that I'll be getting the better truck!

21. The iPhone is obviously better than the Samsung. Just ask anyone.

22. I think that there are space wars between aliens in other galaxies—after all, no one has proven that there are not.

*23. The new Audi Sport gives you all the power you need. Buy one and you will be the envy of your friends. You will know the true joy of power. Audi Sport is the best sports car on the market.

24. *Jayden*: You have been playing poker all night and have lost every hand. Why are you playing another hand?

    *Lincoln*: Well, I know that since I have lost the last several hands, I am guaranteed to win this hand. I just know it!

*25. *Son*: Can I share a beer with you, Dad?

    *Dad*: No son, you are not yet 21.

    *Son*: I don't see what the big deal is that I'm not 21. Making the legal drinking age 21 makes no sense. One day before age 21 wouldn't make a difference, nor would two days. In fact, why does one year make a difference. What is the exact moment, Dad, that will make difference between being able to drink and not? You cannot tell me. So, let's just have a beer together.

26. Look, I happen to know that she had an abortion when she was a teenager, and thus we must pay no attention to her arguments against abortion.

27. All birds are light, and nothing travels faster than light. So, nothing travels faster than birds.

28. You know that Dr. Jones got his new quantum physics idea about the behavior of quarks from watching that science fiction show, right? Thus, we cannot accept that in our physics.

*29. Susan, how can you accept Mary's advice for moving on after your heartbreaking breakup? Mary has never had her heart broken, and in fact she has never even been dumped.

30. There is simply no evidence that humans persist through time by being wholly present at each moment that they exist—that is, there is no evidence that they persist by *enduring*, and therefore, humans do not persist by enduring.

*31. *Senator Moore*: Senator Harris, you are a cold man who does not care about starvation in the world.

*Senator Harris*: Why do you say that?

*Senator Moore*: Because you did not vote for the new bill to give aid to poor countries to help feed the poor.

*Senator Harris*: Look, giving aid to the poor countries is not going to completely eliminate starvation, and so why should we throw away our money on giving aid?

32. *Dylan*: I am a vegetarian because I am opposed to the animal cruelty often involved with the killing of animals, and in fact I am opposed to killing animals in general.

*Julian*: Look, Dylan, your view that animals are sacred and that all living things must be protected is simply untenable. We have to eat and get protein.

# APPENDIX
# ANSWERS TO EXERCISES

## Chapter 3

### EXERCISE 3.1

1. One way to make this statement more precise is as follows:

   **The hurricane will hit the city** *at 5:00 p.m.* **tomorrow.**

4. One way to make this statement more precise is as follows:

   **If you drive** *over 45 mph,* **you will get a speeding ticket.**

7. One way to make this statement more precise is as follows:

   **This movie is intended for audiences** *aged 18 years and older.*

### EXERCISE 3.2

1. (a) This is syntactic ambiguity.
   (b) One way to eliminate the ambiguity is:

   **Betsy told Sally that Sally has a bee on her shoulder.**

4. (a) This is lexical ambiguity.
   (b) One way to eliminate the ambiguity is:

   **The sound of the bark of our dog, Acacia, is unique and healthy.**

7. (a) This is collective-distributive ambiguity.
   (b) One way to eliminate the ambiguity is:

   **Paul and Kyle together rowed a boat.**

### EXERCISE 3.3

1. *Snake* is the general word.

4. **One way of making the italicized expressions more specific is as follows:**

   The bank is at 425 J Street, at the northwest intersection of J Street and Main, but walk up to the bank slowly and quietly because of the large dog outside the southwest side of the bank.

7. Option (b) is the more specific sentence.

### EXERCISE 3.4

1. (a) The word "racism" is being defined.
   (b) This is definition by synonym.

4. (a) The word "Christian" is being defined.
   (b) This is ostensive definition.

7. (a) The word "person" is being defined.
   (b) This is a definition in terms of necessary and sufficient conditions.

### EXERCISE 3.5

1. This definition of "morally right" is **circular**, since to say that something is *morally appropriate* is just another way of saying that it is *morally right.*

4. This definition of "racist" is **too broad and too narrow**.

   It is too broad since it entails, for example, that if someone of a different race than me takes offense at my statement that they are a beautiful person, then I count as a racist, even if I believe that all races are equal and love all people.

   It is too narrow since someone may believe that all other races are inferior to their own race and hate all others, but never *say* anything offensive to others, and the definition would entail that the person is *not* a racist.

7. This definition of "planet" is **too narrow**, since it entails that no other solar system in the universe can have planets, since the definition specifies that a planet orbits the *sun*, which is located in our solar system alone. To make it broader, one should add, "a celestial body that is in orbit around the sun *or some other star.*"

283

## Chapter 4

### EXERCISE 4.1

**1. Statement**

It asserts that something is the case. Either it *says that* there is some objective standard of rating books, and the first rates higher, or it *says that* the person *prefers* the first book. Either way, it is *asserting that something is the case*.

**5. Statement**

It is asserting that it is the case that the *hope* exists.

**10. Not a Statement**

It is a *command*. It is *not* asserting that something is the case, but rather commanding the person to stay away.

**15. Statement**

Either it *says that* there is some objective standard of beauty, and the woman satisfies those standards really well, or it *says that* this person is attracted to the woman. Either way, it is *asserting that something is the case*.

### EXERCISE 4.2

**1. This argument contains *three* statements in its content.**

1. Only fish can sing.
2. Marlin is a fish.
3. Marlin can sing.

**4. This argument contains *three* statements in its content.**

1. If the universe exhibits design, then God exists.
2. The universe exhibits design.
3. God most certainly does exist.

**7. This argument contains *two* statements in its content.**

1. The US leaders had no clear plan for maintaining order once Saddam Hussein's government had been toppled.
2. The United States should not have invaded Iraq.

**10. This argument contains four statements in its content.**

1. If a fetus is a human person, then it is morally wrong to kill it without good reason.
2. If it is wrong to kill it without good reason, then most abortions are morally wrong.
3. Fetuses are human persons.
4. Most abortions are morally wrong.

### EXERCISE 4.3

**1. This argument *is* a *syllogism*, since it has exactly two premises and one conclusion.**

**Premise:** If you have a current password, then you can login to the site.

**Premise:** You have a current password.

**Conclusion:** You can login to the site.

**5. This argument is *not* a syllogism, since it has only one premise and one conclusion.**

**Premise:** It [the car] is red and square-shaped.

**Conclusion:** The car is red.

**8. This argument is a syllogism, since it has exactly two premises and one conclusion.**

**Premise:** Any coach who falls asleep during a game is not a very good coach.

**Premise:** Coach Johnson once fell asleep during a game.

**Conclusion:** He's probably not a very good coach.

### EXERCISE 4.4

**1. This passage contains an argument.**

**Premise:** Any animal that barks is a dog.

**Premise:** That animal is barking.

**Conclusion:** It [the animal] is a dog.

**5. This passage does not contain an argument.**

It is merely a question, and thus does not even contain one statement. But recall that an argument consists of at least two statements.

**15. This passage does not contain an argument.**

While is does have multiple statements, none is a reason for thinking that another statement in the passage is true. Thus, it lacks the required structure to count as an argument.

20. This passage contains an **argument.**

    **Premise:** If a time traveler enters a time machine at one time and arrives at some other time (past or future) five minutes later, then the time between a time traveler's departure and arrival is five minutes.

    **Premise:** If a time traveler enters a time machine at one time and arrives at some other time (past or future) that is separated by millions of years from the time of entry, then the time between a time traveler's departure and arrival is millions of years.

    **Premise:** The time between a time traveler's departure and arrival cannot be both five minutes and millions of years.

    **Conclusion:** Time travel is impossible.

## EXERCISE 4.6

1. These premises provide **independent** support for the conclusion.

   While together they provide *stronger* support to the conclusion, each alone does provide *some* support to the conclusion, and thus the premises provide independent support to the conclusion.

4. These premises **depend** on each other to support the conclusion.

   The premise that *the water either came from the north river or from the south river* by itself does not support the conclusion that *it came from the north river*, and the premise that *it was not the south river* by itself does not support the conclusion that *it came from the north river.* But together they support the conclusion that *it came from the north river.*

7. These premises provide **independent** support for the conclusion.

   The conclusion, *this room contains artists or realists,* is true if the room contains only artists, and it is true if the room contains only realists. Thus, if we had just one, but not the other, of these premises, the conclusion would still logically follow.

10. This premise provides **independent** support for the conclusion.

    Since there is only one premise, and it does support the conclusion, then it provides independent support to the conclusion.

## EXERCISE 4.7

1. The **sub-conclusion** is: *The bees are angry.*

   The **main conclusion** is: *You will get stung.*

4. The **sub-conclusion** is: *Charles is nice.*

   The **main conclusion** is: *He'd [Charles would] make a good friend.*

## EXERCISE 4.8

There are multiple possible implicit premises that can be contained in the argument. Below is one possible *implicit premise made explicit* for each.

1. Any team for which Aaron Rodgers plays quarterback is likely to win.

4. Most two-year-old children can walk.

7. Typically, when people overeat, they suffer from indigestion soon after.

## EXERCISE 4.9

There are multiple possible implicit conclusions that can be derived from the premises. Below is one possible *implicit conclusion made explicit* for each.

1. [Therefore,] **practicing the homework exercises is good preparation for the test.**

4. [Therefore,] **Bill is very wealthy.**

7. [Therefore,] **we will probably buy a Husky for our next dog.**

## Chapter 5

## EXERCISE 5.2

There are multiple possible thought experiments that can be given to show the arguments to be valid or invalid. Below is one possible thought experiment for each of 1, 4, and 8 as a sample.

1. **Invalid**

   (Thought Experiment): **Imagine that the world was such that not only are both plants and** mammals living things, but that all living things have hearts (contrary to reality).

If the conditions of the thought experiment were true, then the premises of argument would be true, but the conclusion would be false. Since the thought experiment presents a *possible* scenario (after all, God *could have* created the world that way), then it is possible for the premises to be true and the conclusion false. Thus, the argument is *invalid*.

**4. Valid**

(Thought Experiment): **Imagine that scorpions really do have 16 legs, and that literally everything with 16 legs is entirely transparent.**

If the conditions of the thought experiment were true, then not only would the premises of argument be true, but the conclusion could not be false. Indeed, there is no possible scenario in which both premises are true and the conclusion false, simultaneously. Thus, the argument is *valid*.

**8. Invalid**

(Thought Experiment): **Imagine that all philosophers really are critical thinkers and that they are all men. Further, suppose that Susana is a woman and a critical thinker.**

If it were true that all philosophers were critical thinkers (and probably most are, though not all always are – but imagine that they all always are), then nobody would be a philosopher and a non-critical thinker. If so, then *only* critical thinkers would be philosophers, and premise 1 would be true. And, of course, we built into the thought experiment that Susana is a critical thinker and a woman. Thus, premise 2 would be true. However, since we also imagined that only men are philosophers, then Susana would not be a philosopher, and the conclusion would be false.

Since the thought experiment presents a *possible* scenario, then it is possible for the premises to be true and the conclusion false. Thus, the argument is *invalid*.

**EXERCISE 5.3**

There are multiple possible abstractions and diagrams that can be given to show the arguments to be valid or invalid. Below is one possible abstraction and diagram for each of 1, 4, and 7 as a sample.

**1. Invalid**

Abstraction:

**Premise**: At time $t_1$, there were only three *x*s in A.

**Premise**: From $t_1$ to the present, no *x* has been removed from A.

**Conclusion**: Presently there are only three *x*s in A.

Diagram showing invalidity:

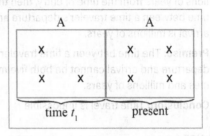

**FIGURE A.1**

Explanation: Notice that there were three *x*s (e.g., cats) in box A (e.g., the house) at time $t_1$ (e.g., last week). Notice further that no *x*s were removed from A from $t_1$ to present. Thus, both premises are true. However, it is false that there are only three *x*s in A in the present. Thus, the argument is *invalid*.

**4. Valid**

Abstraction:

**Premise**: Something is a *P* only if it is an *S*.

**Premise**: *H*s are *P*s.

**Conclusion**: *H*s are *S*s.

Diagram showing invalidity:

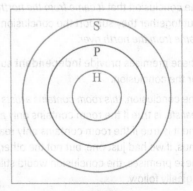

**FIGURE A.2**

Explanation: Notice that something is a *P* (e.g., persisting things) only if it is also an *S* (e.g., thing with a soul), and that all the *H*s (e.g., humans) are *P*s. Thus, it cannot be false that all the *H*s are *S*s. And, there is no possible scenario in which the premises are true but the conclusion false. Thus, the argument is *valid*.

**7. Valid**

Abstraction:

**Premise**: *x* is an A, B, C.

**Premise**: *y* is not an A, B, C.

**Conclusion**: *y* ≠ *x*.

Diagram showing invalidity:

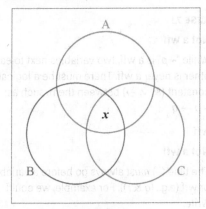

**FIGURE A.3**

Explanation: Notice *x* (e.g., the robber) is an A, B, and C (e.g., wearing a red shirt and glasses, and having a goatee), and that *y* (e.g., the client) is not, and thus the premises are true. Given this, it *cannot* be that the conclusion is false. And, there is no possible scenario in which the premises are true but the conclusion false. Thus, the argument is *valid*.

## Chapter 6

**EXERCISE 6.1**

**1.** (a) This is an **E**-statement.
   (b) This is a **universal** statement.
   (c) This is a **negative** statement.
   (d) The subject term is **computers**, and the predicate term is **thinking things**.
   (e) Both the subject and predicate terms are distributed.

**4.** (a) This is an **I**-statement.
   (b) This is a **particular** statement.
   (c) This is an **affirmative** statement.
   (d) The subject term is **fish that attack people**, and the predicate term is **sharks**.
   (e) Neither the subject nor predicate term is distributed.

**7.** (a) This is an **A**-statement.
   (b) This is a **universal** statement.
   (c) This is an **affirmative** statement.
   (d) The subject term is **large bodies that orbit the earth**, and the predicate term is **planets**.
   (e) The subject is distributed, but the predicate term is not distributed.

**EXERCISE 6.2**

**1.** All BMW i8s are fast cars.

**4.** All statements a person knows are true statements.

**8.** No computers are thinking things.

**14.** All times a tree falls in the forest are times a sound is made.

**19.** All whales are mammals.

**25.** No things identical to my key are things identical to your key.

**EXERCISE 6.3**

**1.** Converse: **All particles are quarks**. The two statements are *not* equivalent.

   Obverse: **No quarks are non-particles**. The two statements *are* equivalent.

   Contraposition: **All non-particles are non-quarks**. The two statements *are* equivalent.

**4.** Converse: **Some square things are not desks**. The two statements are *not* equivalent.

   Obverse: **Some desks are non-square things**. The two statements *are* equivalent.

   Contraposition: **Some non-square things are not non-desks**. The two statements *are* equivalent.

**7.** Converse: **No Germans are Americans**. The two statements *are* equivalent.

Obverse: **All Americans are non-Germans**. The two statements **are** equivalent.

Contraposition: **No non-Germans are non-Americans**. The two statements are **not** equivalent.

11. Converse: **Some electrons are dancers**. The two statements **are** equivalent.

Obverse: **Some dancers are not non-electrons**. The two statements **are** equivalent.

Contraposition: **Some non-electrons are non-dancers**. The two statements are **not** equivalent.

**EXERCISE 6.4**

1. All Muslims are Christians = False

   Some Muslims are Christians = False

   Some Muslims are not Christians = True

5. All pens are blue things = Undetermined

   No pens are blue things = False

   Some pens are not blue things = Undetermined

**EXERCISE 6.5**

1. **Invalid**, which can be seen the Venn diagram:

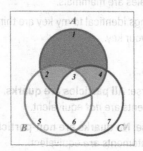

**FIGURE A.4**

4. **Invalid**, which can be seen the Venn diagram:

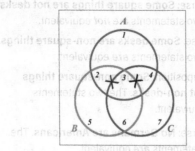

**FIGURE A.5**

7. **Valid**, which can be seen the Venn diagram:

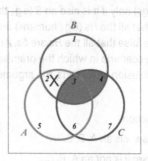

**FIGURE A.6**

## Chapter 7

**EXERCISE 7.1**

1. **Not a wff**

   While "~ $p$" is a wff, two variables next to each other is never a wff. There must be a logical constant (&, ∨, →) between them, such as:

   ~ $p$ → $q$

4. **wff**

7. **Not a wff**

   The tilde (~) *must* always go before a variable, or wff (e.g., ($q$ & $r$)). For example, we could write:

   ~ $p$ & $q$

10. **wff**

12. **Not a wff**

   The reason that #12 it not a wff is that it has two opening parentheses but only one closing parenthesis. Any opening parenthesis must have a closing parenthesis. There are two ways to fix this problem and symbolize to create a wff. First, one could simply remove the first parenthesis so that it reads:

   $p$ & ~ ($q$ → $r$)

   That is the preferred way, since the outer parentheses play no role in clarifying the wff. Second, one could add a closing parenthesis at the end to get:

   ($p$ & ~ ($q$ → $r$))

   While the first way is preferred, the second is not wrong.

**14. Not a wff**

The logical constants &, ∨, → *cannot* go next to each other but *must* always be flanked by exactly two wffs. So, simply place a variable between ∨ and &, and add parentheses, to get a wff. For example,

$(p \vee r) \,\&\sim q$

**EXERCISE 7.2**

Only the final step – the completed wff – for each is provided.

**3.** $(p \rightarrow j) \,\& \, m$

**4.** $p \rightarrow (j \,\& \, m)$

**9.** $p \rightarrow (j \rightarrow m)$

**13.** $\sim ((d \,\& \, t) \rightarrow \sim l)$

**14.** $\sim l \rightarrow (\sim d \,\& \sim t)$

**18.** There are two ways of doing *neither* φ *nor* ψ:

$\sim \varphi \,\& \sim \psi$

$\sim (\varphi \vee \psi)$

So, for 18, there are two correct symbolizations:

a. $l \rightarrow (\sim t \,\& \sim d)$

b. $l \rightarrow \sim (t \vee d)$

**EXERCISE 7.4**

**1. Valid**

**TABLE A.1**

|   | p | q | p ∨ q |
|---|---|---|---|
|   |   |   | **C** |
| 1 | T | T | T |
| 2 | T | F | T |
| 3 | F | T | T |
| 4 | F | F | F |

**4. Invalid**

**TABLE A.2**

|   | p | q | p ∨ q | p → (p ∨ q) | ~p | ~(p ∨ q) |
|---|---|---|---|---|---|---|
|   |   |   |   | **P1** | **P2** | **C** |
| 1 | T | T | T | T | F | F |
| 2 | T | F | T | T | F | F |
| 3 | F | T | T | T | T | F |
| 4 | F | F | F | T | T | T |

**7. Invalid**

**TABLE A.3**

|   | p | q | r | ~r | p ∨ r | (p ∨ r) → q | q & ~r | ~p |
|---|---|---|---|---|---|---|---|---|
|   |   |   |   |   |   | **P1** | **P2** | **C** |
| 1 | T | T | T | F | T | T | F | F |
| 2 | T | T | F | T | T | T | T | F |
| 3 | T | F | T | F | T | F | F | F |
| 4 | T | F | F | T | T | F | F | F |
| 5 | F | T | T | F | T | T | F | T |
| 6 | F | T | F | T | F | T | T | T |
| 7 | F | F | T | F | T | F | F | T |
| 8 | F | F | F | T | F | T | F | T |

**10. Valid**

**TABLE A.4**

|   | p | q | r | q ∨ r | p → q | ~(q ∨ r) | ~p |
|---|---|---|---|---|---|---|---|
|   |   |   |   |   | **P1** | **P2** | **C** |
| 1 | T | T | T | T | T | F | F |
| 2 | T | T | F | T | T | F | F |
| 3 | T | F | T | T | F | F | F |
| 4 | T | F | F | F | F | T | F |
| 5 | F | T | T | T | T | F | T |
| 6 | F | T | F | T | T | F | T |
| 7 | F | F | T | T | T | F | T |
| 8 | F | F | F | F | T | T | T |

**EXERCISE 7.5**

**1. Valid** (There are at least two ways of showing that 1 is valid. Here is one way.)

**TABLE A.5**

| P1 | P2 | P3 | C | Variable Box |   |   |   |
|---|---|---|---|---|---|---|---|
| $p \rightarrow (q \,\& \, m)$ | $(q \,\& \, m) \rightarrow r$ | ~r | ~p | m | p | q | r |
| T T T T | T T T | F T | F T | | T | | F |
| T✓ | T✗ | T✓ F✓ | | | | | |

**4. Invalid**

**TABLE A.6**

| P1 | P2 | P3 | C | Variable Box |   |   |   |   |
|---|---|---|---|---|---|---|---|---|
| $\sim (q \rightarrow m) \rightarrow s$ | $\sim s \vee \sim p$ | $r \rightarrow p$ | $(q \rightarrow m) \vee r$ | m | p | q | r | s |
| T F T T | T T T F F | F F T | T F F F | F | F | T | F | T |
| T✓ | T✓ | T✓ | F✓ | | | | | |

**7. Invalid**

**TABLE A.7**

| P1 | P2 | P3 | C | Variable Box |   |   |   |
|---|---|---|---|---|---|---|---|
| $p \rightarrow q$ | $r \rightarrow s$ | $\sim r \vee \sim p$ | $\sim s \vee \sim q$ | p | q | r | s |
| F T F | T F T | T F F F T | F T T | F | T | F | T |
| T✓ | T✓ | T✓ | F✓ | | | | |

## EXERCISE 7.6

1. **Modus Ponens; Valid**

4. **Disjunctive Syllogism; Valid**

7. **Denying the Antecedent; Invalid**

### Chapter 8

## EXERCISE 8.2

1. Sample: My parents, my friends' parents

   Target: Parents

   Relevant Property: *try to make life better for their children*

   Strength: **Weak**. The sample size is too small, and thus the sample fails to be representative, and it is biased.

4. Sample: Pigeons that Max has observed in Las Vegas and Los Angeles over the past 10 years

   Target: Pigeons

   Relevant Property: *have beaks shorter than one inch*

   Strength: **Weak**. First, we do not know the sample size. It may be large, but we cannot assume that it is. Second, even if is a large sample, the pigeons in Las Vegas and Los Angeles do not represent the pigeons in New York or in other countries. Third, the sample is biased, since only pigeons in Las Vegas and Los Angeles could be part of the sample.

7. Sample: Over 1,500 bull elk were observed in various places in in the United States

   Target: bull elk in the United States

   Relevant Property: *have antlers over 36 inches long*

   Strength: **Strong**.

## EXERCISE 8.3

1. Source Analog: Abortion

   Target Analog: Capital punishment

   Similarities: involve killing a person

   Relevant Property: *morally wrong*

   Strength: **Weak**. There are too many differences between a fetus in the womb and a convicted criminal on death row.

   Added Statement: The added statement further **weakens** the argument, since it is clearly morally wrong to kill an innocent person, but not *clearly* wrong to kill a convicted criminal on death row.

4. Source Analog: Beth as dogsitter

   Target Analog: Beth as babysitter

   Similarities: loves the being

   Relevant Property: *being excellent*

   Strength: **Weak**. There are too many differences between caring for a dog versus caring for a baby, such as that a dog can be left alone, and only needs to be fed and walked, whereas a baby needs much more care.

   Added Statement: The added statement **strengthens** the argument, since it adds an instance of babysitting.

7. Source Analog: Bodybuilders that I follow on YouTube

   Target Analog: Me

   Similarities: maintain calorie deficit and work out regularly

   Relevant Property: *lose body fat and gain muscle mass*

   Strength: **Weak**. There are too many potential differences between the online bodybuilders and me.

   Added Statement: The added statement further **weakens** the argument, since the workout experience plays a role in how effective the workout is.

## EXERCISE 8.4

1. Conclusion: The storms are the cause of the cicadas buzzing loudly

   Method Used: Method of agreement

   Potential Weaknesses: The weakness in this case seems to be that there are other, additional relevant causes that have been overlooked, even if the weather does play a role in the buzzing. It could also be a coincidence that the cicadas are buzzing just before the storm.

4. Conclusion: Dr. Garber laughing at Dr. Smith's theory that the empty tomb is explained by

Jesus' mysterious lost twin brother is the cause of Dr. Smith being cold and distant.

Method Used: Method of difference

Potential Weaknesses: In this case, the causal claim in the conclusion is likely correct. A potential weakness is that there are possibly other, additional relevant causes that have been overlooked.

7. Conclusion: The worms are the cause of the potbelly.

Method Used: Method of residues

Potential Weaknesses: In this case, the causal claim in the conclusion is likely correct. A potential weakness is that there are possibly other, additional relevant causes that have been overlooked, such as malnutrition playing a role.

### EXERCISE 8.5

1. **Analogical argument**
4. **Analogical argument**
7. **Generalization**

## Chapter 9

### EXERCISE 9.2

1. Explanandum: The tree died

   Explanans: The lack of water [to the tree]

4. Explanandum: The appearance of a table there

   Explanans: Simple particles being arranged in a "table-wise" way

7. Explanandum: Your extra belly fat as of lately

   Explanans: Your excessive alcohol use

### EXERCISE 9.3

1. This is a ***repeatable causal*** explanation.
4. This is a ***non-causal, teleological*** explanation.
7. This is a ***non-repeatable causal*** explanation.

### EXERCISE 9.4

1. (i) Explanans 1 (The dog has fleas) is the better explanation.

   (ii) It is better **primarily** because it has greater explanatory power. That the dog would be

biting and scratching itself is more probable if it has fleas than it would be if it was trying to communicate that it wanted to be pet.

Second, and to a lesser extent, explanans 2 is more problematic in that it conflicts with what we have good reason to accept about how dogs communicate that they want to be pet—which does *not* involve biting and scratching itself, but instead involves tapping the owner with its paw, putting its head on its owner's lap, and the like.

4. (i) Explanans 2 (there was an earthquake) is the better explanation.

   (ii) It is better because it has greater explanatory scope. Explanans 2 explains *both* the toppled wall and the crack in the street, whereas explanans 1 does not explain the crack in the street.

## Chapter 10

### EXERCISE 10.1

1. **Appeal to popularity**
4. **Genetic fallacy**
7. **Equivocation**
10. **Inconsistency ad hominem**

### EXERCISE 10.2

1. **False dilemma**
4. **Decision-point fallacy**
7. **Begging the question**

### EXERCISE 10.3

1. **Inconsistency ad hominem**
4. **Equivocation**
7. **Guilt by association**
10. **Poisoning the well**
14. **Straw man**
19. **Fallacy of composition**
23. **Appeal to emotion**
25. **Decision-point fallacy**
29. **Circumstantial ad hominem**
31. **Perfectionist fallacy**